The First Book of

PageMaker® 4
for the Mac®

Carla Rose

SAMS

A Division of Macmillan Computer Publishing

11711 North College, Carmel, Indiana 46032 USA

To
Joey Grimaldi

Trademarks

Publisher
Richard K. Swadley

Publishing Manager
Marie Butler-Knight

Managing Editor
Marjorie Hopper

Acquisitions/Development Editor
Stephen R. Poland

Technical Editor
Tracy Kaufman

Manuscript Editor
Ronda Carter Henry

Editorial Assistant
Tracy Kaufman

Cover Designer
Held & Diedrich Design

Designer
Scott Cook

Indexer
Jill Bomaster

Production Team
*Claudia Bell, Scott Boucher, Brad Chinn, Brook Farling, Bob LaRoche,
Laurie Lee, Julie Pavey, Howard Peirce, Cindy L. Phipps, Joe Ramon,
Tad Ringo, Dennis Sheehan, Louise Shinault, Lisa A. Wilson*

Contents

vi

viii

ix

Introduction

The Evolution of Desktop Publishing

▶ *Using the Macintosh*
▶ *What is Desktop Publishing Anyway?*
▶ *The PageMaker Advantage*

When your office or group needs forms, brochures, newsletters, or flyers, do you reach for the rubber cement bottle and the X-acto knife to put together a paste up? Have you ever thought, there has got to be an easier way?

This book, your Macintosh computer, and Aldus PageMaker, will make preparing all kinds of printed material easier.

Publishing, according to our trusty dictionary, means preparing and issuing information to the public. Therefore, desktop publishing could probably be defined as publishing done on a desktop. Of course, the kind of desktop we're talking about isn't a slab of executive walnut, or even woodgrain Formica. The Macintosh computer has given us a new kind of a desktop—an electronic one. Within the context of the Mac, your desktop is your working (and playing) environment.

PageMaker brings publishing to your fingertips, letting you produce great looking documents quickly and inexpensively. Corporations, advertising agencies, book and magazine publishers, and free-lance artists are using PageMaker for all kinds of projects, from single-page flyers to entire books. This book was produced using PageMaker, with text written in Microsoft Word, and art created with Silicon Beach SuperPaint.

Even though PageMaker is the choice of most graphic design professionals, the program is equally suitable for the beginner. This book will teach you, step-by-step, how to translate your ideas into attractive and functional documents.

If you are unfamiliar with terms or operations mentioned, Chapter 2 gives a brief explanation of some basic Mac operations. For more detailed information, try *The First Book of the Macintosh*. Once you are familiar with the Mac, you're ready to learn desktop publishing with PageMaker.

What is Desktop Publishing?

Desktop publishing, or DTP for short, has been around longer than you think. The first desktop publishers were the ancient Sumerians, writing in cuneiform script on clay tablets, with a reed stylus. Close to a half million of these tablets survived, giving scholars a firsthand look at Sumerian newsletters and flyers 53 centuries old. Figure I.1 shows a piece of a cuneiform publication.

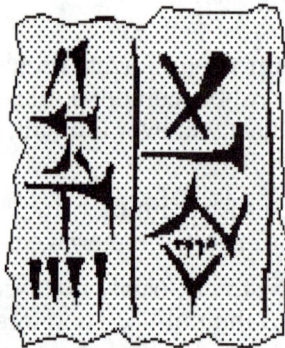

Figure I.1 A fragment of the Sumerian Daily News.

The Hebrew scribes, painstakingly tracing the letters of the Pentateuch onto vellum scrolls, were also desktop publishers, as were countless monks in monasteries all over Europe, who copied and decorated psalms and prayerbooks. At that time, information could be put together by one person, in a form suitable for sharing with others. However, with the advent of Gutenberg's movable type and the printing press, the process changed. It no longer depended on individual effort.

Publishing now required specialists such as artists, engravers, typesetters, and pressmen, and a lot of specialized equipment. Figure I.2 shows one of the first printing presses.

Figure I.2 An early printing press.

As recently as ten years ago, publishing a four-page newsletter required writing the copy, taking the pictures, sending the copy to a typesetting house, and the photos to a photoengraver. Headlines and body copy were returned separately on long strips of paper called *galleys.* After careful proofreading, and assuming the typesetter hadn't made any mistakes, the whole package of type was sent to a paste-up artist. The paste-up artist would mark the size and placement of all the elements in blue pencil on big sheets of white cardboard. Next, he/she would carefully glue everything in place. The paste ups were then sent to the printer, who would photograph them onto either paper or metal printing plates, manually add special effects, high quality photos, or engravings, and print them. It was a time-consuming, expensive, and frustrating process, especially when a misspelled word or a missing comma meant redoing an entire page of type. Printing more than one color was even more complicated.

Desktop publishing as we know it today has come full circle. It still takes specialized equipment, but we've come back to a system in which one person can easily create and publish a document. You don't have to depend on one specialist to set the type, another to stick it down on paper, and a third to smear ink on the printing plate. With your Macintosh, a word processor, a graphics program, PageMaker, and a laser printer, you can do the whole job. Like the Sumerian scribe scratching his slab of clay, you are in control of the process. If you want to change the words or their position on the page, you can. You can even create a new document any time you have something to say. A simple one-page flyer takes only a few minutes to produce, and a four-page newsletter, a couple of hours. With fewer constraints on your imagination, you're able to communicate more effectively.

Computerized DTP became feasible when the personal laser printer was introduced. Instead of being limited to dot-matrix print that wasn't much better than an ordinary typewriter, computer users had a range of typefaces and sizes which looked nearly professional. When Adobe Systems introduced a typesetting language called *PostScript,* which could talk to personal laser printers, professional typesetting equipment, and high resolution devices such as film recorders and plate makers, desktop publishing truly came of age. Now anyone can produce materials with exactly the same look and feel as those of the big publishing facilities.

xiv   Why PageMaker?

Most publications combine text and graphics. For example, newsletters usually have photos or drawings, financial reports include graphs and statistical tables. Even company letterhead generally has a logo. With a sophisticated word processing program, you can set up a two or three-column page, and even paste in a graphic or draw a box around a paragraph. Some graphics programs allow you to enter and edit text as well. So, why do you need PageMaker? Beyond word processing or graphics programs, PageMaker gives you more control over the look of the finished product and makes the job much easier and faster.

In five years, Aldus PageMaker has become the industry standard. PageMaker is easy to use and more versatile than any other leading DTP program. PageMaker is also compatible with QuickDraw, PostScript printers, and Linotronic. It runs in black and white or color on any Mac Plus or higher (a hard drive is recommended). The extra memory of a Mac II speeds up the program, and the ability to use MultiFinder enables you to jump back and forth between programs.

PageMaker gives you far more flexibility than even the most advanced word processor. You can place your words and pictures with absolute precision. You can also experiment without the risk of losing or damaging your document. If you want to see how a headline would look a point larger, it takes just a couple of mouse clicks to change it. And if you don't like the change, it's easy to undo.

PageMaker is designed to simulate the steps a paste-up artist would use to set up a publication. If you've ever put together a page the old-fashioned way, using PageMaker will seem quite natural. Start by defining borders, and pasting the text and graphics electronically on the page. Once the text has been imported into PageMaker, you can:

▶ Reposition an element by sliding the element until it's where you want it.

▶ Resize a picture without distorting it.

▶ Run type around an irregular shape.

▶ Link columns, or even whole pages of text, so that a change in format is automatically carried through.

▶ Shorten or lengthen text, and change the typeface or the amount of space between lines or letters.

▶ Find out how much space a story will occupy by pouring it into PageMaker and letting it jump to as many columns or pages as it needs.

▶ Setup a master page and flow text into it.

▶ Create an index and table of contents, for a book or report, just by selecting the key words to be included. PageMaker will sort, cross-reference, and list the appropriate page numbers for you.

XV

The most surprising thing about PageMaker is that it's not difficult to use. At first glance the package looks complicated. PageMaker comes with four disks and five books. Disk 1 includes an Installer which guides you, step-by-step, through the installation process. (For a detailed explanation of how to load PageMaker onto your hard disk and make backup floppies, see the Appendix at the back of this book.) Before you put the box back on the shelf, however, you may want to flip through the booklet called *Introduction to PageMaker* for inspiration.

A Word About Version 4.0

Since PageMaker first appeared, each succeeding version has included new features. The current release, PageMaker 4.0, is the most powerful yet. This book was written about PageMaker 4.0, but much of the material applies equally to earlier versions of the program. The basic features haven't changed, although some menu commands and keyboard shortcuts may be different. If you have an earlier version of PageMaker, you should upgrade to the current version to use this book effectively. The Story Editor, document linking, and many of the other features you'll learn about in this book are not available in releases prior to 4.0.

PageMaker has just released version 4.01, which fixes a few minor bugs in 4.0. If your disks don't say 4.01, you'll receive the upgrade as soon as you send in your registration card.

Conventions

Q This book employs several conventions to help you understand certain concepts. To ensure that you don't get stranded, text references act as signposts to point you in the right direction for more information on related topics.

One of the most helpful features of this book is the Quick Step. *Quick Steps* provide step-by-step instructions for your own specific PageMaker needs. Look for Quick Step icons to find these instructions.

> ▶ ⊘ **Tips** and **Cautions** appear in boxes with hints to ensure you don't lose your time, documents or sanity.

Some typographical conventions make referencing easier. New terms appear in *italics*, followed by an explanation. Command, file, and menu names are capitalized.

If you see an instruction to press a key combination, such as ⌘+D, hold down the Command key and then press D. (Don't type the plus sign between the two keys.)

Acknowledgments

First of all, thanks to the people at SAMS who made this book possible, especially Steve Poland, Ronda Henry, and Lisa Bucki.

Thank you to Freda Cook at Aldus Corp., for answering questions both silly and serious; and for providing updated software. Special thanks to Elisa Cohen in Aldus Technical Support, for being supportive beyond the call of duty.

Thank you to Marleen Winer of TeleTypesetting in Brookline, Mass. for the guided tour of service bureaus.

Deep appreciation to Dubl-Click Software for producing the wonderful WetPaint series of Classic Clip Art, which is used throughout this book.

Thanks and hugs to Jay for all kinds of help—especially with the printing chapter; and to Josh and Danny for their patience and tolerance of all those late dinners, and to all three for giving me the time and space I needed to finish this project!

xvii

Chapter 1

From Idea to Finished Page

In This Chapter

▶ *Planning Your Publication*
▶ *Setting Up Layout*
▶ *Using Typography*
▶ *Designing Headlines*
▶ *Designing Graphics*
▶ *Printing Your Publication*

In order to translate your ideas into presentation-quality publications, you need to understand the process by which words and pictures are merged to become a finished product. Because PageMaker is designed to electronically replicate the procedures that artists and graphic designers have traditionally used, the basic steps are much the same, whether you're using a Mac, or scissors and glue. Nothing is particularly complicated and, as always, the computer makes the job even easier. Once you have learned the steps and the reasons for following them, you'll be well on your way to designing and producing all kinds of printed materials.

Planning Your Publication

The key to success with DTP is planning. Before working on a publication, consider the following:

▶ Who is your audience? Will the publication be distributed only to members of a particular group, or will it introduce your group to a much larger audience?

▶ Are illustrations needed? What kind? If you are using drawings, how detailed will they be? Will you be using color?

▶ What kind of articles will the publication have? How many? What length? How many pages will you fill?

▶ How many copies will you need? How will they be printed?

▶ Will you mail the publication in an envelope, or will it be a self-mailer?

2

If you know the purpose of your project, you'll probably be able to answer most of these questions right away. Others may take some thought, or even some research. You can learn a lot by looking at other publications. Train yourself to be aware of design, in fact, start right now by taking a look at this book. Notice the running heads at the top of each page, and the use of a second color for headings and page numbers. Look at the space between the lines of type. Is it the same height as the letters? Look at the width of the margins on facing pages. Is the type actually centered on the page, or is there a wider margin on the outside of the pages? These are things you'll need to think about when you start to design pages.

▶ **Tip:** When you become a registered PageMaker user, you'll receive a free subscription to *Aldus Magazine*. In addition to providing helpful hints and how to's, the magazine is full of examples of work from other PageMaker users. It's a great source of ideas.

Layout

Layout is the business of deciding how to put together the jigsaw puzzle of words, pictures, lines, boxes, and so on, on the page. Layout is also designing each page so that the most important elements are read first, and it is attractive to the reader. Laying out pages gives you an opportunity to be creative, experiment, and customize your publication to the needs and taste of your audience.

Before you begin to work with PageMaker, use a pencil and paper to make a rough sketch or *dummy,* as shown in Figure 1.1. This can be as rough as you care to make it. The purpose is to help you decide what will go where.

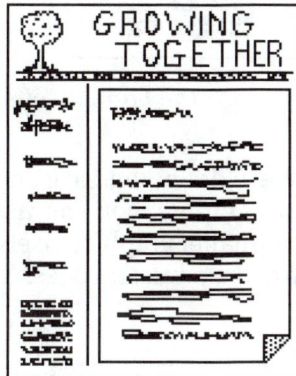

Figure 1.1 A rough dummy.

In the rough dummy shown in Figure 1.1, the *banner,* the name of the publication, is at the top of the page. Although this is traditional, it's not necessary. Figure 1.2 shows one of many alternative arrangements.

The layout must be balanced. This doesn't mean that it needs to be symmetrical. In fact, a completely symmetrical layout generally does not look good. In such a layout, there is no dominant element and nothing to catch your eye. When you're designing a newsletter, a flyer, or anything of that nature, there ought to be one lead story or significant element that is noticed first. The usual place to put this is near the upper left-hand corner, because the English language is read from top to bottom and left to right. The reader's eye automatically goes to this starting point. (If you were laying out a page in Hebrew or Japanese, for example, the rules would obviously be different.) Formal newspapers, such as the New York Times, may put the lead story on the right. The eye tracks across the top of the page and is stopped by the larger headline type. Positioning the story at the edge of the page encourages the reader to turn to the inside pages.

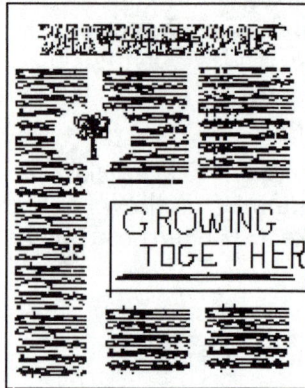

Figure 1.2 A dummy with the banner set at midpage.

4

In order to lead the eye down the page and balance the weight of the dominant headline or graphic, you can use a second element, as shown in Figure 1.3. The smaller graphic offsets the weight of the large black headline at the top of the page, and doesn't fight with the headline for dominance.

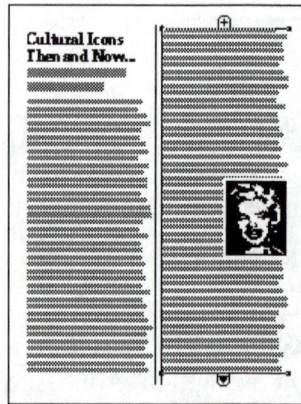

Figure 1.3 The headline balanced against a smaller graphic.

You can also use white space as a design element to add emphasis to the story or graphic it surrounds. A well designed page will create within itself a sort of visual pathway for the eye to follow. The reader sees the main item first, and then follows down to the next and so on, until he reaches the bottom of the page. This is called *eye-leading*. Figure 1.4 illustrates the front page of a newsletter that uses eye-leading successfully. The combination of the margin between the columns and the large, attention-grabbing photograph will bring you to the table of contents beneath.

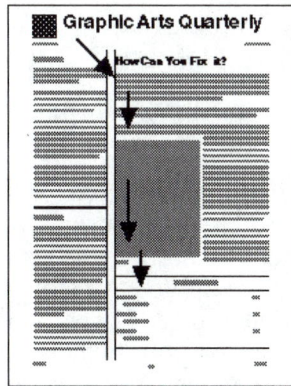

Figure 1.4 Eye-leading used on the front page of a newsletter.

Typography

Design and layout aren't the only important aspects of publishing. You need words as well. If you are the writer as well as the designer, you'll have a lot of work to do. But, there are some advantages. If you discover that a story or headline needs to be shortened to fit or needs to be fleshed out a little further to fill up some space, you can do it yourself with a minimum amount of fuss. You can handle text with the word processor and then import the story into PageMaker. Once you have the text, you need to fit it into the layout in an attractive and legible manner. This is where typography comes in. There are hundreds, if not thousands of different *typefaces*. A typeface is the distinctive design of a set of type, distinguished from its weight (such as bold or italic) and size. Popular faces such as Helvetica, are generally available in a variety of weights and widths, such as Helvetica Light, Helvetica Thin, or Helvetica DemiBold condensed. Some typefaces have a very casual look, others are quite formal. There are typefaces with *serifs* and without. Serifs are the little finishing strokes on the ends of letters. Most designers find that setting large blocks of text in serif type makes them easier to read. Examples of different typefaces are shown in Figure 1.5.

This is 14 point Times.
This is 14 point Times Bold.

This is 14 point Helvetica.
This is 14 point Helvetica Bold.

Figure 1.5 Times and Helvetica typefaces.

Times Roman is an example of a serif face, which was originally designed for the London Times. Times is a very condensed face, meaning that the characters are narrow and set close together. This was done in order to get as many words as possible per newspaper column, while maintaining some legibility. Times Bold is the same face in a *heavier weight.* Using Times for your text gives you a very dense page, perhaps more suitable for a newspaper or technical journal. Bookman is another serif face, less condensed, and often used for books and magazines.

Type without serifs, called *sans serif,* is often used for headlines, advertising, and letterheads. Helvetica, shown in Figure 1.5, is an example of sans serif type. This type has a more modern feel and can be very distinctive. Popular faces such as Helvetica are generally available in a variety of weights and widths.

All typefaces can be modified directly on your Mac. This can be done by selecting bold, italic, or some other modification from the **Type Styles** submenu. You can also expand and condense the letters by using the **Set Width** submenu, as shown in Figure 1.6. When you set width, you can spread out a line or shrink it. Figure 1.6 shows the **Set Width** submenu percentages. Percentages less than 100% *shrink* the line. Percentages greater than 100% *expand* it.

> ▶ **Tip:** Although you have the option of using outline or shadowed characters, these should be avoided under most circumstances, as they are hard to read and don't reproduce well.

6

Type	Element	Windows
Font ▶		
Size ▶		
Leading ▶		
Set width ▶	Other...	
Track ▶	70%	
Type style ▶	80%	
	90%	
Type specs... ⌘T	✓Normal ⇧⌘X	
Paragraph... ⌘M	110%	
Indents/tabs... ⌘I	120%	
Hyphenation... ⌘H	130%	
Alignment ▶		
Style ▶		
Define styles... ⌘3		

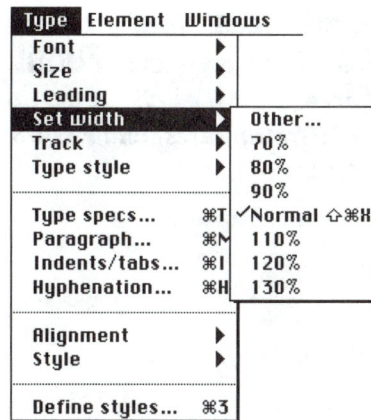

Figure 1.6 The Type menu with the Set Width submenu highlighted and displayed.

Try to limit the number of typefaces you use in a single document to a maximum of three or four. You'll need a face for the text, one for the titles, and one or two for the headings, captions, and charts or tables. If you use more than four different typefaces, however, you'll run the risk of having your document look like a ransom note. Staying within the four face limit still allows you some flexibility in that you can use bold, italic, and normal *fonts* of each face, as well as different sizes. (A font is a typeface of a particular style and size, such as Helvetica Bold 24 pt.)

Headlines need to be written and typeset in a way that will attract attention. It's the headline that makes the reader decide whether or not to read whatever follows. Bookman and Palatino, both serif faces, and Helvetica and Futura, which are sans serif faces, are frequently used for headlines because they are extremely readable.

▶ **Tip:** Bookman, Helvetica, Palatino, New Century Schoolbook, and Courier, which is the standard IBM typeface, are the most legible typefaces for fax transmittal according to a recent study by Adobe Systems.

Harder to read, but fun to play with are the character faces. A few are shown in Figure 1.7. These are often useful for ads or posters, and can work well in a masthead design or logo. Because they are more difficult to read, they shouldn't be used for text.

There are round faces, funky faces, COWBOY FACES, FANCY FACES, Funny faces, Old Faces, Familiar faces, *Strange Faces, Pretty Faces, and* **FACES** for all kinds of places...

Figure 1.7 Examples of character faces.

Graphics

Traditionally, graphics are photographs or drawings produced separately from the text, and pasted into the layout. However, the term graphics, as applied to desktop publishing, actually refers to anything that's not set in type. To further confuse you, charts and tables, which are usually typeset, are thought of as graphic elements as well. A box around a piece of copy is also a graphic, as are the thin lines used to separate columns.

Graphics for DTP are generally produced in another program and imported into PageMaker. There are many ways to do this.

▶ You can use a *paint* program such as SuperPaint or MacPaint. (Paint describes images as individual dots or bits, creating a bit-mapped image.)

▶ You can use a draw program like Aldus Freehand, Adobe Illustrator, or MacDraw, which save images in the *PICT* format. (PICT describes graphics as objects.)

▶ You can also use *Encapsulated PostScript Format* graphics (EPSF), which use the PostScript language to describe a draw type object.

▶ You can import scanned images, using a scanner to copy a photograph or drawing, into the *TIFF* format (Tag Image File Format).

Many publications use *clip art*, which comes from any of the numerous commercially produced libraries of drawings, scanned images, fancy borders, symbols, and designs. You can get useful and unusual clip art libraries as shareware from user groups or on-line services such as CompuServe and Online America.

8

> ▶ **Note:** *Shareware* programs are freely distributed by their authors to anyone interested. Users pay a fee to the creator of the program if they use it. Shareware depends on the honor system. If you use shareware, pay for it!

Computer clip art comes on a disk or on a CD-ROM (compact disk) in Paint, PICT, TIFF, or EPSF. Computer clip art can be pasted directly into a PageMaker publication or *customized* in a graphics program. Figure 1.8 shows the before and after of a single clip art image, customized in SuperPaint.

Figure 1.8 A single clip art image customized in SuperPaint.

9

Noncomputerized users of clip art purchase their libraries as large catalogs, which may be cut out and glued directly into a layout or photocopied for use.

Customizing clip art lets you use unique images with less work than if you had to create them yourself. Use clip art, as done with the George Washington portrait, as a jumping off point for your own creativity. Starting with an existing image, you can add or subtract whatever is needed to make the end result work for you. This is one of the many advantages of computerized clip art. The paper variety can't be adapted as easily. All you can do is cut it and paste it. Customizing is especially important if you want to adapt a piece of artwork to use as your logo. You may not be able to copyright an unaltered piece of clip art. If you make changes, though, you can use it almost any way you see fit, as long as you're not reselling someone else's work as your own clip art.

Using scanned photos successfully depends on how the publication will be printed. Scanning translates the continuous tones of a photograph into a *halftone*. Halftones convert continuous tone pictures, such as black-and-white photographs, into fixed patterns of black-and-white dots, which vary in size to create gray areas. The photographic process for turning photographs into halftones places a screen with lines of a specific density over the photograph so that only dots show through. The density of the screen affects the size of the dots, and the quality of the reproduction. A scanned photo is never as clear as the original or a photographically produced halftone, but can be acceptable for many applications. The photograph shown in Figure 1.9 was created with a video camera and the Computer Eyes scanner and software package. Later it was modified in a Digital Darkroom, before being pasted into this PageMaker publication.

10

Figure 1.9 Scanned art.

▶ **Tip:** A laser printer requires a minimum of four of its dots to make up one halftone dot, so that laser-printed halftones don't equal halftones for quality.

The limitations of laser printing can also mean that the resulting image will be less than ideal quality. You may want to use a scanned picture to show the size and placement of an image, and then have a commercial printer make a halftone version of the picture to be inserted into a paste up before printing.

Printing

When all the type and graphics are placed in the layout, it's time to review everything and add any final touches. You may decide, for example, that a drawing needs a line at the top and bottom to keep it separate from the columns of text surrounding it. This is also the time to do a final proofreading of all copy, and to clean up any mistakes. You should look carefully at the design of the pages, both on-screen and on a printed page. Print proof copies often while you're working to spot errors on paper that you may not notice on-screen. Watch out for pages that are too cluttered, too crowded, or lack a focus of interest. If a story has been continued to a second column or another page, verify that the text has flowed across properly. When everything is in its final form and position, you're ready to print.

How you print depends on what you're printing and how many of them you need. If you want only a few copies of a simple one-color publication, it's probably easiest to run them off on your laser printer. Simply enter the number of finished pages you need and proceed.

11

Photocopying is simple, but not economical for large quantities or appropriate for high quality work. If you're going to be using the services of a commercial printer or a service bureau, it's a good idea to talk to them ahead of time. Find out what your job will cost and what they expect to receive from you. Some printers want camera ready pages. Other printers and all service bureaus, may want your publication on a disk. You'll save time and money by checking.

> ▶ **Note:** Service bureaus are equipped with laser printers of various kinds. Many have very sophisticated (and expensive) imagesetting equipment, which can translate your Mac files into beautifully set pages for a reasonable fee. Some service bureaus even have Macs you can rent by the hour, as well as scanners, photocopiers, binding and collating machines.

If you need more copies than you want to run from your laser printer, and higher quality than is possible by photocopying, try instant printing. Instant printers use an inexpensive paper printing plate for as many as ten thousand copies. It's a kind of offset printing, just like the much fancier jobs done by enormous presses at newspapers, magazines, and book publishers.

Whether you're photocopying or sending your work to a real printer, you'll work from a laser-printed master. Use a good quality copy paper, or a coated reproduction paper for maximum sharpness. You can also take your disk to a larger printing facility, and have them print your publication directly from the disk to a photographic imagesetter. They can even make a printing plate directly from the computer with a laser printer.

If the job involves more than one color, the printing process is more complicated. PageMaker can handle spot color easily. Spot color uses a particular shade of ink to give you a single color. Using spot color separations, you can design your pages with the chosen color(s) in the places desired, and select Spot color overlays in the Aldus Print Options dialog box, as shown in Figure 1.10.

12

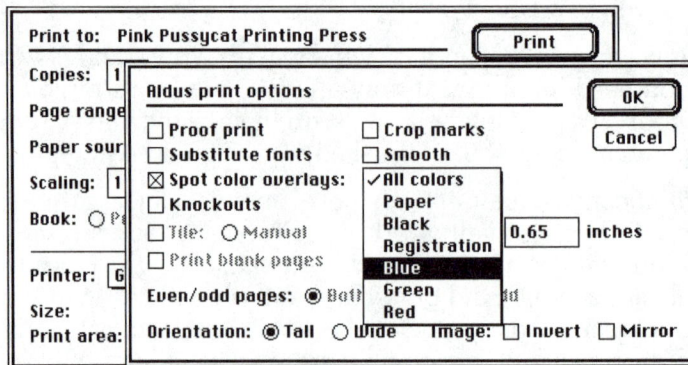

Figure 1.10 The Aldus Print Options box.

Process color, a different color printing method, uses halftone plates and four colors of ink—cyan (blue), magenta, yellow, and black—to create full color photos and illustrations. PageMaker can't manage process color (four-color separations). To handle this, you need a color separation utility such as Aldus PrePrint.

If you print using spot colors, separate the color work from the black ink parts of your publication. The paper will be printed twice for a two-color job; once with red, for example, and again with black. There will be masters and two printing plates, one with only the black ink part of the page, and one with only the red. These are called *separations*. They may also be referred to as overlays, since one is laid over the other.

Add registration marks to help the printer keep everything in line. The registration marks have to be in the same spot on all pages. Figure 1.11 shows sample registration marks. If your publication page is smaller than the print area of the paper you'll be printing on, tell PageMaker to add crop marks and registration marks, along with the name of the second color (or colors). Crop marks show the printer where to trim the finished page. If the printed page is full-size, talk to your printer about the easiest way to assure registration.

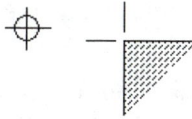

Figure 1.11 Registration and crop marks.

Sometimes you may want to print one color on top of another to give the effect of a third. Other times you want to avoid a second color over the first. In order to keep one color from printing on another, you create a *knockout.* The PageMaker Print Options dialog box gives you this option, and creates the overlays for you. *Trapping* is a way of increasing the boundary of spot colors by a small percentage to avoid leaving a thin white line between colors on a slightly misregistered page. Trapping is discussed further in Chapter 9.

13

Pick a Color

If you use custom printing, consider colored ink. The difference it will make to your publication is generally well worth the additional cost. Consider, for example, brown ink on tan paper, or dark blue on gray. The look is distinguished and tells the reader that you went the extra step. If you are producing a corporate newsletter or another promotional piece for a business, it's especially important to consider the corporate image. With a color Mac, you can preview different ink and paper choices on-screen.

In spite of WYSIWYG (What You See Is What You Get), the colors you see on-screen may not match the colors your printer actually uses (especially if you're working on a black-and-white Mac). Colors always look different on-screen and on paper, because while the monitor produces transmitted light, the paper is seen in reflected light. More importantly, what you call cherry red, for example, may not match either your printer's or your client's idea of this color. To avoid unexpected color variations, use the *Pantone Matching System* (PMS).

There are over 700 different colors in the PMS library and every good printer knows how to match them exactly. PageMaker supports PMS colors, and your printer can give you a PMS color guide to compare to the actual ink the print shop uses.

You can define colors yourself. PageMaker has several different ways of describing colors. You can experiment with these on a color Mac by opening the Define Colors dialog box and changing settings until you have the colors you like.

If you are using PageMaker on a Mac Plus, SE, II, or LC with a monochrome monitor, you can still add spot color. You just won't be able to see it until it's printed. PageMaker will use gray tones to approximate the colors on-screen for you. Use a PMS chart to select the colors you want. Color illustrations appear as gray-scale pictures on a black-and-white laser printer, but they may not reproduce the original tones very well.

14

Choosing a Printing Process

The printing process used depends on the type of job. Four-color printing requires a much more complicated process, elaborate presses, and costs more. Whatever the size of your job, if you need a commercial printing company, talk to them first. You can save a great deal of time and effort by knowing, in advance, that the printer can, for example, make your printing plates directly from your disk. The printer may advise you to output your final copy at twice the size and let them scale it down on the camera when they make the plates for the offset printing. This will effectively double the resolution of the finished piece from 300 to 600 dpi.

Before you decide on a printer, shop around. You'll find quite a range of prices quoted, even though the specs (the specifications for the job) are the same. You'll also find that some printers do a better job than others, even though they're using the same equipment. Ask to see samples. You can judge whether the image is sharp or fuzzy, or the ink looks even or spotty on any areas of flat color. Look on the back of pieces for ghost images caused by sloppy pressroom work. Examine the samples under strong white light or outdoors, to check color purity.

> ▶ **Tip:** Write down all your questions before you go to the printer. If you have a dummy of your project, paper samples to show the stock you want, or anything else that will help the printer figure out what you want, bring it.

Ask for a written bid but understand that, unless you have a signed contract with the printer, the job may exceed the estimate by up to 10%. Ask about discounts, especially if the job is something like a newsletter that will be produced on a regular basis. If you have several different items to be printed, such as stationery, envelopes, bill heads, and business cards, you may be able to negotiate a better price by bringing in several jobs at once. And, if your job involves a second color, ask if there are plans to use that color on any other upcoming work. You might be able to save on setup charges if the press is already setup with brown ink for someone else's job.

If there is any part of the process you don't understand, don't hesitate to ask for help. Most printers are happy to answer all your questions and provide valuable advice. For example, if there are budget constraits, your printer can often show you ways to do the job more economically.

15

A good printer will have a selection of various kinds of paper on hand, and should be able to special order any paper that you specify. If the stock you want isn't readily available, ask the printer to suggest an alternative. Most print shops can also bind reports, drill holes for a three ring binder, run glue down the edge of a stack of paper to make note pads, or arrange for die-cutting of odd shaped pieces.

Find out whether your printer wants the job on a disk or camera ready paste ups. If the printer does accept disks, make up one (or as many as needed) with nothing on it but what's required for the job. Make sure your version of PageMaker produces files that can be read by the printer's Mac, and that the printer has any nonstandard fonts you have included in your design.

If camera ready is specified, it means that the printing plate will be made from the materials exactly as you've submitted them. If there are stray marks or spots on the camera ready pages, they'll be on the finished work as well. Protect your artwork with tissue overlays and carry it flat in a folder to protect it from damage.

Be sure that you and the printer agree, in advance, on schedules and deadlines. You should expect to pay more for a rush job, or for any last minute changes. Before you accept the finished job, look it over thoroughly in the shop. Once you've signed for it, it's yours—mistakes and all. If you find mistakes the printer has made such as smeared ink, or the wrong ink or paper was used, calmly indicate what is wrong and ask the printer to reprint it.

Copyrighting Your Work

When you publish something to be distributed such as a newsletter, you can protect it by placing a copyright bug ©, or the word copyright, along with the year of publication and the name of the owner of the copyright on it. This might be the publisher of a book, the company or group producing a newsletter, or the corporation represented by the flyer or catalog. (The letter (C) in parentheses is not an acceptable substitute.) You must also submit two copies of the work to the Library of Congress within three months. (Failure to do so can result in a fine of $250.) Publishing the notice is sufficient but for further protection, you can register the copyright by requesting the appropriate forms from the Library of Congress. Submit the forms, a fee, and the required two copies of the work to be copyrighted. If you have any questions about copyrights, you may be able to get answers from the Copyright Office at the Library of Congress, or an attorney.

Your responsibilities are different if you're using someone else's copyrighted material. The bottom line here is, don't do it without written permission from the copyright holder, otherwise, you can be sued. For example, suppose you want to reproduce an article called, "Small Rodents and You" from *The Gerbil Journal*. You need a letter from *The Gerbil Journal* giving you permission to use the article in your publication. You must also make a note, on the page in your newsletter, stating the original source and the phrase, *Reprinted by permission*.

If you use clip art files, these are generally safe to reproduce because they were created for that purpose. Copyright, in this case, involves not redistributing the clip art as disks. When in doubt, read the materials that accompanied the clip art. It should give you the guidelines for the ways you can legally use the material without infringing on the copyright.

16

What You Have Learned

Before you start to design a publication, you need to consider how the publication will be used in the form of the following:

▶ Tailor your work to your audience and your budget.

▶ Make a pencil and paper dummy to help you plan the pages. Among the design considerations are balance and eye-leading. Effective use of white space helps your design as well.

▶ When you select type, limit yourself to a few faces. Four is the maximum number for most pieces, but you can use different sizes and weights of type within the same family.

▶ Graphics are everything that is not text. Boxes, lines, logos, charts, diagrams, drawings, and scanned photos are all graphics. Clip art offers an easy way to add images to your pages. Clip art comes in several formats, and can be modified in your paint program before being pasted onto the page. Scanned photos can be imported directly into PageMaker, or retouched in a computer darkroom program.

▶ PageMaker can handle spot color and make separate masters for each color. It won't do four-color process separations, however. For that you need Aldus PrePrint. PageMaker also allows you to use the Pantone color Matching System, which lets you specify exact shades of over 700 colors.

▶ Always do a final check and proof a hardcopy before you take your work to a commercial printer. It's often easier to see mistakes on the printed page than on-screen.

▶ Work with your printer and don't hesitate to ask questions. Printers can give good advice and help you find less expensive solutions to your problems.

▶ When you publish something you want to protect, you can copyright it yourself by using the copyright bug © with the year of publication, and the name of the copyright holder. If you reprint copyrighted material, be sure you have written permission from the copyright holder.

17

Meet the Mac

In This Chapter

▶ *Getting Started with the Mac*
▶ *How to Use the Keyboard and the Mouse*
▶ *How to Use Menus*
▶ *Cutting, Copying, and Pasting*
▶ *Saving Your Work*
▶ *Processing Words and Pictures*

An Introduction to the Macintosh

This chapter is specifically for those readers who have not used a Macintosh before. If you're familiar with basic Mac operations, you may want to skip ahead to the next chapter to start working with PageMaker. If not, this chapter will provide a quick introduction to Mac basics.

There are a number of different Mac models. Some have built-in black and white screens. Others use a separate monitor, which may be black and white or color. Some have more memory, or have built-in hard disks. But aside from these minor differences, all Macs think alike.

Macs and PCs work differently. The IBM PC and its many clones use a system called *DOS*. DOS stands for Disk Operating System. The Mac simply calls its operating system *System*. Instead of having to select from long directories of PC files, with obscure titles like PMNL1.DAT, the Mac allows you to point to a little picture (or *icon*) on-screen, and push a button. This is called a *Graphical User Interface,* or GUI. What it means to the user is that you can see, in pictures, symbols, and words on-screen, exactly what you're doing. It's one of the features that make the Mac ideal for desktop publishing.

> **Tip:** If you are just getting started with the Mac, follow the setup instructions that came with your computer, and take the Guided Tour. It's on a disk called either "Macintosh Basics" or "Guided Tour." It demonstrates the features we'll discuss in this chapter.

20

The Desktop

The *desktop* is the environment in which all Mac operations take place. To get to the Mac's desktop, simply turn on your computer. (What you see depends on what was open when the computer was shutdown.)

On the desktop are icons, which are little symbols or pictures which represent various documents, folders, and applications. At the top of the screen is a *Menu bar,* shown in Figure 2.1, containing the names of various menus. A menu is a list of commands, or things you can do such as opening or saving a file. When you open an application, the Menu bar will change to a different set of menus to use within that program.

In Figure 2.1, there are currently two windows open, Mac's HD and PageMaker. The PageMaker window has a striped *Title bar* at the top showing it is *active,* the window selected for use. You can have many windows open on your desktop, but only one can be active. In Figure 2.1, there are different icons for PageMaker's *applications, folders, disks, files,* and *templates.* (Applications may also be called *programs.* PageMaker is an application.)

Application icons tend to look something like their counterparts in reality. Folder or disk icons hold files and other folders. When you open a folder or disk, what is actually opened is a *window* which lets you see and use whatever's in the open disk or folder. Document icons look like the application which created them. Documents, or files, are the pages you create within an application. (PageMaker refers to its documents as publications.) A template is a format for a publication.

The *Trashcan*, in the bottom right corner of the desktop (shown in Figure 2.1), is for files you don't want to keep. Throw them away in the trash by opening the Trash window and dragging the unwanted files into it. The Trashcan will empty itself when the Mac needs the memory for something else or when you select **Empty Trash** from the **Special** menu.

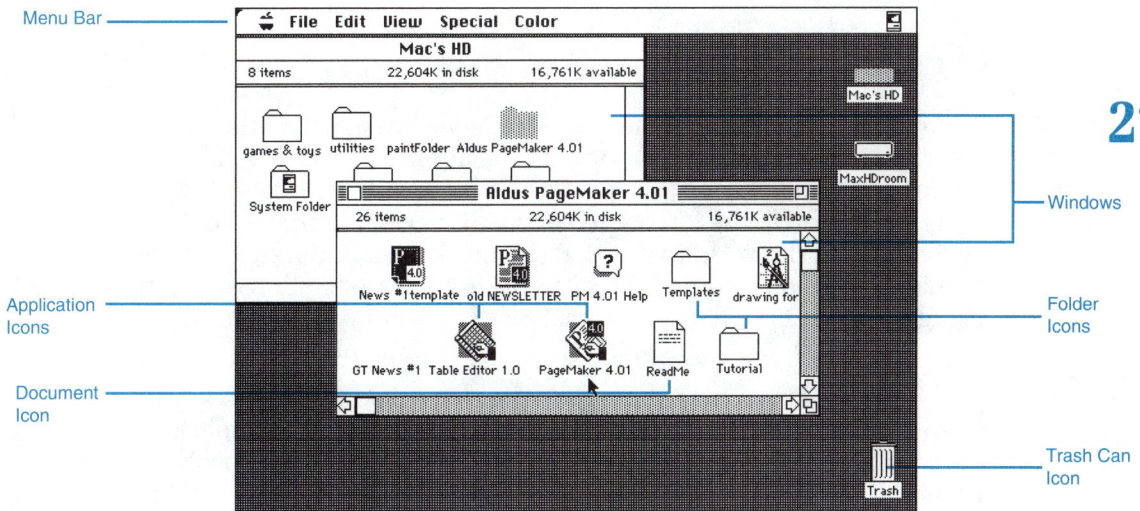

21

Figure 2.1 Open windows on the desktop showing application, document, and folder icons as well as the Trashcan.

Talking Back to Your Mac

There are two ways to communicate with your Macintosh: the *keyboard* and the *mouse*. Not all operations let you use either. There are key combinations for the keyboard, which will perform many functions.

However, any operation which requires moving something, dragging an icon, or locating a particular menu item can only be done with a mouse. When you're using the keyboard to type words into a program, you'll find it much faster to use the key combinations to perform operations such as saving your work, copying a paragraph, and so on. When you're using the mouse as a drawing tool or to rearrange files on your desktop, for example, it's easier to use the mouse to open a publication or to move around the screen. Using both and switching between them will soon become automatic.

Throughout this book the word *select* will be used to indicate that you should use the keyboard or the mouse, in whatever manner necessary, to select an item. If you need help at any point in the book with selecting an item, refer back to this chapter.

Using the Keyboard

There are several different kinds of Mac keyboards. All but the oldest have numeric keypads to the right of the alphanumeric keypad. The optional extended keyboards for the SE and Mac II series also have a function keypad at the top of the keyboard. Several different kinds of keyboards are shown in Figure 2.2. (If your keyboard doesn't include function keys, don't worry. You can perform all Mac operations without using function keys.) No matter what Mac keyboard you're using, there are a few special Mac keys you'll need to know about.

The first key is the *Command key*, also called the Apple key or Clover key. On the two extended keyboards, it has both the Apple logo ( ) and the clover symbol on it (⌘). It's located to the left of the spacebar. Press and hold the Command key and then a letter, number, or symbol key, to tell the Mac to perform an operation or command. Some Mac keyboards include Esc and Control keys, which may be used in advanced applications.

The *Option key* gives you optional characters in most type fonts, and is used to modify some Command key functions as well. For example, you can press ⌘+Option+P to place page numbers.

Most Mac keyboards also have four *arrow keys,* which can be used to reposition the cursor when you're typing. PageMaker also uses the ← and → to adjust the spacing between letters. All of the keys described are shown in Figure 2.2.

Option
Key

Command
Key

Macintosh Plus Keyboard

Numeric
keypad

Arrow
keys

Esc Key

Control
Key

Option
Key

Command
Key

Macintosh SE Keyboard

Numeric
keypad

23

Arrow keys

Function Keypad

Esc Key

Control
Key

Option Key

Command
Key

Macintosh Extended Keyboard

Numeric
Koypad

Arrow keys

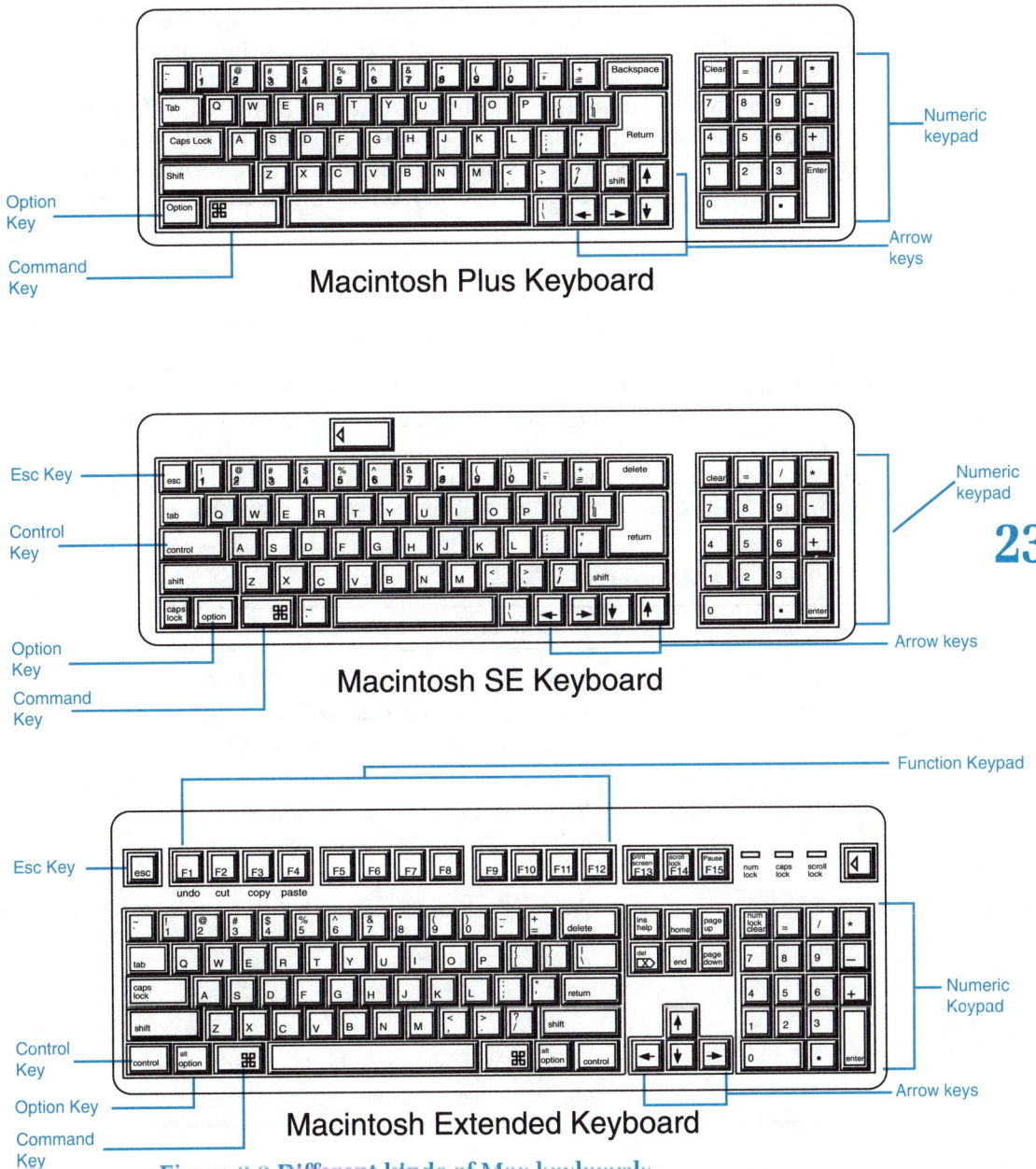

Figure 2.2 Different kinds of Mac keyboards.

Keyboard shortcuts can be used for many menu commands. They are shown on the menus to the right of the actions they represent. Although the Macintosh maintains a fairly consistent pattern of commands, the same combination can mean different things in different programs. As an example, pressing ⌘+I sets the indents and tabs in PageMaker, but selects Print Preview in Microsoft Word. Some basic commands such as **Open**, **Save**, **Cut**, **Copy**, **Paste**, and **Quit** are the same in all programs.

Using the Mouse

The other way to communicate with your Mac is to use the mouse. Computer mice are friendly creatures. To use the mouse with Page-Maker, you'll need to be familiar with the tricks your mouse can do. Table 2.1 lists all mouse procedures that can be used with the Mac and PageMaker, and gives a brief description of how each works.

24

Table 2.1 Mouse Procedures.

Procedure	Description
Pointing	Moves the mouse pointer to an item on-screen.
Clicking	Press and release the mouse button once quickly. Clicking selects an icon, a menu item, a button, or a starting point in the text.
Double-Clicking	Press and release the mouse button twice quickly. Double-clicking opens or activates a selected item.
Triple-Clicking	Press and release the mouse button three times quickly. Triple-clicking selects a paragraph in PageMaker.
Dragging	Press the mouse button and hold it down while you move the mouse. Dragging highlights blocks of text or menu selections, and moves an object to a new position.

When you move the mouse, the mouse pointer moves across the screen. The shape of the pointer can change, depending on what the computer is doing at the time. The *Arrow pointer* can become a *Wristwatch*, which indicates that the Mac is doing something that takes time. It can also turn into an *I-beam*, which means that it's ready to work with text. The Arrow, Wristwatch, and I-beam pointers are shown in Figure 2.3. PageMaker includes other types of pointers which let you draw shapes, lines, selection boxes, and so on (discussed in Chapter 3).

Figure 2.3 The Arrow, I-beam, and Wristwatch mouse pointers.

You can change the speed of clicking and mouse movement by opening the **Control Panel**, which is a **Desk Accessory**. You'll find a list of useful **Desk Accessories** (also called DAs) in the **Apple** menu.

> **Note:** The **Desk Accessories** are small utility programs available under the **Apple** menu, which can be run while using another program. The **Control Panel** is a **Desk Accessory** that enables you to set the volume of sound, the speed of typing and clicking, and the level of other system functions. For more information about the **Desk Accessories** and the **Control Panel**, consult the *First Book of the Mac*.

25

To change the speed of clicking and mouse movement, use the following Quick Steps.

Q Changing the Speed of Mouse Clicking and Movement

1. Position the pointer on the to the left of the Menu bar and press the mouse button.

   The **Apple** menu appears.

2. Select the **Control Panel** option.

   The Control Panel dialog box opens.

3. Click on the **Mouse** icon in the left column.

   You may need to click on the ↓ to scroll to it. The Mouse Control dialog box will open.

4. Click on one of the four circles, from slow to fast.

   Mouse Tracking adjusts the speed at which you can move the mouse. Experiment to find a comfortable speed.

5. Adjust double-clicking speed.

The closer the arrows, the less time between clicks.

6. Click on the square (the Close box) to the left of the Title bar.

This accepts your choices, closes the box, and returns you to the desktop.   □

Selecting Text

The Macintosh can do a lot more than merely emulate a typewriter. If you select text (*highlight* it), you can manipulate it in a variety of interesting ways. Depending on the program, you can change type styles, capitalize initial letters, sort or number the lines, or reorganize the text as an outline, just to name a few.

To select a single word, move the I-beam to a word and double-click. The Mac *highlights* the nearest whole word to show it's selected. (Highlighting means that a color Mac outlines a selection with a contrasting color. A black-and-white Mac inverts selected text to highlight it.)

You can select anything from a single letter to a group of words or paragraphs by holding down the mouse button and dragging across the desired text. When you release the button, the Mac selects everything you dragged over. PageMaker gives you additional ways to select text by triple-clicking, or searching for a particular word. But double-clicking and dragging work in every program, in every situation where you can edit text.

Working with Windows

If you look at an open Macintosh window, like the one in Figure 2.4, you'll discover some features that are common to many Mac programs. The window has several square boxes at the corners. The *Close box,* in the upper left corner, closes the window when you click on it with the mouse button. The *Size box,* in the lower right corner, lets you stretch and shrink the window so that it takes up more or less space on the desktop. And, clicking on the *Zoom box,* in the upper right corner, will expand the open window to full-screen size, or shrink it down again.

Whenever there is more in a window than can be seen, the *scroll bars* turn gray and become active. The scroll bars are found on the right and bottom sides of the window and have their own *scroll boxes*. Use the scroll boxes to move more of the window into view.

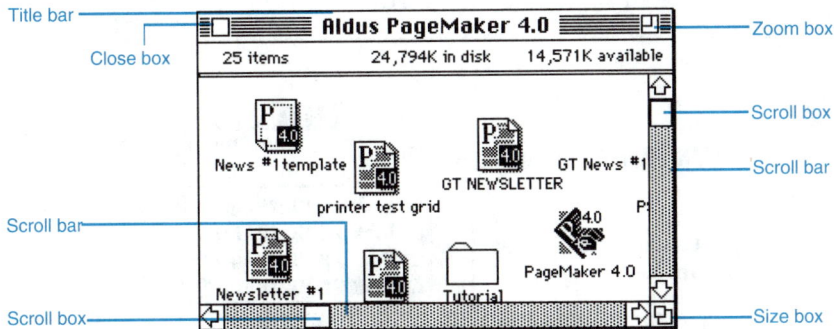

Figure 2.4 Window boxes and bars.

27

Menus and Dialog Boxes

The **Apple** menu and other menus like it are *pulled down* from the Menu bar to access commands and options. There are also pop-up menus, scrolling menus, and submenus.

▶ Pop-up menus and scrolling menus are found in dialog boxes. Pop-up menus let you move between folders, and may offer you other choices in other applications. Scrolling menus let you select from a list of files or folders.

▶ Submenus are subsidiaries of other menus, indicated by a *triangle*. When you click on the triangle, the submenu appears.

Select options from pull-down, pop-up, and submenus by clicking on them and releasing the mouse button when the desired choice is highlighted (changes color). To select an item on a scrolling menu, click once to select it and then click on the Open button in the dialog box, or simply double-click on the selection. Figure 2.5 shows the different kinds of menus.

> ▶ **Note:** You can use shortcuts for some menu choices by using key combinations, but you can't select menu items from the menu with the keyboard.

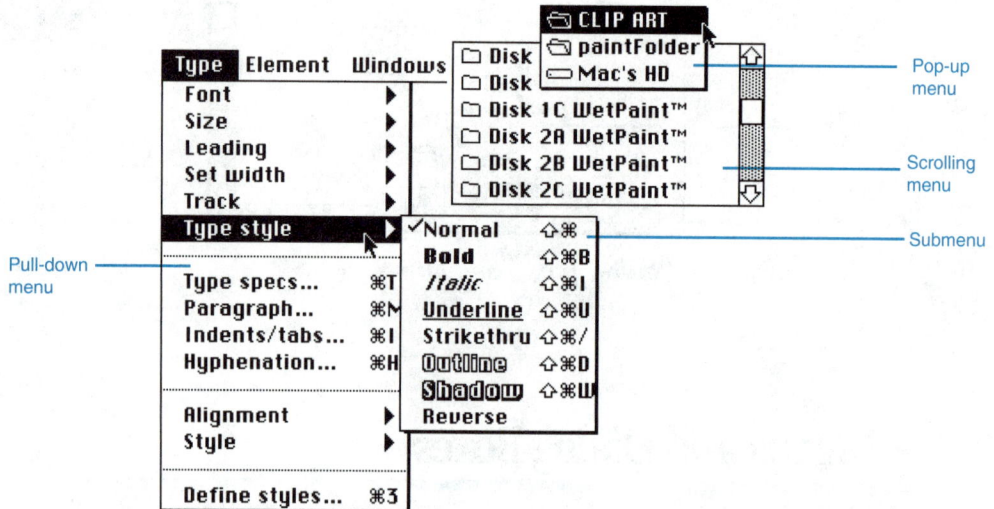

Figure 2.5 Pull-down menus, pop-up menus, scrolling menus, and submenus.

In Figure 2.5, **Type style** on the **Type** menu and **Clip Art** on the pop-up menu are highlighted. Highlighting lets you know when a menu or icon is selected.

A menu command with an ellipsis (...) after it means that, upon selecting this command, a *dialog box* will appear. Dialog boxes appear on-screen whenever there is an action to perform, information to enter, or a question to answer. Dialog boxes also give warnings. Figure 2.6 shows the Mac's Page Setup dialog box. In this box the Mac wants you to tell it how to set up a page for printing.

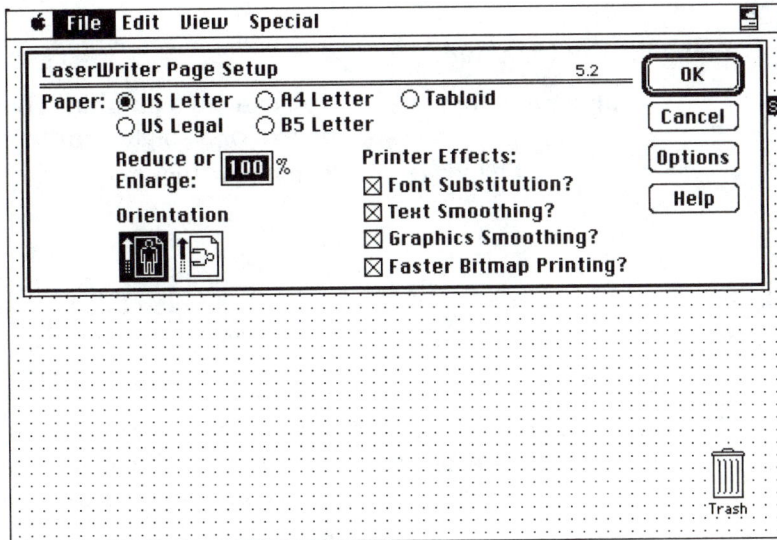

Figure 2.6 The Page Setup dialog box.

29

Cut, Copy, and Paste

The **Cut**, **Copy**, and **Paste** commands are in the **Edit** menu. These choices aren't active on the desktop itself, but they're useful in virtually every Mac application and in many **Desk Accessories**. Anything cut or copied is held on the *clipboard* until you replace it with something else, or until you shutdown. You can paste a clipped item into a publication, and then paste it again into your scrapbook.

The **Cut** command removes the selected text or art and holds it on the Mac's clipboard, just as you might cut a piece out of a page and tack it on the bulletin board until you are ready to use it. The clipboard can hold text or art that has been cut or copied from a publication. However, the clipboard can only hold one item, large or small, at a time, and the contents of the clipboard are lost whenever you shutdown the Mac. Use the following Quick Steps to see how the **Cut** command and clipboard work.

Q **Using the Cut Command**

1. Select the item or text to be cut.

   You can cut a graphic, a block of text, or a single word.

2. If you are cutting text, drag the I-beam cursor over it while holding down the mouse button to select it.

   The text is highlighted.

3. Press ⌘+X.

   The selected item disappears. (It has been cut to the clipboard.) □

The **Copy** command works just like the **Cut** command, only it transfers a duplicate of the selected text or art to the clipboard. Use the following Quick Steps to see how the **Copy** command works.

30

Q **Using the Copy Command**

1. Select the item or text to be copied.

   You can copy a graphic, a block of text, or a single word.

2. If you are copying text, drag the I-beam cursor over it while holding down the mouse button to select it.

   The text is highlighted.

3. Press ⌘+C.

   You won't notice any difference, but the selection has now been copied to the clipboard. □

The **Paste** command takes whatever is on the clipboard and inserts it into your publication. If the paste job involves text, it will be pasted where the I-beam is located. You can continue pasting the same piece of text or art over and over, as long as you don't cut or copy anything else. Use the following Quick Steps to paste text into your publication.

Q **Using the Paste Command**

1. Position the cursor at the point you want to insert the contents of the clipboard.

   If you're pasting from the scrapbook, simply open it from the Apple menu.

2. Press ⌘+V. A copy of whatever was on the clipboard is now on-screen.

You can paste multiple copies of the same item. Just keep pressing ⌘+V. □

> ▶ **Tip:** To see what's on the clipboard, select **Show Clipboard** from the **Edit** menu.

The Scrapbook

If you want to **Cut** and **Copy** several different elements, use the *scrapbook*. The scrapbook is one of the **Desk Accessories** available under the **Apple** menu. You can store as many pictures or pieces of text as you like in the scrapbook. They will be saved until you cut them out or delete them. Figure 2.7 shows a typical scrapbook page. The fraction in the bottom left corner of the screen indicates the page number and the total number of pages in this particular scrapbook. For example, in Figure 2.7, the fraction indicates that the tiger is on page 1 of 8 pages. The words *LINK* and *PICT* indicate that the picture is part of a publication and that it is a PICT, or picture file. Use the following Quick Steps to paste to the scrapbook.

31

Ⓠ Pasting to the Scrapbook

1. Open the scrapbook from the **Apple** menu.

The first page will automatically be displayed.

2. Press ⌘+V.

The Mac will create a new page and paste the contents of the clipboard on it. □

To **Cut** or **Copy** from the scrapbook, use the following Quick Steps.

Ⓠ Cutting or Copying from the Scrapbook

1. Open the scrapbook from the **Apple** menu.

2. Use the scroll bar to locate the item to be cut or copied.

Slide the white box right to turn pages.

3. Press ⌘+X to **Cut** or ⌘+C to **Copy** to the clipboard.

The item is placed on the clipboard. □

Figure 2.7 A scrapbook page.

32

Although you can only have one scrapbook active at a time, you can keep several different scrapbooks for different purposes. The one you are using should be in the **System Folder**, and should be called *Scrapbook File*. The **System Folder** is always present. It's the brains of the Mac. The Scrapbook File is a file in the **System Folder**, which the Mac automatically creates and maintains when the scrapbook is one of the available **Desk Accessories**. (It's included on all systems unless somebody deliberately deinstalls it.)

To start a special scrapbook for a project such as a newsletter, use the following steps:

1. Open the **System Folder** and change the name of the *Scrapbook File* to something like *Old Scrapbook File*.
2. Close the folder.
3. Open the scrapbook from the **Apple** menu. You'll get an empty scrapbook. Paste as many items in it as you want.

To go back to your previous scrapbook:

1. Open the **System Folder**.
2. Rename the current scrapbook file. You might call it *Newsletter Scrapbook*.
3. Change the name *Old Scrapbook* back to *Scrapbook File*.
4. Close the **System Folder** and go back to work.

Undo and Redo

One of the single most important commands on the **Edit** menu is the **Undo** command. The **Undo** command undoes the results of the most recent operation you performed. For example, if you just deleted your headline by accident, you can fix it by using the **Undo** command. However, if you delete a headline and then type even one letter, all the **Undo** command will do is remove that letter.

> ▶ **Tip:** If you **Undo** something and then decide you want it back, **Undo** it again. It will be redone. (As soon as you **Undo**, the command changes to **Redo** on the **Edit** menu.) A quick way to use **Undo** and **Redo** is to press ⌘+Z.

33

If you've been saving your work, and you can't **Undo** something because you performed another operation before you tried to use the **Undo** command, there's another way to undo it. The **File** menu has a **Revert** command, which undoes everything that has happened since the last time you saved. For example, if you want to experiment with setting a story in a different typeface or size, always save first. And, if you don't like the result, simply use the **Revert** command and you'll be back where you started from.

When it's not possible to perform an edit function, the commands will still be visible, but they'll be disabled. *Disabled commands* are grayed out on the menu to show you they're temporarily not available as choices. Figure 2.8 shows PageMaker's **Edit** menu with disabled commands. Since we copied this menu at a time when nothing was selected in our publication, there was nothing to **Cut** or **Copy**, so those commands are disabled.

Most users prefer to learn the key combinations for **File** and **Edit** menu commands. In general, they're the same in all programs. If you accidentally type the combination for a disabled command, nothing will happen. If you type the wrong key combination—**Cutting** when you meant to **Copy**, for example—just use the **Undo** command.

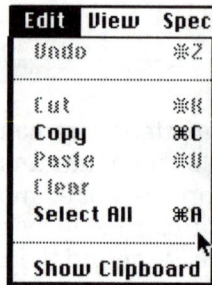

Figure 2.8 Commands displayed in gray type are disabled and cannot be selected.

PageMaker's Writing and Drawing Capabilities

PageMaker is intended to help you put words and pictures together. Even though you can type text in PageMaker, you will find it easier to use a word processing program to do the actual writing, especially if your project involves long pieces of text. PageMaker's built-in *Story Editor* can be used for checking spelling and making minor changes; however, it wasn't designed as a tool for writers and doesn't have the power of the more sophisticated word processing software.

PageMaker can import or copy text from most of the commonly accepted word processing applications. Which one should you use? Try several until you find one you're comfortable with. This book was written in Microsoft Word 4.0 on a Mac IIsi. The layout was done in PageMaker.

Drawing in PageMaker

Paint programs are also used in conjunction with PageMaker. The Mac's graphic capabilities are limited only by the skill of the user. There are many graphics programs that work with PageMaker. The most expensive ones aren't necessarily the best for all users. Silicon Beach Super-Paint is one of the most versatile, but select a paint program according to your needs. You might prefer Aldus Freehand or the advanced color capabilities of Electronics' Art Studio/32. There are also image processing programs such as Silicon Beach's Digital Darkroom, which are used to edit scanned images. Image processing programs will be described in more detail when we discuss scanners and images.

Mac programs are very compatible. Once you learn how to use one, it is easy to apply the same techniques and principles to a new program; there is a consistent user interface. For example, once you've learned how to **Cut**, **Paste**, and **Save** in WordMuncher, you've also learned how to do it in PicassoPaint. The compatibility factor also makes it easy for the user to switch from one program to another and accept text or pictures in various formats.

Before delving into PageMaker, spend some time getting acquainted with your Mac.

Saving Your Work

Computers are unpredictable, so experienced Mac users save often. If you save every few minutes when something goes wrong, you'll only lose a few minutes worth of work instead of the whole project. If you haven't saved the publication you are currently working in and you try to **Quit**, the dialog box shown in Figure 2.9 will appear. The OK button has a heavy line around it showing that it is the *default* button. To save an existing publication before quitting, simply click on OK or press Return. If you want to get rid of publications or files, you can use the Trashcan.

> ▶ **Note:** The default is an action, command, or specification the computer will carry out unless you specify otherwise. For example, plain type (as opposed to boldface or italic) is the default type style in most word processing programs.

The first time you save, you'll get the Save As dialog box, slightly different in each application. You can use the pop-up menu to save the file to a different folder. Once your file has a name, you can save it quickly by pressing ⌘+S.

Quitting shuts down the application open and takes you back to the desktop. To quit a Mac application, simply press ⌘+Q or select **Quit** from the **File** menu.

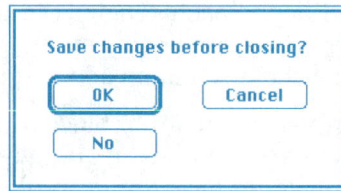

Figure 2.9 The Save changes before closing dialog box.

To shut off your computer, open the **Special** menu and select the **Shutdown** command. Always use the **Shutdown** command, instead of just flipping the switch.

What You've Learned

36

This chapter taught you some basic Mac operations. Specifically, you learned about:

▶ The Macintosh's Graphical User Interface, which uses symbols and pictures on-screen.

▶ How to use the desktop. Menus are lists of commands. Icons represent applications, files, and folders. Opening a folder gives you a window that lets you see what applications and documents are available inside.

▶ How to use the keyboard and the mouse. Keyboard shortcuts can be used for most commands. And, the mouse can be used to select, move, and open files by pointing, clicking, double-clicking, and dragging.

▶ How windows can be opened, closed, resized, and scrolled, using the mouse and the boxes at the corners and sides of the window.

▶ How the **Edit** menu commands let you **Cut**, **Copy**, and **Paste**, within a page, to the clipboard or scrapbook. The clipboard only holds one item. The scrapbook holds many.

▶ How to use **Undo** and **Redo** to rescue work you've changed by accident. If you can't **Undo**, you can use the **Revert** command to revert to the last version you saved. Commands that look gray on the Menu bar are disabled and not available as choices.

► How to save your work often. Throw away unwanted files in the Trashcan. Choose **Shutdown** from the **Special** menu to turn off the computer correctly.

37

Getting Started in PageMaker

In This Chapter

▶ *Starting a New Publication*

▶ *Using the Toolbox*

▶ *Viewing Your Work in Different Ways*

▶ *Printing*

▶ *Saving and Quitting*

▶ *Getting Help*

Once PageMaker is installed on your Macintosh, you are ready to open the application and start laying out pages. For purposes of illustration, this chapter, and the ones following it, will show the creation of a four-page newsletter. This process will involve importing text from several different word processing programs and pasting in graphics created in SuperPaint and MacPaint II. Clip art files will also be used.

> ▶ **Note:** If PageMaker is not installed on your computer, refer to Appendix A for installation instructions.

Starting a New Publication

Like any other Macintosh application, PageMaker can be opened from the desktop in one of two ways:

▶ By double-clicking on the **Application** icon.

Or,

▶ By selecting the application and pressing ⌘+O or choosing **Open** from the **File** menu.

When you open the application, the start-up screen appears showing a picture of a happy PageMaker user, and a legal disclaimer about Pantone. This screen soon changes to one showing your registration information. When this disappears, the PageMaker Menu bar and your desktop fill the screen, as shown in Figure 3.1.

40

> ▶ **Note:** If you're curious about the people who developed PageMaker, hold Shift as you open **About PageMaker**. The credits will appear. The last name on the list is Rocky. Sources at Aldus say the mysterious Rocky is Rocky the Flying Squirrel, mascot for the original PageMaker development team.

You might think, at first, that the application has bombed or refused to open. However, if you look at Figure 3.1, you'll see that the Menu bar is different from the desktop Menu bar, and that the dotted PageMaker icon shows that the program is in use. Before PageMaker will open a publication for you, you must tell it whether the publication is an existing one or a new one. If it's a new publication, you need to specify page size and format. PageMaker will then create the work area, according to your specifications, on the *pasteboard*. The pasteboard is like a large, slightly sticky, drawing board. Anything you put on it will stay there until you move it. The pasteboard surrounds the pages of your publication and extends beyond what's immediately visible in the window.

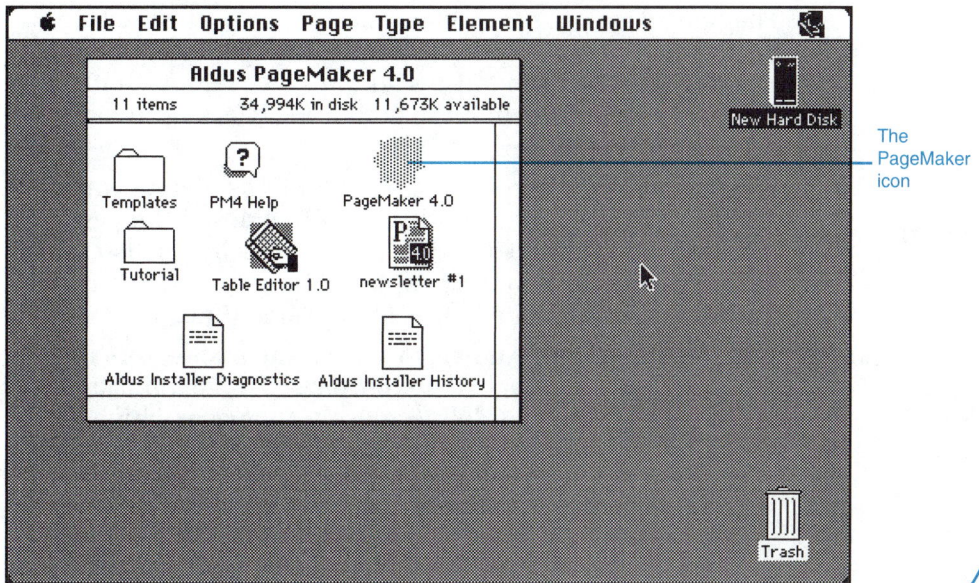

The
PageMaker
icon

*Figure 3.1 The PageMaker desktop. (The dotted outline of the
icon shows that PageMaker is in use.)*

The Page Setup box, shown in Figure 3.2, enables you to set up
your publication. Select **New** from the **File** menu or press ⌘+N. The
options in this dialog box tell PageMaker how to set up the pasteboard,
on which you'll assemble your layout. These options include:

The *Page* option: A menu which lets you select the size of
your publication. The choices include Letter, Legal, Tabloid
(11 x 17), or Custom. If you select a traditional size, the
dimensions will appear in the dimension boxes. If you
choose Custom, you can type in the size of the pages you
want to use.

The *Orientation* option: Allows you to select Tall, for a
vertical page or Wide, for a horizontal page. You cannot mix
the two in one publication.

▶ **Tip:** If you want to use a single horizontal page in a
vertical publication for a chart or wide graphic, import
the page to a graphics program such as SuperPaint or Aldus
Freehand. Rotate it to the proper orientation, and then import
it into PageMaker as a graphic.

The *Start Page* option: Allows you to type in the starting page number and the ending page number. If you don't know, guess. You can always add more or remove unused pages when you finish, by selecting Add Page or Remove Page in the Page menu.

The *Double-sided* and *Facing pages* options: Allow you to choose whether or not to print on both sides of the page. Working with double-sided pages is easier if you also select Facing pages. Choosing this option allows you to see both the left and right facing pages at the same time.

The *Margin* option: Allows you to set the inside, top, outside, and bottom margins of your page. The margins are indicated as dotted guidelines within the page, which don't print. You can set margins in thousandths of an inch, millimeters, and picas (a printer's unit of measure, equaling $1/16$ of an inch).

The *Numbers* button: When selected, this button opens the Page Numbering box, as shown in Figure 3.3. (The ellipsis (...) after a word indicates that choosing it will give you a dialog box.) This dialog box allows you to select the type of page numbers (Normal, Roman numerals, and so on) you wish to use. You can also set a prefix for numbers on the table of contents and index pages.

42

> ▶ **Tip:** In PageMaker, any time you have more than one dialog box open on-screen, you need to close all of them in order to return to the program. To do this, click on OK or press Return for each box or simply press **Option+Return** to close all the boxes.

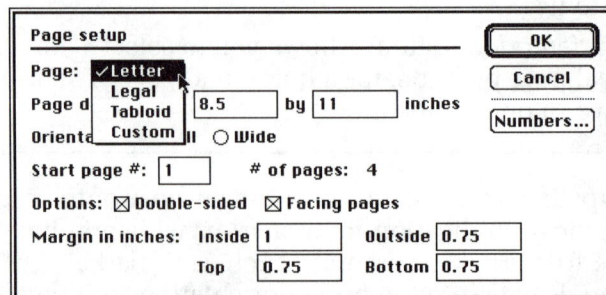

Figure 3.2 The Page Setup box.

```
┌─────────────────────────────────────────────────────┐
│ Page setup                              ┌────────┐    │
│                                         │   OK   │    │
│ Page: │Letter  ┌──────────────────────────────────┐  │
│                │ Page numbering              ┌────────┐│
│ Page dimensi   │                             │   OK   ││
│                │ Style: ● Arabic numeral   1, 2, 3, ... └──────┐
│ Orientation:   │        ○ Upper Roman      I, II, III, ... │Cancel││
│                │        ○ Lower Roman      i, ii, iii, ...  └──────┘
│ Start page #:  │        ○ Upper alphabetic A, B, C, ... AA, BB, CC, ...
│                │        ○ Lower alphabetic a, b, c, ... aa, bb, cc, ...
│ Options: ☒ D   │                                          │
│                │ TOC and index prefix: │            │     │
│ Margin in inch │                                          │
│              ▲ └──────────────────────────────────────────┘
└─────────────────────────────────────────────────────┘
```

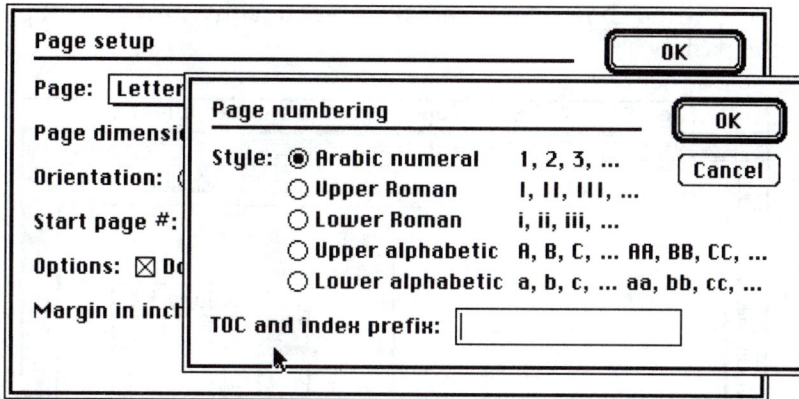

Figure 3.3 The Page Numbering box.

Use the following Quick Steps to setup a publication on the pasteboard.

43

Q Setting Up a New Publication

1. Double-click on the **Program** icon.

   Wait for the start-up screen to disappear.

2. Select **New** from the **File** menu or type ⌘+N.

   The Page Setup box appears.

3. Select from the options described previously.

4. Click on OK or press Return.

   PageMaker accepts your changes and creates the pasteboard work area to your specifications. ☐

Q Opening an Existing Publication

1. Locate the publication icon on the desktop.

   It will have whatever name you saved it as.

2. Double-click on the icon.

   You'll open PageMaker and go to whatever page you were working on when you closed the file. ☐

Figure 3.4 shows the PageMaker screen with a new page in place on the pasteboard.

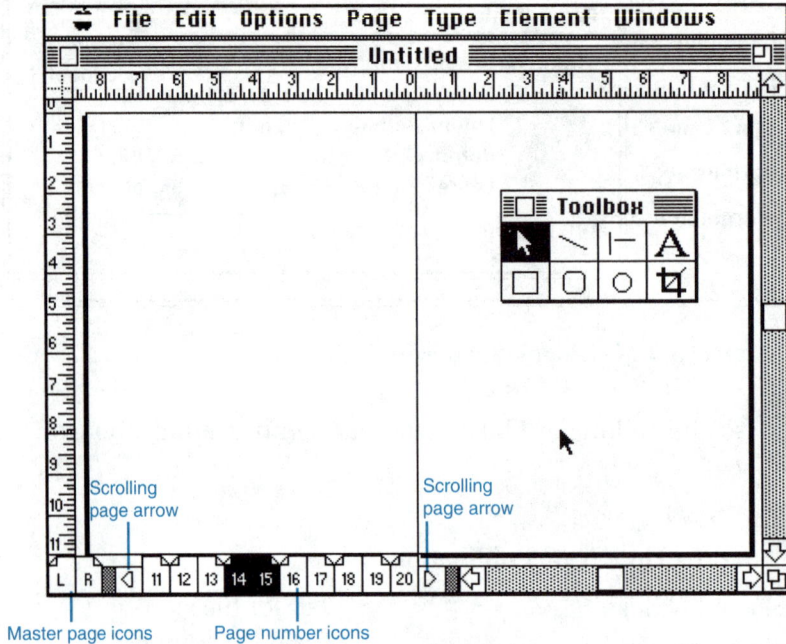

Figure 3.4 A new page on the pasteboard.

Using the Pasteboard

The pasteboard can also be used to store a text block or graphic until you decide where you want to paste it. When you change pages within the publication, anything sitting on the pasteboard will remain there, just like scraps of type or artwork taped to the edges of a drawing board. If you close a publication with items still stored on the pasteboard, they'll be saved along with it. Use the following Quick Steps to place an item on the pasteboard.

Q **Placing an Object on the Pasteboard**

1. Select the text or graphic to be removed from the layout with the Pointer tool.

2. Drag the text or graphic beyond the edge of the publication.

The text or graphic moves across the page to the position you are dragging it to. A blank area shows in the publication where the item used to be.

3. When you are ready to place the removed text or graphic, select it and drag it to its new position.

The text or graphic moves from the pasteboard to the new position in the publication that you are dragging it to. □

Changing Pages in Your Publication

The *Page icons*, in the lower left corner of the screen, are dog-eared pages indicating the number of pages in a publication. Clicking on a page number takes you directly to that page. If the publication is longer than the number of icons that can be displayed, PageMaker will add scrolling arrows at both ends of the page list. You can flip forward or backward by clicking on the scrolling arrows. If you hold down the Command key while clicking the appropriate arrow, PageMaker will take you to the beginning or end of the publication.

45

The *Master page icons* are the pair of page icons which appear to the left of the Page icons (if you are viewing facing pages). If you're working on a single-sided page, select **New** from the **File** menu and deselect the Facing Pages box. Then only one Master page icon will appear. Master pages contain any elements you want to repeat on every page, such as the date, page number, or title of the publication. Click on these icons to go directly to the master pages. Setting up a master page will be discussed in Chapter 5.

The PageMaker Toolbox

The PageMaker *Toolbox* appears in the upper right part of the screen, as shown in Figure 3.5. The Toolbox contains eight tools, some similar to those found in graphics programs.

Use the following Quick Steps to open and close the Toolbox.

Q **Opening and Closing the Toolbox**

1. Press ⌘+6.   The Toolbox appears
                                                 on-screen.

2. Press ⌘+6 or click on the   The Toolbox disappears
   Toolbox's **Close** box to hide   from the screen.
   the Toolbox.
                                                                          □

The eight Toolbox tools include:

The *Pointer tool:* The Pointer tool, shown in Figure 3.5, is shaped like an arrow. You can use it to move and resize text or graphics. To move an item with the pointer:

1. Position the arrow on the text block or graphic and click to select it, as shown in Figure 3.6a.

2. Hold down the mouse button and drag the item to its new location. Notice that the pointer changes shape when you're repositioning, and becomes a four-headed arrow, as shown in Figure 3.6b.

3. If you hold down Shift while you drag, the object will move only on a vertical or horizontal axis.

4. If you click and drag on any of the handles, which are the little black boxes at the edges of the object, you can stretch the object, as shown in Figure 3.6c. Notice that the pointer changes shape to show the direction that the object is being stretched in. Holding down Shift while you stretch keeps the object in the same proportions.

46

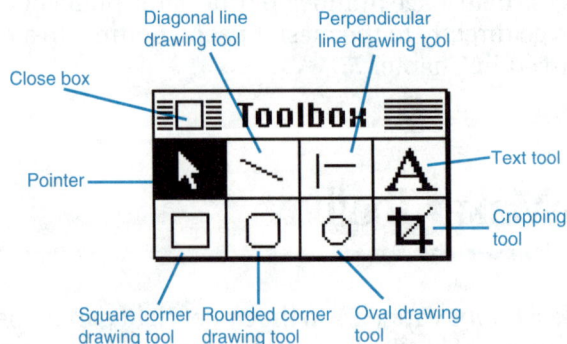

Figure 3.5 The Toolbox.

Selecting
an object
with the
pointer

Object
handles

Repositioning an object
with the pointer

Stretching an object with
the pointer

a

b

c

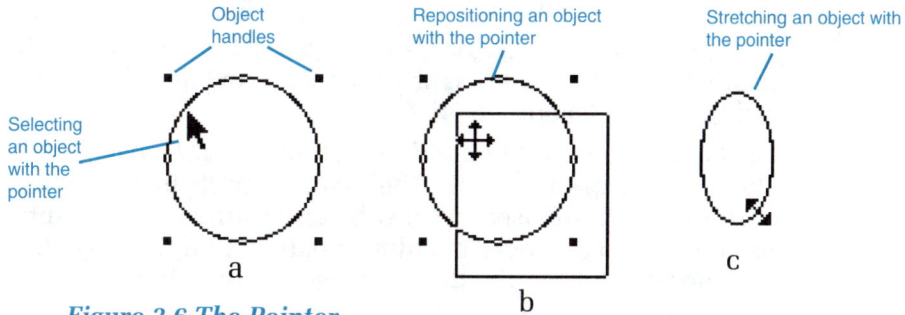

Figure 3.6 The Pointer.

The *Line Drawing tools:* Both tools, shown in Figure 3.5, can draw a straight line at any angle. Use the *Diagonal Line Drawing tool* to draw lines in any direction. Use the *Perpendicular Line Drawing tool* for greater precision. With the Perpendicular tool, you can draw lines which are perfectly vertical, horizontal, or a precise 45° angle. This is especially useful when creating forms and rules between columns. To change the weight of a line, select **Line** in the **Element** pull-down menu, as shown in Figure 3.7. To draw a line, select the Line tool from the Toolbox. The pointer becomes a cross. Position the cross hairs on the page and hold the mouse button down to anchor one end of the line. Now drag the line until it's the right length. When you release the mouse button, the line will remain.

47

ons Page Type	Element Windows
None	Line ▶
Hairline	Fill ▶
.5 pt ———	
✓1 pt ———	**Bring to front** ⌘F
2 pt ———	**Send to back** ⌘B
4 pt ▬▬▬	
6 pt ▬▬▬	Text rotation...
8 pt ▬▬▬	**Text wrap...**
12 pt ████	Image control...
	Rounded corners...
═══════	
═══════	**Define colors...**
═══════	
═══════	Link info...
– – – – –	Link options...
▬ ▬ ▬ ▬	
▪▪▪▪▪▪▪▪▪▪	
••••••••••	
Reverse line	

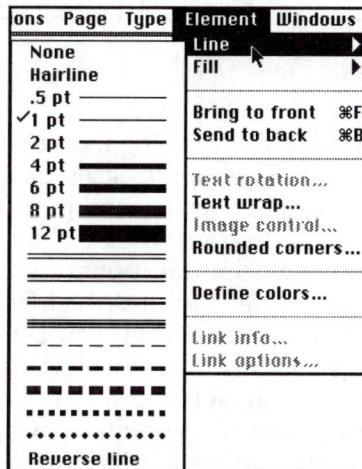

Figure 3.7 Changing the weight of a line.

The *Text tool:* The letter A, shown in Figure 3.5, represents the Text tool. The Text tool is used to create new text or edit existing text. We'll discuss working with text and the Text tool further in Chapter 7.

The *Square Corner, Rounded Corner* and *Oval Drawing tools:* These tools work much like their counterparts in a graphics program. They are used to draw boxes around text or graphics, and to create blocks of color or patterns on the page. If you choose **Fill** from the **Element** menu shown in Figure 3.8, you can change the pattern in the box.

48

File	Edit	Options	Page	Type	Element	Windows

Untit... | Line ▶
None | Fill ▶
Paper
Solid | Bring to front ⌘F
10% | Send to back ⌘B
✓20%
30% | Text rotation...
40% | Text wrap...
60% | Image control...
80% | Rounded corners...

Define colors...

Link info...
Link options...

A drawn box filled with a 20% solid pattern

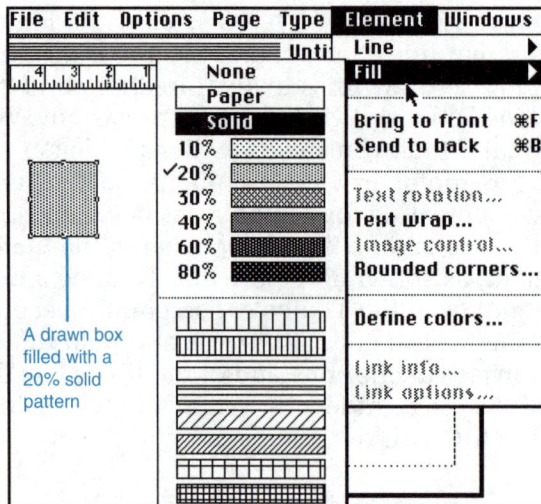

Figure 3.8 Changing the pattern in a box.

The *Cropping tool:* The Cropping tool lets you select portions of a graphic to crop. The tool is based on the traditional cardboard frame used by artists and photographers, and can be moved in and out to frame a particular section of a picture. Figure 3.9 shows the traditional tool and the PageMaker Cropping tool. Move the handles (the black dots) to reduce or enlarge the picture area. When you use the Cropping tool, the picture itself remains the same size. You just see less of it. If you decide to change the cropping later on, you can reveal the hidden parts of the picture by sliding it around inside the cropping frame, or enlarging the frame to reveal more of the picture.

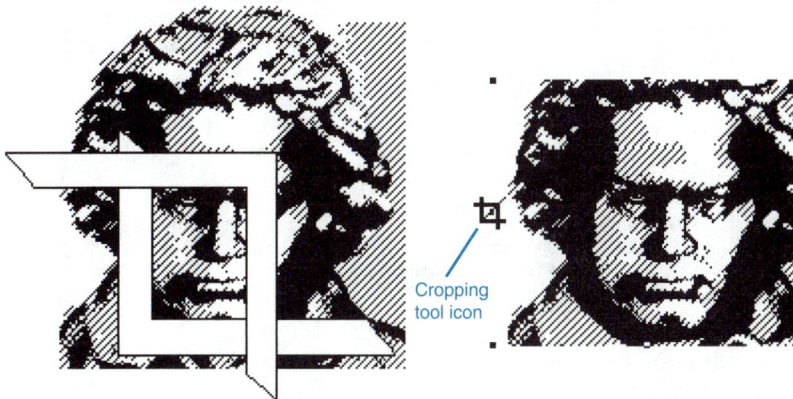

Cropping
tool icon

Figure 3.9 The Cropping tool icon.

The Rulers   49

The vertical and horizontal rulers at the edges of the pasteboard appear by default, but you can turn them off by pressing ⌘+R or by selecting **Rulers** from the **Options** menu. You can display the rulers in inches, picas, millimeters, or even ciceros (a European standard for type measurement). The measurement unit you choose will appear in future dialog boxes. If you choose Custom for the vertical ruler setting, you can type in the point size of the spacing betwen the lines of type. The marks on the vertical ruler will then correspond to the line spacing. Line spacing will be discussed further in Chapter 6.

You can set your horizontal ruler to inches and your vertical ruler to picas, or any other combination you like. The measurments on the rulers are changed in the **Edit** menu's Preferences box, as shown in Figure 3.10. The zero point on both rulers is at the upper left-hand corner of the page. Select **Zero lock** from the **Options** menu to lock or unlock the zero point on the ruler. You can reset zero (when it is not locked) by clicking on the dotted cross hairs in the upper left corner of the screen, where the rulers intersect. Now drag the intersection point to the place where you want to set zero. This is useful when you need to measure the specific size of an element. For example, if you are creating a flyer with a tear-off postcard and you need to make the postcard exactly 3" x 4", drag the intersection point down to the upper left corner of the postcard and measure it. Reset the zero point when you are done.

```
┌─────────────────────────────────────────────────────────────┐
│ Preferences                                    ┌────────────┐ │
│ ─────────────────────────────────────────────  │    OK    │ │
│ Layout view:                                    └────────────┘ │
│   Measurement system: │ Inches │                ┌────────────┐ │
│   Vertical ruler:     │ Inches │                │  Cancel  │ │
│                                        ┌──────────┐          │
│   Greek text below:   │ 9 │  pixels    │          │ points  │
│                                        └──────────┘          │
│      Guides:      Detailed graphics:    Show layout problems: │
│      ● Front      ○ Gray out            □ Loose/tight lines  │
│      ○ Back       ● Normal              □ "Keeps" violations │
│                   ○ High resolution                          │
│   Story view:                                                │
│      Size: │ 12 │ ▷ │ points   Font: │ Optima │             │
└─────────────────────────────────────────────────────────────┘
```

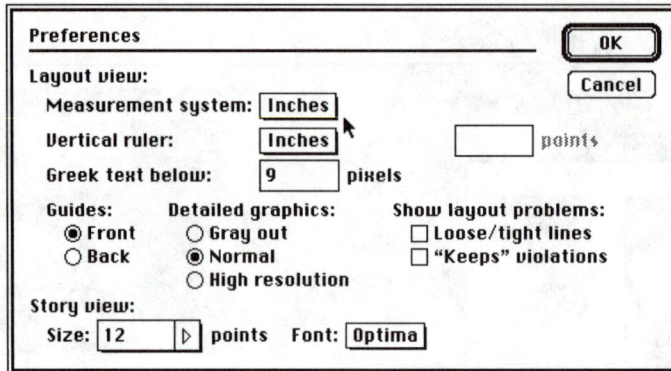

Figure 3.10 The Preferences box.

You can also use the Preferences box to tell PageMaker whether to put the nonprinting guidelines in front or behind the text and graphics you paste down. This is strictly a matter of individual choice. You can switch between front and back at any time.

50

Setting Up a Grid

When you design a publication in PageMaker, you begin by setting up a layout grid. PageMaker draws the grid to your specifications as a set of nonprinting dotted lines. The grid consists of nonprinting margin lines, and column and ruler guidelines. These guidelines help you place and align graphics and text blocks on the page. (They'll appear in light blue on a color Mac screen.) If you were doing a layout the old-fashioned way, you would draw your guidelines in non-reproducing blue pencil on each page, or use preprinted grid sheets.

Setting Margins

The first step in setting up a grid is defining the margins. There are four margins: top, bottom, left, and right. If you're using facing pages, inside and outside margins take the place of left and right margins. (Because of the binding process, you may want to leave more space in the inside margins.) The area between two facing pages is called the *gutter*.

You've already set the margins in the Page Setup box (earlier in this chapter), and you can see them on-screen as the dotted rectangle inside the page outline in Figure 3.11. You can change the margins at any time by returning to the Page Setup box, and entering new numbers.

Margins apply to every page in your publication. If you have text or graphics that need to extend past the margin, all you need to do is put it there. As long as it's within the print area of the printer you are using, it will appear.

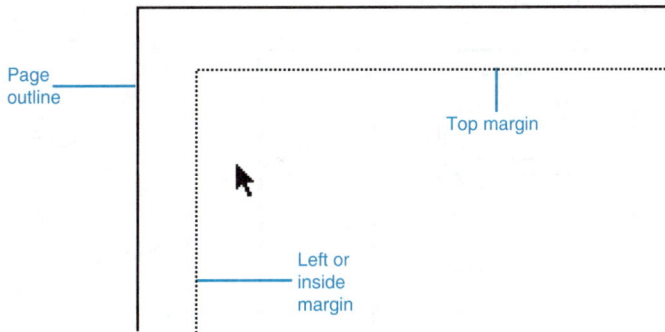

Figure 3.11 The top and left margins inside the page outline.

51

When you set the margins, PageMaker assumes, by default, that you'll be setting one column of type between these margins. So it places a set of column guidelines over the margin lines. You may want to relocate these column guidelines. To do so, point to them and hold down the mouse button. A double-headed arrow appears, which indicates in what direction you can move the line. Next, a dotted line scrolls across the ruler as you drag, so that you can set precise measurements. Figure 3.12 shows a column guideline being realigned.

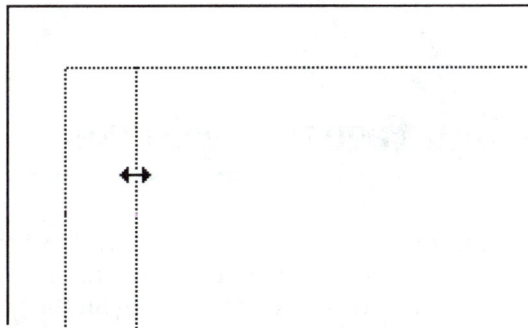

Figure 3.12 Realigning a column guideline.

Changing Vertical and Horizontal Guidelines

You can add vertical and horizontal guidelines by placing the pointer anywhere on the appropriate ruler. The pointer will become a double-headed arrow, centered over a dotted line. Hold down the mouse button as you drag the line into the correct position. You can add and remove guidelines as needed. To remove a guideline, simply select it and drag it from the page to the pasteboard. It will disappear. In Figure 3.13, guidelines have been placed for the masthead, dateline, two columns of text, and a graphic, of a newsletter.

Top margin
guideline

Right
margin
guideline

Ruler
guidelines

Left margin
guideline

Column
guidelines

Bottom
margin
guideline

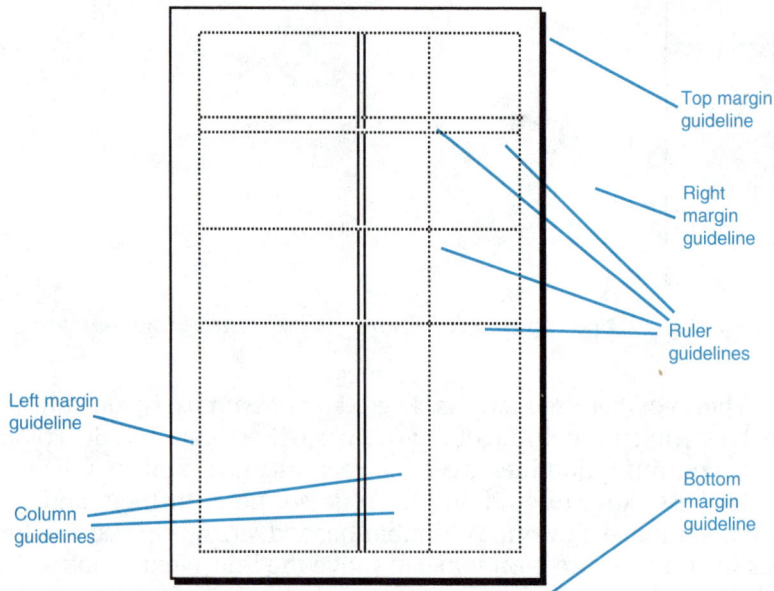

Figure 3.13 Guidelines set for a two-column newsletter.

Resizing Your Page in PageMaker

In the **Page** menu, you can select several ways to view your publication. The Fit in Window view allows you to see the full page and part of the pasteboard area. This view is best for working on the general layout of a page. However, at this size, it's impossible to read type or to see anything in great detail. It is also difficult to align grid lines or objects with precision because the rulers are so small.

> ► **Tip:** To view the entire pasteboard area, press Shift + ⌘ + W
> or hold down Shift and select **Fit in Window** from the **Page**
> menu. This view is useful if you think you've stored something
> on the pasteboard but don't immediately see it.

Figures 3.14 through 3.17 show a sample page at various magnifications.

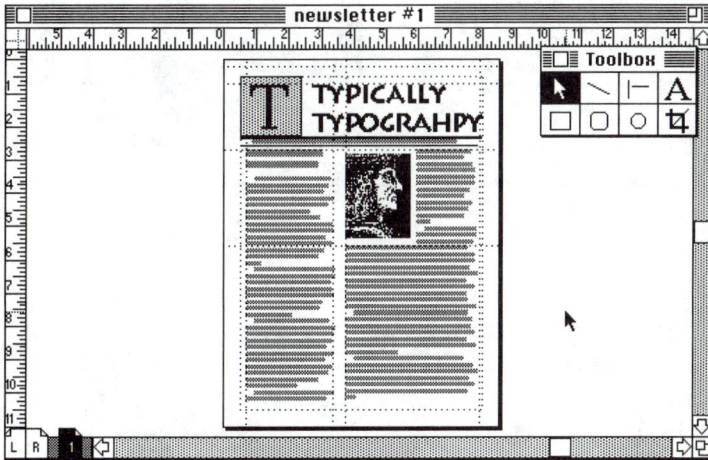

Figure 3.14 A sample page in Fit In Window view.

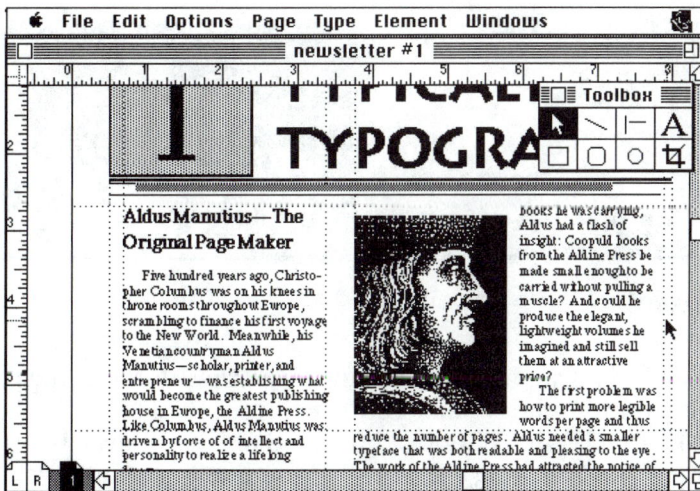

Figure 3.15 A sample page 75% of actual size.

53

Figure 3.16 A sample page 100% of actual size.

54

Figure 3.17 A sample page at 200% magnification.

Some sizes are better for editing text, others for aligning graphics and fine-tuning the layout. You can jump quickly back and forth between the Fit in Window and Actual size views by pressing Option+⌘ and clicking the mouse. If you point to a particular spot on the Full page view, when you press Option and click, PageMaker will expand your view at that spot. Use the following Quick Steps to experiment with resizing your page.

Q Experimenting with Resizing the Page

1. Press ⌘+W to see the whole page. Or, select ⌘+Option and click to go back and forth from one view to the other.

   The whole page appears with text grayed out.

2. Press ⌘+1 to see the page at actual size.

   Part of the page displays in full size.

3. To resize from actual size to 200%, press ⌘+shift+Option, and click on the part of the screen to be magnified.

   A close-up view of the page appears.

   □

55

Moving Around the Page in Magnified View

Use the scroll bars or the *Grabber Hand* icon to move around the page in magnified view. The Grabber Hand icon, as shown in Figure 3.18, appears when you press Option, and hold down the mouse button. As long as the mouse button is held down, the Grabber Hand will move you around the page. The Grabber Hand is available no matter what tool is selected at the time. When you release the mouse button, you'll return to whichever tool you were using. This feature is especially useful if you want to create or modify something on the pasteboard, rather than within the page. For example, you can use the Grabber Hand to move yourself to a clean spot on the pasteboard, or locate something stored on the pasteboard you want to move into the layout.

Saving Your Publications in PageMaker

One of the single most important things you can do in PageMaker is to save your work frequently. If you don't save and you get a message like *The application PageMaker has quit unexpectedly*, you will lose all of your work since the last save. This message can appear if you run out of memory, or if there are too many applications running in MultiFinder.

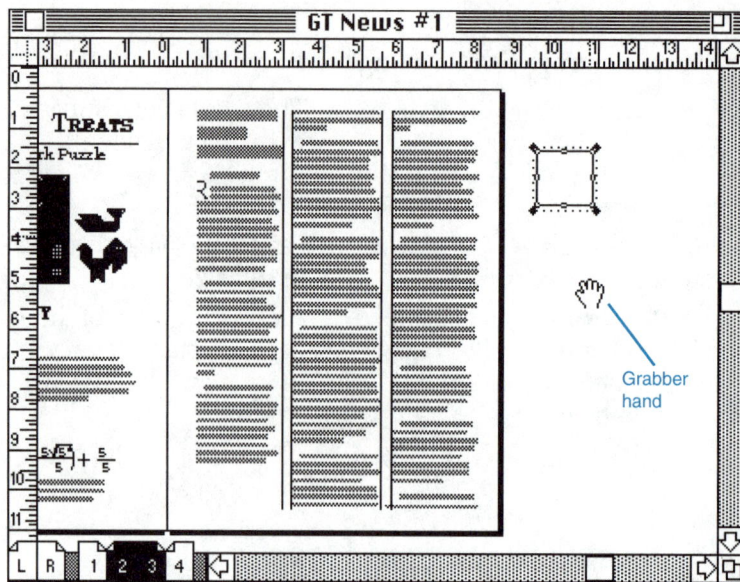

Figure 3.18 The Grabber Hand icon.

In addition to saving your publication, the Save As box, shown in Figure 3.19, gives you another interesting option. You can also save various master layouts or anything else you've created, as a *template*. Templates are publications that automatically open as unnamed copies of themselves rather than originals. The original remains on the desktop to be reused. Because the copy opens as untitled, there's no chance of altering it by mistake. You can use a template as a basis for a series of similar publications. A newsletter template, for example, might contain the masthead and grids for columns. From the desktop you can easily determine, by looking at the icons, which of your files are templates and which are publications. Figure 3.20 shows a template icon, with empty margins indicated, and a document icon with grayed areas representing type in place. Creating and modifying templates will be discussed in Chapter 4. Use the following Quick Steps to save a template or publication.

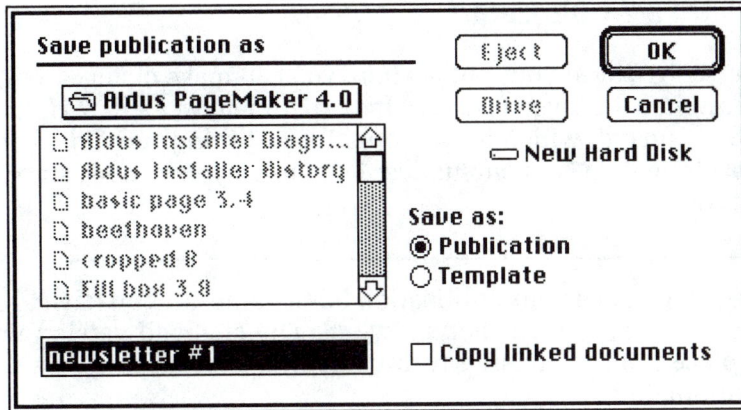

Figure 3.19 The Save As box.

Template icon — Newsletter 1

Newsletter #1 — Document icon

Figure 3.20 The Template and Publication icons.

Q Saving a Publication

1. Select the **File** menu and **Save As**.

   The Save As box appears, as shown in Figure 3.19.

2. Enter the name of the publication in the field at the bottom of the box.

   Your publication now has a file name.

3. Click on the pop-up box on top of the scrolling menu to save in a different folder. Click on **Drive** to save it to a different disk.

   You can place the file anywhere you choose by selecting different folders and disks.

4. Click on the **Publication** button to save as a publication or click on the **Template** button to save as a template.

   Your publication is saved in the folder and form you chose.

57

The Revert Command

Once you've saved your publication, you can make changes to it, and then *revert* to the saved version if the experiment was a flop. Unlike the **Undo** command, which only *undoes* the last thing you did, choosing **Revert** from the **File** menu undoes everything you've done since your last save.

> ▶ **Tip:** Once your publication has a name, all you have to do to save changes is type ⌘+S. The changed version will replace the previously saved version each time you type this combination.

58

Printing in PageMaker

Until you actually print it, you don't have a publication. All you have are points of light on a screen. Don't wait until your publication is finished to print it. Printing draft copies as you go along is helpful for many reasons. You might find it easier to proof a hard copy instead of proofing directly on-screen. This way you can get a better sense of the appearance of your chosen typeface and leading. When you see the whole page in print for example, you may decide that the type blocks are too dense and need to be opened up more, or changed to a lighter face. A printed copy can also show design flaws you hadn't noticed on-screen, such as a crowded headline, too much space between elements, or margins that are too big.

If you print and check your work at various stages, you'll be able to make changes that affect other pages without having to completely redo everything. Even if you don't have access to a laser printer, an ImageWriter (dot-matrix printer) proof will be somewhat helpful. However, with a dot-matrix printer, use Adobe Type Manager (ATM) or TrueType, to minimize the jaggies (enlarged pixels which make type look like it's set with Lego blocks.) Figure 3.21 shows the effect of Adobe Type Manager on large type.

With Adobe Type Manager ———— **B B** ———— Without it

Figure 3.21 Large type with and without Adobe Type Manager.

> ▶ **Tip:** Using Adobe Type Manager will slow down your Mac. Consider installing it but turning it off from the **Control Panel** when you don't need it. (Many professional artists and designers with faster Mac IIs leave it turned on all the time, because of the improvements it can make to on-screen type.)

To print a copy of a PageMaker publication, first check the Page Setup to verify the printer settings. Then select **Print** from the **File** menu, or press ⌘+P. If you have more than one printer, use the **Chooser DA** in the **Apple** menu to select the appropriate one. When you installed PageMaker, you installed a special Aldus Printer Driver that talks to your printer. You must select a printer because PageMaker needs to know which Aldus Printer Driver to use to match its output to the characteristics of that printer.

When you select **Print** from the **File** menu, a dialog box appears, as shown in Figure 3.22. At the top of the Print box is the name of the selected printer.

> ▶ **Note:** If you want to use the Apple Print Driver rather than the Aldus APD, hold down Option as you select **Print**. PageMaker will give you a series of dialog boxes for print options and page setup and finally the Apple Print box. (The Apple driver, unlike APD, supports background printing under MultiFinder and may handle PICT images better than the APD on some printers.)

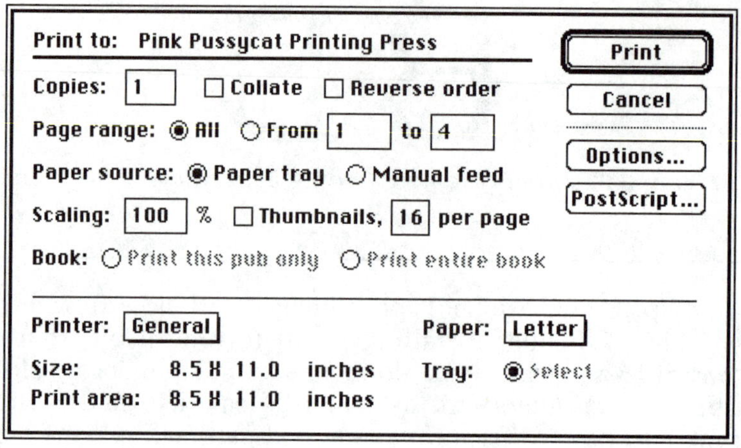

```
┌─────────────────────────────────────────────────────────────┐
│ ┌─────────────────────────────────────────────────────────┐ │
│ │ Print to:  Pink Pussycat Printing Press    ┌───────────┐ │ │
│ │                                            │   Print   │ │ │
│ │ Copies:  │ 1 │   ☐ Collate  ☐ Reverse order└───────────┘ │ │
│ │                                            ┌───────────┐ │ │
│ │ Page range: ⦿ All  ○ From │1│  to │4│      │  Cancel   │ │ │
│ │                                            └───────────┘ │ │
│ │ Paper source: ⦿ Paper tray  ○ Manual feed  ┌───────────┐ │ │
│ │                                            │ Options...│ │ │
│ │ Scaling: │100│ %  ☐ Thumbnails, │16│ per page└──────────┘│ │
│ │                                           ┌────────────┐ │ │
│ │ Book: ○ Print this pub only  ○ Print entire book        │ │
│ │                                           │PostScript..│ │ │
│ │─────────────────────────────────────────────────────────│ │
│ │ Printer: │General│              Paper: │Letter│          │ │
│ │ Size:       8.5 X 11.0   inches    Tray:  ⦿ Select       │ │
│ │ Print area: 8.5 X 11.0   inches                          │ │
│ └─────────────────────────────────────────────────────────┘ │
└─────────────────────────────────────────────────────────────┘
```

Figure 3.22 The Print box.

The Print box offers you the following options:

The *Copies* option: Allows you to print as many as 100 copies at one time; however, photocopying may be more economical.

The *Collate* option: Allows you to collate multiple copies as they're printed. Ordinarily, PageMaker would print the determined number of copies of one page, and then go on to the next, and so on. If you select the Collate box, it will print one complete set of pages, in order, and then repeat the process until it has made the number of copies requested. However, collating takes longer to print, since each page must be loaded into the printer's memory all over again.

> **Tip:** To move quickly from field to field in a dialog box that asks for numbers, use Tab.

The *Reverse* order option: Allows you to tell the printer to print the last page first, and the first page last. Normally, a printer adjusts itself to end up with a stack of pages which has the top page on top. However, on older printers, the first page printed is on the bottom and the last page is on top. In this case, Reverse order allows you to lift a stack of pages off the tray in the correct order, with no paper shuffling.

The *Page range* option: Allows you to tell the printer which pages to print.

The *Paper source* option: Allows you to change the paper source, if your printer offers this feature. This option is useful when you want to print one page on special paper without having to reload the tray.

The *Scaling* option: Allows you to tell the computer to rescale the entire publication proportionately. This is helpful if, for example, you've designed your layout to print on a Linotronic 300, which can print right to the edge of the paper. However, you're proofing it on a LaserWriter II, which leaves a margin. To fix this, you can simply scale down the publication a few percent, until it fits into the LaserWriter's print area. The *Print area* is shown beneath the type of printer at the bottom of the dialog box.

The *Thumbnails* option: Allows you to save paper when you're checking on page layouts, by asking PageMaker to print miniature pages just under two inches high. Because type smaller than 18 point is virtually illegible to the average eye, you won't tend to get caught up in the content of the words and can focus on the weight of the type and the flow from one page to the next. Figure 3.23 shows a set of thumbnails for a catalog.

61

The *Printer* option: The Printer box shows which printer has been selected, and which Aldus Printer Driver PageMaker is using. That printer's specific page size and print area are shown below.

The *Paper* option: The Paper box indicates what size paper the printer should be set for.

The *Tray* option: The Tray option is enabled if the chosen printer has more than one paper tray, as it might if it handles several paper sizes.

The *Options* and PostScript buttons will be covered later.

Use the following Quick Steps to print a copy of your publication.

Printing Your Publication

1. Select the **File** menu and **Print** or press ⌘+P.

The Print box appears, as shown in Figure 3.22.

2. Select the appropriate options.   If you use the default settings, one copy of the whole publication will be made, without enlargements or reductions.

3. Click on **Print** or press Return.   PageMaker accepts your choices and prints your publication.   ☐

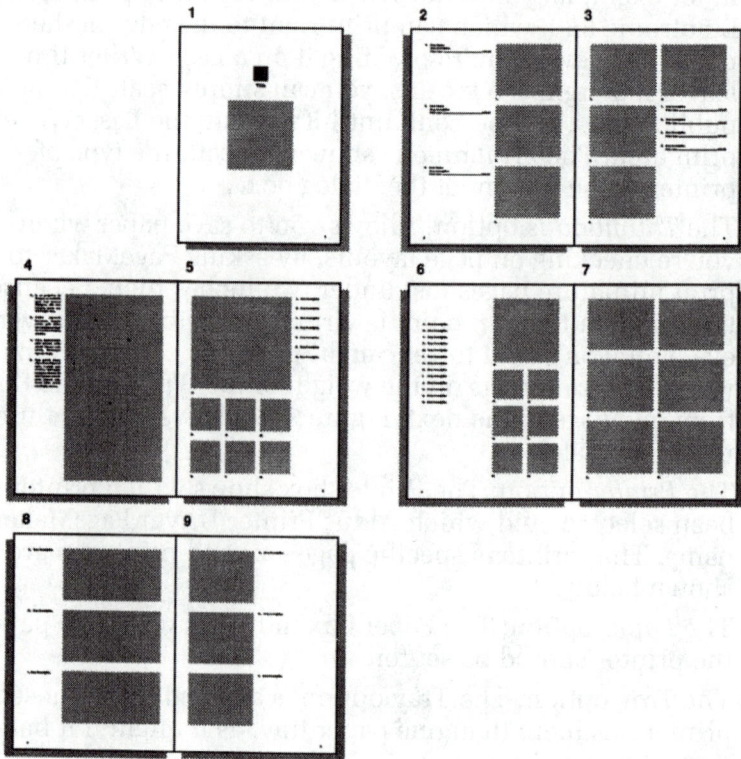

Figure 3.23 Using the Thumbnails option.

WYSIWYG

WYSIWYG stands for What You See Is What You Get. It is true for most Mac applications, most of the time. In PageMaker, however, there are some exceptions to this rule. Sometimes you don't get even a close resemblance of what you see. Some problems that can arise include:

▶ *The Linotronic vs. the LaserWriter problem:* Since PageMaker is a professional page make-up program, it lets you paste graphics or text all the way out to the edge of the paper. This is useful because the professional output devices, such as the Linotronic, can print from one edge of an $8^{1}/_{2}$ x 11 page (or larger) to the other. Desktop laser printers, such as the Apple LaserWriter, can't. Because of the mechanics of the process and the construction of the laser printer, it has a limited print area. It's quite possible that you'd set up a publication to be printed on a Linotronic or other brand of imagesetter, using full bleed (the print area comes right to the edge of the paper). However, when you try to proof it on your trusty desktop LaserWriter, you'll get a warning that the page was composed for a different printer. If you try to print on the LaserWriter anyway, there will be a half inch of white space all around your art and copy, and your publication will look different on-screen. What has happened is that PageMaker has recomposed the entire page for your LaserWriter, using the laser printer's font and page size information to correct the kerning, spacing, and justification. In order to keep your original layout unchanged when you use a different printer, open a copy of the publication file and print from that copy.

▶ *The PostScript error:* This error is caused by some incompatibility between the pieces of the PostScript code. It can make objects disappear on paper that you can see plainly on-screen, or shift the position of a line of type for no apparent reason.

▶ *The Font ID error:* This problem manifests itself when two fonts on your system have the same number. This causes PageMaker, when it sends data to the printer, to pick up the wrong font. Your beautiful Lithos Bold masthead might come up as Hobo, or even Geneva. There are ways to check your font list for conflicts. Chapter 9 gives instructions for doing this.

63

▶ *Incompatible font IDs:* Even though you may have verified the specifications of the service bureau printer and imagesetter, something could go wrong. Aside from the font ID conflicts described above, it's quite possible that you might use fonts your service bureau doesn't own. In such a case, PageMaker looks for the closest available font to the one you've specified. This could cause you to lose a line or two of type if the new font is less condensed. Keep a list of the fonts you're using, and check to be sure your service bureau has them. You may be asked to submit your publication as a PostScript file, by telling the Mac to print to a disk. The best way to guard against these kinds of errors is to insist on seeing a proof, and to examine it very carefully. Never let the printer go ahead and run ten thousand copies of your flyer without checking a proof.

Quitting PageMaker

As with other Mac programs, you have the option of closing the file or quitting the application. Either way unless you've just saved, you'll get a box asking whether you want to save changes. In addition to saving as a template, which we described earlier, you have the option of copying *linked documents.* This copies any and all external files linked to your document into the same folder to which you're saving. A linked document is one that PageMaker automatically retrieves from its creator application. After you've pasted a story into PageMaker, if you make changes in the original text in your word processor, the PageMaker version will reflect the changes. The Copy Linked Documents command makes copies of these files and stores them in the folder with your PageMaker publication. Doing this is necessary if you're taking the publication to a service bureau for printing, or to another computer. Just copy the folder onto a floppy disk. Linked documents and restoring broken links will be explained in Chapter 8.

PageMaker automatically performs a mini-save every time you move to another page of your publication, click the page icon, print, copy, insert, delete, or change the page setup. These mini-saves require more memory. To compress the size of the file you're saving, use the **File** menu's **Save As** command, and save your publication with the same name. Figure 3.24 shows the Save As box. Use the following Quick Steps to reduce the size of your publication.

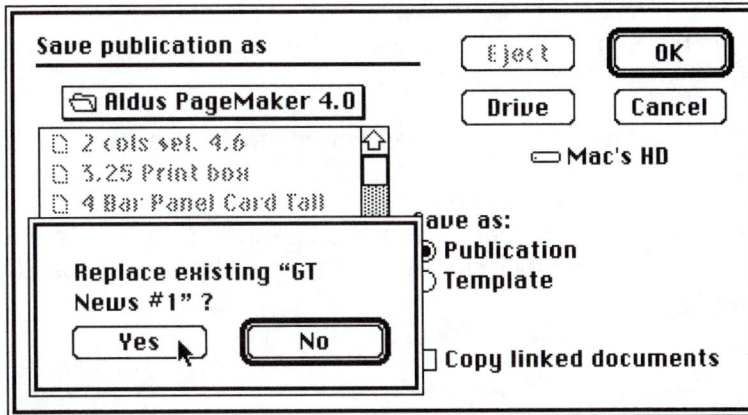

Figure 3.24 If you want to replace the existing file with a smaller version of it, click on Yes.

65

Q Reducing the Size of a Saved File

1. Select **Save As** from the **File** menu.

   The Save As box, with your publication's name entered in the field, will appear.

2. Click on OK or press Return.

   The Alert box, shown in Figure 3.24, appears.

3. Click on Yes.

   The publication will be saved as a much smaller file. □

Getting Help

While you are working in PageMaker, if you get stuck or wonder how to do something, help is available. There are two ways to access a menu of helpful information.

▶ Select **Help** from the **Window** menu to go directly to PageMaker's Online Help screen. Click on the button that accesses the general area of the problem, and scroll through the list of topics until you find one that relates to your question.

▶ Open the **About PageMaker** box in the **Apple** menu, and click on the **Help** button. You'll access the same Help screen system described above.

Get specific help about any command by pressing ⌘+?. The cursor will beome a large question mark. Then select the menu item about which you want information. In Figure 3.25, we have accessed help about Zero lock. The screen shown in Figure 3.26 explains the function of the Zero lock command. Use the following Quick Steps to practice getting help.

Q Getting General Help

1. Choose **Help** from the **Window** menu.	The Online Help Screen window will appear.
2. Click on the appropriate buttons for help.	Commands and Topics will give you scrolling menus of specific items.
3. Select the item about which you have a question.	The menu will be replaced by a text screen explaining the function.
4. For more help, click on the **More Help** box at the bottom of the screen.	A pop-up menu of related topics appears.
5. Select a topic. When finished, click on the **Quit Help** button.	You will be returned to the page you were working on. □

To get specific help, use the following Quick Steps.

Q Getting Specific Help

1. Type ⌘+?.	Whatever tool you're using will turn into a question mark.
2. Select the menu command with which you need help.	You'll get the Online Help screen for that item.
3. When finished, click on **Quit Help** to return to the page.	□

```
Options  Page  Type
✓Rulers              ⌘R
 Snap to rulers      ⌘[
 Zero lock  ?

✓Guides              ⌘J
✓Snap to guides      ⌘U
 Lock guides
 Column guides...

 Autoflow

 Index entry...      ⌘;
 Show index...
 Create index...
 Create TOC...
```

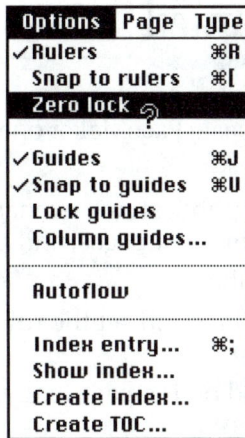

Figure 3.25 Asking for Help about the Zero Lock command.

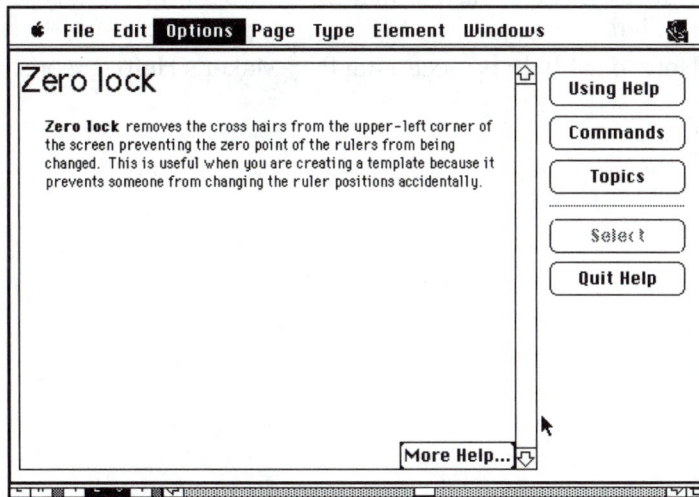

```
 🍎  File  Edit  Options  Page  Type  Element  Windows        🦅

Zero lock                                        ⇧   ┌─────────────┐
                                                     │ Using Help  │
  Zero lock removes the cross hairs from the upper-left corner of
  the screen preventing the zero point of the rulers from being    │ Commands    │
  changed. This is useful when you are creating a template because it
  prevents someone from changing the ruler positions accidentally. │  Topics     │
                                                     ┈┈┈┈┈┈┈┈┈┈┈┈┈
                                                     │  Select     │
                                                     │  Quit Help  │
                                                     └─────────────┘
                                        More Help... ⬇
```

Figure 3.26 The Zero Lock Help screen.

No matter what PageMaker operation you're working with, the Help screens are available.

What You've Learned

This chapter taught you basic PageMaker operations. Specifically, you learned about:

▶ How to open a new publication, set margins, select the appropriate page size, number of pages, and page orientation.

▶ How to use the Toolbox.

▶ How to draw guidelines and set the rulers for your preferred unit of measurement.

▶ How to move around on the page and view the page at different magnifications.

▶ How to save your work and save disk space by resaving your publication.

▶ How to print proofs and make changes for different types of printers.

▶ How to get help by accessing PageMaker's Help screens.

Chapter 4

The Birth of the News

In This Chapter

- ▶ *How to Create a Multipage Newsletter*
- ▶ *Planning and Design Considerations*
- ▶ *Numbering Pages and Placing Footers*
- ▶ *Changing and Using Default Settings*
- ▶ *How to Format a Template*

According to the market research staff at Aldus, more copies of PageMaker are bought by people intending to produce newsletters, than for any other reason. Even if your main interest is designing business forms, packages, or ads, as opposed to a literal interpretation of desktop publishing, the newsletter format is a good way to explore many of PageMaker's features. As you set up the pages and assign page numbers, planning and design considerations will be discussed, which apply to all kinds of page layout projects, not just the task at hand.

Planning Your Publication

The most important part of producing a newsletter happens long before you turn on your Macintosh and open PageMaker, or it's supposed to happen. The mistake that too many of us make is to plunge right in, figuring that we'll somehow make up a design as we go along. At best, getting everything put together creatively, on time, and within a budget, is a challenge. But to try to do it without advance planning is like trying to prepare dinner without looking to see what's in the icebox. Sometimes you get lucky, and all the ingredients come together in a harmonious whole. However, more often, you end up with hash in print, as well as on the table.

Look at the steps in planning, as applied to a semi-fictitious newsletter. There are four things to consider:

1. What?—What materials will you need? How many articles? Of what length? What kind of artwork? What about other graphic elements, charts or diagrams?
2. Who?—Who will be responsible for creating or otherwise providing each item?
3. When?—When must each of these items be ready in order to be included in the newsletter?
4. How much?—Will you need to pay for any of these materials? How many copies of the finished product are needed, and what will the printing cost be? Can you afford to proceed?

70

For example, suppose a local group has decided to produce a newsletter for parents and teachers of gifted children. What will go into this newsletter? With only four pages, there's not much space. They decide to use one long article and two shorter ones, plus a fun page of puzzles for various grades. The newsletter won't have room for a great many graphics, but using some bits of clip art help make it interesting, and the puzzles can be graphics rather than word problems.

Who will provide these items? The articles will be contributed by group members, two of whom have access to Macs and will submit their work on disk. One may send text files by modem. Some art will be provided, and the rest can be produced on the Mac. The contributors have agreed to a deadline. The task of laying out the newsletter can begin as soon as all the pieces arrive.

What about the cost? In this case, there's no need to pay the writers or artist. The clip art files exist. There are no photographs, which could add to the printing cost. So, the only expenses will be printing and mailing. The newsletter will be printed on single sheets of 11 x 17 paper and folded to make four 8 $\frac{1}{2}$ x 11 pages. Future issues may add a separate *middle* page, making a total of six. There's enough information now to sketch out a dummy and talk to the printer, who provides a written estimate. The job can't cost more than 10% over the estimate, and it's within the budget.

Design Considerations

Once you have the materials in hand, or at least, an idea of what they'll look like and how much space they'll need, you can begin to design the pages. To do this, you'll make up a dummy of your newsletter with pencil and paper. You might actually make two or three different versions so you can try different arrangements of columns, and different story placements. Dummies don't need to be full size, since you're just scribbling in the shapes of pictures and text blocks, and not writing every word. For a tabloid size (11 x 17) newsletter, make the dummy half size on a sheet of typing paper, cut down so that the pages are 4 ¼ x 5 ½. (Just folding the paper in half doesn't give you the right proportions.) Be sure that your dummy includes the following:

- ▶ Text blocks (columns) for all the stories you're using.
- ▶ Picture blocks roughly the right size and shape for all the art you're using.
- ▶ Space for the address, postage, and return address if the publication is a self-mailer.
- ▶ The banner with the name of the publication, and the masthead.
- ▶ Table of contents, if any.

By starting with a dummy, you know you won't accidentally leave out any of the important parts. The dummy can be, and generally is, very rough. Figure 4.1 shows the two double pages of a dummy for a four-page newsletter. There's not much detail.

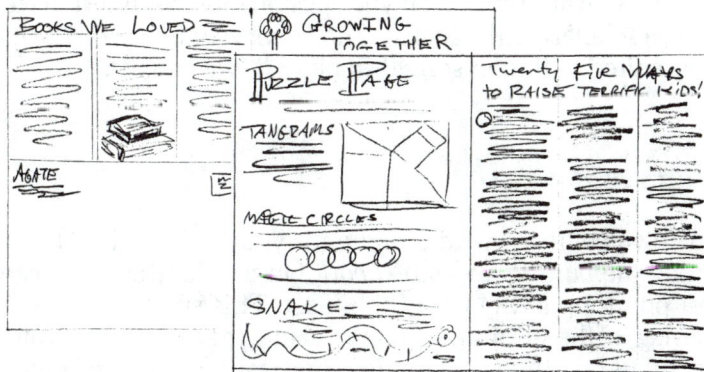

Figure 4.1 Dummies for a four-page newsletter.

71

When you study a dummy, you can see all the flaws in your design. For example, looking at the two inside pages of the dummy shows that a whole page of type is going to be overwhelming. Using a *pull quote*, a block of copy *pulled* from the text and enlarged, may help relieve the monotony of the page. Fortunately, the page opposite has plenty of white space and will help to balance out the dense text on the right. It's important to layout facing pages together, since they're usually viewed together. PageMaker is designed to let you work on both facing pages at once. You can also see the visual effect of the *gutter*, the double-width margin between the two facing pages. Normally, the inner margin has to be generous, if the publication is a book or pamphlet that is bound or stapled together. Otherwise, the words would be impossible to read. If your newsletter, like the example, is folded, you may decide to make the inside margins smaller, to make the gutter less of a gap.

What's in a Name?

72

One of the first things a magazine or newsletter needs is a name. Here's a chance to be creative! The name should fit these criteria:

▶ It should suggest the subject of the newsletter.
▶ It should be easy to remember.
▶ It should attract attention.

Which of these has more appeal: *The Journal of Astrophysical Technology*, or *Skywatcher*? Look for short, catchy names when possible, and when appropriate. If your publication has a serious tone and purpose, a scholarly title, such as *The Pennsylvania Journal of Law* may be more suited to it than something like *Philly Lawyer*.

Banners and Mastheads

After you've come up with a name for your publication, think about designing the *banner* and *masthead*. On a ship, the masthead is the highest point, up at the top of the mast. This spot is reserved for the "house flag" of the shipping line. On a yacht, the owner's "private signal" banner would fly there. These flags and banners were unique to their owners and helped to identify the vessel from far away. The masthead and banner on a publication are similar in several respects. They sit in a prominent spot on the page, and carry information about the publisher and the publication. A banner should be unique and recognizable at a distance.

Although the terms banner and masthead are sometimes used interchangeably to refer to the design for the title of a newspaper or newsletter, banner is the correct word. The masthead is the box which carries the name and address of the publisher and editors, possibly the volume or issue number, and even subscription rates and other information.

Logo Graphics

Banners often contain a logo or graphic symbol (some examples are shown in Figure 4.2) of some sort, as well as the name of the publication. Your company or group may have a logo that you want to use, or you might decide to create a unique one for the publication. This task is best done in a graphics program such as Aldus Freehand or SuperPaint. For better resolution, the logo should be drawn larger and reduced. To begin, measure the space available on your pencil and paper dummy, and square it. If the logo is to fit into a one inch square on the finished banner, create it twice as large or within a two inch square.

73

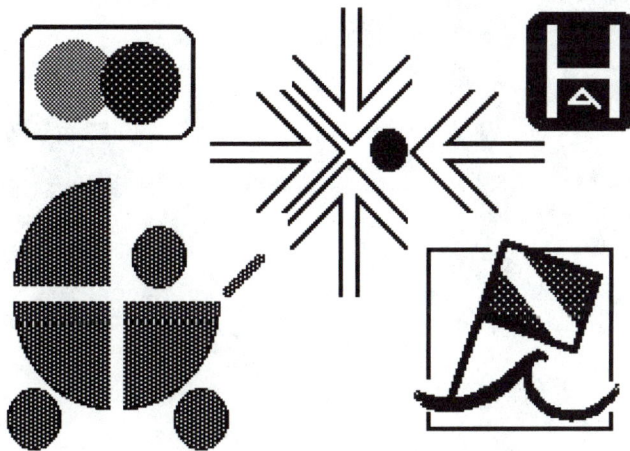

Figure 4.2 Logo designs.

Since you're going to be changing the size of the drawing, save the file as a draw-type graphic, rather than as a paint image. Paint programs create bit-mapped images with a resolution of 72 dots per inch (dpi).

Although they look fine when printed full size on a 300 dpi laser printer, paint graphics will distort when enlarged or reduced to an inexact multiple of the original dimensions. This is because in order to print correctly, the computer has to translate whole pixels into half pixels, quarter pixels, or some other fraction. Because it can't do this, the fractional pixels are either omitted or left as whole ones, causing lumps and bumps in outlines, and strange plaids and checkerboards in dot patterns.

> ▶ **Note:** For a complete explanation of the different types of graphic images, see Chapter 8.

If you create the logo in a draw program, such as MacDraw or SuperPaint's draw layer, you can reduce it as a PICT object and it won't distort. Figure 4.3 shows a newsletter logo copied to SuperPaint's draw layer and resized to 50%. The type for the banner could be added in the graphics program, but in most cases, it's easier to do it in PageMaker.

74

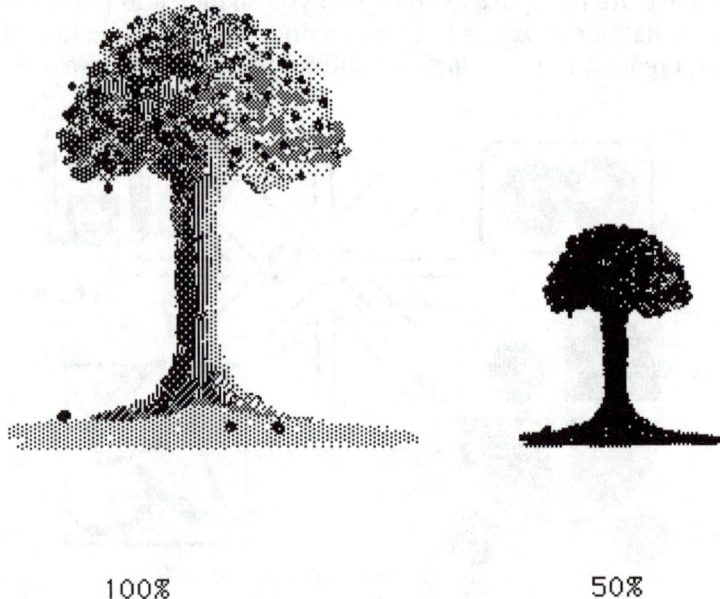

100%   50%

Figure 4.3 Logo at full size and scaled 50% in a draw program.

Since much of the overall design of the newsletter will remain the same from one issue to the next, you'll be able to set up master pages and keep them as a template, saving a good deal of time on future issues. You can incorporate the masthead and page numbers into the master layout, and define margins and columns, knowing that you will be able to change them if you want to. If you add another two, four, or more pages, they'll appear in the same format, with no additional work needed. PageMaker will allow you to use as many as 20 evenly spaced, equal-width columns per page. This is more than you'll probably ever need unless you're setting financial data, or some kind of catalog format.

As you're setting up the master pages, you can place *hairline rules* between columns, and you can even create and save the style sheets for your typography, once you decide on the fonts to use. When it's time to publish the paper, all you'll need to do is place the stories and pictures, and print it.

You need to use margins that will be acceptable to your laser printer, and you also need to be sure to leave a *gripper* for the printer. The gripper is a margin, at least three-eighths of an inch wide, on the top or bottom of a page. You need to leave one so the printing press can grip the sheet of paper to move it from the stack to the printing plate, and then off to the pile of finished sheets without smearing the ink.

75

If you wanted to use a *bleed*, which means there's printing right up to the edge of the paper, you'd have to use a different kind of printer. The Linotronic can print out to the edges, but you'd still have a problem giving the printer his gripper if you chose full bleed, and ran to the edge on all four sides. One way to achieve this would be to use larger paper and cut it down after printing. All you'd need to do, beyond making sure that the right size paper was available and that your printer could handle the job, would be to indicate crop marks at the corners of the pages so the printer would know where to trim the pages. Figure 4.4 shows the use of crop marks and a bleed.

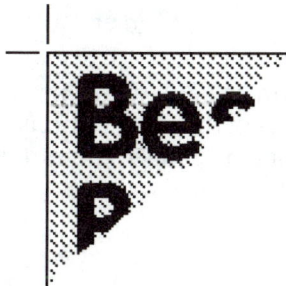

Figure 4.4 The crop marks mean cut here.

Setting Up the Page

Now, you're ready to open PageMaker and get started. When you choose **New** from the **File** menu or press ⌘+N to start a new publication, you'll get the Page Setup dialog box. Even if your newsletter will be printed on paper that's 17 inches wide, you need to specify an 8 $^1/_2$ x 11 page because that's the size of the individual pages. The orientation is tall, and there are four pages. If PageMaker's default margin settings (3/4" outside, top, and bottom, and 1" inside) are too wide, you can reduce them by entering new numbers in the boxes. Select the number to be changed and type in a new value. Figure 4.5 shows the Page Setup box with the appropriate numbers inserted. While you're here, open the Numbers box to make sure that Arabic numerals are selected, since you won't need Roman numerals or Alphanumerics for this job.

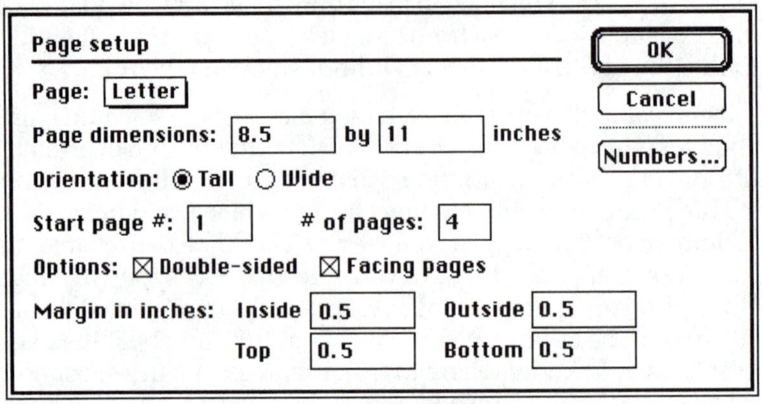

```
┌─────────────────────────────────────────────────────────┐
│ Page setup                              ┌──────────────┐  │
│                                    ─────│      OK      │  │
│ Page: │Letter│                          └──────────────┘  │
│                                         ┌ ─ ─ ─ ─ ─ ─ ┐   │
│ Page dimensions: │8.5   │ by │11    │ inches  Cancel      │
│                                         └ ─ ─ ─ ─ ─ ─ ┘   │
│ Orientation: ◉ Tall  ○ Wide            ┌──────────────┐   │
│                                        │  Numbers...  │   │
│ Start page #: │1     │   # of pages: │4    │          │   │
│                                        └──────────────┘   │
│ Options: ☒ Double-sided  ☒ Facing pages                   │
│                                                           │
│ Margin in inches:  Inside │0.5   │   Outside │0.5   │     │
│                       Top │0.5   │   Bottom  │0.5   │     │
└─────────────────────────────────────────────────────────┘
```

Figure 4.5 Change the margins from PM's defaults to the appropriate newsletter settings.

If you were creating a book with a preface and a table of contents, you would choose some of the other options in the Number box, shown in Figure 4.6. You'll actually place the numbers when you have your master pages open on-screen.

> ▶ **Note:** If you were creating a book or other very long document, you could number up to 999 pages. For the sake of disk space, and to simplify the process of scrolling through long documents, it's easier to divide the material into sections or chapters, and save them as separate documents. The Book command assembles the pieces and keeps the numbering straight.

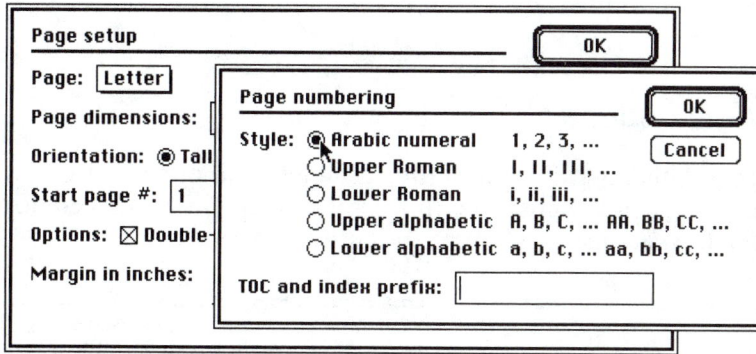

Page setup   [OK]

Page: [Letter]

Page dimensions:

Orientation: ⦿ Tall

Start page #: [1]

Options: ☒ Double-

Margin in inches:

Page numbering   [OK]

Style: ⦿ Arabic numeral   1, 2, 3, ...   [Cancel]
       ○ Upper Roman   I, II, III, ...
       ○ Lower Roman   i, ii, iii, ...
       ○ Upper alphabetic   A, B, C, ... AA, BB, CC, ...
       ○ Lower alphabetic   a, b, c, ... aa, bb, cc, ...

TOC and index prefix: [   ]

Figure 4.6 The Numbers box.

To set up a multipage publication, use the following Quick Steps.

Q **Setting Up a Multipage Document**

1. Open PageMaker from your desktop.

   If it's already open, select **New** from the **File** menu or press ⌘+N. The Page Setup dialog box appears.

2. Change the settings as needed. Enter the number of pages.

   If you're using double-sided pages, always click on the box to show **Facing pages**.

3. Click on the **Numbers** button to open the Page number box.

   Verify that the page numbers are the right kind.

4. Press Option+Return to close both boxes.

   The pages on the pasteboard will reflect your settings. ☐

77

Defining the Grid Lines

Now you can start creating your actual pages on the pasteboard. Begin by setting up a grid. This is a system of dotted lines, which include the *margin lines*, *column guides*, and *ruler guides*. Grid lines don't print, but they help you to align columns of type and graphics as you place them on the PageMaker page. The margin lines are already in place. You located them when you entered the numbers in the Page Setup box. The edge of the page is a solid black line, and the margins are represented by a dotted line a half inch inside the page outline. (If you have a color Mac screen, margin lines appear in pink.)

Adding Columns

Click on the left and right master page icons to open them. You can define the left and right pages differently. Open the **Column guides** box on the **Options** menu, shown in Figure 4.7.

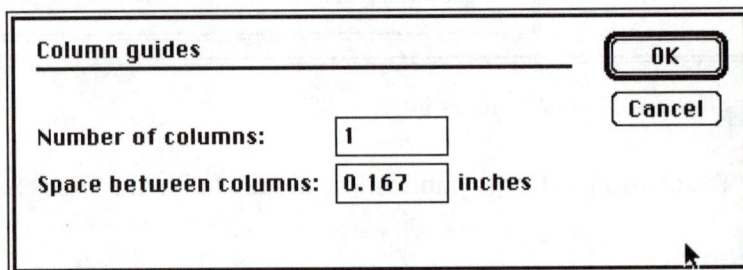

Figure 4.7 The Column guides box.

The default settings shown in Figure 4.7 refer to the current default page setup, with only one column per page. You may change this by selecting Set left and right pages separately at the bottom of the dialog box, shown in Figure 4.8. Two sets of boxes appear, one for each page. You can leave a single column on the left, and change the right page to two columns. You could also change the default spacing between columns to give a little more room. When you're through making changes, click on OK. When the dialog box closes, the changes will be made on the page.

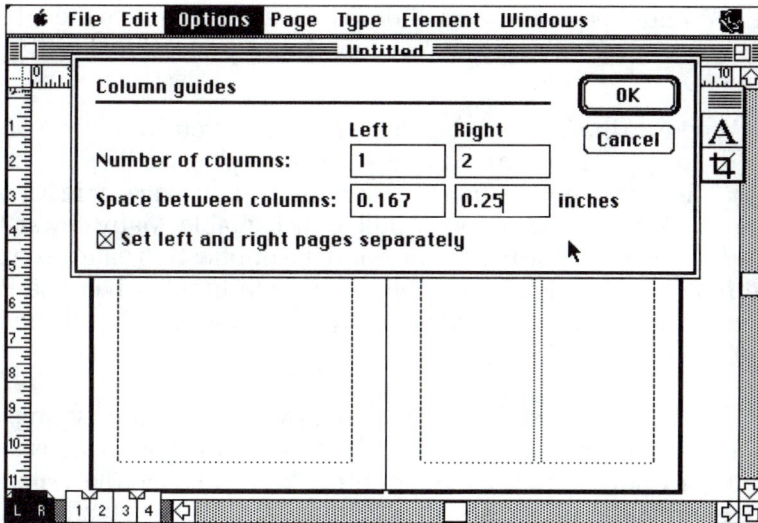

Figure 4.8 Setting left and right pages separately in the Column guides box.

Use the following Quick Steps to set columns.

Setting Columns

1. Open **Column guides** in the **Options** menu.

   The Column guides dialog box appears.

2. To set up facing pages differently, click on the **Set left and right pages separately** checkbox.

3. If you're changing a setting, click on it to select it, and type new numbers into the box.

   When you're finished, click on OK to close the box and let PageMaker make your changes. ☐

Numbering Pages

If your publication has only a couple of pages, it's probably not necessary to number them. However, with a longer publication, it's mandatory, particularly if you want to use a table of contents or an index. Without page numbers, there's no way to reference the articles. Even a four-page newsletter will look more professional with page numbers.

Where do the numbers belong? There are several options. You can stick them out in the margin at the side of the page (as they are in this book). They could go in a footer at the bottom of the page, or in a header at the top. Any of these options would be acceptable. Many newsletters include the name of the publication and the publication date next to the page number. You don't have to type in each number because Page-Maker will number pages automatically. Use these steps to create a page footer.

1. Zoom to Actual size so that you can see what you're typing. Place the cursor at the bottom left edge of the page. Choose **Type** from the **Type** menu, or press ⌘+T to open the **Type Specifications** box, shown in Figure 4.9. When you click on any of the words in rectangular boxes or the triangles after boxes, you'll get a pop-up menu. Select a typeface from the **Font** pop-up menu. Then set the type size. Since the information will be a single line at the bottom of the page, fairly small type, such as 10 point Palatino, would be a good choice. Click on OK.

2. Place an automatic page number marker by pressing ⌘+ Option+P. PageMaker displays the marker **LM** to indicate a page number on the left master page, as shown in Figure 4.10. Type in the name and date of your publication on the same line, or any information you want to put there.

3. Using the pointer, click on the footer you've created. You'll see it encased in two parallel lines, with handles at the top and bottom, as shown in Figure 4.11. This indicates that it's a text element. If you need to move it so that it lines up with the bottom of the page margin, use the pointer to drag it around. For example, you could move the page/date line to the top of the page, if you chose.

4. To duplicate the footer, press ⌘+C to copy it, and then scroll to the right master page, and press ⌘+V to **Paste** it. Exact positioning isn't possible until it's pasted, so just plunk it down anywhere, and use the pointer to move it. When you position the pointer inside the text box and hold down the mouse button, you get a four-headed arrow, shown in Figure 4.12. This arrow lets you move the box in any direction. Note that the page number marker has changed. Now instead of LM, it says **RM** for right master. (It switched automatically, when you pasted it onto the right hand page.)

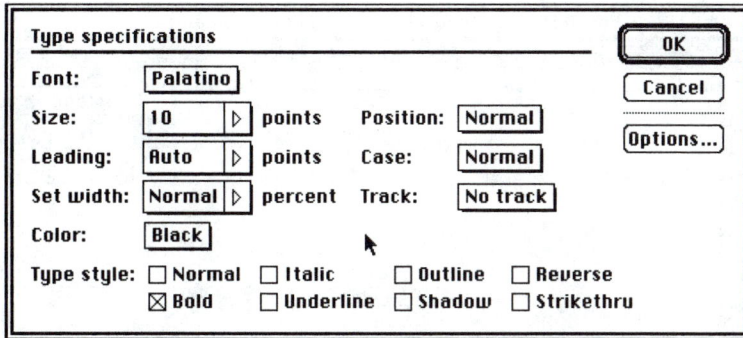

Figure 4.9 The Type Specifications dialog box.

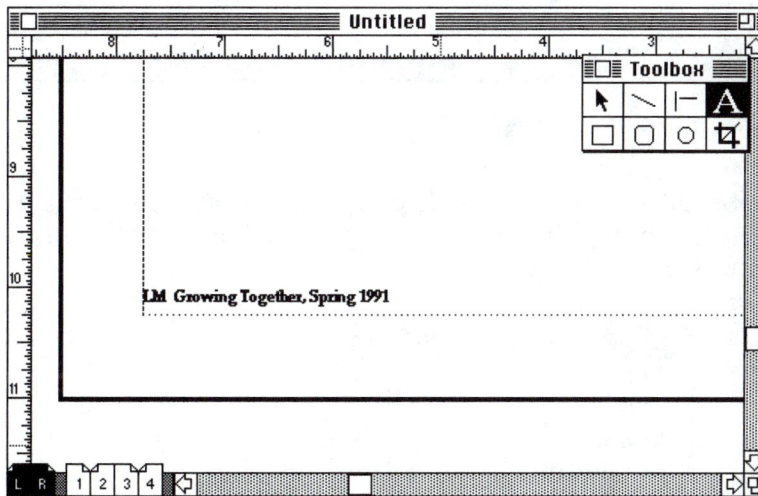

81

Figure 4.10 LM stands for left master.

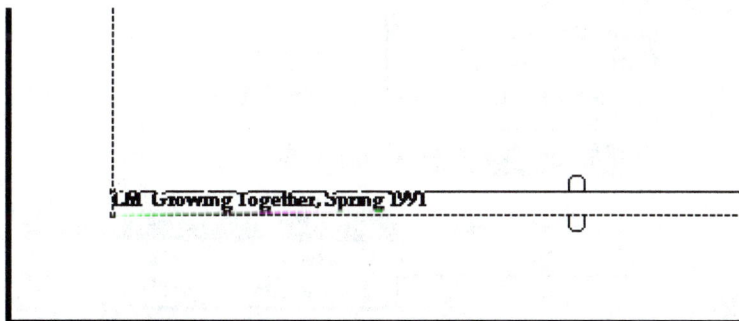

Figure 4.11 The footer has been selected.

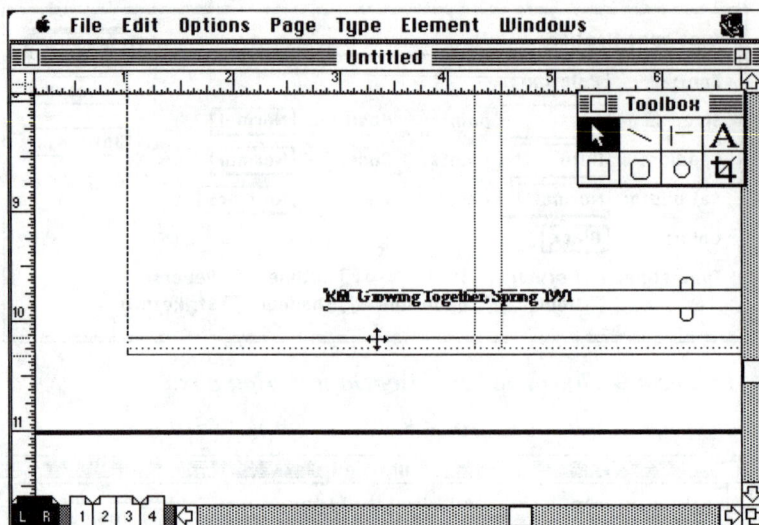

Figure 4.12 Moving the text box.

82

Since this block, in the right corner of the page, must mirror the left side, select the type by dragging across it, and then open the **Alignment** menu, as shown in Figure 4.13.

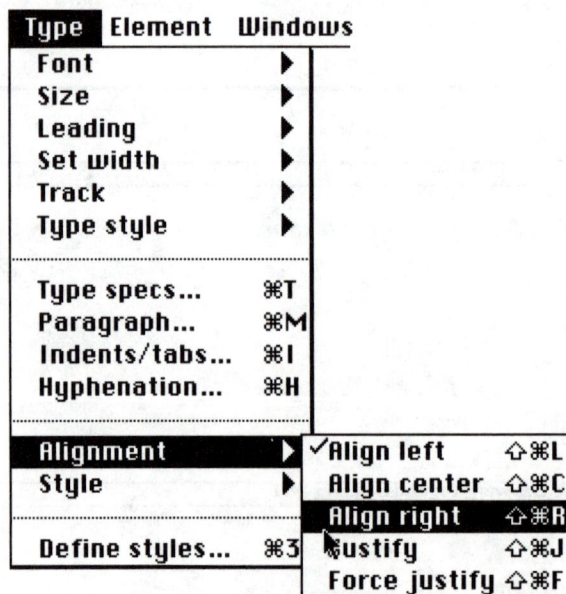

Figure 4.13 The Alignment menu.

When you choose Align right, the type scoots across the page and positions itself against the right page margin. There's still a minor problem however. The page marker belongs on the outside edge. So simply cut it using ⌘+X, insert the cursor where you want the number to appear, and **Paste** by pressing ⌘+V. Figure 4.14 shows the final result.

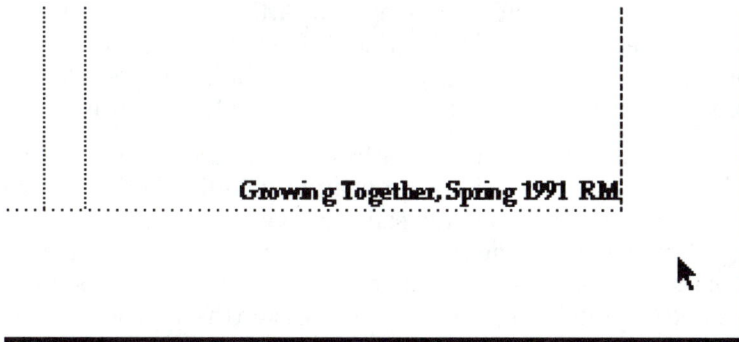

Growing Together, Spring 1991 RM

Figure 4.14 The completed footer.

83

Use the following Quick Steps to setup page numbering.

Page Numbering

1. Set the cursor on the left master page where the page number should appear.

   This could be at the top, bottom, or center of the margin.

2. Press ⌘+Option+P. The letters **LM** indicate the left page marker.

   Add the name, date, or other information you wish to include with the page number.

3. Copy and reposition the footer, as needed, on the right master page.

   LM automatically becomes **RM** on the right hand pages.

Remember to make frequent saves as you proceed, in case of a power failure, system crash, or other disaster. Since you started a new publication, use Save As to give your file a title. Save it as a document for now, and after you've put the banner, masthead, and other repeating elements in, save it again as a template.

Defaults and How to Change Them

PageMaker has preset options and settings called *defaults*, for most of its operations. You've already seen the column and page numbering defaults, and the defaults in the Page Setup box. You can change any of these defaults while you're working on a particular document, and save the revised settings with the document. They then become publication defaults, specific to that publication. So whenever you start a new document, PageMaker reverts to its original default settings.

If you change default settings from the desktop, when no publication is open, you're changing application defaults, and your changes will become the new default settings every time you open a new publication. Customizing PageMaker in this manner can save a great deal of time. For example, if you only use PageMaker for documents to be printed on your laser printer, you can assign the appropriate margins and page setup specifications and not have to think about them each time you start a new project. Or, if you have a "corporate identity" typeface that's used on all your printed material, or a "corporate color" that you'll use for accents on your publications, you can set these as application defaults.

When you create a template for a specific purpose such as a newsletter, any publication defaults you've put in will be saved along with it. You can also use templates from other sources. Many come with dummy text and graphics placeholders installed, so you need only replace them with your own words and pictures. Your PageMaker package comes with templates for various purposes, including several different newsletter designs, business forms, catalog pages, business cards, and corporate reports. Each also has a Style palette, which defines the type font (face, size, and weight) for each different kind of type used in the publication. (Creating your own Style palette is discussed in Chapter 6.) You can use these premade templates just as they come, or customize them by changing their defaults and rearranging the page layouts to suit your needs.

Figure 4.15 shows the PageMaker template identified on the disk as *Newsletter 1*. Notice the filler, or dummy text, used as a placeholder. This dummy text is also called *greeking*, or *Lorem Ipsum*. (I've often wondered why "Greeking" instead of "Latining"?) PageMaker gives you a Microsoft Word file titled *Lorem Ipsum*, in the template folder. You can use this to fill out your own templates if you choose. A sample of Lorem Ipsum is shown in Figure 4.16.

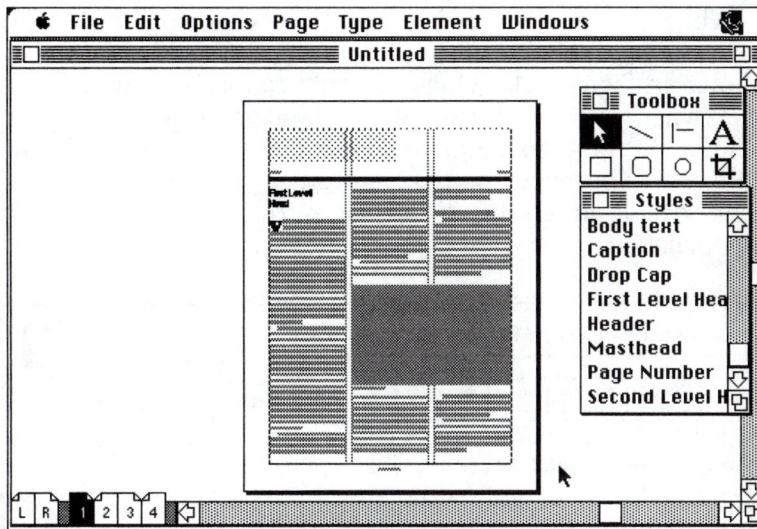

Figure 4.15 PageMaker's Newsletter 1 format.

85

Subhead

Lorem ipsum dolor sit amet, consectetuer adipiscing elit, sed diam nonummy nibh euismod tincidunt ut laoreet dolore magna aliquam erat volutpat. Ut wisi enim ad minim veniam, quis nostrud exerci tation ullamcorper suscipit lobortis nisl ut aliquip ex ea commodo consequat. Duis autem vel eum iriure dolor in hendrerit in vulputate velit esse molestie consequat, vel illum dolore eu feugiat nulla facilisis at vero eros et accumsan et iusto odio dignissim qui blandit praesent luptatum zzril delenit augue duis dolore te feugait nulla facilisi Lorem ipsum dolor sit amet, consectetuer

Iam sol, Aethiopas fugiens Tithoniaque arva, Flectit ad Arctoas aurea lora plagas. Est breve noctis iter.

Brevis est mora noctis opacae, Horrida cum tenebris exulat illa suis. Iamque Lycaonius plaustrum caeleste.

Subhead

Boötes Non longa sequitur fessus ut ante via, Nunc etiam solitas circum Iovis atria toto Excubias agitant sideraara polo. Nam dolus et caedes, et vis cum nocte recessit, Neve Gigante um Dii timuere scelus. Forte aliquis scopuli

Figure 4.16 It's all Greeking to me.

You can also find useful templates in *shareware libraries*. If you belong to CompuServe, America Online, or GEnie, you can find templates in their desktop publishing libraries, which you can download to your Mac. If you create a particularly interesting template, and you're in a generous mood, it would be nice to upload it to one or more of the on-line services so others can try it.

When you use a premade template or when you create and save one of your own, check the Template button in the Save As dialog box, as shown in Figure 4.17. Once the publication is saved in template format, when you open it from the desktop you'll be opening a copy, rather than the original template. This protects it so you can't unintentionally erase your work, or make unwanted changes. The copy opens as *Untitled* and you can alter it, add to it, and resave it again as a template or a publication.

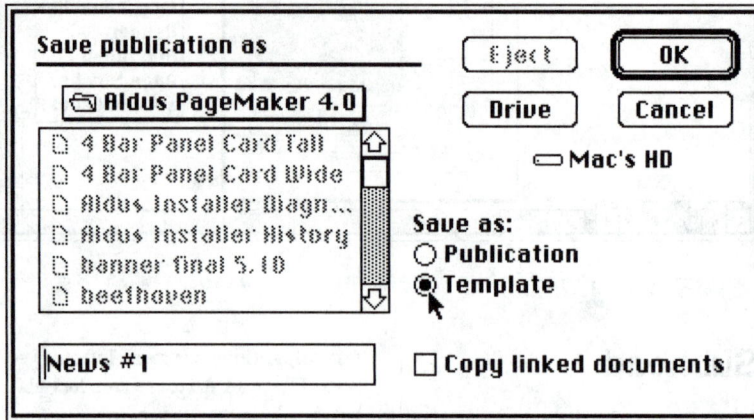

Save publication as

☐ **Aldus PageMaker 4.0**

☐ 4 Bar Panel Card Tall
☐ 4 Bar Panel Card Wide
☐ Aldus Installer Diagn...
☐ Aldus Installer History
☐ banner final 5.10
☐ beethoven

〔 Eject 〕 〔 **OK** 〕

〔 Drive 〕 〔 Cancel 〕

▭ Mac's HD

Save as:
○ Publication
◉ Template

☐ **Copy linked documents**

News #1

Figure 4.17 Checking the Template button to save and protect your template.

To save your template, use the following Quick Steps.

Q Saving a Template

1. Select **Save As** in the **File** menu.   The Save As box appears.

2. Type a name into the field.   This names the template.

3. Click on the **Template** button.   This will tell PageMaker to open a copy of the template each time you use it.

4. Click on OK.   The Template icon looks different from the document icon, shown in Figure 4.18. ☐

Figure 4.18 The Template icon is hollow, while the publication icon is full.

Word Processor Templates

If you enter your text first in a word processing program such as Microsoft Word or WriteNow, you can save time by creating a template in that program for text to be imported into PageMaker. Setup a word processor page with the type style and sizes you'll use for your newsletter copy. Save it with a name like *Newsletter Worksheet*. From the desktop, open the **Get info** box in the **File** menu, and click on the Lock box to lock the document, as shown in Figure 4.19. Now you can use the document like a template, and save your work by giving it a new title.

87

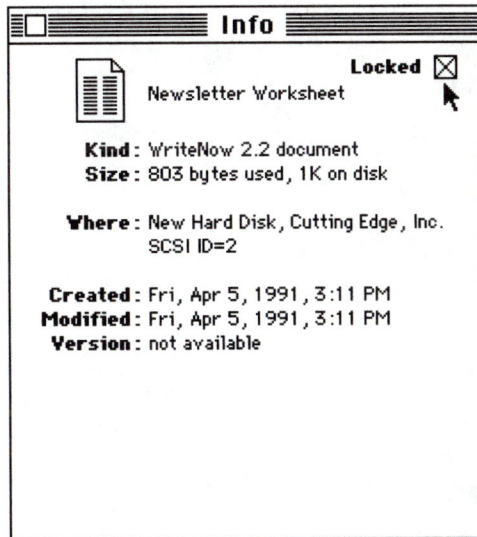

Figure 4.19 Locking a document by clicking on the Get info box.

What You've Learned

Planning is the key to a successful publication. In this chapter, you learned:

▶ How to plan ahead by asking what, who, when, and how much.

▶ How to make a pencil and paper dummy as a guide for laying out your publication.

▶ How to set up a multipage publication.

▶ How to number pages automatically by placing number markers on the master page layout.

▶ How to change the number of columns per page, by using the Columns dialog box.

▶ How to use and change default settings.

▶ How to save your work as a publication or as a template.

Creating Master Pages

In This Chapter

▶ *Ruler Guides and Alignment*
▶ *Working with Layered Objects*
▶ *Adding a Masthead and Banner*
▶ *Adding Pages and Removing Pages*

In the previous chapter, you began to create the master template for a multipage publication. The page number blocks are placed and columns are assigned. In this chapter, you will finish the master layout by placing all the elements that will be repeated from one issue to the next. There's an important distinction that must be made between master pages and the master template. *Master pages* are provided for you in every PageMaker publication you open. They're represented by the L and R page icons at the bottom left of your PageMaker screen. Every item you place on a master page will be repeated on every (same side) page in your publication. Placing page number markers on the master pages, as you saw in the previous chapter, placed a number on each page of the publication. *Master templates* are files you create using master pages and customizing individual pages, as a basis for setting up publications with repeating elements like a newsletter or a book.

In order to position the banner and other repeating elements where they belong on the page, PageMaker lets you place *ruler guides* wherever you need them. Ruler guides are nonprinting lines which align with the rulers at the top and left sides of the page. These guidelines are part of the layout grid, along with the nonprinting margin and column guides. You've already seen the margin lines and column guides defined on the page, which appeared when you assigned columns on the master pages.

Using a layout grid helps assure that your publication sticks to the design you've planned out for it. Traditionally, paste-up artists either used preprinted grid sheets or drew the lines they needed in light blue pencil. (Light blue doesn't reproduce when photographed to make a printing plate.) PageMaker makes it even easier to set up a grid. And unlike the preprinted sheets, PageMaker can remove these grid lines when you no longer need them, or hide them for an unobstructed view of the page.

A Guide to Guidelines

On a color Mac you'll see each of the different kinds of guidelines in a different color. The margins are pink, columns dark blue, and ruler guides turquoise. On a black-and-white screen, they'll show up as dotted or dashed lines. To create a ruler guide, click on the appropriate vertical or horizontal ruler, and drag a line from it to the exact spot on the page where you want the guide. As you drag the line, you'll see a dotted line move across the ruler indicating the distance from the zero point (the corner of the page, unless you've changed it). Figure 5.1 shows a guideline about two inches down from the top of page 1.

This guide was placed on the regular first page rather than on the master page, because it will only be used on this page. To work on a particular page, go to the lower left corner of the screen and click on the icon for the page you want to open. Place guides that you'll use repeatedly on the master pages so you won't have to redraw them each time. Then you can add supplementary guides on regular pages later on, as you need them. You can always choose to ignore the guidelines if something needs to be placed close to, but not directly on one.

Line Up and Make it Snappy!

When you select the **Snap to Rulers** and **Snap to Guides** commands under the **Options** menu, it is as if your nonprinting guides are magnetic. When **Snap to Guides** is turned on, anything you place on the page close to a guideline, will attach itself to that guideline. **Snap to Rulers** aligns any text, graphic, or tool (other than the pointer or Text tool) to an invisible grid composed of the tick marks on the rulers. Snapping elements to ruler marks places them with accuracy to 1/2880th of an inch, .00882 of a millimeter, or with similar precision within whatever scale of measurement you are using.

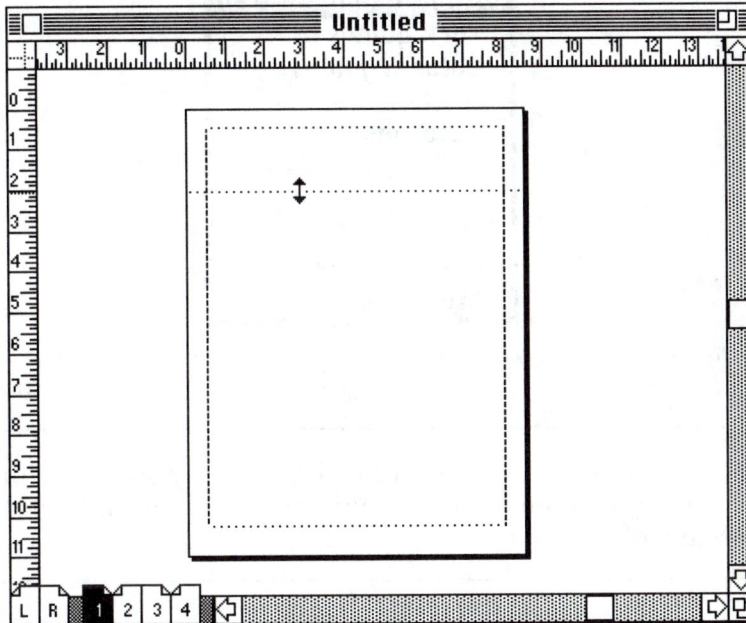

Figure 5.1 Placing a ruler guide.

As shown in Figure 5.2, the **Snap to** commands are selected from the **Options** menu or by pressing ⌘ + [for rulers and ⌘ + U for guides. When selected, they have checkmarks beside their names.

There are times when you might want to place an item close to, but not quite on a guideline. With the Snap to feature turned on, it's very difficult to do. Every time you come close to the guide, the item is magically drawn to it, like the author's white dog to black slacks. If you turn off the **Snap to** command either by pressing the ⌘ combination again or by deselecting it from the menu, you can position the item wherever you want it. Turning on **Snap to** again won't move it once it's placed.

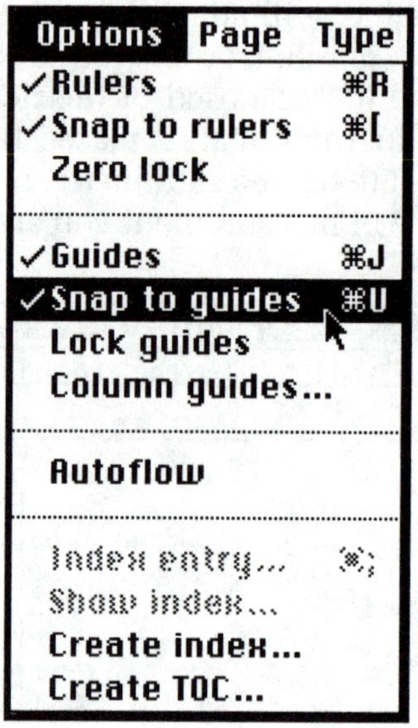

```
┌──────────────────────────────────┐
│ Options  Page  Type              │
│ ✓Rulers          ⌘R              │
│ ✓Snap to rulers  ⌘[              │
│   Zero lock                      │
│ ·································· │
│ ✓Guides          ⌘J              │
│ ✓Snap to guides  ⌘U              │
│   Lock guides                    │
│   Column guides...               │
│ ·································· │
│   Autoflow                       │
│ ·································· │
│   Index entry...    ⌘;           │
│   Show index...                  │
│   Create index...                │
│   Create TOC...                  │
└──────────────────────────────────┘
```

92

Figure 5.2 Snap to.

> ▶ **Tip:** If you place a thin ruled line directly on a guideline, it may be hidden by the guideline. Hide the guidelines to see any missing lines.

Use the following Quick Steps to use the **Snap to** commands.

Q **Drawing Guides**

1. Place the pointer on the ruler. Hold the mouse button down and drag the guideline into position.

   The line will scroll across or down the screen as you drag the mouse.

2. Press ⌘+U to activate **Snap to guides**.

   When you position something near a guideline, it will try to align itself with the guideline. ☐

Lay Down Layers

Other elements you might want to place on a master page are dot patterns, colored lines, or blocks to accent a block of text. For example, if you'll always place your table of contents in the same spot and want to make it stand out, you can fit a block of color or a dot pattern behind it, as shown in Figure 5.3. The dot pattern could go on the master page or on a regular page of your newsletter template. Then, in each issue, you can add the appropriate text block as a second layer on top of the dot pattern.

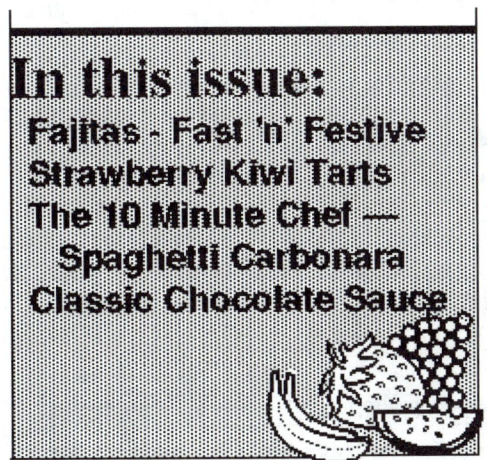

Figure 5.3 The dots are a 20% screen, which could be printed in a second color.

93

Another trick is also shown in Figure 5.3. The picture has been placed over the dots but they don't show through it as they normally would. To create this kind of electronic white out, use the following Quick Steps.

Q Placing a Graphic on Top of a Colored Block, While Keeping the Dots From Showing Through

1. Select **Paper** from the **Fill** menu and **None** from the **Line** menu under **Elements**.

   This will give you an **invisible** shape.

2. Select the appropriate shape tool and draw a mask to cover the unwanted part of the background.

   You'll be able to locate it by its handles as long as the shape is selected.

3. If the shape isn't selected it will be invisible against the background. In case you lose it, click on the approximate area where it is.

   When you click on the shape, it will be selected again.

4. Drag the graphic over the mask frequently to check the fit, and move it out to the pasteboard again if the mask needs more adjustment.

   Try to choose graphics with simple shapes for this treatment, or you'll drive yourself crazy trying to mask them. □

This particular graphic, being an irregular shape, needed several pieces of mask. A close-up with the graphic removed and the masks selected is shown in Figure 5.4. You can also restore a piece of pattern in the middle of the mask by selecting the pattern as **Fill** and placing it with the appropriate shape tool. Once you've placed an object, you can press ⌘+B to send it to the back layer. Then you can place something else on top of it. Pressing ⌘+F brings a selected object, text block, or graphic to the front layer.

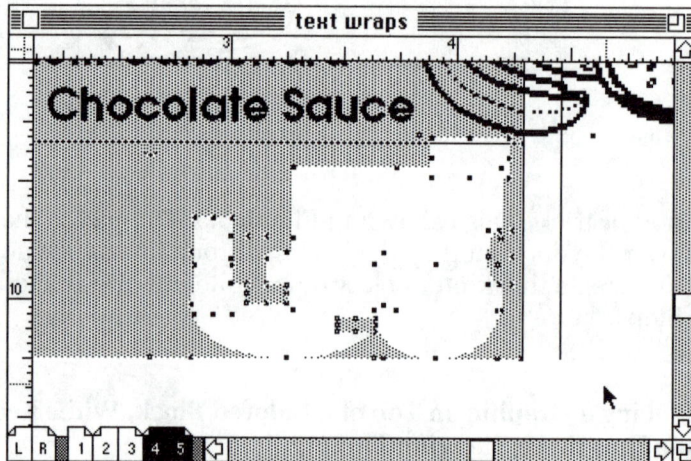

Figure 5.4 The mask is the middle layer and the graphic goes on top of it.

You can use layering to create many interesting effects. What you bring to the front will overlap whatever is behind it. Overlapping lets you simulate shadows and other special effects, and can create a three-dimensional effect on the page.

⊘ **Warning:** If you're overlapping blocks of color on the page, be careful how you do it. Colors may mix strangely when printed. Check with your printer before you set up a page with overlapping colors.

Creating a Masthead

95

The masthead and banner will remain essentially the same from one issue to the next. Only the date and volume number will change so these elements can be part of your master publication. Laying out a masthead is simple since it's really just a block of text. The masthead should include the following information:

- ▶ The name of the publication.
- ▶ Name and address of the publisher.
- ▶ Copyright notice.
- ▶ Credits—editor, reporters, designer, photographer, and so on.
- ▶ Subscription information may also be included.

Once you've decided where on the page to locate the masthead, select the Text tool, and type the information into PageMaker. Format it so it fits the space available and remains legible. It should either be encased in a box or set in very different type so it's clearly not part of the editorial material (the main text) of your publication. Figure 5.5 shows the text of a typical masthead.

The masthead is generally placed somewhere near the front of a publication. However, you may place it anywhere it fits; there's no real rule. Newspapers frequently run the masthead with the index on page two or on the editorial page. In the example in Figure 5.6, it's being used as a design element and will be placed on the first page of the newsletter. The table of contents runs down the left side of the page, with the masthead below it. Since the masthead is an area of fairly dense type, it will help balance the other items on the page. The arrangement of columns on page one of this sample newsletter has been changed to create a narrow and a wide column. To change the column size, simply click on the edge of the column and drag it to its new position.

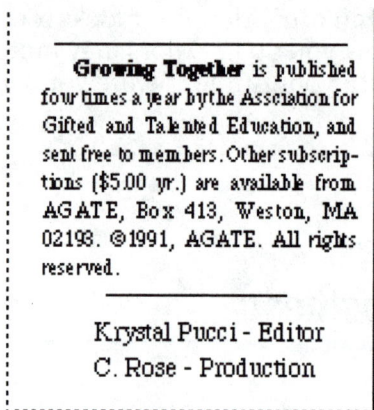

Growing Together is published four times a year by the Association for Gifted and Talented Education, and sent free to members. Other subscriptions ($5.00 yr.) are available from AGATE, Box 413, Weston, MA 02193. ©1991, AGATE. All rights reserved.

Krystal Pucci - Editor
C. Rose - Production

Figure 5.5 The masthead tells who's in charge here.

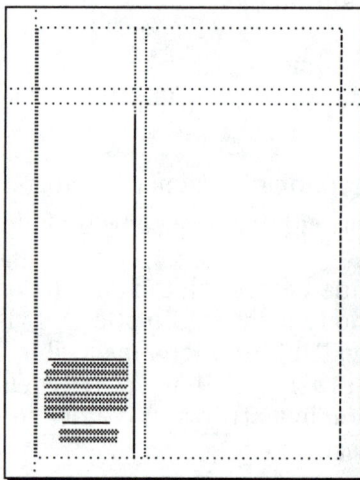

Figure 5.6 The front page of a sample newsletter with the masthead placed.

Mastheads and other text blocks which remain unchanged are called *boilerplate.* You can either put these items on the master page template, save them in your scrapbook or as text files, and paste them down as needed. Retyping them each time is tedious and unnecessary, and is practically guaranteed to introduce mistakes at some point.

> ▶ **Tip:** If you save boilerplate text or graphics as files rather than keeping them in a scrapbook, save them as **BP/...** or use a distinctive symbol such as * or # at the front of the file name. This way, even if you have a lot of files in your newsletter folder, you'll be able to view by name and find the files you need quickly.

Creating a Banner

There's another element on the first page that can be part of a master layout; it's the banner. Aside from inserting a new date for each issue, the banner will remain the same. Your publication must be immediately recognizable. Keeping the banner in the same place and trying to achieve a consistent look by following the same basic layout and design from one issue to the next, will help you achieve this goal. Changing the appearance of your publication from one month to the next confuses the reader.

To create a banner, decide where on the page it should be. Most banners run across the top of the front page, but it could also go across the bottom or even down the edge. In the following examples, the traditional top of the page format is used, and a guideline has been placed to show the bottom edge of the banner.

Banners often include a logo. To place a logo, follow these steps:

1. Open the Place box by selecting it from the **File** menu or by pressing ⌘+D. Select the graphic to be placed, as shown in Figure 5.7.

2. Click on OK to close the selection box. The pointer will change to the Place document icon, shown in Figure 5.8. Position it approximately at the upper left corner of the area where you

want the logo to appear. When you click, the graphic appears (for this example, the tree would appear). Now you can make whatever adjustments are needed.

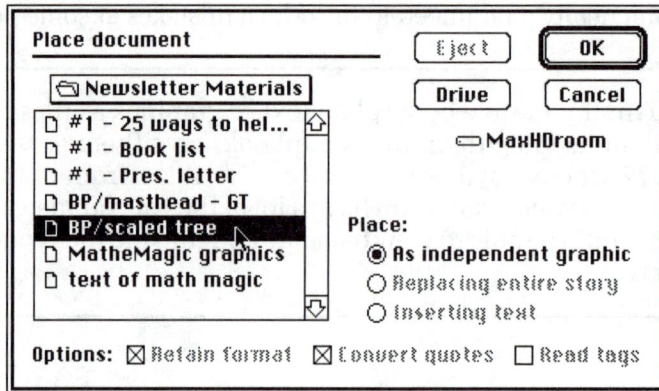

Figure 5.7 Pick the graphic to be placed.

98

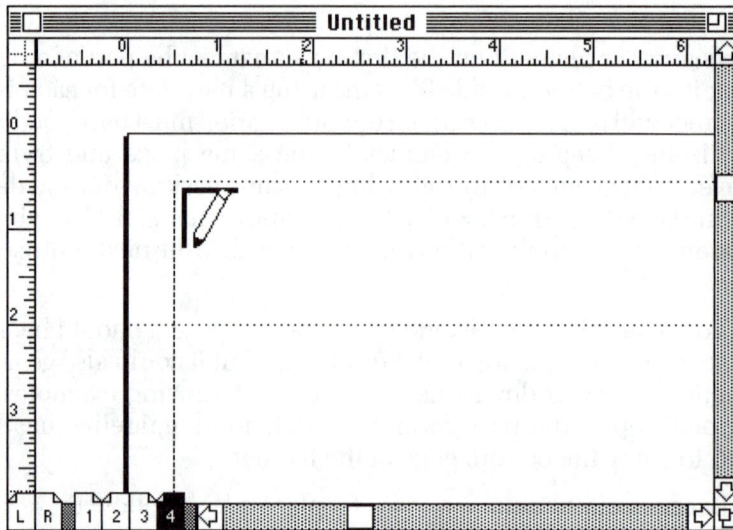

Figure 5.8 The Place graphics icon.

The first adjustment you may need to make is done with the Cropping tool. When you transferred the graphic into PageMaker, the whole page was copied in from the paint program. This means there's a lot of blank space around the logo. To avoid confusion, it's best to crop it out. You can use the Cropping tool as a pair of scissors to trim away the unneeded parts of the page. Figure 5.9 shows the Cropping tool in use.

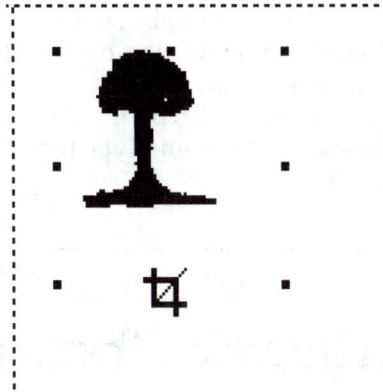

Figure 5.9 Is this cropping, trimming, or pruning the tree?

99

To crop a logo, use the following steps:

1. Select the Cropping tool and click on the graphic. You'll see little black boxes (handles) at the edges and centers of each side.
2. Click on any handle and drag to move the edge of the page. Dragging the edge in makes the page smaller. You can drag all four sides of the page in so the edges are right at the edge of the picture.
3. If you put the Cropping tool in the middle of the graphic box, it changes to a hand and lets you slide the image around within the box.

> ▶ **Tip:** To avoid the need for cropping, open your paint program and select only your graphic. Copy it into the scrapbook and place it into the document from there, or paste it directly from the clipboard. (You won't be able to maintain links to a graphic pasted this way, however.)

After you've placed the logo, you're ready to add the type. PageMaker gives you several options for determining types sizes and fonts. The easiest is to use the **Type** menu's various submenus to select the font, size, and other attributes you want to use. Remember, banners need to be distinctive, but easy to read. Choose a relatively large type, perhaps 48 points or more, depending on the length of the name. PageMaker lets you choose any type size, not just the ones listed on the menu. If you want to use a different size, choose **Other** and type it into the little box. You can choose sizes in whole numbers and tenths. So if 48 point is just a bit too large, try 47.5 points. After you set the attributes for your type, choose the Text tool and type the name into the banner, as shown in Figure 5.10.

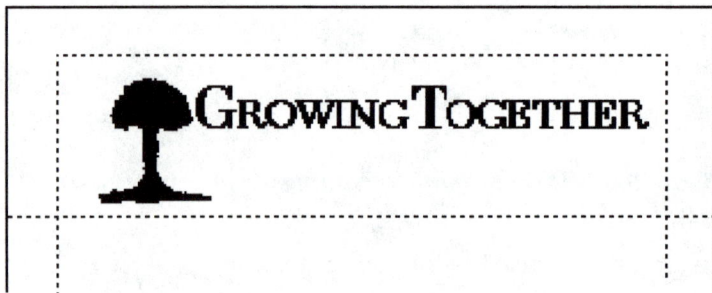

Figure 5.10 Inserting the text for the banner.

Don't be disappointed if the banner doesn't look right the first time you place the type. The illustrations that follow show some of the stages our sample banner went through before reaching an acceptable design.

In Figure 5.10, the banner looks rather crowded, and leaves too much empty space underneath the name. Perhaps we might try moving it to two lines, shown in Figure 5.11.

How about reversing the positions of the name and tree? It's easy to select the elements and try them in various combinations. You can move things around until you're satisfied. In Figure 5.12, we've added other elements to create the final version of the banner. The date, which was added to balance the tree, is in a separate text block making it easier to change from one month to the next.

Most publications add a *dateline,* a line of type below the banner that generally contains the date and name of the publishing group sponsoring the newsletter. Since this information is already on the first page of our example, the dateline can be used for other purposes. Figure 5.13 shows one possibility.

Figure 5.11 Two lines of larger type for the banner makes a better design.

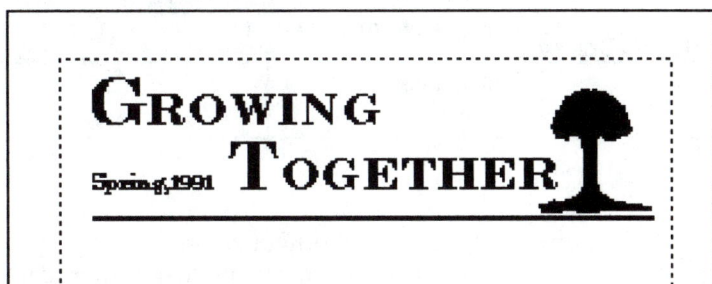

Figure 5.12 The final version of the banner.

Figure 5.13 Placing a motto in the space for the dateline.

When the type isn't long enough to fill out the line properly, there are several solutions. You could use a longer sentence, center the type you have, add bullets or decorative devices at the ends of the line, or expand the width of the type by selecting a larger percent on the **Type width** menu. Figure 5.14 shows the **Type width** menu and the expanded line beneath.

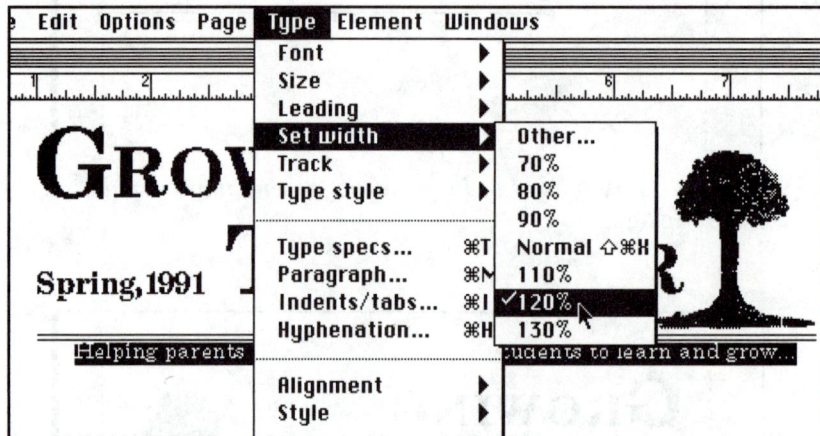

Figure 5.14 The Type width menu.

Study your dummy to see what other elements are likely to repeat from one issue to the next. The more you can do to complete a template, the quicker you'll be able to put together the monthly, weekly, or daily news.

> **Note:** Perhaps even the hourly news! The Pan Am Shuttle from Washington to New York and Boston now distributes a PageMaker set publication, aptly called *The Latest News*. It's laser printed and ready for free distribution fifteen minutes before each of the hourly shuttle flights, and includes stories from the UPI news wire and Macintosh graphics.

Setting Up a Self-mailer

If your production is to be a self-mailer, you can set aside the addressing area and set up the return address block and mailing indicia on your master page layout. A self-mailer, logically enough, is a publication that doesn't get mailed in an envelope. The usual way to produce a self-mailer is to dedicate half of the last page to addressing and mailing requirements. Figure 5.15 shows a self-mailing newsletter. The last page has been divided in half, with copy on the upper half and the return address and mailing information on the bottom.

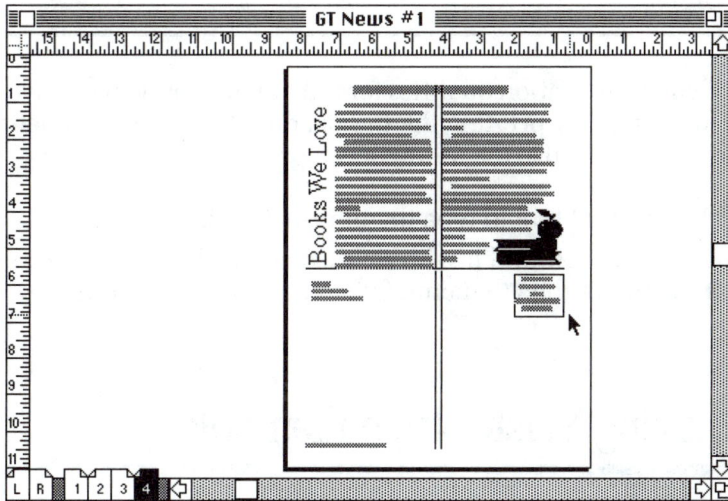

Figure 5.15 An example of a self-mailer.

To add the return address block to the master page layout, use the following steps:

1. Begin by drawing a ruler guide halfway down the page at 5 $1/2$ inches, the point where the newsletter will fold for mailing.

2. Place a thin line as a folding guide, and to mark the limit for anything placed on the top half of the page.

3. Select the Text tool, drop down to leave a reasonable margin, and insert the return address.

Mailing Indicia

The United States Postal Service allows bulk rate (third class) mailing of a minimum of 200 pieces of identical mail. Permit mailers must use postage meter imprints, precanceled stamps, or print the bulk rate permit number *indicia* on the envelope. The indicia is a small block that includes the words Bulk Rate, US Postage, and the permit number.

> ▶ **Note:** Postal regulations are subject to change without notice. Check with your Postmaster before planning to use bulk mail and for information on obtaining the necessary permits.

If your publication qualifies for bulk mail rates, you can avoid the need for stamps by printing the indicia directly on the newsletter. To create the indicia, use the following steps:

1. Use the Text tool to type the information into a text block.
2. Draw a box around it with the Rectangle tool. Be sure to select **None** under the **Fill** menu. Otherwise, you'll cover up the text.

Removing Master Page Elements

Any elements such as the page number blocks, which were placed on PageMaker's left and right master pages, will appear on every page of your publication. If they aren't wanted on a particular page for some reason, you may remove them from that page. To do so:

1. Go to that page and then open the **Page** menu. There will be a check next to the words Display master items.
2. Click on Display master items to remove the check mark. Anything that was created on the master page will be removed.

If you have placed guides on the master pages, you may choose whether or not to apply them by selecting or deselecting **Copy master guides**, also on the **Page** menu.

Adding Pages

The example template is for a four-page newsletter. If your next issue has a lot more material, you might need to make it six pages, or maybe even eight. To insert additional pages, select **Insert pages** from the **Page** menu, and indicate the number of pages and their position in the box, as shown in Figure 5.16. The pages you insert will renumber themselves automatically. If the next month's newsletter has fewer pages, you delete the unneeded ones by choosing **Remove pages** from the **Page** menu.

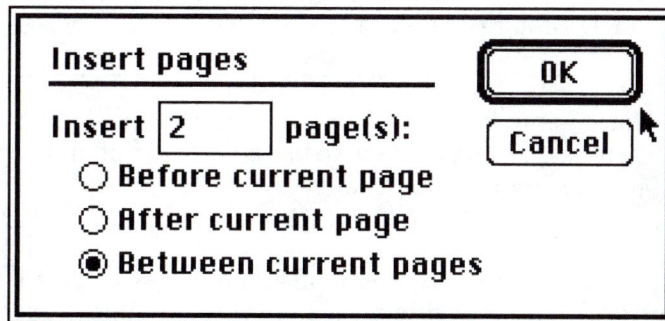

Figure 5.16 Adding pages to a newsletter.

When you add pages, remember that your newsletter is printed on both sides of the page so you are actually adding two pages at a time. You'll want to add these pages in the middle of the existing ones. To add or remove pages, use the following Quick Steps.

Adding and Removing Pages

1. To change the number of pages in an existing publication, choose **Insert** or **Remove** from the **Page** menu.

   The Insert or Remove pages box appears.

2. Type the number of pages to add or page numbers to delete.

3. Click on where to add, if needed.

4. **Click on OK.**

The New page icons appear at the bottom of the screen and pages display on-screen with column guides and master page elements in place. ☐

If the newsletter is printed on 11 x 17 inch paper, and folded in half to make four 8 ½ x 11 letter sized pages, you can add a single letter size sheet to make six pages. Tucked into the outer pages, it will stay in place without being stapled. Should you increase the page count to eight, simply print a second double sheet and fold one inside the other. For ten, add the single center page again.

> ▶ **Note:** Ten pages is the practical limit for this. With more than ten pages, you need to use some kind of binding even if it's just a staple in the middle.

If you're working with more than a couple of pages, it's a good idea to make up an *imposition dummy* to help you assemble the pages in the right order for printing. Make a little book and number its pages. When you unfold them you may be surprised to see which pages are adjacent! The term imposition dummy is an old one, going back to the early days of printing. It's probably called this because the page order is imposed by the manner in which the publication is put together. Figure 5.17 shows an 8-page dummy, set up to print on two sheets of 11 x 17 paper. Incidentally, selecting Tabloid from the Page Setup box will not give you the two page spread you're looking for. If you give separate pages to your print shop, the printer will assemble them in the right order. Or, if you have access to one of the larger photocopiers which uses 11 x 17 paper, and you're going to do your own reproduction, you can take your laser printed master pages and paste them onto large sheets of white board following the layout of your dummy.

After you place all the elements which will repeat every time you revise the newsletter, stop your work temporarily and save it as a template. After saving as a template, you must close the document and reopen it so that you're working on a copy. Otherwise, you could end up creating your newsletter on the template itself.

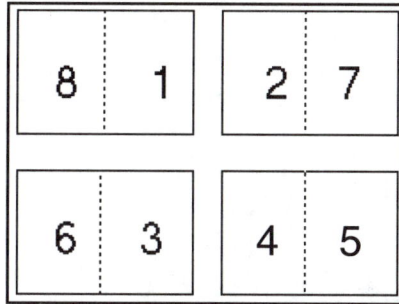

Figure 5.17 With a longer publication, making an imposition dummy is the only way to figure out what goes where.

What You've Learned

107

In this chapter, you learned how to set up master pages for a newsletter. Master pages hold all the information, graphics, and setup instructions you'll use over and over. Master pages should be saved as a template. Specifically, you learned:

► How to place ruler guidelines.

► How using **Snap to Guides** makes elements attach to the nearest guideline.

► How **Snap to Rulers** creates an invisible grid from ruler tick marks. Elements will snap to this grid.

► How to assemble layers of text and graphics, as if they were printed on cellophane, and how to use masks as electronic white out.

► How to set up a masthead and what should be included in it.

► How to construct a banner.

► How to add and remove pages using the **Page** menu.

► How to use an imposition dummy.

Working with Text Files

In This Chapter

▶ *Preparing Text for Importing*
▶ *Formatting Paragraphs*
▶ *Linking Columns*
▶ *How to Flow Text Into Multiple Columns*
▶ *Using a Style Sheet*
▶ *Placing and Designing Headlines*

Although you can use the Text tool in PageMaker to type directly into your publication, it's easier to use a word processing program for anything more than a few sentences. Word processing programs, such as MacWrite, WriteNow, or Microsoft Word, allow you to do more editing, and do it faster, than a page layout program can. Most word processors come with built-in shortcuts and key combinations to make editing easier. And, since you're used to using your word processor, typing and editing the story in a more familiar format won't get in the way of creating it.

Using a word processor also gives you the ability to run grammar and spell checking programs before you add the story to your publication. Most word processors include spelling dictionaries. Grammar checking programs, in addition to catching common grammar errors,

help eliminate the kinds of mistakes spell checking programs sometimes miss. For example, no spell checker can catch this kind of error:
Sum people make this mistake *two* often. There are several good
grammar checking programs commercially available.

> ▶ **Note:** PageMaker has its own spell checking program
> which is part of the Story Editor function (discussed in
> Chapter 7).

Importing Text

110

PageMaker can import files from all of the popular word processing
programs and can accept standard ASCII text as well. ASCII is the
handiest way to import text sent via modem from another computer, or
transferred from a PC or laptop to the Mac.

> ▶ **Note:** A program called MacLink Plus/PC allows your Mac
> to connect to a PC, PS/2, NeXT, or Sun computer and
> translate files into your word processor with the original
> formatting and fonts.

When you installed PageMaker on your computer you selected the
proper filters to translate your word processor's documents into Page-
Maker documents. PageMaker's installer created a folder called *Aldus
Filters,* which holds the filters that interpret your words into a form that
PageMaker can handle.

> ▶ **Tip:** To see what filters are installed, press ⌘ as you select
> **About PageMaker** from the **Apple** menu. A scrolling list of
> all the currently installed import and export filters will appear.

Once the correct filters are installed you can forget about them. They work in the background making no difference at all in the way the program operates. What the filters actually do is to take the formatting commands from your document and translate them into PageMaker's commands. Most of your formatting will come through exactly as you had written it. A few special word processing formats, like double-underlining and hidden text, will not carry into PageMaker. Nor will headers and footers.

Placing Text with the Place Command

The Place dialog box can be used to place both text and graphics. Before importing text into PageMaker, make sure that you've planned the layout and determined the arrangement of columns on the page where the text will be placed. Making a dummy, as explained in Chapter 3, will help you decide on the position of your elements and the overall layout of your publication. In the following examples, stories will be placed into a newsletter. Very wide columns have been set on the first page because this section of text is to look like a typewritten letter. For specific information on defining columns and drawing grid lines, refer to Chapter 3.

111

Text Flow Options

There's one more thing to think about before placing the text. Do you want to place it a column at a time or all at once? PageMaker gives you three ways to flow text into a publication. You might think of them as three *speeds* of text placement.

▶ *Manual text flow* is the slowest method. The text stops flowing at the bottom of the column. If there's more to the story, you must click at the bottom of the column to get the Manual text placement icon shown in Figure 6.1 again. Manual text flow is PageMaker's default. Text flow is manual as long as Autoflow is not checked on the Options menu.

▶ *Semi-automatic text flow* fills a column of text and stops. If there's more text to place the icon reappears, letting you fill columns at your discretion. To use Semi-autoflow, select Autoflow from the Options menu. When you begin to place text, hold down Shift. This changes the Autoflow text icon to the Semi-autoflow text icon shown in Figure 6.1. After you place the first piece of text, the flow of words stops at the end of the column, and the text icon returns to the screen so you can place more text.

▶ *Automatic text flow,* or Autoflow is the fastest way. The Autoflow text icon is shown in Figure 6.1. As the arrow in the icon suggests, once you position the icon, text keeps on flowing until it's all placed. PageMaker even creates new pages, if the text is longer than the space available. Autoflow is turned on by selecting it in the Options menu. Highlighting the word will add or remove a checkmark. When Autoflow is checked it's turned on.

Semi-Automatic

Manual ——— Automatic

Figure 6.1 The Manual, Semi-automatic, and Autoflow text placement icons.

112

Using the Place box

Since our first story is quite short we'll leave **Autoflow** turned off and place the text manually. To open the Place dialog box, select it from the **File** menu or type ⌘+D. The Place box, shown in Figure 6.2, enables you to select the story you want to place and gives you three other options:

Retain format preserves the same type style and formatting that was used in the word processor's version of the story. When a story has extensive formatting such as tabs and bulleted lists, various sizes or styles of type, or other formatting that you want to keep, check this option. PageMaker will import the formatting commands with the story.

Convert quotes changes *straight quotes* to *curly quotes.* One of the things which distinguishes word processors from typewriters are the quotation marks. Typewriter quotes and apostrophes are straight. You use the same set of quotes at either end of the quotation. Typographic quotes; however, are different. We think of them as "66" and "99" quotes. In the very early days of typesetting, printers used upside-down commas for the front-end quotes and apostrophes for the rest. When Linotype machines came along, they had the 66 and 99 quotes designed in because that was how the inventors of the machine thought typeset quotation marks were supposed to look. And, so the standard for printed (as opposed to typed) copy became curly quotes. For professional-looking text, always leave Convert quotes checked.

Read tags lets PageMaker use style names and attributes you assigned in your word processor. Read tags will be discussed in detail in Chapter 7.

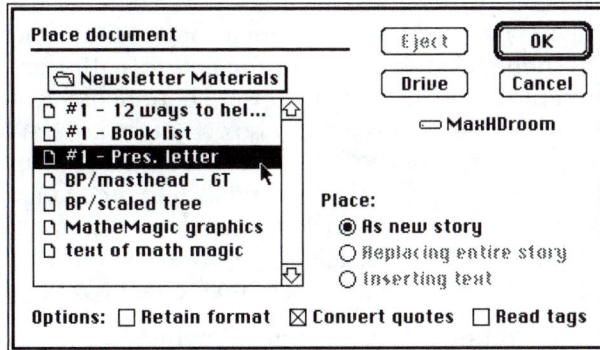

Figure 6.2 The Place dialog box.

113

After the appropriate options are checked, use the following Quick Steps to place text manually.

Placing a Story with the Manual Text Flow Icon

1. Verify that **Autoflow** is not checked on the **Options** menu.	If **Autoflow** is checked select it to remove the check.
2. Press ⌘+D.	The Place dialog box opens as shown in Figure 6.2.
3. Select the story to import.	A file has been selected.
4. Click on the appropriate boxes and buttons and then click on OK.	Choose whether or not to import formatting, use curly quotes, and read tags. When the dialog box closes, the Manual text icon will appear.
5. Position the icon at the head of the column and click.	Text will flow into the column.

Working with Longer Text

Many stories, or other blocks of text, are longer than a single column. When you have more text than will fit in one column, obviously you need to continue the flow into as many more as are needed. PageMaker lets you handle long stories as easily as short ones.

When you place text into a column it comes with what PageMaker calls *windowshade handles* at the top and bottom of the text block. The handles are centered on lines at the top and bottom of the block, which define the ends of the text selection box. By moving the little boxes or handles, at the ends of the line, you can adjust the width of your column of text. The windowshade handles let you change the length of the column by dragging it up or down. If the top handle is empty it indicates the top of the article. The lower windowshade handle will have an arrow in it if there's more text to be placed.

To place additional text, use the following steps.

1. Look at the bottom of the text block. If there's an arrow in the windowshade handle, as shown in Step one of Figure 6.3, this indicates there's more text to be placed. When you place the pointer on the arrow and click, it changes to the Manual text placement icon.
2. Clicking at the head of the next empty column will place the unpasted text in that column, as shown in Step two. Again there's an arrow at the bottom of the column, indicating that there's more text to be placed.
3. The unpasted text can be placed using the steps above to create a third column of text, as shown in Step three.

114

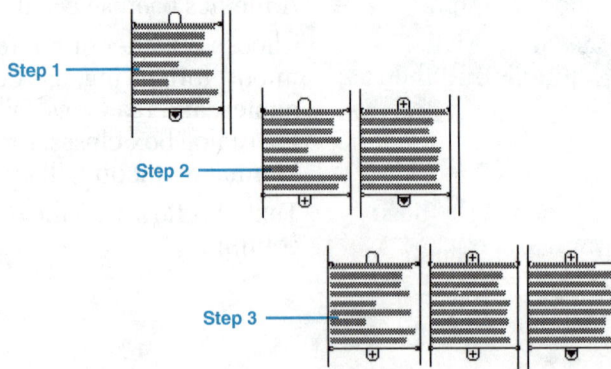

Figure 6.3 The steps in placing additional text.

Using Semi-Automatic Text Flow

Sometimes you want to retain some control over the placement of your text, but not so much that you need to stop and pick up the icon again after each column. This is the situation in which you would use Semi-automatic text flow. Use the following Quick Steps to place text with Semi-automatic text flow.

Q **Using Semi-Automatic Text Flow**

1. Turn on **Autoflow** from the **Options** menu.

   A checkmark appears on the menu when it's on.

2. Press ⌘+D for the **Place** box, select the story, and set the preferred options. Click on OK.

3. Position the Autoflow icon at the top of the first column, press Shift, and click.

   The Autoflow icon will change to the Semi-autoflow icon. The first column of text will flow and stop, leaving the icon on-screen.

4. Position the icon at the next column. Press Shift and click.

   Repeat this step until all the text is placed. □

115

You can reflow a text block if you decide, for example, that your page should have been set up as two columns instead of three, or if you want to relocate it to a different place. Simply close up the window-shade handle by placing the pointer on the bottom handle and dragging upward, and then click on the empty top handle. You'll get the Text placement icon again and you can reposition the text wherever you want it, or store it on the pasteboard until you're ready for it.

Using Autoflow to Place Text

To place text automatically, use the following Quick Steps.

Q **Placing Text with Autoflow**

1. Turn on **Autoflow** from the **Options** menu.

   A checkmark appears on the menu when **Autoflow** is on.

2. Press ⌘+D for the **Place** box, select the story, and set the preferred options. Click on OK.

> This step is the same in all text placement modes.

3. Position the Autoflow icon at the top of the first column and click.

> The text will fill as much space as it needs.
>
> □

If the text is longer than the number of pages you specified in the Page Setup box, PageMaker will add as many additional pages as the story requires, formatting them like your master pages and flowing the type into them. If you're flowing text automatically, you can stop the flow by pressing Shift+⌘. PageMaker will automatically revert to **Autoflow** when you start placing text again. Change **Autoflow** to Manual flow by holding down ⌘ and clicking the icon.

> ▶ **Note:** In Automatic text flow mode the text stops flowing if you manually interrupt it, if the publication reaches 999 pages (its maximum length), or if you run out of text to place.

116

If you decide not to place the text you've imported, click on the Pointer tool to cancel the placement. If text is already placed press ⌘+Z to undo the placement, or ⌘+A (for select all) and delete.

Threading and Unthreading

Text that has been flowed into two or more blocks or columns is said to be *threaded*. Threaded text is electronically joined together. If you shorten the length of the first column, the excess words will jump to the head of the next and so on. It has a sort of ripple effect. This has its good and bad points. A good point is that you're not likely to lose a line from the middle of a story. Text will get pulled back or pushed ahead to the next linked text block. A bad point is that this ripple effect may interfere with formatting, as a change in one line changes all the others.

Threaded text is identified by the plus symbol (+) which appears in both the upper and lower windowshade handles when the text block is selected. The text we placed in Figure 6.3 was threaded. Figure 6.4 also shows columns of threaded text. The first column has no plus symbol at the head of the story. That's because the thread starts there. Notice the arrow at the end of the third column. It tells us there's more text left to place.

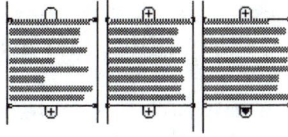

Figure 6.4 These columns are threaded together. Changes in one affect all three.

If you make a change in one block that you don't want to carry all the way through, you can isolate or unthread that particular block. To do so, follow these steps:

1. Select the block you wish to isolate with the Pointer tool and cut it to the clipboard using ⌘+X, or by selecting **Cut** from the **Edit** menu.
2. Now, using ⌘+V or the **Paste** command from the **Edit** menu, replace it where you cut it. The thread is now broken.

Any changes you make in this text block now will affect only this block. To rethread it back into the story:

1. **Cut** the block to the clipboard as before. Create an insertion point at the end of the previous text block or at the beginning of the next, by positioning the I-beam cursor and clicking. A blinking vertical line will appear in the text.
2. **Paste** the block back in. The text will rethread itself into the story starting at the insertion point.

117

▶ **Note:** When you isolate one text block the rest of the text remains threaded. If you make editing changes or formatting changes that move lines of text from one block to another, your isolated block could come back in out of sequence. To avoid this, unthread all blocks if you unthread any.

Replacing and Inserting Text

If you have an existing story you want to replace:

1. Click anywhere in the story with the Text tool. Press ⌘+D to open the **Place** box, select the replacement story, and click on the **Replacing Entire Story** button.

2. Click on OK or press Return. When the dialog box closes PageMaker removes the old story and inserts the new one.

If the new story is shorter, any excess text blocks will be deleted. PageMaker adds more text blocks or pages, if the new story is longer, when **Autoflow** is selected. If **Autoflow** is not selected the last text block will have an arrow in the lower handle, indicating that there's more text to place. You can also insert new text into an existing story by using the Text tool to create an insertion point, and then following the previous steps but clicking on the Inserting text button instead of the Replace button.

Adjusting Text and Customizing Paragraphs

118

When you click on a block of text with the pointer you'll see two sets of handles. The black boxes at the four corners of the text block are handles, which you can drag to widen or narrow a column of text. The windowshade handles in the middle of the lines at the top and bottom of the column allow you to lengthen or shorten the column. If you want to shorten a column of type:

▶ Click on the bottom handle and move it up, as if you were raising a windowshade.

To shrink or expand the width of a column of text:

▶ Click on one of the handles at the end of the top or bottom line, (shown in Figure 6.5) and drag the handle in (to shrink) or out (to expand). PageMaker will automatically reflow the text to fit the new column size. If there's more text than will fit, a triangle will appear in the bottom windowshade handle.

To move the whole section of text around within the page, or to drag it out to the pasteboard:

▶ Click anywhere inside the text and hold the mouse button down while you reposition it.

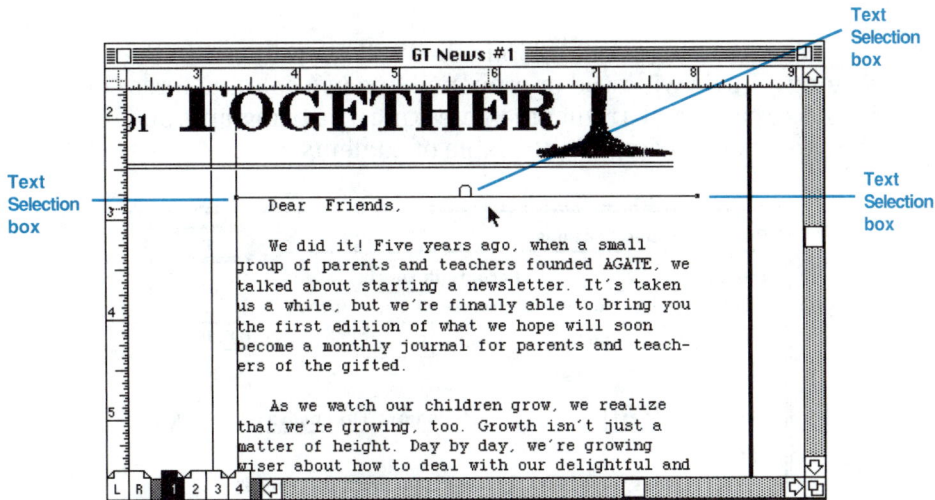

Figure 6.5 The Text selection boxes.

119

Paragraph Specifications

PageMaker gives you a number of different options for customizing paragraphs in the Paragraph Specifications dialog box, shown in Figure 6.6. To open the dialog box, select **Para** from the **Type** menu or press ⌘+M. Within it you can change PageMaker's default settings for the options listed below in Table 6.1.

Table 6.1 Default settings in the Paragraph Specifications box.

Option	PageMaker default
Indents	Left, First, and Right, 0 inches
Paragraph Space	Before, After, 0 inches
Alignment	Left
Dictionary	English

You can also select options that will keep lines together, avoid leaving a single widowed or orphaned line in a column, force column breaks or page breaks rather than breaking up a paragraph, and include the specified paragraph in the table of contents.

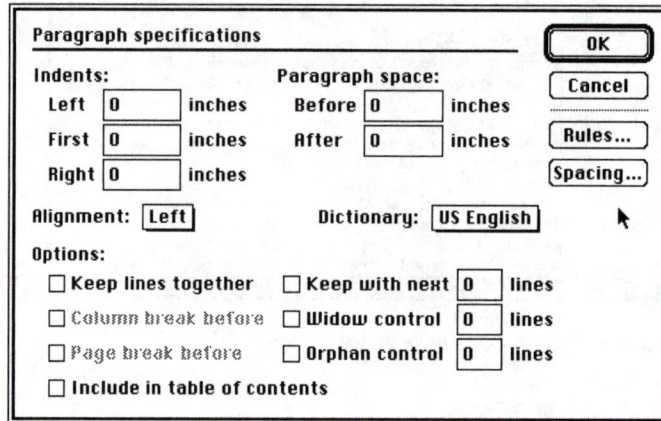

```
┌──────────────────────────────────────────────────────────┐
│  Paragraph specifications                    ┌──  OK  ──┐  │
│                                              └──────────┘  │
│  Indents:              Paragraph space:      ┌─ Cancel ─┐  │
│    Left  [0]   inches    Before [0]  inches  └──────────┘  │
│                                              ┌─ Rules...─┐ │
│    First [0]   inches    After  [0]  inches  └──────────┘  │
│                                              ┌Spacing...─┐ │
│    Right [0]   inches                        └──────────┘  │
│  Alignment: [Left]          Dictionary: [US English]    ▶  │
│  Options:                                                  │
│    □ Keep lines together   □ Keep with next [0]  lines     │
│    □ Column break before   □ Widow control  [0]  lines     │
│    □ Page break before     □ Orphan control [0]  lines     │
│    □ Include in table of contents                          │
└──────────────────────────────────────────────────────────┘
```

120

Figure 6.6 The Paragraph Specifications dialog box.

▶ **Note:** You can also set indents and alignment options independent of the Paragraph Specifications box. They may be accessed directly from the **Type** menu.

Indents and Tabs

To indent or not to indent? It's a question worthy of consideration. Many publications are now set *flush left*, meaning that the type is set up against the left hand margin. (You may come across the term *ragged right*. It means the left side is flush with the margin, and the right is ragged.) Some publications use what's called a *hanging indent* for added emphasis. In a hanging indent, the first word or words of the paragraph hang to the left of the main body of the text. There are *normal indents*, in which the first word of the first line begins a few spaces in. And, finally *nested indents*, commonly used to set apart a piece of text, such as a quotation. Figure 6.7 shows examples of the different styles of indent.

Hanging
Indent

Normal
Indent

Flush
Left

Nested
Indent

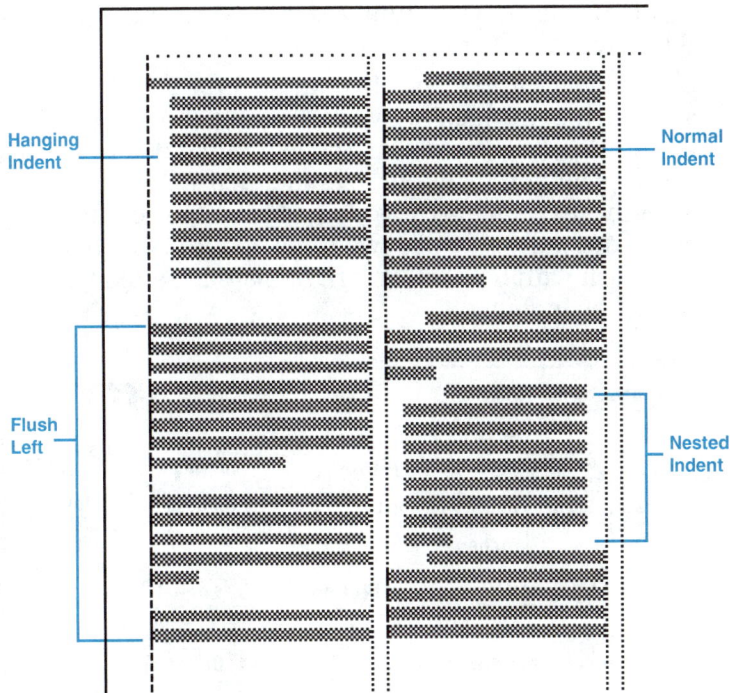

Figure 6.7 Types of indents.

Entering numbers into the box with nothing selected sets up a format for any additional text you place in PageMaker. To assign any of these indent styles to a specific paragraph you need to select it first. Typing into the Paragraph Specifications box with text selected affects only the paragraphs selected. Select the text to be formatted by placing the cursor within it, pressing ⌘+M to open the dialog box, and following these instructions:

► *Flush left:* To set type flush left simply set indents in the Paragraph Specifications box to zero inches.

► *Hanging indents:* The first line of type remains at the margin or to the left of it, with the rest of the paragraph indented. These are produced by making the Left indent a positive number greater than zero. This moves the body of the paragraph in from the column edge the amount you've specified. Next, enter a zero or a minus number for the first line indent. If you enter zero as a first indent it will hold the line of type at the column edge. A negative number, as shown in Figure 6.8, will move it even further left into the margin.

▶ *Normal indents:* Enter a number for the indent in the first line field. Leave the other values at zero.

▶ *Nested indents:* Enter a positive number for the left indent, again moving the main body of the paragraph in from the column edge, but also use the same number or a larger one, for a first line indent. In addition, as Figure 6.7 shows, the right side of the text can also be indented from the column edge. This is especially effective when the text is justified. *Justified text* is flush with both left and right margins, although the first line may be indented.

122

```
┌──────────────────────────────────────────────────────────────┐
│  Paragraph specifications                          ( ▸ OK ◂ )  │
│  ────────────────────────────────────────────                 │
│  Indents:              Paragraph space:            [ Cancel ]  │
│    Left [0.25]  inches    Before [0]    inches     ...........  │
│    First [-0.25] inches   After  [0]    inches     [ Rules... ]│
│    Right [0]    inches                             [Spacing...] │
│                                                                │
│  Alignment: [Justify]          Dictionary: [US English]        │
│  Options:                                                      │
│    □ Keep lines together    □ Keep with next [0]  lines        │
│    □ Column break before    □ Widow control  [0]  lines        │
│    □ Page break before      □ Orphan control [0]  lines        │
│    □ Include in table of contents                              │
└──────────────────────────────────────────────────────────────┘
```

Figure 6.8 The numbers in the fields indicate a hanging indent.

▶ **Tip:** Any time you need to select a single paragraph, place the Text tool cursor anywhere within it and triple-click (just like double-clicking only three quick clicks). The whole paragraph will be highlighted.

Setting Indents on the Screen

If you prefer to set the paragraph indents on-screen with a ruler to guide you there's an easy way. Select **Indents/Tabs** from the **Type** menu or press ⌘+I (for Indents) to place a ruler at the head of the column of type, as shown in Figure 6.9.

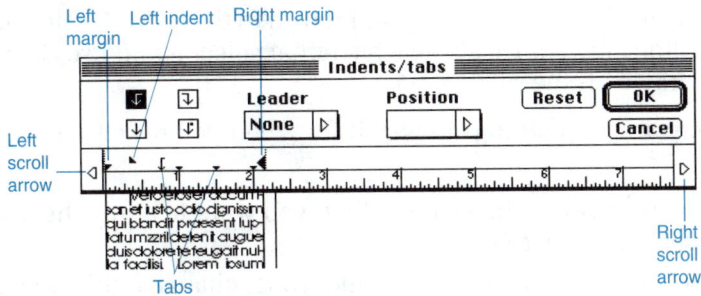

Figure 6.9 The Indents/Tabs ruler lets you see where you're placing tabs and indents.

At the left side of the ruler there are two triangles. The lower triangle marks the left margin indent (or the edge of the column), and the upper triangle shows the first line indent. The large triangle on the right side of the ruler shows the right indent (or the right margin). The zero point on the ruler automatically aligns itself with the left corner of a selected text block. If no text was selected, no insertion point is present so the ruler simply centers itself on the page. You can also use the small hollow arrows at the ends of the ruler to scroll left or right as you need to. The ruler may be moved wherever it's needed by clicking on it and dragging it to a new location.

123

Using Tabs

PageMaker has default tab settings every half inch (or half centimeter). As many as 40 tab stops may be set on the ruler including left justified, right justified, centered, and decimal tabs. To simplify locating the tabs and indents whenever one is selected, its position can be read in the Position box on the ruler. To rearrange the tabs and indents, use the following steps.

1. Click on the tabs and drag them to a new location. As you drag the numbers in the Position box change. The Position box gives the exact position of the marker in whatever unit of measurement you've specified in the Preferences dialog box. Use the numbers to guide you in placing markers accurately.

2. You may also place a tab by clicking in the arrow on the Position box to get a menu of tab options, selecting one and entering a position for it in the box.

3. When you're done click on OK or press Return, and the text will move to reflect your changes.

To cancel your tab settings and return to the defaults click on the Reset button. To remove a single tab either select it and use Delete, or simply drag it off the ruler.

Here are a few things to watch for when you're setting tabs and indents.

▶ Be sure to select the text to which you want to apply the tab or indent. Otherwise nothing will move.

▶ You won't see the position of the words change until you click on the OK button or press Return.

▶ If you imported text that already has tabs or indents applied to it, you must remove them before PageMaker can place its own tab and indent indications.

▶ You can only set indents within existing page margins or column guides.

▶ If you add more text to an existing story PageMaker automatically assigns to it the same indents that were used in the preceding paragraphs.

▶ PageMaker sometimes has problems with imported first line indents. Normal indents and hanging indents can produce strange errors if the first line indent is wider than the column into which the type is being placed. Figure 6.10 illustrates this kind of error.

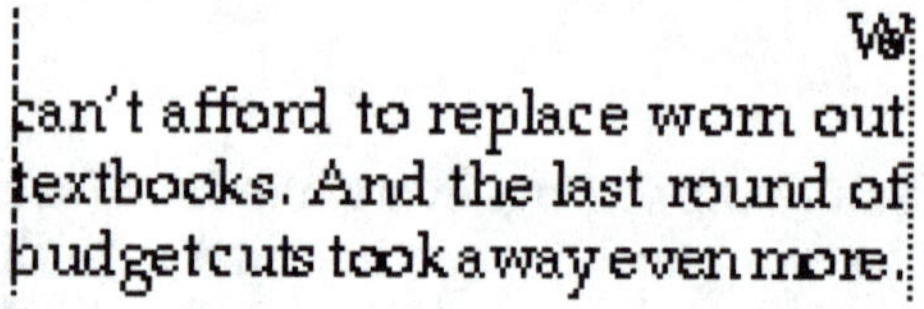

124

can't afford to replace worn out textbooks. And the last round of budget cuts took away even more.

Figure 6.10 The type gets scrunched into whatever space is available.

Use the following Quick Steps to set indents on the ruler.

Q Setting Indents

1. Select paragraphs to be indented.

   The selected text will be highlighted.

2. Press ⌘+I to place the Indents/Tabs ruler at the top of the column.

   The ruler will be aligned with the selected text.

3. Drag the first line indent marker (upper of two triangles at the left) to the desired location.

Remember, the type will not move until you click on OK.

4. Move the left indent marker if the entire paragraph is to be indented.

5. Move the right triangle in if the right side of the paragraph is to be indented.

6. Click on OK or press Return when finished.

The type will move to the new positions. ☐

Leaders

Use the ruler to set the type of *leader* to use between tabs. Leaders are repeated dots or dashes used between tabs in a chart or table to help the reader see the relationship between columns. The leader fills in any space between the end of the text and the next tab stop. Figure 6.11 shows various kinds of leaders. Leaders are set in the Leader box on the Indents/Tabs ruler. Select **Custom** from the **Leaders** menu to invent your own leaders as long as they're standard keyboard characters. For example, $>>>$ or $\approx\ \approx\ \approx$ can be used for special effects. (You can adjust the spacing of these characters by using the Tracking command discussed later in this chapter.)

125

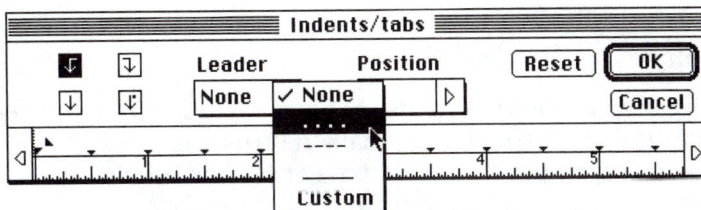

Figure 6.11 The Leaders pop-up menu.

To specify a leader style, use the following Quick Steps.

Q Setting Leader Styles

1. Select the text to which you want to add leaders.

   If none is selected Leader style will be applied to subsequent tab settings.

2. Press ⌘+I to open the Indents/Tabs ruler.

3. Click on the triangle in the Leader box to get a pop-up menu of leader styles.

   Choose the style you want or choose **Custom**.

4. If you choose **Custom**, type the characters you want to use as a leader into the Leader box.

   If you don't want to use leaders select **None**.

5. Now set the tabs as described earlier.

   When you click on OK leaders will appear before tabs. □

> ▶ **Tip:** Remember to select text before entering changes to it. Otherwise the new settings will only apply to the next text entered.

Paragraph Spacing

When you type a page with a number of paragraphs, you double-space between them by using two carriage returns. One of the differences between using an old-fashioned typewriter and a word processor or page layout program, is that you are able to specify the exact amount of space between paragraphs, and whether to insert it before or after the paragraph. To set the amount of space between paragraphs, use the following steps.

1. Press ⌘+M to open the **Paragraph Specifications** dialog box or select it from the **Type** menu.

2. Enter the amount of space desired into the Data field for Before or After.

3. Click on OK or press Return. PageMaker will insert the space each time you press Return.

> ▶ **Tip:** If you've selected text before setting paragraph speci-
> fications, the text will change to suit the values specified
> as soon as you click on OK. If no text is selected the values will
> apply to the next text you enter. PageMaker will not automati-
> cally space before the first paragraph of a text block, nor will it
> space after the last paragraph of a text block.

You can save yourself a great deal of trouble if you always use PageMaker's Paragraph Specifications box to set paragraph spacing rather than a double carriage return. Adding extra carriage returns can cause alignment problems, especially if the carriage return accidentally gets tagged with a style different from that of the surrounding text.

Alignment

127

Alignment refers to the way in which a column of type is placed on the page, relative to the margins on either side of it. PageMaker offers you several alignment choices available as a separate pop-up menu under the **Type** menu, as well as in the Paragraph Specifications dialog box. Open the Paragraph Specifications box from the **Type** menu or by pressing ⌘+M. To apply any of these alignment options first use the Text tool to position the cursor anywhere within the block of text to be aligned. Then select the desired option from the menu, or type its command key shortcut listed below. Figure 6.12 shows the effects of the various alignment options.

▶ *Left-aligned type* (⌘+Shift+L) is the easiest to read because all the spaces are even. It is the default for PageMaker and virtually every other text handling program.

▶ *Centered type* (⌘+Shift+C) is useful for headlines and cap-tions.

▶ *Right-aligned type* (⌘+Shift+R) can be used in small amounts as a design element, but right alignment is seldom used for an entire story.

▶ *Justified type* (⌘+Shift+J) means that both left and right sides are aligned to their respective margins. Justification automati-cally adjusts the amount of space between letters and words to make each line the same length. Longer text blocks are often set justified for a more uniform page.

▶ *Force-justified type* (⌘+Shift+F) is new to PageMaker 4.0. It forces justification of the last line of a paragraph. It's not always desirable, as Figure 6.12 shows.

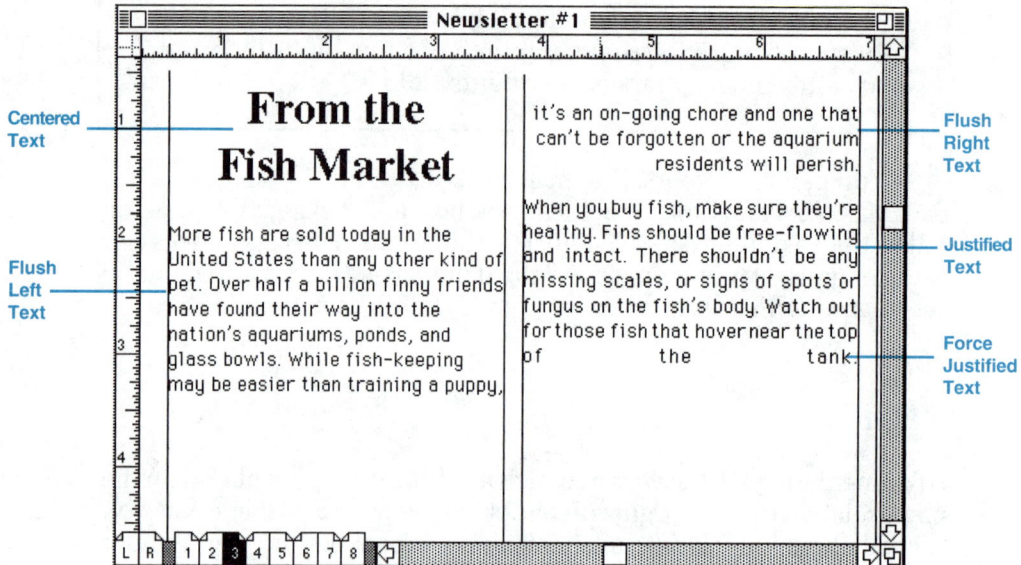

Centered Text

Flush Left Text

Flush Right Text

Justified Text

Force Justified Text

Newsletter #1

From the Fish Market

More fish are sold today in the United States than any other kind of pet. Over half a billion finny friends have found their way into the nation's aquariums, ponds, and glass bowls. While fish-keeping may be easier than training a puppy,

it's an on-going chore and one that can't be forgotten or the aquarium residents will perish.

When you buy fish, make sure they're healthy. Fins should be free-flowing and intact. There shouldn't be any missing scales, or signs of spots or fungus on the fish's body. Watch out for those fish that hover near the top of   the   tank.

Figure 6.12 The various types of alignment.

Widows and Orphans

There's a simple rule in typography: Avoid widows and orphans. Lest you think me heartless, may I explain? *Widows* are the final lines of paragraphs that end up starting new columns rather than being kept with their "husband" paragraphs. *Orphans* are lines that should lead off a new column or page, but somehow get tacked onto the preceding one. In most instances, widows and orphans are lines of type that are separated from the paragraphs to which they should belong. They dangle in mid-story looking lost and forlorn, and spoiling the page design. PageMaker lets you control the unsightly effects of widows and orphans on your page makeup. Within the Paragraph Specifications dialog box you can set limits for widow and orphan control, as shown in Figure 6.13. Enter a number from 1 to 3 in the boxes for widows and orphans, to define how many lines you want to begin or end a column with.

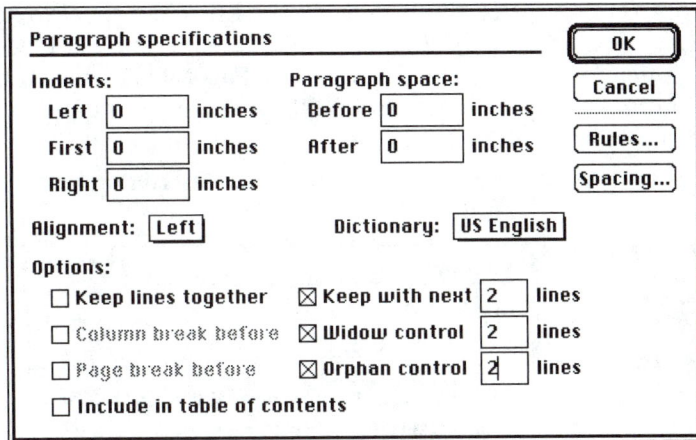

Figure 6.13 Controlling widows and orphans.

PageMaker can also keep paragraphs together if you select the Keep lines together option. However, if you choose this option, your columns may become uneven in length because paragraphs won't break where the column normally ends in the page.

129

Paragraph Rules

Use the Paragraph Rules feature to place thin lines between paragraphs. While this is not very useful within the body of a news story, it's nice in a catalog. It can also be used to separate entries in a table of contents or other listing, as shown in Figure 6.14. Use the following steps to place rules on the page.

1. Select the text to have rules applied.
2. Press ⌘+M to open the **Paragraph Specifications** dialog box or select it from the **Type** menu. Click on the **Rules** button to open the **Paragraph Rules** box.
3. Decide whether to use lines above or lines below the paragraph. If you use both you'll have two rules.
4. Choose the line style and color by clicking on the pop-up menus in the appropriate boxes. Click on a button to set line width.
5. If lines are to be indented, enter indent amounts in the Indent boxes.

6. Click on the **Options** button to set the lines to a specific height, above or below the baseline of the line of text closest to the rule, or enter Auto in the Height box to let PageMaker place the lines. (Ignore the Align to Grid option. It's used in setting up a ruled form, which will be discussed in Chapter 10.)

7. Press Option+Return to close all the nested dialog boxes.

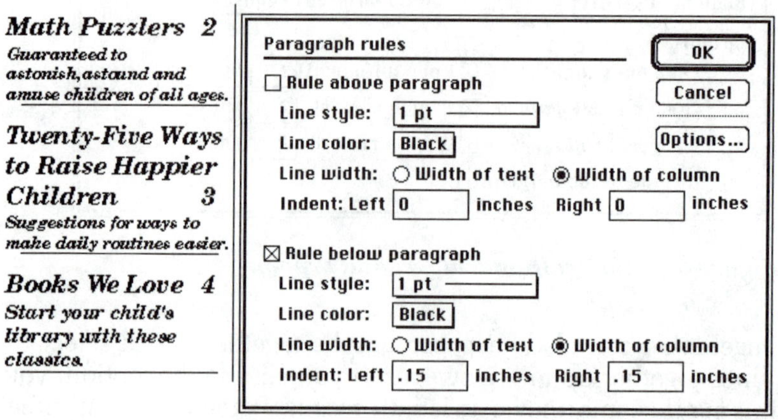

Figure 6.14 Placing paragraph rules.

Specifying Type

So far the text we've placed in PageMaker has all appeared in the default type font, 12 point Times. If it's not the look you had in mind, you can specify any typeface that's installed in your Macintosh and select all kinds of style variations. This is done in the Type Specifications dialog box under the **Type** menu. Open the box from the menu or by pressing ⌘+T. Figure 6.15 shows the Type Specification box which contains the type options as pop-up menus. To view your options under any category, put the pointer on the word or number in the box and press the mouse button. A list will appear. Move up or down the list until your choice is highlighted. Use the Type Specifications box to define the following choices:

Font: Use this menu to select the name of the typeface you want to use. The default is Times.

Size: Type sizes are measured in points. When a box has an arrow, as this one does, click on the arrow to see a list or type your choice in place of the entry in the box. 12 points is the default size.

Leading: Leading is the amount of space between lines. Auto, the default setting, adjusts the leading automatically to an appropriate height.

Set Width: PageMaker will expand or condense the type by a percentage determined in this box. Choose 10% increments from 70-130%. 100% is normal, neither condensed nor expanded. Normal is the default.

Color: If you want to set your type in another color or use *reverse* (white on black) type, use this box to change the type color. Black is the default setting for color.

Position: This refers to the position of the type relative to the baseline. The options are normal (the default), subscript, and superscript. The latter two are used primarily in scientific notation and footnotes.

131

Case: PageMaker gives you three choices. Normal, the default setting, lets you enter upper and lowercase letters. All Caps disables the lowercase letters. Small Caps gives you two sizes of capital letters, the smaller being (by default) 70% of the larger. The percentage may be changed in Type Options.

Track: This adjusts the closeness of the letters on each line. No track is the default, meaning that no adjustment is made.

Type style: Click on the box or boxes for the styles you wish to use.

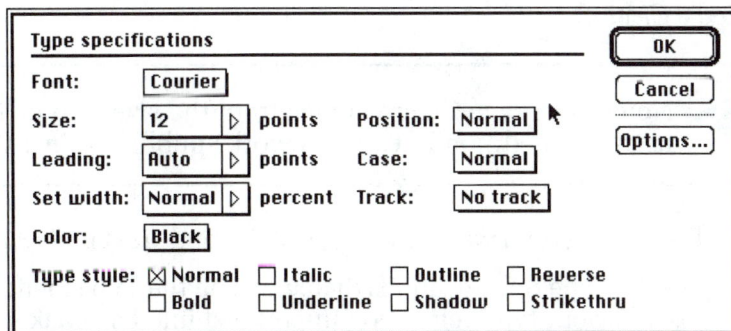

Figure 6.15 The Type Specifications dialog box.

> ▶ **Note:** You can determine the type specifications before you import text. Press ⌘+T to open the Type Specifications box. Select settings and then place the text.

Fonts

There's often a good deal of confusion about the difference between typefaces and fonts. PageMaker helps contribute to the confusion by identifying the name of the particular typeface to be selected in the Type Specifications dialog box as a font. A font is actually the complete character set for a particular typeface, size, and style such as Helvetica Bold 12 point. The font includes both upper- and lowercase characters, punctuation marks, numbers, and any special characters like $ % £ π, and so on, which may be included with it. In the Type Specifications box, what PageMaker asks you to select as a font is really a typeface. When you click on the Font box you'll see a pop-up menu listing all the kinds of type currently installed on your Macintosh. Simply select the one you want to use.

Type Measurement

In the United States type is measured in units called *points*. PageMaker also supports the slightly larger European type measurement unit called a *Cicero*.

> ▶ **Note:** The name Cicero comes from the size of type first used in an edition of Cicero's works published in 1458.

There are several ways to set type styles and sizes in PageMaker:

▶ Use the Type Specifications dialog box on the Type menu to describe your type before you import text into PageMaker.

Or,

▶ Select the type once it's in position and either change the specifications in the box, or use the pop-up menus under the Type menu, to change individual attributes such as point size.

In general you'll use 10 or 12 point type for body copy and larger sizes for headlines. You can use fractional points too. To change point sizes in the Type Specification dialog box, use the following Quick Steps.

Q Changing Type Size

1. Select the type you want to change.

   If none is selected, changes will apply to the next text brought in.

2. Press ⌘+T or select **Type Spec** from the **Type** menu.

   The Type Specifications dialog box will open.

3. Type the desired point size into the Size box or click on the triangle at the right of the box to display a menu of type sizes. Click on OK or press Return when done.

   You may enter sizes in whole points and tenths of a point for example, 29.1 points. When the dialog box closes the type will change to the new point size.   □

133

Leading

Back in the old, precomputer days of typesetting, words were set in type one letter at a time and fastened down into a wooden frame. The typesetter used variously sized strips and blocks of lead to maintain the spaces between the words and lines of type. Although PageMaker does it electronically, the vertical spaces between lines of type are still called *leading,* (pronounced to rhyme with sledding). The amount of leading used affects both the appearance and the readability of your publication. Too little leading makes a very dense page. The lines are crowded too closely together and the reader feels cramped and uncomfortable. Too much leading means there's too much space between lines so the reader's eye has a hard time following the flow from one line to the next. There's no clear sense that individual lines of text are related. The reader becomes distracted. Figure 6.16 shows some examples of leading.

For standard *body copy,* the main text of the story, the amount of leading is correct when it's not noticeable. The casual reader shouldn't be aware of space, or lack of space, between lines of type. In general, the rule is to make the leading 20% greater than the height of the type. As Figure 6.16 shows, the type in the $^{12}/_{14}$ example looks best.

This is a block of text in 12 point type. The leading used is 10 points, a *negative* leading. The type is cut off in places, and is hard to read. This is sometimes refered to as 12/10, or "twelve on ten".

This is a block of text in 12 point type. The leading used is 14 points, a *normal* leading. The type is easy to read. This is called 12/14, or "twelve on fourteen".

This is a block of text in 12 point type. The leading used is 12 points, a *tight* leading. The type appears cramped, and is still hard to read. This is called 12/12, or "twelve on twelve".

This is a block of text in 12 point type. The leading used is 18 points, a *loose* leading. The type is, once again, hard to read. This is called 12/18, or "twelve on eighteen".

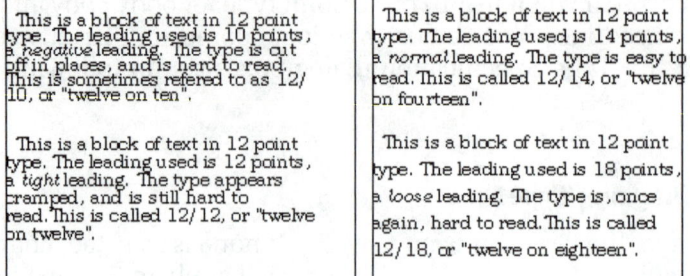

Figure 6.16 When you're reading between the lines, maybe you're looking at the leading.

134

> ▶ **Note:** The $^{12}/_{14}$ combination of type size and leading height is called *twelve on fourteen,* not twelve fourteenths. Others might be thirty on thirty six and so on. Even though they look like fractions, they're not.

Of course, what's right for one type font and one purpose might not be right for another. Some fonts can tolerate less leading while still maintaining readability. Others need all the help they can get. Page-Maker allows you to adjust leading in very small increments, as little as a tenth of a point or $^{1}/_{720}$ of an inch. If you needed to squeeze in an extra line of type at the bottom of a column, you could reduce the leading for the entire column or story by a fraction of a point and gain enough space to fit the extra line in.

> ▶ **Tip:** It's not a good idea to change the leading for only a few lines of text. The differences, even though small, will be apparent. Uneven line spacing looks sloppy and detracts from the readability and the appearance of the page.

If you don't change the leading when you enter text, PageMaker's default is to automatically compute 120% leading, which would give you the normal 10/12 or 12/14, and so on. Of course, this doesn't mean that there is a space 12 points high between two lines of 10 point type. It means that the line of type, including its leading, is 12 points high but the characters themselves are 10 points high. To see this, highlight a line of text. Surrounding the letters is a horizontal bar called a *slug.* Figure 6.17 shows what a slug looks like.

Leading is the
space between
the lines.

Top of Caps

Descender

Ascender

Baseline

This is a slug.

Slug

x-height

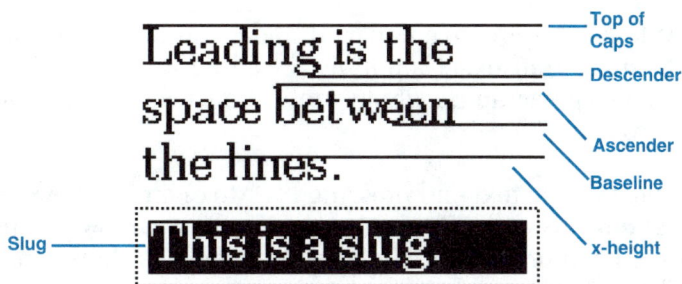

Figure 6.17 Anatomy of a slug.

The height of the slug indicates the amount of leading. In Figure 6.17 the slug is 18 points high. Within it the characters are aligned on a common *baseline,* which is a reference line that allows for precise horizontal alignment. To have PageMaker automatically calculate and place leading, use the following steps.

▶ Select the text and press ⌘+Shift+A (all together).

135

Or,

1. Select the **Leading** menu under the **Type** menu, as shown in Figure 6.18, and choose **Auto**.
2. The type will automatically be leaded to 120%.

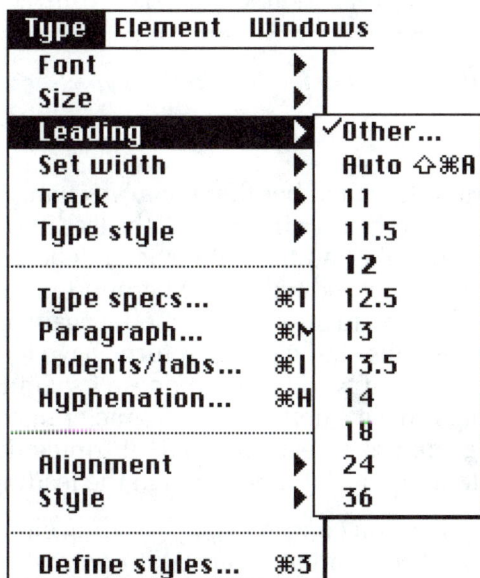

Type	Element	Windows
Font	▶	
Size	▶	
Leading	▶	✓Other...
Set width	▶	Auto ⇧⌘A
Track	▶	11
Type style	▶	11.5
		12
Type specs...	⌘T	12.5
Paragraph...	⌘M	13
Indents/tabs...	⌘I	13.5
Hyphenation...	⌘H	14
		18
Alignment	▶	24
Style	▶	36
Define styles...	⌘3	

Figure 6.18 Leading may be set on the Leading pop-up menu.

Auto-leading is convenient and is adequate for most layouts. If you wish to specify an exact amount of leading for any section of text whether it's a paragraph, a whole publication, or a single character, you may do so by:

▶ Selecting the text and pressing ⌘+T to open the **Type Specifi-cations** box. Select a point size from the **Leading** pop-up menu or enter your own setting in the Data field as shown in Figure 6.19.

Or,

▶ Select Leading under the Type menu and choose a point size from the list, or choose Other and enter your setting in the box. Remember, you can specify leading in tenth of a point increments.

136

```
┌─────────────────────────────────────────────────────────────┐
│  Type specifications ─────────────────────────    ┌────────┐ │
│                                                    │   OK   │ │
│  Font:      [Trajan]                               └────────┘ │
│                                                    ┌────────┐ │
│  Size:      [18  ] ▷ points   Position: [Normal]   │ Cancel │ │
│                                                    └────────┘ │
│  Leading:   [20  ] ▷ points   Case:     [Normal]   ┌────────┐ │
│                                                    │Options…│ │
│  Set width: [Normal]▷ percent Track:    [No track] └────────┘ │
│                                                               │
│  Color:     [Black]                                           │
│                                                               │
│  Type style: ☒ Normal  ☐ Italic     ☐ Outline  ☐ Reverse     │
│              ☐ Bold    ☐ Underline  ☐ Shadow   ☐ Strikethru  │
└─────────────────────────────────────────────────────────────┘
```

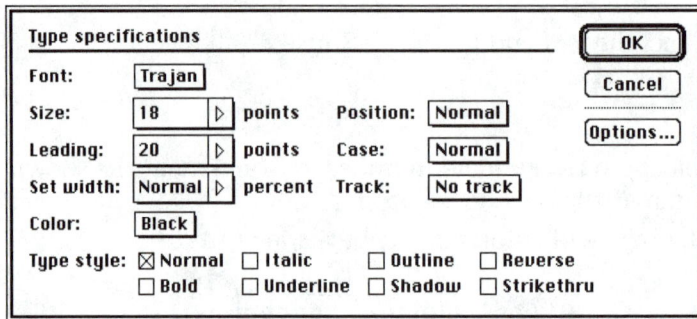

Figure 6.19 Specifying leading in the Type Specifications dialog box.

It's important to remember that if you've changed the leading for a character or a word within a line of text, the leading for the whole line will change to the higher number. If the larger character moves to the next line because you've edited the text around it, the leading for the previous line will revert to the smaller amount again. Even nonprinting characters, spaces, tabs, and carriage returns have leading assigned to them. If the text you're working with doesn't seem to have the right leading, you might have a nonprinting character imbedded in the line with the wrong amount of leading. To fix it triple-click the paragraph with the Text tool to select it, and reassign the leading.

PageMaker lets you choose to place leading either proportionally or from the tops of the capital letters. With *proportional leading,* two thirds of the assigned line spacing lies above the baseline, and the remaining third below it. Proportional leading allows you to use different fonts on the same baseline while keeping the overall line spacing the same. This works because all the characters are sitting on a baseline that is always the same distance below the top of the slug.

Top of caps leading uses the height of the tallest ascender to position the baseline. The distance from the top of the slug to the baseline equals the height of the tallest font ascender in the particular face, whether it's actually used in the text or not. Figure 6.20 shows the relationship of the letter and its baseline, to the slug in both leading methods.

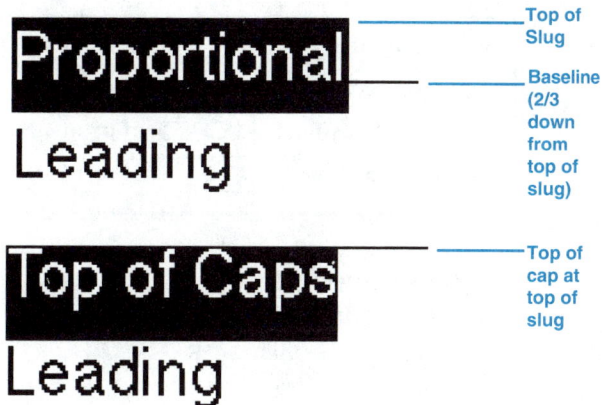

Figure 6.20 The relationship of the leading to the baseline. The type in both examples is 24/36.

Leading methods are selected in the Spacing dialog box which is accessed by a button in the Paragraph box. Press ⌘+M and then select Spacing.

> ▶ **Tip:** The best rule is to stick with Proportional leading unless you have some reason not to. Top of Caps may be easier to work with if you're trying for special typographic effects.

Subscript and Superscript

The Options box (within the Type Specifications dialog box) lets you define exact positions for *subscript* (words below the baseline) and

137

superscript (words above the line). You can also define a percentage size for small caps. Figure 6.21 shows the settings and some possible results. If subscripts and superscripts are set in the same size type as the rest of the line, they will affect the leading. If you choose to use them on a tightly leaded page, you can reasonably expect them to force a gap between the lines. The alternative is to let them run into the line above or below, or to use a much smaller type font. PageMaker's default size for subscript and superscript is 58.3% of the point size.

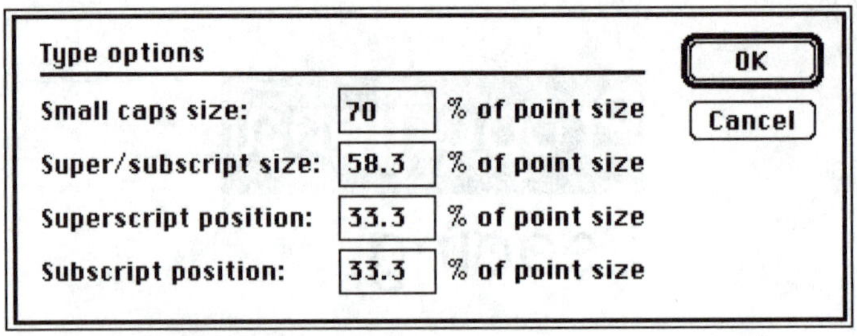

Type options

		OK
Small caps size:	70	% of point size
Super/subscript size:	58.3	% of point size
Superscript position:	33.3	% of point size
Subscript position:	33.3	% of point size

Cancel

138

An example of ₛᵤᵦₛ꜀ᵣᵢₚₜ.
An example of ˢᵘᵖᵉʳˢ꜀ʳⁱᵖᵗ.
THESE ARE SMALL CAPS

Figure 6.21 Examples of subscript, superscript, and small caps.

Tracking

No, it's not what a bloodhound does, nor is it the act of leaving muddy footprints on the kitchen floor. *Tracking*, or track kerning, refers to the spacing between the letters and words on the line. Use the Track command to tighten or loosen the space between letters. Track kerning is selected from the **Type** menu. PageMaker applies predetermined values to each font on your system to determine how much tracking is normal for that font. It then compensates as you specify for "very loose", "very tight", or somewhere in between. You can also specify No track. Figure 6.22 shows the effects of different track kerning. Normal track improves the visual appearance of letter spacing by reducing the amount of space on larger point sizes and increasing it on smaller point sizes. Generally, at a medium point size, tracking has little or no effect because the type is already spaced properly.

Type | Element | Windows

Cultural Icons ———— Very Loose

Then and Now...

Track ▶ No track ⇧⌘Q
Very loose
Loose
✓Normal
Tight
Very tight

Cultural Icons ———— Normal

Then and Now...

Cultural Icons ———— Very Tight

Then and Now...

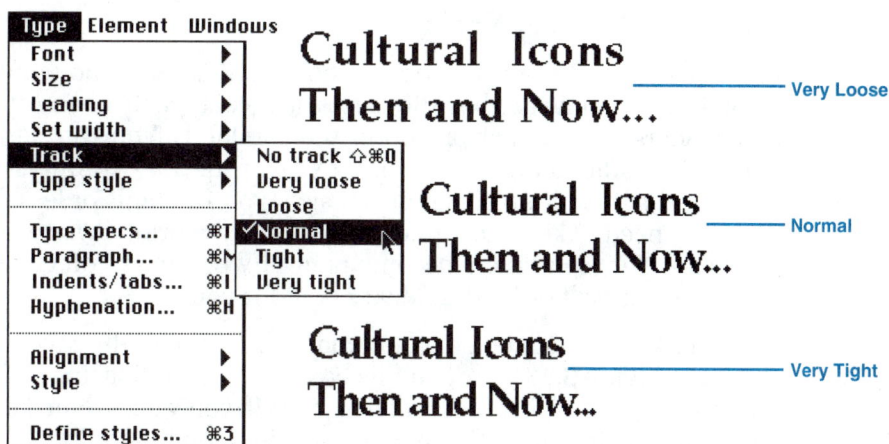

Figure 6.22 Examples of tracking.

To apply tracking, follow these steps:

139

1. Select the type to which tracking is to be applied.
2. Open the **Type Specifications** dialog box by selecting it from the **Type** menu or by pressing ⌘+T.
3. Click on the **Track** box to bring up the **Tracking** menu. Select the appropriate amount of tracking. Click on OK or press Return to close the dialog box and apply the tracking to the selected type.

Or,

1. Select the type to which tracking is to be applied.
2. Select **Tracking** from the **Type** menu and choose the desired tracking from the menu.

▶ **Tip:** If you've specified track kerning it will take Page-Maker much longer to redraw the page whenever you change from one view to another. This is because it must recalculate the tracking each time. To work faster, specify track kerning only for selected lines of very small or very large type such as photo captions or headlines. Apply No track to normal text.

Manual and Automatic Kerning

Kerning adjusts the space between individual letters. The word kern actually is the name for the little pieces of metal type that hang out over other letters like the bar on top of the capital T. You can kern text manually or automatically, as well as by using the track kerning system. Kerning has little or no effect on text size type 12 points or less. You'll generally need to kern headlines and other large print. At larger point sizes gaps between letters become painfully obvious. You can either kern type yourself or let PageMaker do it for you.

Pair kerning can be done automatically through the Spacing box shown in Figure 6.23. To open this box click on the Spacing button in the Paragraph Specifications dialog box. If you check Pair kerning, PageMaker will automatically kern specific combinations of letters. Kerning information and tracking information are built into each font of type, and PageMaker can use this information to kern whatever combinations need to be kerned. Such combinations as Tr, Te, WA, We, and Yo all benefit from having the gaps closed up, especially at headline sizes where the open space is even more distracting. If you select Pair kerning, all specified character pairs will be kerned if they're of the same font size, and if they are larger than the minimum point size you indicated in the Spacing dialog box.

140

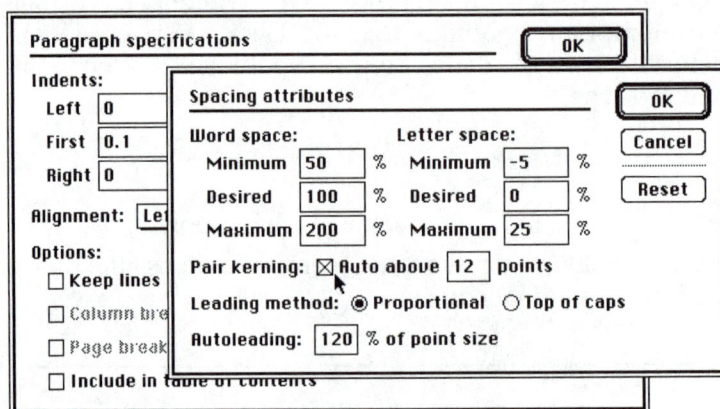

Figure 6.23 The Spacing dialog box.

▶ **Tip:** Kerned text, like tracked text, takes longer to redraw on-screen. If you kern only larger text such as headlines, your pages will be redrawn faster.

Use the following Quick Steps for kerning pairs of letters.

Q **Kerning Letter Pairs**

1. Press ⌘+M to open the **Paragraph** dialog box. Click on the **Spacing** button and select the **Pair kerning** option.

   The Pair kerning option kerns all the common combinations automatically.

2. Set the minimum point size to be kerned. Enter a number in the Auto above points box.

   Only kern larger type sizes (Over 18 points in most fonts).

3. Manually kern any letters that still don't look right using the steps described earlier for manual kerning.

   Manually adjusts any individual spacing problems.

   □

You may also kern letters manually. PageMaker adjusts the space by either a large (¹⁄₂₅th of an em) or small (¹⁄₁₀₀th of an em) increment. An *em*, by the way, is a square the width of the letter m in whatever font you're using. The em is not a fixed measurement since it's related to the particular font. To kern any two letters, place the Text tool cursor between them and type the following keystrokes:

► To tighten a pair of letters press ⌘+Delete (or ⌘+left arrow) for a large decrease in space, or Option+Delete (or Option+left arrow) for a small decrease.

► To loosen the space press ⌘+Shift+Delete (or „+Shift+right arrow) for a large increase, and Option+Shift+Delete (or Option+Shift+right arrow) for a small one.

► To remove all kerning, select the text and press ⌘+Option+K. Figure 6.24 shows the results of kerning several letter combinations on a banner. Space was closed up between the G and R, the O and W, and the T and O. The other letters looked fine.

You can manually kern combinations that have already been automatically pair kerned if you want to change the spacing. Pair kerning doesn't work well for all fonts so you may want to make some adjustments. You can even kern punctuation marks, spaces, or nonprinting characters such as carriage returns. Since manual kerning is fine tuning, it's generally done as the last step in adjusting letter spacing. If you're kerning type smaller than 25 points, you might not be able to see the effect on-screen unless you're working in an enlarged view. For best results do manual kerning at the 200% or 400% page view.

141

GROWING

Spring, 1991 TOGETHER

Before
Kerning

GROWING

Spring, 1991 TOGETHER

After
Kerning

Figure 6.24 Before and after manual kerning.

> **Warning:** Manual kerning may be inaccurate if you've used odd sized type without Adobe Type Manager or Macintosh's System 7 TrueType. If the type looks jaggy on the screen, don't try manual kerning.

142

Headlines

"It's what's up front that counts" was a popular advertising slogan a few years back. Although the product itself is long forgotten, (the slogan was memorable, but not very effective) the principle it expressed applies wonderfully to the creation of headlines. The headline determines whether or not the reader is going to pay attention to the text which follows. A good headline is bait that hooks the reader and tells, in a few words, what the story will be about. Here are some tips for effective headlines:

▶ Make your headlines larger than the body text and set them in a contrasting typeface for maximum clout. Using boldface type also helps.

▶ A headline has to be brief to fit the space available with large size type. Often you have room for only a few words. That's why you need to make them the right words.

▶ Ideal point sizes for headlines range from 36 to 72 points, depending on the size of the publication. If you're setting up an ad and the first word is "Sale", it ought to be in big, bold type. Don't overdo it though. Headlines larger than 72 points are hard to read at normal viewing distances.

▶ Don't capitalize every word of a headline. Capitalize only the most important words and leave the smaller ones in lowercase. Capitalizing every word slows reading comprehension.

▶ Beware of using fancy typefaces for headlines unless there's a really good reason for it. They're better suited for ads and posters than newsletters or corporate reports.

▶ Headlines should contrast with body copy. If you're using a serif face for the text, you might use a sans serif face like Helvetica or Optima for the headlines.

▶ In making up pages with several stories on the same page, don't make all the headlines the same size. You should have one obvious lead story per page. The other, less important stories can have more modest headlines. The idea is to keep the stories from competing with each other for the reader's attention.

143

▶ Never set headlines in capital letters unless they're only a word or two long. Words set in capital letters are hard to read. Most people read words by recognizing the shapes of their outlines as much as by learning the sounds of the letters. When words are set in capital letters the reader loses this visual clue, since all the letters are the same height. Figure 6.25 shows the difference in readability of uppercase and lowercase letters.

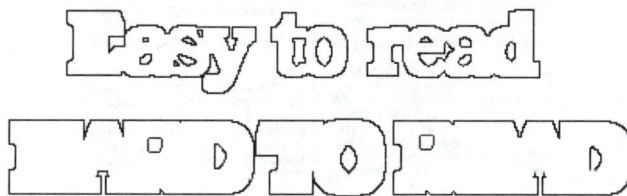

Figure 6.25 Which of these is hard to read?

Placing a Headline

When you are placing a headline always make it a separate text block from the body copy which follows. You can do this in either of two ways:

▶ By typing your headline directly into a new text block.

Or,

▶ By cutting the headline from the story you've imported and pasting it into a new block.

Cutting and pasting an existing headline will unthread it from the text which follows so you can work with it without affecting the formatting of the story. Once you have the headline in its own text block you can extend the block across the page or make it span two columns by selecting it with the pointer, and dragging on a handle. Select it also to change the size and style of type to something suitable for headline use.

Using headlines in a multi-column format can be tricky. Be careful not to place headlines next to each other as they're likely to be read as one continuous line rather than two. This, by the way, is called *tombstoning* because it's reminiscent of the side-by-side stones in old cemeteries. Of course, this can make for some unintentional humor as shown in Figure 6.26.

144

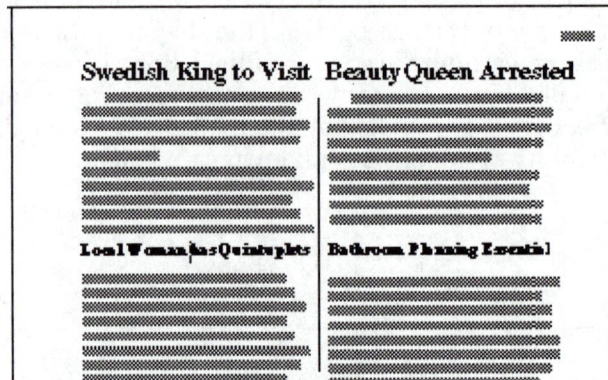

Figure 6.26 A double dose of tombstoning.

The headline should extend over the whole story. If you have a three-column story don't give it a two-column headline. If there's a photo that's part of the story, make sure the headline covers it too. Conversely, make sure the headline doesn't extend out over a story that's not related to it.

Text Rotation

There's a guaranteed way to make a headline get noticed—run it sideways. PageMaker lets you rotate a text block 90° so that it runs along the side of the page instead of across it. Figure 6.27 shows a headline turned on its side. It becomes a design element and has more visual impact than it would if it were just placed at the top of the column. To do this, use the following steps.

1. Select the text block to rotate and select **Text rotation** from the **Elements** menu.

2. The Text Rotation dialog box contains icons showing the four possible rotations. Be sure that your headline is kerned and sized before you rotate it. After it's turned you can't edit it.

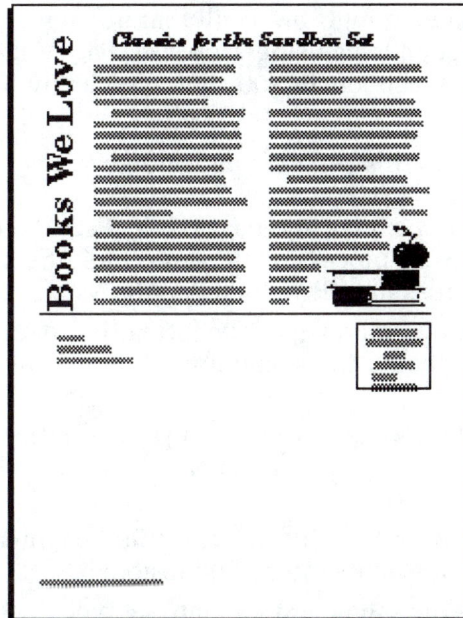

145

Figure 6.27 The headline runs up the page instead of across it.

Figure 6.27 also shows a subhead, a second level or subsidiary headline. We've stretched it across the tops of two columns. To do this, use the following steps.

1. Separate the text block containing the subhead from the rest of the copy by cutting it and repasting it.

2. Select it with the pointer and drag a corner text block handle as needed, until the subhead fits the space available.

To center a headline:

▶ Select it and press ⌘+Shift+C or choose **Center** from the **Alignment** menu.

What You've Learned

Many of the skills you need to work with text in PageMaker are skills you've already mastered using a word processor. Formatting paragraphs and specifying fonts aren't all that different, no matter which program you happen to be using. However, PageMaker is designed to handle certain aspects of the job more efficiently and with greater flexibility.

Specifically in this chapter you learned:

▶ How to import stories into PageMaker. PageMaker accepts text from most word processing programs and ASCII files via modem, or files from PC's linked to the Mac.

▶ How to place a story, adjust the formatting, define the type and paragraph specifications, and import the text in the designated style.

▶ How to import longer stories using the **Autoflow** option to bring in all the text at once. PageMaker will create and fill columns or pages as needed.

▶ How to import a story into several columns threaded together, and how to break the thread and restore it.

▶ How to use the **Alignment** menu to set type flush with either margin, centered, or justified. You can force justification to space a headline across a column of text. Use the Indents/Tabs ruler or the Paragraph Specifications dialog box to set indents and tabs.

▶ How type heights are measured in points. The space between lines of type is called leading. You can adjust the leading to give more or less space. 120% of the type point size is a good leading size. Thus, 10 point type looks good with 12 point leading.

146

▶ How to set the sizes of subscript, superscript, and small caps using the Type Specifications dialog box.

▶ How to adjust the spacing between paragraphs by using the Paragraph Specifications dialog box rather than using double carriage returns.

▶ How to avoid creating widows and orphans, which are misplaced lines of type, by setting a minimum number of lines per paragraph at a column or page break.

▶ How to track the space between letters and words on a line of type. Kerning is the spacing between individual pairs of letters. PageMaker will kern common pairs automatically or you can kern them manually.

▶ How to design headlines that are appropriately large and easy to read and how to place headlines over the stories they relate to.

▶ How to rotate a text block to run along the side of a page by using the Text rotation option.

147

Styles, the Story Editor, and Type Tricks

In This Chapter

▶ *Using a Style Sheet*
▶ *Using the Story Editor*
▶ *Spell Checkers and Dictionaries*
▶ *Hyphenation*
▶ *Creating Dropped Caps*

Style sheets are not designer bed linens. In PageMaker terms, a *style sheet* contains predefined specifications for headlines, captions, and body copy. These predefined specifications are called *styles*, and you can save time by using them to format your publication or make global changes. These are not type styles, such as bold or italic. PageMaker maintains a selection of styles in a *palette*. Select styles from the palette and apply them to your pages, much as you would apply colors to a canvas from a paint palette. PageMaker's Style palette is a small window, like the Toolbox window, and is accessed through the **Windows** menu or by pressing ⌘+Y. Within this window, you can select from PageMaker's default settings or from styles you've added to the palette yourself. New styles can be defined and named within Page-Maker, or imported from your word processor along with the text.

Working with Styles

Use the Style palette to apply styles to text that's already placed in PageMaker. PageMaker has included several default style settings on the Style palette. For example, there's a headline style, one for body text, two styles for subheads, and a style for captions. Even before you learn how to add your own styles to the list, you can practice applying one of these default styles to your text. Use the following Quick Steps to apply a style which already exists on the Style palette.

Q Applying an Existing Style

1. Select the text or headline to which you'll apply the style.

   The text or headline is highlighted. If the text you happen to be working with hasn't been formatted with the style sheet, No style will be selected, as shown in Figure 7.1.

2. Press ⌘+Y.

   The Style palette appears.

3. Click on the name of the style to apply.

   The selected text or headline will change to that style. □

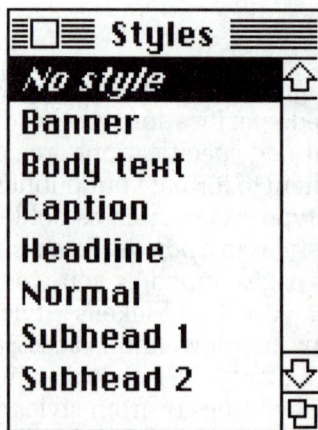

Figure 7.1 The Style palette.

Changing Existing Styles

When you set up a style sheet, it will be kept with that publication (or template). Each new PageMaker publication that you open has a set of default styles built-in. You can use these as a jumping off point in creating your own. To change an existing style, use the Edit Styles box. You can reach this box in one of two ways:

▶ By selecting **Define styles** from the **Type** menu, selecting the name of the style to edit, and then clicking on the **Edit** button.

Or,

▶ By pressing ⌘ and clicking on the name of the style to change in the Style palette.

The Edit Style dialog box, shown in Figure 7.2, appears. The buttons on the right bring up the Type and Paragraph Specifications boxes, the Hyphenation box, and the Indents/Tabs ruler that you've already learned to use through the **Type** menu. The difference between settings you make here, through the Edit Styles box, and settings you've previously made in the **Type** menu, is that the settings you make now will apply to the style you're creating, and not to a specific piece of selected type.

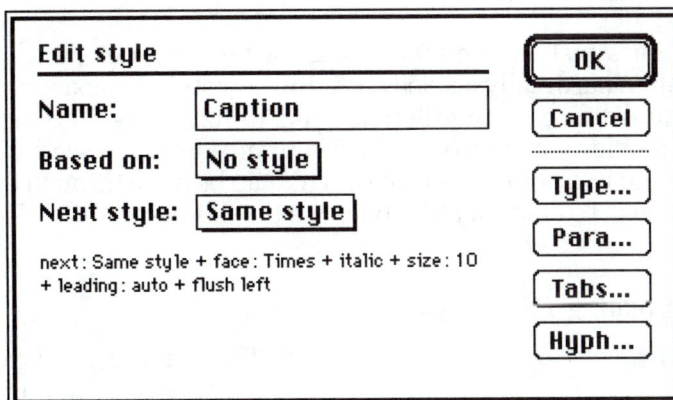

151

Edit style

Name: Caption

Based on: No style

Next style: Same style

next: Same style + face: Times + italic + size: 10 + leading: auto + flush left

OK
Cancel
Type...
Para...
Tabs...
Hyph...

Figure 7.2 Editing a style.

Within the Edit Style box, there's a pop-up menu called **Next Style**. Its purpose is to automate the process of applying styles by letting you specify not only the style you're defining, but the one that will follow it and be applied to the next paragraph. For example, if you define a headline, you can make the next style automatically a subhead. If you've just defined a subhead, you might want to assign body text as the next style. Since the style is applied every time you change paragraphs, you may want to specify same style as next, especially in the case of body text, where you could have many paragraphs of the same style. Use the following Quick Steps to edit a style.

Q Editing a Style

1. Press ⌘ and click on the name of the style to edit.

   The Edit Style box opens with the existing parameters of that style.

2. Enter your changes using the buttons in the dialog box.

   The buttons will give you the appropriate dialog boxes to make changes in.

3. Click on OK or press Return when finished.

   The changes will be applied to all text in the publication to which the style was applied.   □

152

Creating a New Style

Sometimes making a minor change or two to an existing style isn't enough. What's really needed is a brand new style. For example, say you want to define several different kinds of headlines. PageMaker's defaults provide you with one which you can edit as you see fit, but you'd like to add two or three new ones. This can be done through the Define Styles box. To create a new style, use the following Quick Steps.

Q Creating a New Style

1. Press ⌘+3.

   The Define styles box appears, as shown in Figure 7.3.

2. Select an existing style from the pop-up menu to base a new style on.

   If there's no style you wish to base the new style on, select **No style**.

3. Type in the name of the new style.

4. Use the buttons to open the and paragraph specifications, and so on.

Verify all the attributes of your new style or PageMaker will use the default settings.

5. Click on OK or press Return when done.

☐

Define styles

| Style: | OK |
| | Cancel |

Selection
Body text
Caption
Headline
Normal
Subhead 1
Subhead 2

New...
Edit...
Remove
Copy...

next: Normal + face : N Helvetica Narrow + size : 12 +
leading : auto + flush left + hyphenation

153

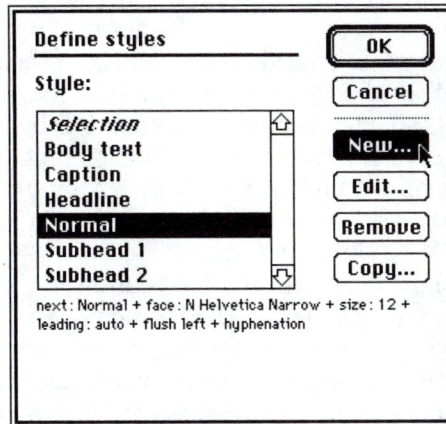

Figure 7.3 The Define Styles box.

The Define styles dialog box contains a list of all the styles in the Style palette. To base your new style on an existing one:

1. Open the **Define styles** box by pressing ⌘+3.
2. Select the style you want to use as a basis for your new one by clicking on it in the scrolling menu. After the style is high-lighted, click on the **New** button.
3. The **Edit** box opens with the Style name box empty.
4. Enter the name for your new style, and then make whatever changes are needed to the specifications for the new style.

If you want to save a paragraph as a style:

1. Select the paragraph or click an insertion point anywhere within the text.
2. Open the **Define styles** box. The style attributes for your chosen text will be listed in the lower part of the dialog box.
3. Open the **Edit** box to make any additional modifications.

4. Assign the style a name and click on OK to save it to the style sheet.

Keeping a style sheet helps you avoid using the wrong font for a headline or text block. For example, if you set up a subhead style in Helvetica Bold 14 point, and apply the style to all subheads, your publication will end up with a more consistent look. However, there are a few pitfalls in using the style sheet. If you make additional changes (through the **Type** menus or Type Specifications box) in a text block that has style sheet formatting applied, you will lose these changes if you then make any other changes that affect the style sheet. For example, suppose your style sheet definition of subheads is based on the Normal body copy style, using Helvetica as the normal text and subhead face. You then change one subhead to Helvetica Medium italic, using the **Type** menu. Now you decide that the body copy should be in a serif face, and you change the style sheet to make Palatino 12 your normal font. Suddenly, your Helvetica Medium italic subhead, and everything else in your document with a style based on some variation of normal, turns into Palatino. New styles, which are based on existing styles become permanently threaded to a *style chain*. If you change the style at the head of the chain, all other styles threaded to it will change accordingly.

Copying a Style Sheet

After you've created a set of styles for a publication, you can reuse that style sheet in your next publication. This will save you from having to reenter the styles again. You can just copy them from one PageMaker publication to another. Use the Copy styles feature when your publication is part of a series (a monthly newsletter or one of several business forms), to maintain a consistent look. You can also use the Copy Styles feature if you are creating a long document, such as a book or instruction manual, that might be set in several chapters and you need to maintain the same styles throughout. You can copy a style sheet from another PageMaker publication by:

1. Clicking on the **Copy** button in the **Define styles** box, shown in Figure 7.4.
2. Choose the publication whose style sheet you want to copy.
3. Click on OK. PageMaker will copy all of that publication's styles into the current document. If any styles have the same names, an Alert box will appear asking whether you want the

154

new styles to replace the existing styles. Click on OK to continue and the styles will be copied into your current document, where you can use and modify them.

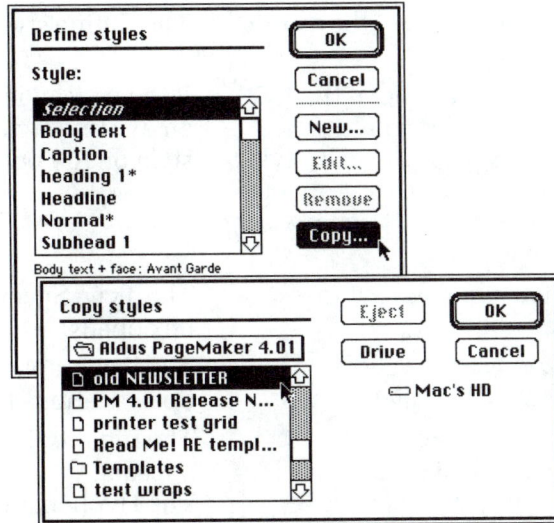

Figure 7.4 The Copy styles dialog box.

> ▶ **Tip:** You can use the Copy styles feature when your publication is part of a series (like a monthly newsletter or one of a series of business forms) to maintain a consistent look.

To import styles you've created in your word processing program, be sure to click on the Retain Format button in the Place document box. When you place the document into PageMaker, the styles will come through along with the words, as long as they're compatible with PageMaker's styles. PageMaker will add the word processor's styles to its style sheet and **Style** menu, with an asterisk after the name to distinguish them from PageMaker's own styles.

> ⊘ **Warning:** Be careful. If imported styles have the same name as PageMaker's own styles, it will use its own styles and ignore the imported ones.

155

Use the following Quick Steps to define styles.

Q **Defining Styles**

1. Press ⌘+3 to open the **Define styles** box.

   The Define styles box opens.

2. Click on **New** to open the **Edit style** box. Enter a name for the new style. If the new style is based on an existing style, select it from the Based on pop-up menu.

   If the new style isn't based on an existing style, select No style on the pop-up menu.

3. Click on **Type** and set the type attributes.

   The Type Specifications box opens.

4. Click on **Para** to set the paragraph attributes.

   The Paragraph Specifications box opens.

5. Click on **Tabs** to set the indents and tabs.

   The Indents/Tabs ruler appears.

6. Click on **Hyph** to specify hyphenation attributes.

   The Hyphenation box opens.

7. Press Option+Return to close the dialog boxes and save the style.

   Whenever you have more than one dialog box open, clicking Option+Return confirms the settings and closes all of the boxes at once. □

Using Style Name Tags

If you're working in your word processor and want to save time when placing text into PageMaker, enter the copy as plain text, unformatted, and put a style name tag at the head of the copy in angle brackets (**<>**). For example, start a story like this:

<headline> Challengers Sweep Town Election

<subhead> Incumbents stunned at loss

<normal> In a "throw the bums out" mood, local voters elected two new Aldermen, three new library trustees, new school committee members, and a new town clerk yesterday, in the only election in town history in which all of the incumbents lost.

Following paragraphs, as long as they use the normal format, don't need additional tags. When you get ready to place the story into your PageMaker publication, check the Read tags option in the Place box. PageMaker locates the tags, and applies the designated styles to each paragraph. Use the following Quick Steps to apply styles.

Q Applying Styles

1. Select the text to which you want to apply a style.

   You must always select something before you change it. Place the I-beam cursor anywhere within the paragraph to be changed.

2. Press ⌘+Y to open the Style palette. Press Shift to preserve any styling that exists in the text, such as italics, and click on the style to apply.

   As soon as you click the style name, the paragraph will change to that style. (Only the selected paragraph will change.) □

157

⊘ **Caution:** Be careful when assigning styles because you *cannot* undo them. The only way to return to your previous formatting is to select Revert from the **File** menu, and go back to the last version saved. It's a good idea to save frequently while you work, and always save before experimenting with styles. If you are a novice user of style sheets, it's advisable to use them for only one or two styles at first, defining the other formats directly from the Type and Paragraph Specifications boxes. Since styles are not undoable, you can make major mistakes if you aren't sure of what you're doing. As you become more comfortable with the Style palette, you can begin to use it to copy more of your styles.

Overriding Styles

Sometimes you'll want to change a single word within a formatted paragraph. There may be a phrase, such as a title, that needs to be italicized or a word that needs to be in boldface for added emphasis. Do this by selecting the word or words to be changed, and modifying them as needed. When you modify a style, a plus sign (+) will follow the name of the style in the Style palette and **Style** menu, when those words are selected, to indicate that the style has been overridden. Such overrides are permanent which means that they'll remain if you change the format of the paragraph. For example, if you format a paragraph in Helvetica medium and you make a single word bold, when you change the face from Helvetica to Palatino, the emphasized word will switch to Palatino bold.

> ▶ **Note:** An exception to permanent override occurs when, for example, you've italicized a few words in a paragraph, and then decide to set the whole paragraph in italics. The previously italicized words will become plain text, since Page-Maker seeks to preserve the contrast in styles.

158

Type style (italic, bold, and so on) is a permanent attribute but other changes you might make, such as point size, hyphenation, leading, tabs and indents, are all temporary overrides. If you later apply a style having the same attributes, you'll remove your changes. For example, if you had a line of 12 point type, and you wanted to say WOW! in the middle of it in 14 point type, you'd change the word WOW to 14 points. That would be a temporary override. Suppose later that you decided to make that whole paragraph 14 point type, or even 10 point type. The WOW, even though you'd intended it to be two points larger, would change to the same size as everything else. So changing the rest of the paragraph removes the previous change.

> ▶ **Tip:** There's a way to preserve temporary spacing overrides when you change styles. To keep them intact when you apply a new style, hold down Shift while you click on the style name in the Style palette. Your paragraphs will change to reflect the new style, but the temporary overrides will remain unchanged.

The Story Editor

Although PageMaker makes it easy to edit text while you're looking at pages, this isn't always the most convenient way to do it. Every time you do something that changes the page, PageMaker has to stop and redraw it. This can take a while and after the tenth redraw, it gets annoying (especially on an older, smaller, slower Mac). Fortunately, Aldus has given PageMaker 4.0 an easy-to-use *Story Editing function*. Earlier versions of PageMaker didn't include this feature, but in PageMaker 4.0, the Story Editor enables you to open a text-only window, with powerful word processing capabilities. You can open a window for each story in your publication.

Opening Story Editor

To edit a story, position the cursor anywhere within it and either select Edit story from the bottom of the Edit menu, or press ⌘+E. Your story will appear in Story Editor format, as shown in Figure 7.5. Story Editor opens as a text-only window on top of the Page layout view, with the first few words of the story as the title. PageMaker considers text blocks that are threaded together to be a single story. Because the story is saved as part of the publication, it doesn't need a separate title. Pressing ⌘+E when you're in Story Editor will take you back to your publication, as will clicking anywhere outside the Story window.

159

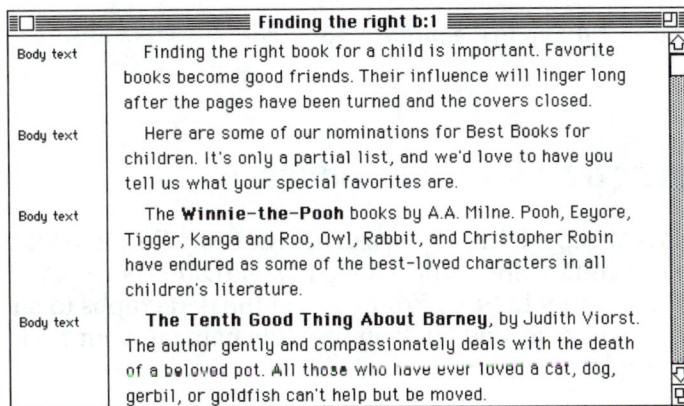

	Finding the right b:1
Body text	Finding the right book for a child is important. Favorite books become good friends. Their influence will linger long after the pages have been turned and the covers closed.
Body text	Here are some of our nominations for Best Books for children. It's only a partial list, and we'd love to have you tell us what your special favorites are.
Body text	The **Winnie-the-Pooh** books by A.A. Milne. Pooh, Eeyore, Tigger, Kanga and Roo, Owl, Rabbit, and Christopher Robin have endured as some of the best-loved characters in all children's literature.
Body text	**The Tenth Good Thing About Barney**, by Judith Viorst. The author gently and compassionately deals with the death of a beloved pet. All those who have ever loved a cat, dog, gerbil, or goldfish can't help but be moved.

Figure 7.5 The Story Editor view.

The Story Editor doesn't show your formatting, except for type styles such as bold or italic. Instead, it uses a generic font like Geneva and lists the names of your assigned paragraph styles, if any, to the left of the story. (You can change the font and point size which Story Editor displays in, by using the Preferences box. You can also use this method to preview a headline in a particular size and style.) If you haven't formatted your text, there will be a dot next to each paragraph or headline, and no style will be highlighted on the Style palette. It just means that the text has not had a style sheet attached to it, even though you might have designated a particular face and size using the Type Specifications box. Empty lines also have dots indicating No style. If the style has been applied, it will be highlighted on the Style palette, as shown in Figure 7.6.

160

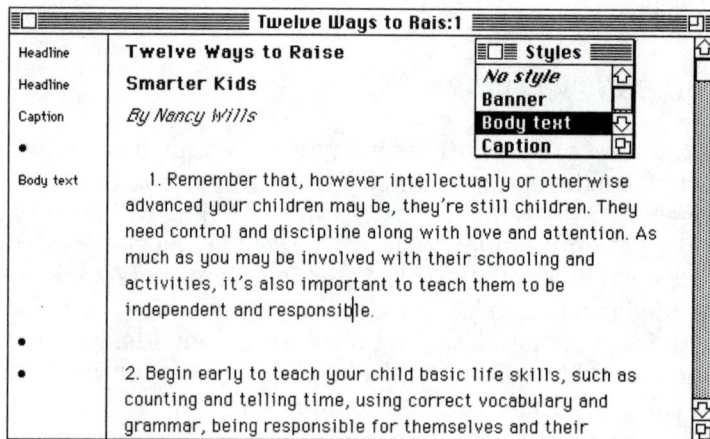

Figure 7.6 The Style palette highlights the style of selected text.

Assigning a Style in Story Editor

If a style is already defined, you can use the Story Editor to assign it. For example, if you've already designated a style called body copy, it's easy to open your story in Story Editor, select the paragraphs to be put into the body copy style, and click on the style name in your Style palette.

Word Processing in Story Editor

Once you're in the Story Editor, you can add, remove, cut, copy, and paste text as much as you like, just as you would with any other word processing program. Any changes you make in the Story Editor will immediately be reflected in your copy. You probably won't see them; however, as PageMaker grays out the corresponding text blocks in the Layout window, as shown in Figure 7.7.

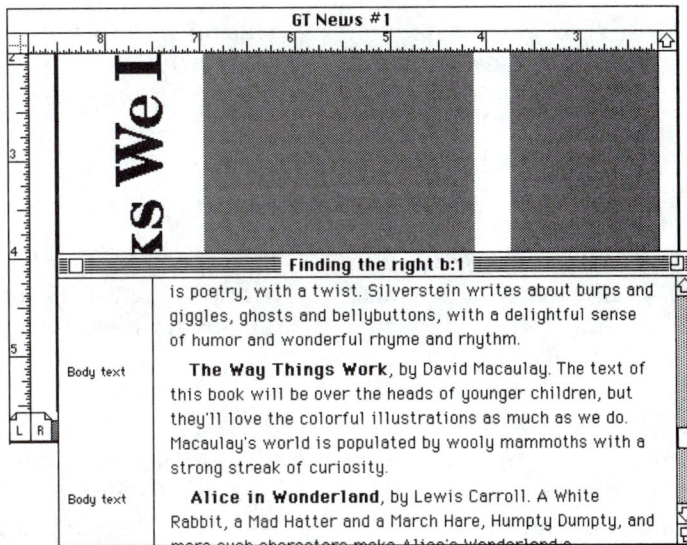

161

Figure 7.7 Text in the page layout grayed out behind the Story Editor window.

You can toggle back and forth between Story Editor view and Layout view by pressing ⌘+E to see how your changes are affecting the rest of the page. When you leave the Story window, the text automatically reflows back onto the page. Any changes you've made in Story view will appear in Layout view. If you're not finished editing, leave the Story window open. Pressing ⌘+E always takes you to the same point in Layout view that you were at in Story view.

If the story is new and you want to place it on the page, press ⌘+D or choose **Place** from the **File** menu. The Story window closes and you'll be back in Layout view with a loaded Text icon.

If you change your mind about placing a story after you've gotten the Text icon, just click on the Pointer tool in the Tool box and you'll return to Story view so you can continue to edit.

PageMaker lets you open several Story windows at the same time, making it easy to cut, copy, and paste between them. Each window holds one story. To work with several Story windows at once, use the following Quick Steps.

Q **Working with Several Story View Windows**

1. Select a story to edit and press ⌘+E to edit it in Story Editor.

   The first Story window opens.

2. Choose **New Story** from the **Story** menu and create one using Story Editor as your word processor. Or, choose Import and bring in a story from a word processing file to edit.

   This opens a second Story window.

3. If the other story you want to edit is also in your PageMaker publication, return to Layout view without closing the first Story window, select the additional story, and press ⌘+E.

   This opens another Story window. Figure 7.8 shows the possibilities.

4. Now you can cut and paste between the windows and make any changes you wish. When you're done editing, close the Story window.

   Already placed stories will reflow in Layout view. You'll be asked to place or discard any new stories. □

162

> ▶ **Note:** When you have two windows with the same name, the second will be called **:2**. To return to Layout view, click on it or choose it from the **Windows** menu.

Starting a New Story

You can also start a new story by pressing ⌘+E while you're in Layout view with no text selected. An untitled story window opens. Once your story is written, place it in your publication. To do this press ⌘+D to get the Place icon. If **Autoflow** has been selected, it will create new columns or pages as needed. Otherwise, you must place the story manually.

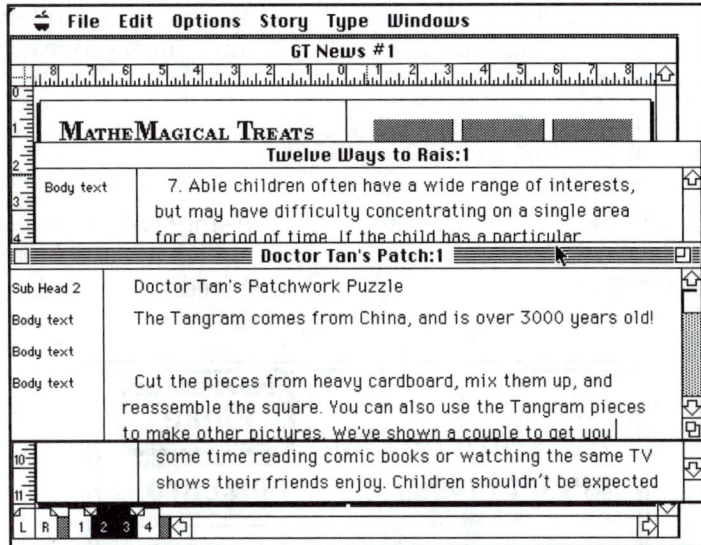

Figure 7.8 Multiple Story windows opened.

163

If you attempt to close a Story window without placing the story, you'll get the Alert box shown in Figure 7.9. PageMaker forces you to make a decision. Choosing Place gives you the Place icon so you can proceed as explained earlier. Discard closes the window and erases your story. If you click on Cancel, the story will remain in the Story window and will be saved, unplaced, with the publication. But suppose your answer is None of the above, because perhaps you want to keep the story for a future issue. Saving it with this publication is a good way to misplace it. Since it wouldn't have a separate title, you'd have no way to locate it without opening the publication and hunting for it. What you should do, in this case, is save it separately in the folder of newsletter materials. This is easy thanks to PageMaker's Export function. You can save whole stories or selected blocks of text. The latter is especially helpful if you have a story that's too long for your present publication, and you decide to break it up and run it in two consecutive issues.

Use the following Quick Steps to export a story.

Q **Exporting a Story from PageMaker**

1. Choose **Export** from the **File** menu.

   This command is disabled if no story is selected. The Export box appears, as shown in Figure 7.10.

2. Locate the folder or disk to save to, and give the story a name

3. Select the word processing format to use or choose **Text only**.

4. Click on OK when finished.

Click on the Export tags box if you're using style tags.

The story will be saved as a file in whatever folder you assigned it to. □

164

Figure 7.9 The Alert box forces you to decide what to do with the story.

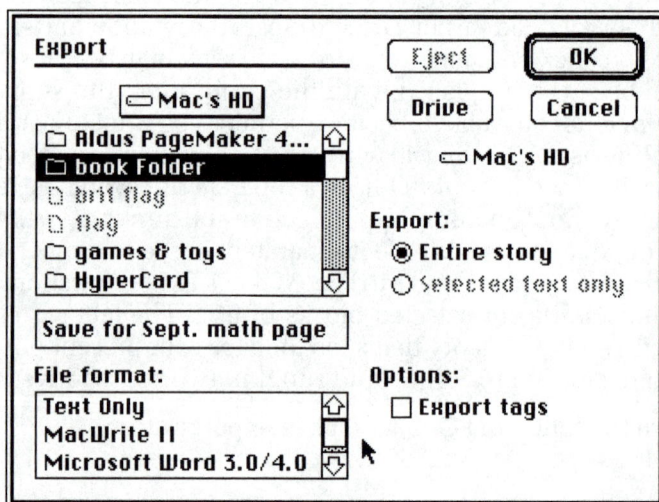

Figure 7.10 The Export dialog box.

> ▶ **Note:** When you installed PageMaker you selected import/ export filters, which convert your word processor's text into PageMaker, and vice versa. If you use several different word processors, you can choose between them or save your file as text only. If you've done a lot of formatting, Microsoft Word 4.0 and *RTF* (Rich Text Format) will preserve the majority of all formatting commands. (RTF is an interchange format, used primarily to transfer files back and forth to a PC. Microsoft Word also lets you save and open files in RTF.)

Occasionally you may encounter the box shown in Figure 7.11. A story may fail to import if the Mac's memory is already full. This can happen when you are running PageMaker, and one or two other applications such as Microsoft Word and SuperPaint, all at the same time under MultiFinder. In such a case, place the story on the pasteboard or just leave the file open, and close down the other applications. Then try again. It should export without any trouble.

165

Figure 7.11 If you see this Alert box you're probably out of memory.

Find and Change

On Story Editor's **Edit** menu, there are two functions familiar to everyone who uses word processors: **Find** and **Change**. Find and Change are a big help in editing text. They can help you locate a key word in a long story without needing to read through the entire piece.

Change can correct spellings of names, or other words that you don't want to make a permanent part of your dictionary. You can make changes either case by case or globally, meaning at every occurrence throughout your story. Figure 7.12 shows the Change box. **Find**, **Change**, **Change and Find**, and **Change** all work exactly as they do in a word processing program.

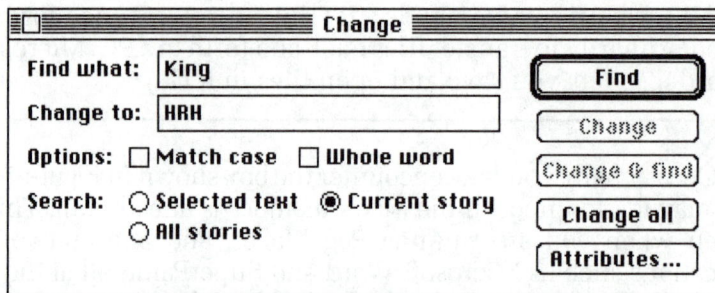

Figure 7.12 The Change dialog box.

PageMaker also lets you find and change text by its type font, size, style, or formatting. PageMaker lets you look not only in a text block or story being edited, but also in every story in your publication. It can't, however, search for text that was placed as part of a graphic, because it doesn't recognize the difference between pictures and words within the graphic block.

> ► **Tip:** The Change box can remain on-screen in the background while you use menu and editing commands. You can move it to an unoccupied corner of your screen and bring it forward when you want to use it.

Finding and **Changing** text by its attributes is done through the Attributes box and its pop-up menus. If you're changing text format attributes:

► Leave the **Find what** and **Change to** boxes empty and click on **Attributes**.

To change a formatting attribute:

► Select the attribute to be changed from the pop-up menus, and then indicate the changes. In Figure 7.13, underlined words are being changed to italics.

```
┌─────────────────────────────────────────────────────────┐
│  Attributes ─────────────────────────      ┌─────────┐   │
│                                             │   OK    │   │
│  Find:                                      └─────────┘   │
│     Para style: [Normal]                    ┌─────────┐   │
│                                             │ Cancel  │   │
│     Font:       [Any]                       └─────────┘   │
│     Size:       [12      ▷]                               │
│     Type style: [Underline]                               │
│                                                           │
│  Change:                                                  │
│     Para style: [Normal]                                  │
│                 ┌──────────────┐                          │
│     Font:       │   Any        │                          │
│                 │   Normal     │                          │
│     Size:       │   Bold       │                          │
│                 │ ✓ Italic   ▖ │                          │
│     Type style: │   Underline  │                          │
│                 │   Strikethru │                          │
│                 │   Outline    │                          │
│                 │   Shadow     │                          │
│                 │   Reverse    │                          │
│                 └──────────────┘                          │
└─────────────────────────────────────────────────────────┘
```

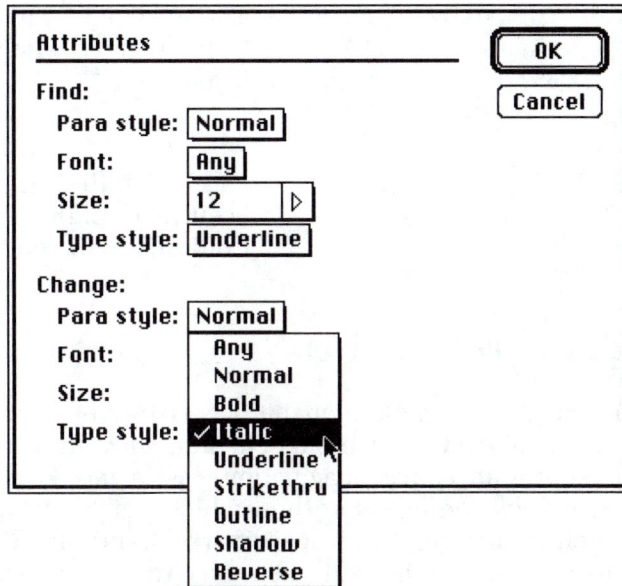

Figure 7.13 The Attributes box provides an easy way to correct minor formatting errors.

167

If you enter a word in Find what and then select Match case, PageMaker will find only words which appear exactly as you've typed them. A word typed in lowercase will be missed if it happens to be capitalized because it starts a sentence. A search for *Pagemaker* will not find *PageMaker*. Use the following Quick Steps to find and change a word.

ⓠ Changing a Word

1. Press ⌘+E to enter Story view.

   Change and Find doesn't work in Page view.

2. Press ⌘+9.

   The Change box appears.

3. Enter the changes in the fields.

4. Choose **Whole word** and **Match case** if desired.

   Not choosing whole word means PageMaker will find your word inside other words. (for example, changing *in* to *out* could give you *outtroduction* or turn *fine* into *foute*.)

5. Select the text to be searched and press Return, or click on **Find** or **Change all**, if you are sure you want to change every occurrence.

The searched for word will be highlighted when it is found.

6. Click on **Change** or **Find next**.

PageMaker finds the next occurrence of the word. Continue until you are done. ☐

Viewing Invisible Characters

No we don't mean seeing pink elephants or even Harvey (the six foot tall white rabbit whom Art Carney brought to life). These invisible characters don't require an active imagination, just a few keystrokes. In PageMaker, *invisible characters* are those which don't print but do affect your text, such as carriage returns, space markers, and tabs. Story Editor lets you see them, which is helpful when you have a line of type that just doesn't seem to be leaded correctly. It could be that one of these invisible characters is upsetting the leading or spacing because it's in the wrong font. Once you find the tab, return, or other invisible character which is messing up your text, you can change or remove it.

168

To show invisible characters, use the following Quick Steps.

Q Showing Invisible Characters

1. Open the story in Story view.

Place the I-beam anywhere in it and press ⌘+E.

2. Select **Display** from the **Options** menu.

The hidden characters will appear. The spaces between words are represented by dots, paragraphs by the ¶ symbol, and tabs by arrows.

3. To solve the leading problem shown in Figure 7.14, isolate pieces of the line and look at the **Point size** menu, shown in Figure 7.15.

If the words selected are in the same point size, they will be checked.

4. When you find a space and word that isn't checked, you've found the problem. To fix it, delete the space and the letters on either side and retype them.

By replacing a space in the wrong point size with one in the right size, you've solved the leading problem.

☐

**The Tenth Good Thing About
Barney**, by Judith Viorst. The author

gently and compassionately deals with

the death of a beloved pet. All those
who have ever loved a cat, dog, gerbil,
or goldfish can't help but be moved.

Leading
problem

Figure 7.14 Text with a leading problem.

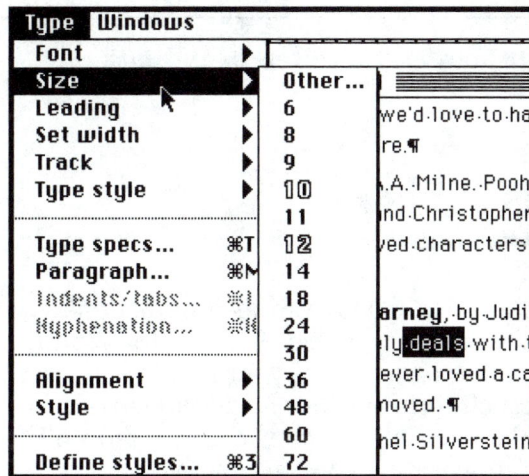

169

Type	Windows			
Font		▶		
Size		▶	**Other...**	
Leading		▶	6	we'd·love·to·ha
Set width		▶	8	re.¶
Track		▶	9	
Type style		▶	10	.A.·Milne.·Pooh
			11	ind·Christopher
Type specs...	⌘T		12	ved·characters.
Paragraph...	⌘M		14	
Indents/tabs...	⌘I		18	arney,·by·Judi
Hyphenation...	⌘H		24	ly·deals·with·t
			30	ever·loved·a·ca
Alignment		▶	36	noved.·¶
Style		▶	48	
			60	hel·Silverstein
Define styles...	⌘3		72	

Figure 7.15 The Point size menu.

Story Editor will also display invisible characters to show the
position of inline graphics, page numbers, and index entries. You can
cut, copy, paste, and delete these characters, and the elements they
represent will be moved or removed on the layout. You can also import
pictures into the Story Editor although you won't see them. They'll
appear as inline graphics characters in Story Editor, and as the actual
graphics in your layout when you place the story. Figure 7.16 shows the
different kinds of markers you're likely to use.

```
┌──────────────────── Imsep pretu tempu :1 ──────────────────┐
│ □□                                                      ◻◻ │
│  •   Imsep·pretu·tempu·⬚rolf··bileg·rokam·revoc·tephe·rosve· │
│      etepe·tenov·sindu·turqu·brevt·elliu·repar·tiuve·tamia·queso·¶ │
│                                                              │
│  •   ▨·Anetn·bisre·freun·carmi·avire·ingen·umque·miher·muner· │
│      veris·adest·duner·veris·adest·iteru·quevi·escit·billo·isput· │
│      tatqu·aliqu·diams·bipos·¶                               │
│                                                              │
│  •   ¶                                                       │
│  •   ▨▪                                                      │
│          Character       Symbol                             │
│          Normal space       ·                               │
│          Tab               →                                │
│          Return            ¶                                │
│          Page number       #                                │
│          Index entry       ◊                                │
│          inline graphic    ▨                                │
└──────────────────────────────────────────────────────────┘
```

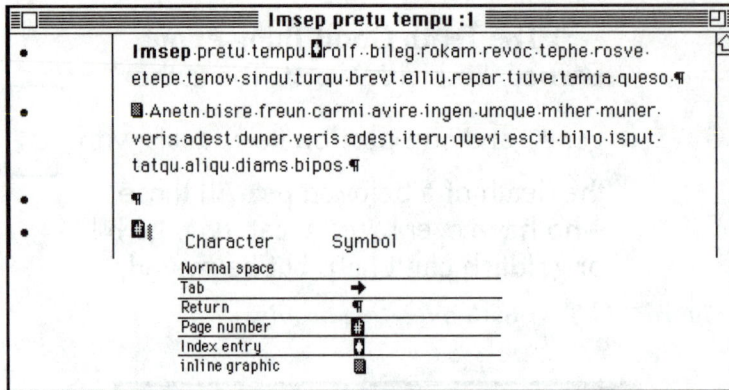

Figure 7.16 Invisible characters of all kinds.

The Spell Checker

170

PageMaker includes a 100,000 word spelling dictionary, which you can use while you're working in the Story Editor. You can also install dictionaries in other languages if your publications are multilingual. You can check spelling in only one language at a time, however. It is *un poco* nuisance for *todos el mundo* who like to show off their linguistic *savoir faire*. Dictionaries, if you have more than one, are chosen from the pop-up menu in the Paragraph Specifications dialog box, shown in Figure 7.17. The grayed out dictionaries in the list are not currently installed.

Additional dictionaries are available directly from Aldus Corporation. Sets include Central European (French, Italian, German, Dutch); Scandinavian (Swedish, Norwegian, Danish); Spanish & Portuguese (includes Brazilian Portuguese); American English, and British English. Both English versions include your choice of a free Legal or Medical supplement. The Legal dictionary covers over 28,000 words from law, accounting, and finance. The Medical dictionary contains over 35,000 entries from Webster's Medical Desk Dictionary including biology and chemistry terms, and abbreviations used in prescriptions. Each dictionary package includes complete installation instructions. Installation is simple and requires only a minute or two.

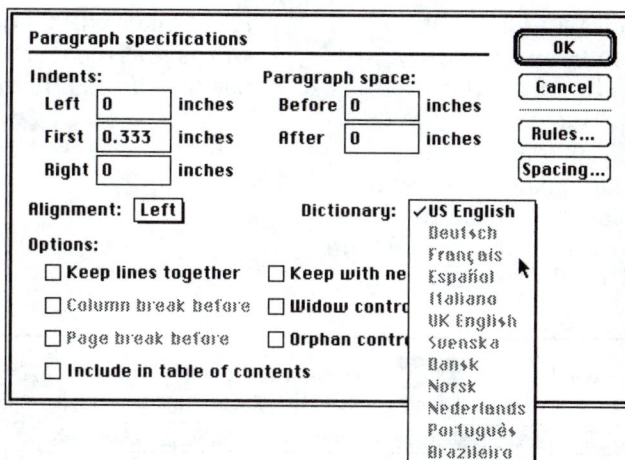

Figure 7.17 Choosing dictionaries from the Paragraph Specifications box.

171

Checking Spelling

To check spelling, use the following Quick Steps.

Q Checking Spelling

1. Choose the **Spelling** command from the Story view's **Edit** menu, or press ⌘+L.

    The Spelling box, shown in Figure 7.18, appears. (You must be in Story Editor.)

2. Check a specific word or paragraph by highlighting it. Use the buttons in the Spelling box to check the story you're working on, or even all the stories in your publication. Click on Start or press Return to begin the spelling check.

    PageMaker scans for unrecognized words in the selected text block or stories. As with most spell checkers PageMaker highlights the unrecognized word and displays it in the Change to field. The window will scroll to display the misspelled word, although you may have to move the Spelling box to see it. The questioned word is also displayed in the Unknown word field, and a list of possible substitutes is given.

3. If your word is correct, click on the **Ignore** button or just press Return. Otherwise, select the correct word from the list PageMaker gives you. If none of PageMaker's guesses are correct, type the correct word into the Change to field, and click on the **Replace** button.

PageMaker will ignore correct words that reoccur after it has questioned them once.

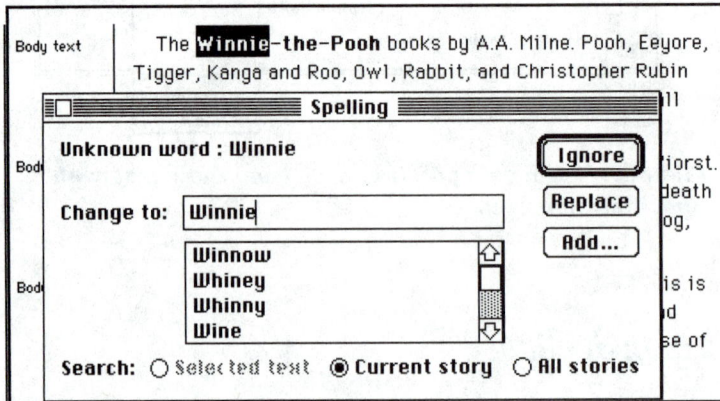

□

172

Figure 7.18 The Spelling dialog box.

If you want PageMaker to add your word to its dictionary, use the following Quick Steps.

Adding a Word to the Dictionary

1. Click on the **Add** button.

PageMaker opens the dialog box shown in Figure 7.19. It verifies the spelling and case of the word and shows you its correct hyphenation, according to grammar rules programmed into PageMaker. (PageMaker uses the same dictionary to check spelling and hyphenation.)

2. If you select Exactly as typed, PageMaker will query the word whenever it doesn't exactly match the entry.

   For example, if the word is capitalized, it will be questioned.

3. Click on OK or press Return to enter the word and close the box.

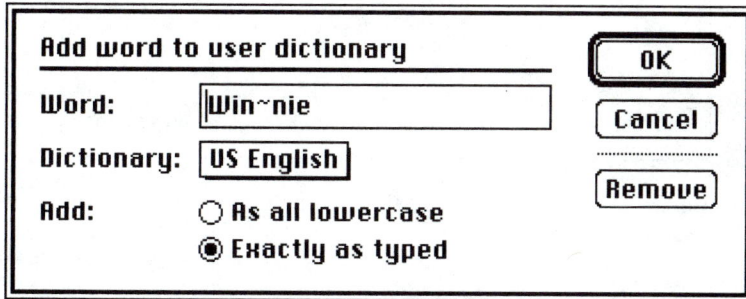

   □

```
┌─────────────────────────────────────────────────────────┐
│  Add word to user dictionary            ╭──────────╮      │
│                                         │    OK    │      │
│  Word:       │Win~nie                │  ╰──────────╯      │
│                                         ╭──────────╮      │
│  Dictionary: │US English│              │  Cancel  │      │
│                                         ╰──────────╯      │
│  Add:        ○ As all lowercase        ╭──────────╮      │
│              ● Exactly as typed        │  Remove  │      │
│                                         ╰──────────╯      │
└─────────────────────────────────────────────────────────┘
```

Figure 7.19 Teach PageMaker any words you think it needs to know.

173

If you tell PageMaker once to ignore a word, it will continue to ignore it for as long as the program remains active. If you quit and then reopen PageMaker, when you do another spelling check, words previously ignored will be queried again. PageMaker will give you an appropriate message if no errors are found.

PageMaker can also catch a few other errors, as Figure 7.20 shows. In this case, a typographical error was made because a sentence was started with *he* instead of *The*. PageMaker queried the mistake. However, PageMaker won't catch errors in plurals of words unless the plural form has been entered separately in the dictionary. For example, if you entered the word *cat* in the dictionary, and then typed *ctas*, it wouldn't automatically offer you *cats* as a corrected spelling. You would have to enter *cats* separately if you expected it to correct *ctas*.

Unlike most Macintosh dialog boxes which demand immediate responses, you can leave PageMaker's Check Spelling and Change dialog boxes active while you work on other parts of your publication. You can't resize the boxes, but you can use menu commands and editing procedures while they are on-screen. With MultiFinder you can also use other applications without closing the boxes. They may remove themselves to a layer behind the active window, but pressing ⌘+L or ⌘+9, brings the Spelling or Change boxes to the front again.

Mad Hatter and a March Hare, Humpty Dumpty, and more such
characters make Alice's Wonderland a wonderful place. The
book is pure whimsy, and endures. Every educated person

Spelling

Possible capitalization error.

Change to: |h

H

[Ignore]

[Replace]

[Add...]

Search: ○ Selected text ⦿ Current story ○ All stories

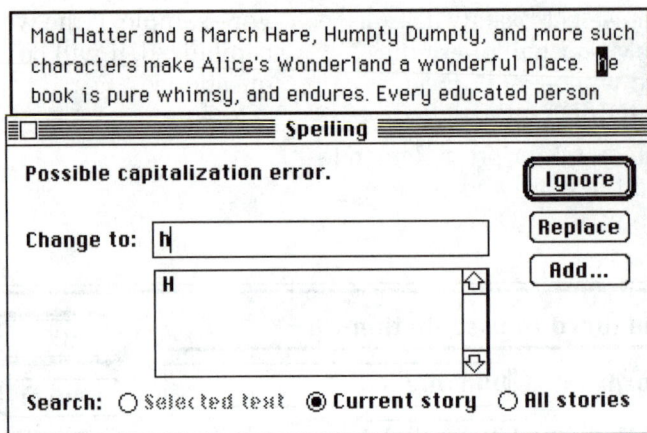

*Figure 7.20 PageMaker searches for caps at the beginning of
sentences.*

174

▶ **Tip:** When you are working on a Mac with a small screen,
such as an SE or a Mac Plus, you might find it more
convenient to move the Spelling box to the bottom of the screen
and resize the Story window so you can see both at the same
time. Documents which have a lot of spelling errors may need
to have their formatting adjusted. Adding or removing even one
character can throw off a line of text, especially if the text is
justified.

Hyphenation

Hyphenation helps your text to flow into nice, even columns. Unfortunately, hyphenation is distracting to read. Ideally, only a few words
should be broken up, so your page can look good without putting a strain
on the reader. But column widths and word lengths are not always ideal.
Hyphenation is a compromise between design and readability. Page-
Maker offers several different ways to handle hyphenating words: you
can do it yourself; let PageMaker do it, according to the hyphenation

information in its dictionary; or use a set of rules built into the dictionary, which can even hyphenate unknown or nonsense words. To use hyphenation:

▶ Press ⌘+H or select it from the **Type** menu. The dialog box shown in Figure 7.21 appears.

To turn on automatic hyphenation:

▶ Click on the **On** button. Automatic hyphenation will remain on until you turn it off. (When you open a new publication, it's on by default.)

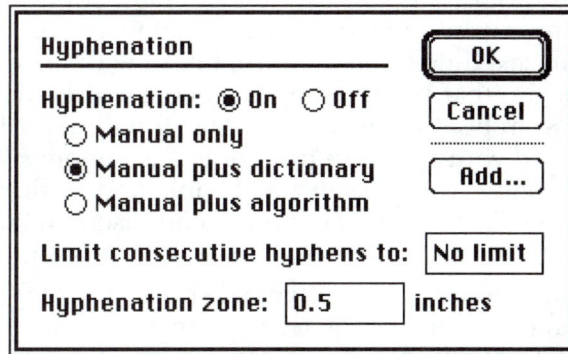

Figure 7.21 The Hyphenation dialog box.

In the Hyphenation box you can choose any of the following options:

Manual Only: means that PageMaker will break words only where you have inserted *discretionary hyphens* by typing a hyphen (-). Discretionary hyphens are invisible unless needed. If you reflow the text, you won't end up with a hyphen in the middle of the line, as you would if you simply broke it. Manual gives you the most control over how your page will look. You can fit copy more accurately than when PageMaker is doing the job automatically. Of course it takes longer, but on the other hand, you don't have to clean up mistakes PageMaker has made. (Algorithms aren't perfect.)

Manual Plus Dictionary: This tells PageMaker to use its dictionary for hyphenation. Any discretionary hyphens you've inserted manually will also be used, if needed. The words will be broken based on the priorities given within the dictionary. A word may have several places at which it could be broken. Depending on the space available, PageMaker will choose the most preferred hyphenation first. You can also insert discretionary hyphenation breaks and assign your own priorities, in the PageMaker dictionary. To assign hyphenation priorities, click on Add in the Hyphenation box or choose the Spelling command in the Story Editor. Enter the new word adding one, two, or three *tilde (~)* symbols where you want a word to break. The single tilde break has the highest priority. If you have a trademark or other word you don't ever want hyphenated, add that word without hyphens and place a tilde directly in front of it, with no space in between. What you're doing is placing a discretionary hyphen in front of the word. PageMaker will never hyphenate any word with a tilde in front of it. Discretionary hyphens you've added to your story will apply only within the publication you're working on. Words and discretionary hyphens added to the dictionary are part of it, unless removed.

Manual plus algorithm: PageMaker uses not only the dictionary and your discretionary hyphenations, but goes to the rules programmed into it to see how a word not in the dictionary, is hyphenated within the grammar of whichever language you're using. Each PageMaker dictionary contains hyphenation *algorithms* for its language. This choice obviously gives you the most flexibility. You can always override PageMaker's hyphenation by inserting a discretionary hyphen where you'd rather have the word break. You can remove a discretionary hyphen at the end of a line by backspacing over it. This will force the word to the next line. To remove a discretionary hyphen in a word in the middle of the line, select the word, delete it, and retype it.

176

> ▶ **Note:** Algorithms are formulas that a computer uses to compute things like hyphenations. They're rules expressed in an if:then format.

To set automatic hyphenation, use the following Quick Steps.

Q **Setting Automatic Hyphenation**

1. Use the Text tool to select paragraphs to be hyphenated.

   Hyphenation will apply only to selected text.

2. Press ⌘+H to open the **Hyphenation** dialog box.

3. Click on the **On** button and choose **Manual plus dictionary** or **Manual plus algorithm**.

   Either of these will hyphenate pages automatically.

4. Click on OK or press Return.

Setting the Hyphenation Zone

You may set an amount of space to consider a *hyphenation zone*. In a nonjustified (ragged right) line, the raggedness is a function of how large or small an area you specify. Allowing fewer picas will give you a more even right edge. Justified text is not affected by a hyphenation zone, as all words needing to be broken will be and the spacing will be adjusted to make them fit.

Set a limit for the number of consecutive lines PageMaker can hyphenate. When you have a large number of consecutive lines of type hyphenated, the row of dashes at the right of the column tend to look like fringe, or possibly rungs of a ladder. Figure 7.22 shows an exaggerated example. To prevent this, set the limit for consecutive hyphens to some reasonable number such as two, even though PageMaker allows you to have up to 255! You can also type No limit, if you don't want to limit the number of hyphenated lines. Typing 0 instead of No limit makes a dialog box appear reminding you that 0 is an invalid number. Use the following Quick Steps to adjust the hyphenation zonc.

177

```
Lorem ipsum dolor sit amet, con-
sectetuer adipiscing elit, sed nonu-
mmy nibh euismod tincid laoree-
amm dolore magna aliquam volu-
tpat. Ut wisi enim ad minim venia-
manno nostrud exercitation ullam-
coper suscipit lobortis nisl ut aliqui-
```

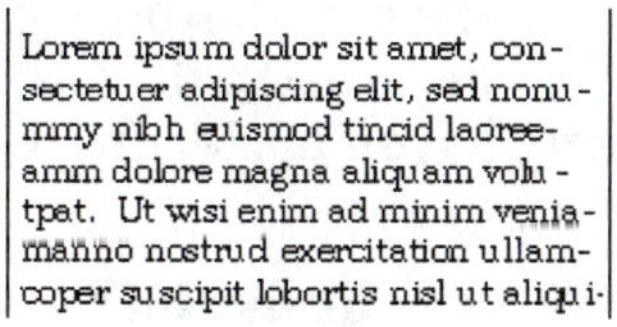

Figure 7.22 Too much hyphenation!

Q **Adjusting the Hyphenation Zone**

1. Press ⌘+H to open the **Hyphenation** box.

    Remember, hyphenation zones don't apply to justified text.

2. Enter a new value into the Zone field.

    The smaller the number, the less ragged the right margin will be.

3. Click on OK or press Return to confirm your settings and close the box.

    The new hyphenation zone will be applied to the selected text. □

Linking Your Stories

It's probably a mistake to call this section "Linking Your Stories," because it implies that it's something you have to do. It's not. It's actually something that PageMaker does for you. Before we get too heavily into linking, let's back up a little and think about what PageMaker is. It's a program that you use to combine the text and graphics files you've created in other programs. Its purpose is to assemble pages, not to be a word processor or a paint program. Because of this, it's able to do a clever trick.

Let's say, for the sake of illustration, that you write a book using Microsoft Word. You create your diagrams and pictures in SuperPaint. You plan to use PageMaker to combine them and set up pages in a ready to print format. Now, you open a new file called *Chapter 1* in PageMaker, and you place the text of Chapter 1 from the file you saved in Word. (You haven't trashed the Word file, just basically copied it into PM.) You do the same for the diagrams and pictures. The graphics are still out there somewhere on your disk called *PICTS*, and you've copied them into PM and placed them in the middle of text. Now when you placed the text into PM, it gave itself a little note that said, "Text came from a Word file called Ch.1, in the Book folder, on the Mac's HD disk." Only it did it in shorthand, like this:

Location: Mac's HD: Book folder: Ch.1.
Kind: Text

Size: 50 K

And, for each graphic, it made a similar note. So when you go open the PageMaker file called *Chapter 1*, the first thing PageMaker does is to check its notes and take a quick peek at the original files. It's looking to see if there's something new in the Word file called *Chapter 1* that it hasn't been told about. If there is, PM automatically updates its file or you get an angry note on your screen asking if you want to update.

This process is called *linking* and it's the clever trick mentioned earlier. The notes Pagemaker keeps about which of the stories and graphics you've placed, came from its link information. It keeps track of all this automatically, whether you need it or not. Sometimes it's unnecessary if you're the only one using PM, entering data for the publication and managing to do all your editing in Story Editor instead of your word processor. On the other hand, if you're editing Chapter 1, while the graphics department is creating the art, and the layout people are doing the page makeup in PageMaker, and everyone's sending files back and forth like crazy, PageMaker's link function is absolutely the only way to make sure that the current version of the words you're editing are going into the book. Because PageMaker is used by people at all levels of publishing, it has some tools that aren't necessary in all situations. Still, links can be helpful for all kinds of publications so it's a good idea to learn how to use them.

179

Getting Link Information

To get information about linked stories, open the Links dialog box in the **File** menu, or press ⌘ + = . The Links box shown in Figure 7.23 appears. To get more detailed information on any of your source files:

▶ Double-click on the file name or click on **Link info**.

Or,

▶ Select the item itself, within your publication (not in the dialog box), and choose **Link info** from the **Element** menu. The dialog box shown in Figure 7.24 appears. (You can get information about linked files of both text and graphics.)

Once the box is open, you can see the status of your links by the presence or absence of the following symbols next to the file name. (If no symbol is shown, either the link is current or no link has been established.)

A *question mark* means that PageMaker can't locate the file. You've either moved it from its original location, changed its name, or thrown it away.

A *black diamond* indicates that the file has been modified. You've added or removed something and resaved it. Page-Maker will automatically update its version the next time you open your publication.

A *hollow diamond* means that the file has been modified but you haven't specified that PageMaker can update automatically. The next time you open the publication, PageMaker will ask you for permission to update its version of the file.

A *hollow triangle* indicates that both the internal PageMaker version and the original word processor or paint version of the element, have been modified independently of each other. If you update the internal version, you'll lose any changes you may have made to it that haven't also been made to the external one. In this case, you'll have to decide which version's changes have priority.

180

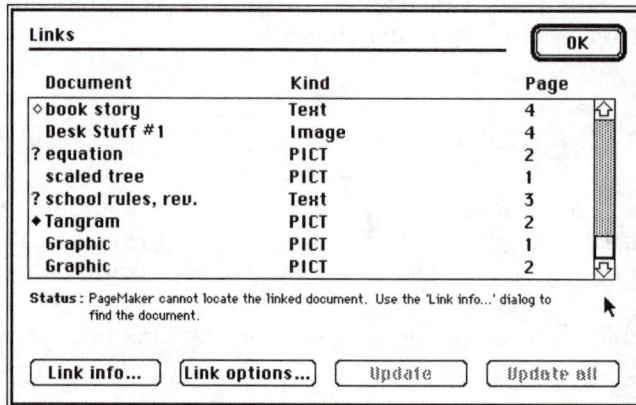

Figure 7.23 The Links box.

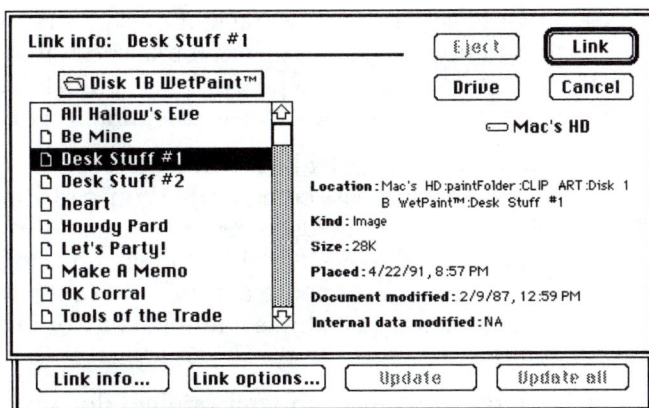

Figure 7.24 The Link information box.

The Links box also tells you where in the publication you placed each story or graphic. You'll see page numbers or the following notations:

181

> *LM and RM:* Left Master means you placed it on the left master page. Right Master means you placed it on the right master page. Items you placed here would probably be a company logo or small picture of some kind, rather than a text file.
>
> *PB:* Pasteboard means your item is on the pasteboard, not placed in the publication.
>
> *X:* X means the story is open as a new story created in Story Editor but not placed in the publication yet. It's not anywhere except in a Story window. (You won't find it on the pasteboard, clipboard, or scrapbook, because you haven't put it there.)
>
> *Page#?:* Page#? refers to a linked inline graphic you've inserted into an unplaced story. The story itself has the X marker and the linked graphic gets this marker. Once you place the story, you'll be placing the inline graphic as part of it.
>
> *OV:* OV stands for overlaid and means there's a piece of text or a graphic on the pasteboard, but placed in such a way that it's touching the page. This graphic or text is not properly placed. Maybe a corner of it is overlapping the page you're working on.

The reason that PageMaker keeps track of these things is to help you locate specific items within what may be a very large or busy publication. If you think you placed a particular graphic, for example, and you can't remember where, you can use this function to find it.

PageMaker automatically establishes links for every story you import using the **Import** or **Place** commands. You can link stories you've created in Story Editor by using the **Export** command and saving them outside of PageMaker. PageMaker will establish links to both text and graphics created within it and exported from PageMaker. To choose whether to have PageMaker update links automatically or to alert you first, open Link options.

If you make frequent changes in your original documents, it's a good idea *not* to use PageMaker's automatic updating feature. Otherwise, you could open up a finished layout and find that it has been totally corrupted by the update. For example, if you've added more text, your document might be a page longer than you had intended. If you've cut out a piece, you might find a large, gaping hole in the middle of page one. If you changed a graphic, you might have messed up the text flow around it. Other changes could undo your formatting.

When you have already applied type or style modifications such as kerning a headline, changing tracking, or adjusting spacing, updating will lose all of these changes as well. Fortunately, PageMaker warns you of the consequences before going ahead and lets you choose not to update. Figure 7.25 shows the Alert box.

182

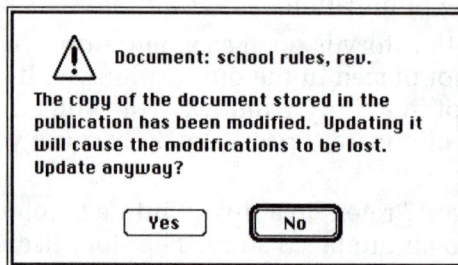

Figure 7.25 This box lets you choose whether to let PageMaker update linked files.

If you like to work on your layout a little bit at a time, you'll have the most success with PageMaker if you make sure your text files are essentially complete before you import them, and then ignore the links. You can still do last minute editing in Story Editor but the goal is to avoid the need to recompose your layouts over and over because your copy has grown or shrunk. On the other hand, should you prefer to do most of your formatting within a compatible word processor, such as Microsoft Word, and polish and format your pages just before printing them, PageMaker's Link feature can save you a good deal of time and energy.

PageMaker will look for links when you ask it to. It checks them automatically when it opens a publication and when you attempt to print. If it can't find a link or finds one that hasn't been updated, the Alert box shown in Figure 7.26 will appear, asking you whether to print or cancel. What you do next depends on the nature of the text or graphic file involved. If it's a missing link to an original word processing document, which you threw away after you imported it into PageMaker, there's no problem. Go ahead and print. If it's a question of not having the latest version of the document, you'll need to decide whether the changes are important. If so, cancel the printing, update the file, and adjust the formatting before printing.

183

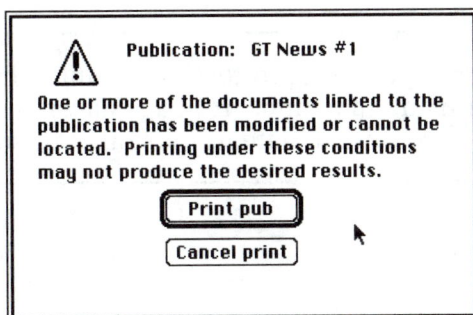

Figure 7.26 Alert box asking you whether to go ahead and print or cancel.

> ▶ **Tip:** Graphics use linking somewhat differently. A missing graphic link can, as the Alert box indicates, produce undesirable results. Linked graphics will be explained in the next chapter.

In addition to throwing away a file, you can accidentally break a link by moving the linked external file to a new folder, changing its name, changing the names of any of the folders in which it's nested, or changing the name of the disk it's on. What happens is that PageMaker keeps a record of the *file path*, the route it must travel to locate that file. The file path of each linked file is shown in the Link info box as Location. For example, this chapter's file path on the author's Mac IIsi is as follows:

Mac's HD:PM Book folder:Work in process:Ch. 7:Ch. 7text

Mac's HD is the name of the hard disk. *Ch. 7text* is the name of the document. All the other phrases, separated by colons, represent folders (and folders within folders). There's a folder called *PM Book folder* and inside it a folder called *Work in process*, and so on.

If you change any of the file or folder names, or if you move the document called *Ch. 7 text* out of the *Work in process* folder, PageMaker would be unable to find it. The changes you make to that file would never make it into the finished book. If a file has been moved or renamed, you can reestablish the broken link by locating the file in the Link info box's scrolling menu and clicking on the Link button.

184

> **Warning:** If you bring in text or a graphic from another program using the clipboard, PageMaker can't track the link and therefore can't update its version of the material.

Dropped Caps

Type is more than just words on the page. Properly used, type can be a design element. For example, in medieval manuscripts, the calligraphers of the time delighted in using ornate capitals. Modern typographers often use a similar device to mark the first word of a paragraph or story. The dropped capital effect is easy to achieve and can add a great deal to the appearance of an otherwise dull page. Figure 7.27 shows a dropped capital.

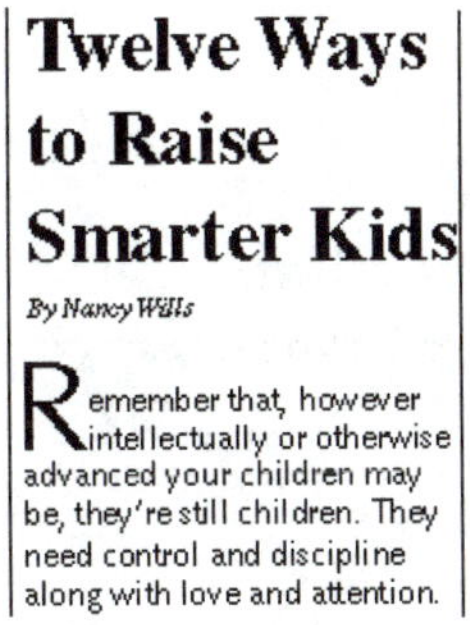

**Twelve Ways
to Raise
Smarter Kids**

By Nancy Wills

Remember that, however intellectually or otherwise advanced your children may be, they're still children. They need control and discipline along with love and attention.

Figure 7.27 Dropped cap.

In Figure 7.27, the same typeface (Optima) was used for the text and the dropped cap. You can also use a more decorative typeface just for the initial letter. Some fonts have versions with swashes added which give a nice effect. You can often use a character face for a dropped cap making it a graphic element in the design, although it's still handled as text. Of course, you can also use the Mac's built-in bold, outline, italic, and shadow options, to add more character to initial letters.

185

There are several ways to handle placing a dropped cap. The following steps are probably the simplest method:

1. Use the Text tool to type the initial letter somewhere on the pasteboard, giving it the size, style, and other characteristics you want.

2. Remove any indent from the line where you'll be adding the dropped cap.

3. Drag the cap into position as its own text block, on top of the existing text.

4. Select the existing text and resize the column to fit the first two lines, or as many as fit, next to the cap. Be sure to delete the letter the dropped cap is replacing.

5. Click on the bottom windowshade handle to get the Text placement icon and reflow the remaining text under the cap.

6. To preserve the correct line spacing, pull down a ruler guide to align with the bottom of the first text block's windowshade. When you place the second text block, position it so that its top line is on the ruler guide, as shown in Figure 7.28. Use the Pointer tool to select both text blocks. (Remember to hold Shift as you click on the second text block so the first remains selected.)

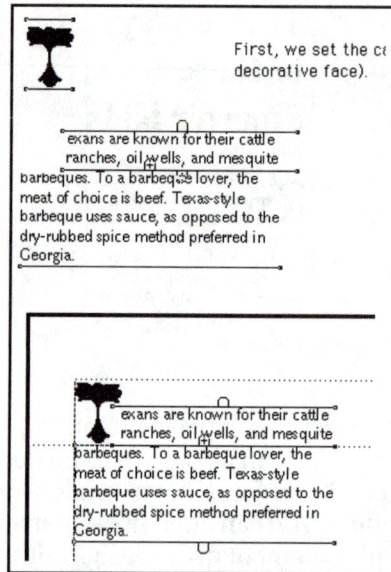

Figure 7.28 Creating a dropped cap.

Another way to create a dropped cap is to turn it into a graphic. To do this, use the following steps.

1. Create the capital letter as a separate text block on PageMaker's pasteboard, using the right style and font.
2. Press ⌘+C to **Copy** it, open the scrapbook and press ⌘+V to **Paste** it in.
3. Use the **Place** command, open the scrapbook file in the **System Folder**, and place the letter as a graphic.

Now you can treat it as a graphic, resizing it if needed, and using PageMaker's Text wrap option (which will be described more completely in the next chapter) to fit the type around it.

What You've Learned

In this chapter you explored other ways in which PageMaker can handle text. Style sheets, link capabilities, and PageMaker's built-in word processor, the Story Editor, were explained. Specifically, you learned:

▶ How to work with styles on the Style palette and how to modify existing styles and create new ones. You also learned how to apply styles to text.

▶ How to use Story Editor, PageMaker's built-in word processor, the **Find** and **Change** feature, and how to save stories you create in Story Editor by pasting them into the publication, or by exporting them as a separate file in your choice of formats.

▶ How to access PageMaker's 100,000 word dictionary and how to check spelling in a paragraph, a single story, or throughout your publication.

▶ How to use PageMaker's dictionary to hyphenate words, and how to add words to it. You learned how to tell PageMaker how many consecutive lines it may hyphenate, and how large a gap to leave at the end of a line.

▶ How PageMaker automatically maintains Links with documents you've imported into it. Links are broken when a file is renamed, moved, or thrown away. You learned how to restore a broken link and when you can safely ignore links.

187

▶ How to add interest to a page by using dropped caps. A dropped cap may be in the same style as the body copy but much larger, or you may use a decorative face.

Working with Graphics

In This Chapter

▶ *Kinds of Graphics Files (Paint, PICT, EPS, and TIFF)*

▶ *Positioning and Manipulating Images*

▶ *Working with Inline Graphics*

▶ *Text Runarounds*

▶ *Linked Graphics*

▶ *Little Boxes and Other Nonpictorial Graphics*

▶ *Shades and Screens*

▶ *Image Control on Halftones and Photographs*

▶ *Adding Color to Your Publication*

"A picture," it's said, "is worth a thousand words." (Of course, it all depends on the picture.) Pictures and other graphic embellishments can, and generally do, make the difference between a bland, boring, newsletter and one that's interesting and appealing to the reader.

PageMaker supports four different formats for importing graphics from other programs. You can use art from any or all of the sources which follow. Each has advantages and disadvantages.

Paint Images

A Paint picture is a *bit-mapped* illustration. This means that it's composed of dots, called *bits* or *pixels*. The first Paint program, MacPaint, was bundled with the early Macintoshes. In the beginning it was the only graphics program for the Mac. As other graphics programs came along, they adopted the Paint file format. It had the advantage of being compatible with the Mac's scrapbook and other applications, and is still the standard for the interchange of bit-mapped graphics. All Mac programs that handle bit-mapped graphics can support Paint, including SuperPaint, Canvas, and, of course, MacPaint II. Artists like MacPaint. Being able to manipulate individual pixels means that they can do detailed drawing, and use electronic *tools* very similar to their real brushes, pens, and spray cans. Bit-mapped art can be richly detailed and quite effective.

190

The major drawback to Paint images is that the pixels, which form them, have square corners. Why is this a problem? Because if you enlarge a Paint image, you don't get more pixels. You get a larger pixel. So, if you need to resize a Paint image in PageMaker, the jagged edges will appear at a greater magnification. Figure 8.1 shows an example of jaggies in bit-mapped art. Seen small, the globe looks reasonably good, but if you blow up the world, you get hit with a ton of bricks! Even at best, the jaggies are obvious and the higher quality your printer, the more they seem to stand out. The Smooth option (in the Print dialog box) may help a little, but jaggedness is still apparent. You may prefer to use Paint graphics only in their original size.

Figure 8.1 Jaggies make some pictures look like they're drawn in bricks.

PICT Images

With the introduction of MacDraw, the computer art world gained a second valuable tool, the *object-oriented graphic*. With PICT images, each object is described by its outline in a series of mathematical vectors. The drawing is saved as instructions, rather than as a string of patterns. Because of its precision, its ability to stack elements in layers while maintaining their separateness, and the ease of modifying line widths and fill patterns, the object-oriented graphic is preferred by engineers and architects. MacDraw lets you save a drawing as a MacDraw file or a *PICT* file. PICT is a standard for transferring object-oriented drawings between applications. Some programs can also save files in a slightly modified PICT format called *PICT2*, which can handle color and more complex formatting. PageMaker can import both PICT and PICT2 drawings.

When you create a shape in PICT, the computer keeps a relatively small amount of data on hand. Objects are saved as descriptions of themselves, in the shortest possible terms. The code includes the type of shape, the screen location of a corner of it, and one dimension, generally a radius or diagonal. Fill and line width are also saved. Since the representation is based on math, rather than a dot by dot description of the object, it's easy for the computer to resize or reposition it. Distortion isn't a problem because the computer can keep things in their original proportions. You don't have to deal with jaggies.

191

On the other hand, Draw-type programs simply don't have the flexibility that Paint programs have. There are object drawing tools similar to the architect's triangles and t-squares, but no pencil, brush, or eraser. You can draw only lines, shapes, or *bezier curves*. A bezier curve (pronounced bez-yay) is one that's mathematically described as a series of control points. Freehand drawings are nearly impossible. Figure 8.2 shows illustrations created for a newsletter in the PICT format.

There are ways to get the advantages of both Paint and PICT. One way is to use Silicon Beach's SuperPaint as your graphics program. SuperPaint can handle both Paint and PICT files, but in an interesting way. The program has a split personality. It can be both an artist's drawing board and an engineer's drafting table, and can copy from one to the other. You can create an image in SuperPaint's Paint layer, and then copy it to the Draw layer to resize it. When you save it from the Draw layer as a PICT file, all the dots in the Paint image become parts of the PICT shape. It can be scaled without added distortion.

Scaling a solidly filled object has different effects, depending on whether it was originally created in Paint or in PICT. A PICT object uses the pattern definition in the program and fills the object with that pattern. The pattern itself remains the same, whether the object box is enlarged or reduced. A Paint object, transferred into PICT, contains the pattern as part of the object. When the object is scaled, the pattern is scaled along with it. Figure 8.3 shows examples.

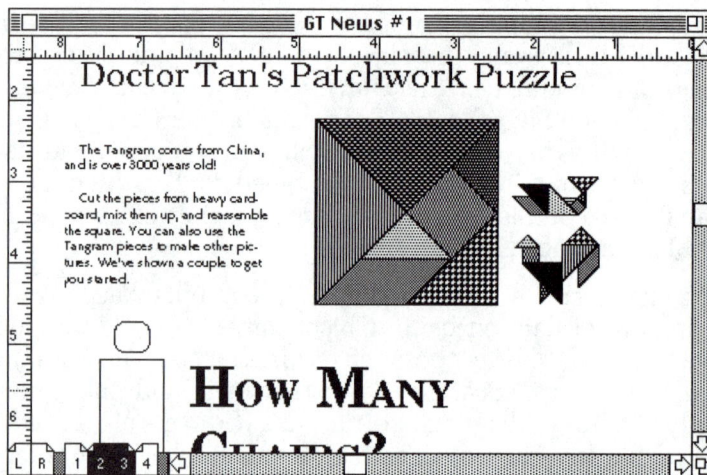

Figure 8.2 Geometric shapes are simple to draw in PICT.

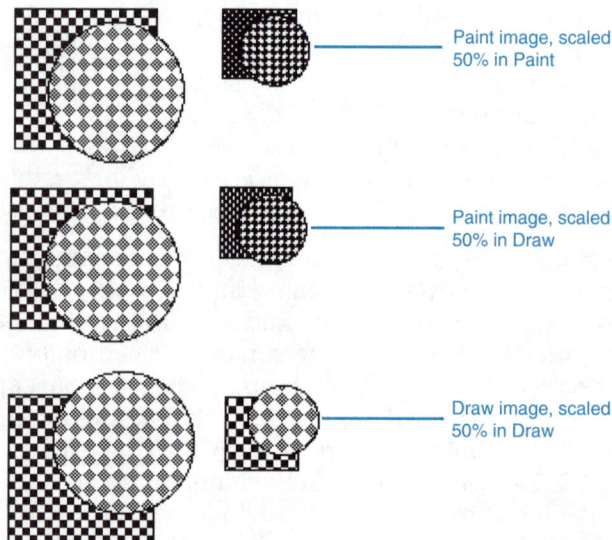

Paint image, scaled 50% in Paint

Paint image, scaled 50% in Draw

Draw image, scaled 50% in Draw

Figure 8.3 Scaling a filled PICT object retains the same size pattern.

EPS

EPS stands for Encapsulated PostScript, a way to define a graphic in the Adobe Systems PostScript language used by many laser printers. Adobe Illustrator and Aldus FreeHand are the two most often used graphics programs which can create EPS files. (Most scanning programs also can create EPS.) Like Paint programs, EPS Drawing programs give you great flexibility with a wide range of tools and special effects, including fine lines, curved text, and graduated shadings. Because these programs speak PostScript, there's never a problem making the image compatible with the printing method. The PostScript interpreter is built into most Mac compatible laser printers, including high resolution ImageSetters such as the Linotronic. The image will print at the maximum resolution of whatever printer you're using, whether it's a Macintosh LaserWriter at 300 dpi, a service bureau's 400, 600, or 1,000 dpi laser printer, or the Linotronic L300 which prints at 2,540 dpi, giving you magazine quality images in your publication.

193

PostScript images are stored as text files and can be read and edited if you know how to do it. (Of course if you do, it's more likely that you're programming computers rather than pasting up a newsletter.) But the PostScript image alone, although it talks to your printer with no difficulty, doesn't give you a picture on-screen. The *encapsulation* in an EPS file allows a PICT version of the image to be included along with the PostScript description, so you can have a screen representation of the image as well as a file for the printer to use. Some Drawing programs support EPS but will give you only a gray box, rather than the actual image, when you import the file into PageMaker. You can use the box to position and resize the graphic but you won't see the picture until you print it. Figure 8.4 is an example of an EPS file placed in a PageMaker publication.

Scanned Images

Although the computer is capable of producing some very nice art, there will be times when you'll want to use a photograph or a piece of art, which wasn't produced on the computer. How can you bring these images into your Mac? The answer is to use a *scanner*. There are various types of scanners, but essentially they all work in a similar fashion to translate your photo or artwork into a set of digital signals, which produce a bit-mapped version of the original.

Figure 8.4 An example of an EPS image.

Flat Scanners

One type of scanner, called a *flat* (or flatbed) scanner, looks and works like a photocopying machine. The original is placed face down on a sheet of glass, and when you turn on the scanner, a bright light moves across the document and 2,500 or more photosensors capture the changes from light to dark as *ons* and *offs*.

High resolution scanners can see up to 256 shades of gray, and some can do color scans too. Files are generally saved as TIFFs (Tagged Image File Format), and can be edited in a digital image processor such as Silicon Press Digital Darkroom or Adobe PhotoShop, before being placed in PageMaker. Figure 8.5 shows a typical TIFF file created by scanning a photograph. (PageMaker also accepts Color TIFF and compressed TIFF files.)

Flat scanners are highly accurate and provide excellent resolution. The main drawback is that they tend to be quite expensive. You would be far more likely to use one at a service bureau than to purchase a flatbed scanner for yourself.

Figure 8.5 Never get in a TIFF with a tiger.

195

Print Head Scanners

Print head scanners are a less costly alternative for those who want the convenience of scanning at home. They do require that you have an ImageWriter, however. To use it, remove the ribbon from your ImageWriter and insert the scanner cartridge. ThunderWare's ThunderScan comes with its own software, which allows you to scan 64 levels of gray and edit up to 256 levels of gray scale on any Mac Plus or higher. It scans at 300 dpi, and is able to save in all major file formats, including TIFF and Paint. Its only real handicap is speed. Scanning a full page of art can take a very long time and the resolution is only 72 dpi. You may decide to use a ThunderScanned picture for position, and instruct the printshop to use a screened halftone when it's printed.

Hand-Held Scanners

Hand-held scanners cost about twice as much as a print head scanner, but they can do some amazing things. ThunderWare's LightningScan 400, which looks something like an overgrown electric razor, scans at 400 dpi. You can join the files from several passes of its four inch wide scanner, into a full page picture. It comes with a plastic guide to help you get a steady, straight scan—important for all hand-held scanners.

Caere's *Typist* scans graphics at 300 dpi but its primary use is as a text scanner. It will input up to 500 words per minute into a word processor or spreadsheet program. The Typist includes OCR (Optical Character Recognition) software, which can translate a bit-mapped image of a letter into an ASCII character, which can be imported into virtually any application that accepts text files including PageMaker. If you have large amounts of material which have been hand typed or created on a noncompatible word processor, the Typist could save you many hours of retyping. It scans at two inches per second and is remarkably accurate on clean, typed, or printed copy. It can recognize eleven Western-European languages, and scans nonstylized fonts from 6 to 72 points. The Typist scans images into TIFF or PICT formats, and can separate graphics from text.

Hand-held scanners require patience, especially when you're just learning to use them. The scanner must be rolled across the text at a steady pace, neither too fast or two slow and not at an angle. Side to side motions or jerkiness will result in an uneven scan. With an OCR program, you'd get unintelligible text. Once you've mastered the technique, these devices can solve many problems, especially if you're working on a newsletter or similar publication, with text from many sources.

Video Digitizers

Another alternative for low-cost scanning combines a little box called a *video digitizer* with a video source you might already own, such as a portable VHS camcorder, a video disk player, or an ordinary TV camera pointed at a still image. The video source needs to be able to give you a good, steady, flickerless still frame. (A VCR deck is not a good source unless it has built-in digital editing, because VHS still frames tend to jiggle.) The digitizer looks at the video signal and translates it into digits, ones and zeros to be specific, which turn back into pixels on the Mac screen.

196

The two most popular video digitizer packages, Digital Vision's Computer Eyes and Koala's MacVision, come with hardware and software. If you're using it with your camcorder, all you do is plug everything in, open the scanning program, and capture an image. You can crop the photo, adjust brightness and contrast, and convert it to a Paint document or save it as a TIFF, PICT2, or EPS file, which can go directly into PageMaker or be retouched in a darkroom program like PhotoShop. How good are they? A lot depends on the quality of the image you're scanning. Most of the photographs in this book were produced with Computer Eyes, and a VHS camcorder.

Color Scanners

Color scanners let you take a color photo and put it into your PageMaker document. Even though they cost about four times as much as gray scale scanners, they are well worth it to the printing and publishing industry. When you need a color scan, look for a service bureau or printer who uses the *Barneyscan* system. Barneyscans can handle either flat art or 35mm slides, and can produce four-color separations for the printer. Adobe PhotoShop can do any necessary color retouching on scanned color images. Color TIFF files can take up a great deal of memory. You'd need a Mac II with 4 or 5 meg of RAM to view your work while scanning a color photo. Save it as a linked file with your PageMaker publication, rather than within the PageMaker file itself. Otherwise, you could end up with a publication too big to fit on a disk.

197

Speaking of file sizes, you can save disk space by scanning your images at the lowest acceptable resolution. Detailed art is best scanned at the resolution of your printer. For example, if you are using a LaserWriter or a similar printer, scan at 300 dpi. If your art is very simple, you may be able to get away with using a lower resolution scan which will give you a much smaller file. Scanning images at the size you want to print them saves time and helps avoid distortion.

If you are dealing with especially large files, you can place linked documents on a different disk, and restore the links before printing by opening the publication and verifying them. You can also use a utility such as CompactPro or Stuffit Deluxe to compress files so they'll fit on the disk. However, you'll need to uncompress them again at the service bureau.

> ▶ **Tip:** Since TIFF, like Paint, is a bit-mapped format, you risk distortion if you scale a TIFF image unless you plan your enlargement or reduction to a percentage of the resolution. For instance, if you intend to reduce the scanned image by 50% when you move it into PageMaker and you'll print it on a 300 dpi laser printer, scan it full-size, at half the desired resolution or 150 dpi. You'll have a smaller file and when you shrink the image, you'll be back at the desired 300 dpi resolution.

Positioning Graphics

198

When you have created, scanned, or taken a graphic from a clip art file, you need to put it into the PageMaker publication. The way to do this is to use the Place box, just as you did to import text. Graphics can be placed from their own files or from the scrapbook. There are several different Place graphic icons shown in Figure 8.6. The one you see depends on the source of your graphic.

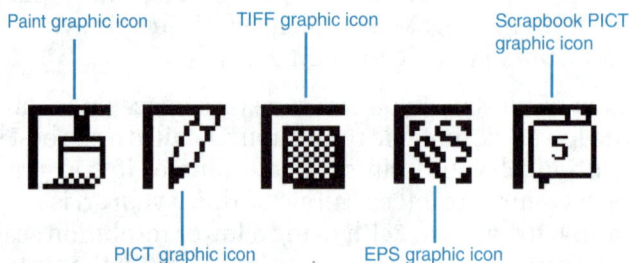

Figure 8.6 The Place graphic icons.

Placing from the Scrapbook

Placing a graphic from the scrapbook is best done with the **Place** command rather than by opening the scrapbook and clipping the image. Once you've opened the Place box, open the **System Folder** and locate the scrapbook file. Opening it will give you a Place icon with a number in it. The number tells you how many graphics there are in the scrapbook. You can place as many of these as you like. When you've finished placing graphics from the scrapbook, click the icon on the Pointer in the Toolbox. To place an image from the scrapbook, use the following Quick Steps.

Q **Placing a Scrapbook Image**

1. Press ⌘+D to open the **Place** box.

   Or, select Place from the **File** menu.

2. Open the **System Folder** and select the scrapbook file.

   Your **System Folder** is on the desktop so you may have to use the pop-up menu to reach it, and the scrolling menu to find the scrapbook file.

3. Double-click on the scrapbook file on the scrolling menu.

   The box will close and your pointer will turn into the Place scrapbook icon with a number inside it. The number indicates how many pages are in the scrapbook.

4. To place the first scrapbook page, move the icon to the upper left corner of the spot where you want the image to appear and click.

   The image will appear and the number in the Place scrapbook icon will be one less.

5. Place additional scrapbook pages by positioning the icon and clicking.

   You can place unwanted images on the pasteboard and delete them later.

6. When you're done placing scrapbook pages, position the icon on the Pointer tool in the Toolbox and click.

   This will restore the Pointer tool.

   □

199

If you only wanted one piece of art and it happens to be somewhere other than first in the scrapbook, you'll have to place and delete the ones in front of it until you reach the page you want. It's a bit of a nuisance but there's no other way to flip through the pages of the scrapbook.

Placing from a Graphics File

It's easy to place a graphic that you've created with any of your graphics programs. You'll even be able to tell what kind of a graphic you're placing because PageMaker uses different Place graphic icons for Paint, PICT, and so on. The following procedure describes placing an image as an independent graphic, which means one that's not tied into the text around it. Later on you'll learn how to place inline graphics too. Use the following Quick Steps to place a graphic.

Q **Placing a Graphic**

1. Press ⌘+D.

    The Place box appears.

2. Select the file to import.

    Use the pop-up menu and scroll bars to locate it.

3. Click on the **As independent graphic** button.

    This determines that you're placing the graphic independent of the text, not as an inline graphic.

4. Click on OK.

    The cursor becomes an icon.

5. Position the icon where you want to place the upper left-hand corner of the graphic and click to paste it.

    The graphic is placed.

Modifying Images

PageMaker lets you modify the graphics you import in several ways. You can resize, reshape, and crop them to suit your needs. You can also move them around within the publication as you would if you were using paper and rubber cement.

Repositioning a Graphic

Moving an image is simple. Just click on it. The pointer will change to a four-headed arrow, indicating that you can drag it in any direction. If you want to place it on a different page of your publication, the easiest way is to drag it from the old page out to the pasteboard. (Make sure none of it is touching the page.) Then, click on the Page number icon at the lower left for the page you want to move to. The page will open and you can drag the image onto it. Place the image where you want it.

Resizing an Image

When you select an image, you'll see resizing *handles*. Use the Pointer tool to grab one of the handles and drag it. The Pointer will change to an arrow, indicating which direction(s) the handle may be moved. A *side handle* will stretch the picture to that side, for example, vertically or horizontally. A *corner handle* will stretch both vertically and horizontally. Whenever you resize an image, PageMaker temporarily displays a *boundary box* around it, showing you the amount of space it occupies. The boundary box vanishes when you release the mouse button.

You can also resize a paint type graphic to match your printer's resolution by holding down ⌘ as you drag. PageMaker will check to see what type of printer is indicated in the Page Setup box and will scale the graphic appropriately for a 300, 450, or 1200 dpi printer. To return a distorted picture to its original proportions, use the following Quick Steps.

201

Q To Resize a Picture (Nonproportional)

1. Point to the corner handle of the selected graphic.

2. Hold down the mouse button.   The Pointer will become a double-headed arrow.

3. Drag the arrow until the graphic is the desired size and shape.   The graphic will change size and shape.   ☐

Q Resizing a Picture (Keeping Proportions)

1. Select the graphic and hold down Shift.   Pressing Shift keeps the height/width ratio constant.

2. Point and drag the corner handle.

A double-headed arrow indicates the change in diagonal measurement.

3. Release the mouse button and Shift when the size is correct.

☐

Q To Resize Proportionally and Match Printer Resolution

1. Hold down **Shift**+⌘ while dragging.

The boundary box snaps to the next size appropriate for the selected printer.

2. Release the mouse button, Shift, and ⌘ keys when the graphic reaches the desired size.

☐

202   *Restoring a Distorted Image*

Sometimes, even though you meant to resize a graphic proportionally, you forget and just drag on it. The result is that the graphic becomes distorted. To return a distorted picture to its original proportions, use the following Quick Steps.

Q Returning a Distorted Image

1. Click on the graphic with the Pointer tool to select it.

When it's selected it will have handles, little black squares at the corners.

2. Hold down Shift, point to any handle, and hold down the mouse button.

The pointer will become a double-headed arrow and a boundary box will appear around the graphic. It may take a couple of seconds.

3. When the box appears the graphic will snap back into shape inside it.

When you release the mouse button the graphic will be left in its original size and shape.

☐

Figure 8.7 shows the steps in this process.

Figure 8.7 Undistorting an image.

203

Cropping A Graphic

To crop a picture use the Cropping tool. As explained in the section on the Toolbox, the Cropping tool's real world analogy is not scissors or a knife, but rather a moveable cardboard frame. When you crop a graphic don't be afraid that you're throwing away a piece of it that you might need later. PageMaker's electronic cropping is far superior to the traditional method of trimming off what you don't want to see. If you change your mind in PageMaker, it's easy to reposition the graphic. You just point to it with the Cropping tool and slide it around inside the frame. Use the following Quick Steps to crop a graphic.

Q **Cropping a Graphic**

1. Select the Cropping tool from the Toolbox and click on the graphic.

   Handles will appear.

2. Point to the handle and hold the mouse button down.

   The Cropping tool will change to a double-headed arrow and a boundary box will appear around the graphic.

3. Drag the boundary box to the desired size and release the mouse button.

The boundary box will shrink as you move it but the graphic will remain in the same size and place. When you release the mouse button, the box will disappear. ☐

Q **Repositioning Cropped Graphic within Boundary**

1. Select the Cropping tool.

2. Click on the graphic.

A four-headed arrow will appear along with the boundary box.

3. Hold the mouse button down and slide the graphic within the frame.

When the graphic is where you want it release the mouse button. ☐

204

Figure 8.8 shows several stages of cropping. The excess background is taken away, leaving the cat in the larger boundary box on top. Then reselect the boundary box and shrink it some more. The cat remains the same size although the box is smaller. Now position the Cropping tool on the graphic itself, instead of on a handle, and slide the cat around inside the box. Even though the cat's paw is cut off (Ouch! Pffft!) in the previous crop, you can get it back by sliding his body to the right.

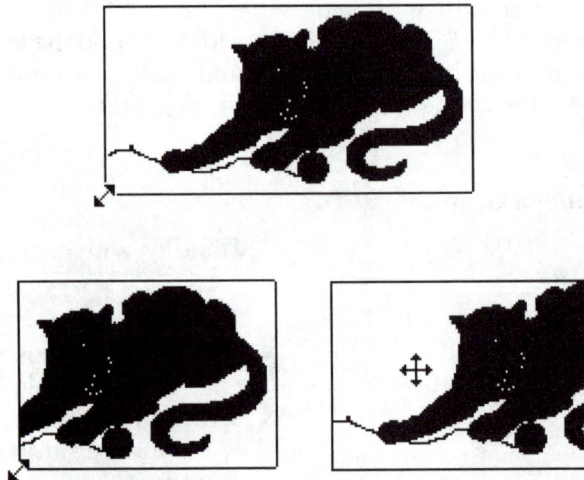

Figure 8.8 Cropping a picture from large to small and repositioning the picture inside the new, small frame.

Electronic Coverups

It sounds like something from the plot of a high-tech thriller but an *electronic coverup* is really a simple trick that can solve a lot of problems when you're working with graphics. Sometimes you bring in a piece of clip art and then discover that cropping it to size isn't enough. There's something in the frame that shouldn't be there. In order to conserve disk space, many clip art libraries fit as many drawings on a page as they possibly can. It's fine in theory but it can be hard to isolate the picture you want to use. Cropping lets you shrink the rectangle that your picture's in, but doesn't let you cut out something that's in the way. Use the following Quick Steps to cover up unwanted parts of a graphic.

Q Covering up Unwanted Items

1. Choose an appropriate Shape tool.

    You may need to combine several boxes or a box and circle, depending on the shape to be covered.

2. Choose **None** from the **Line** menu and **Paper** from the **Fill** menu.

3. Draw the shape over the object you want to cover.

    The unwanted object will be hidden but you'll see the handles from the cover up box. Click anywhere outside of the page to hide the handles. ☐

205

Figures 8.9 through 8.11 show the steps involved in this process.

When an object is oddly shaped, you may need several cover up boxes to blot it all out. If you're working on the pasteboard or if you need to move the art once it has been covered, be sure to select the cover up boxes along with it. Otherwise, you'll have to slide them back into place afterward. If the boxes get lost on the page, it's most likely because they've gotten behind the graphic they're supposed to be in front of. If this happens, select the graphic and press ⌘+B to send it behind. ⌘+F brings anything selected to the front.

Figure 8.9 The objects on either side of the graphic are too close to crop out.

206

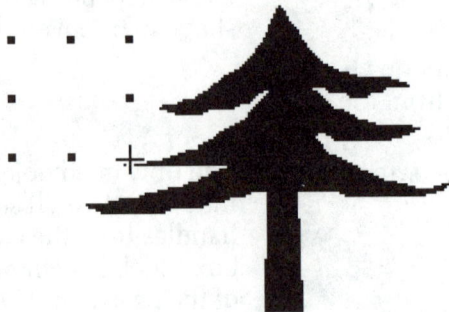

Figure 8.10 A little rectangle of paper has been drawn over one of the objects, and a circle over the other.

Figure 8.11 Now only the tree remains.

> **Warning:** A lot of coverups on complicated graphics may make the PageMaker file unnecessarily large. If you need to do a lot of selective pruning on that tree import it to a graphics program.

Inline Graphics

Inline graphics are placed inside the text so they always remain in the same position relative to the words. This feature is especially useful if you're dealing with a chart, or something similar, which needs to stay with its explanation. If you were to simply place it as an independent graphic and flow text around it, and then decided to add a paragraph at the beginning of your story, you'd have to do extensive reformatting of one or more pages to keep the chart together with its explanation. Inserting it as an inline graphic, however, means that no matter how much you add or remove at the beginning of the story, the words on either side of your chart will remain with it. PageMaker treats the graphic as a single character, no matter how large or small it is.

207

Inline graphics are an ideal solution for those times when you need to add a symbol, icon, or trademark that's not available as a regular key character. You can also use inline graphics as design elements to add interest to a page. Figure 8.12 shows some examples of ways you might use inline graphics.

Placing an Inline Graphic

Graphics are automatically placed inline whenever you use the **Place** command after using the Text tool to select an insertion point. You can also copy a graphic from the scrapbook to the clipboard, and paste it inline. Once the graphic is in place, you can resize it, stretch it, scale it to your printer, or crop it as needed. Use the following Quick Steps to place an inline graphic.

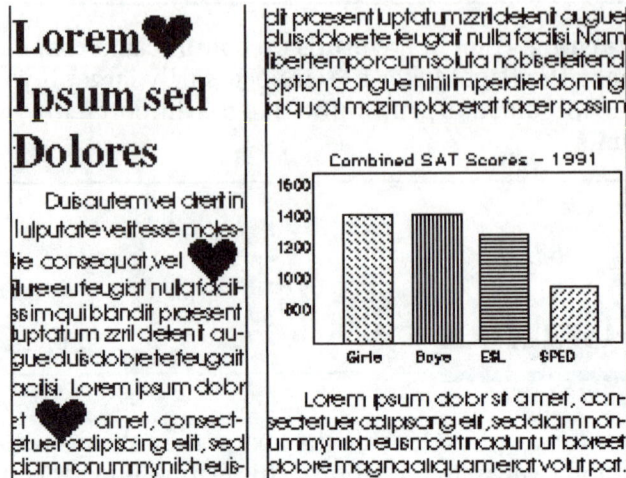

Figure 8.12 Inline graphics can be little spots of color, big charts, or anything else that needs to remain in a specific position.

Q Placing an Inline Graphic

1. Select the Text tool from the Toolbox and put the I-beam cursor where the graphic will be.

   This creates an insertion point for the graphic.

2. Press ⌘+D.

   The Place box appears with the Inline graphic button enabled.

3. Select the graphic and click on OK.

   When the box closes, the graphic will appear where you put it. ☐

You may find, when importing a graphic from a Paint or Draw program such as SuperPaint, that you've brought in a lot of white space along with the selected item. This becomes more obvious when you're attempting to place something inline, as the text which is supposed to follow the graphic, is forced to move a full page away. The solution is simple. Use the Cropping tool to get rid of the excess space. Use the following Quick Steps to close the gaps.

Q Resizing an Inline Graphic

1. Position the insertion point as shown in Figure 8.13.

   Use the I-beam cursor.

2. Use the Place box to select the graphic.

   Note that the inline button is automatically selected.

3. The graphic comes in with a full page of white space as shown in Figure 8.14.

   The white space has pushed the text off the page.

4. Select the Cropping tool from the Toolbox and crop away the extra space.

   Now the graphic fits on the page.

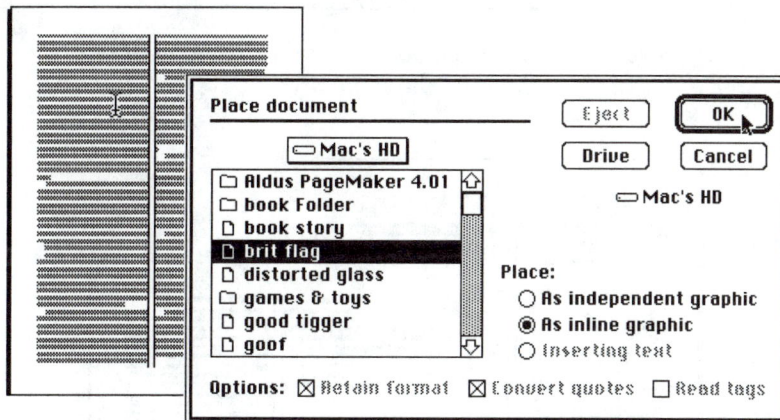

5. Resize it as needed. Figure 8.15 shows the finished inline graphic.
   □

Place document

| Eject | OK |

☐ Mac's HD

| Drive | Cancel |

☐ Aldus PageMaker 4.01
☐ book Folder
☐ book story
☐ brit flag
☐ distorted glass
☐ games & toys
☐ good tigger
☐ goof

☐ Mac's HD

Place:
○ As independent graphic
⦿ As inline graphic
○ Inserting text

Options: ☒ Retain format ☒ Convert quotes ☐ Read tags

Figure 8.13 Position the insertion point.

Inline graphics have a baseline which lines up with the baseline of the adjacent text, if any. By default, the baseline is two thirds the distance from the top of the boundary box to the bottom. Adjust this, if necessary, by dragging the graphic up or down with the pointer. You might need to do this, for example, if the graphic is something like a mathematical formula which needs to be aligned with the rest of the line. You can also apply paragraph attributes such as track, kerning, and leading to the graphic as needed.

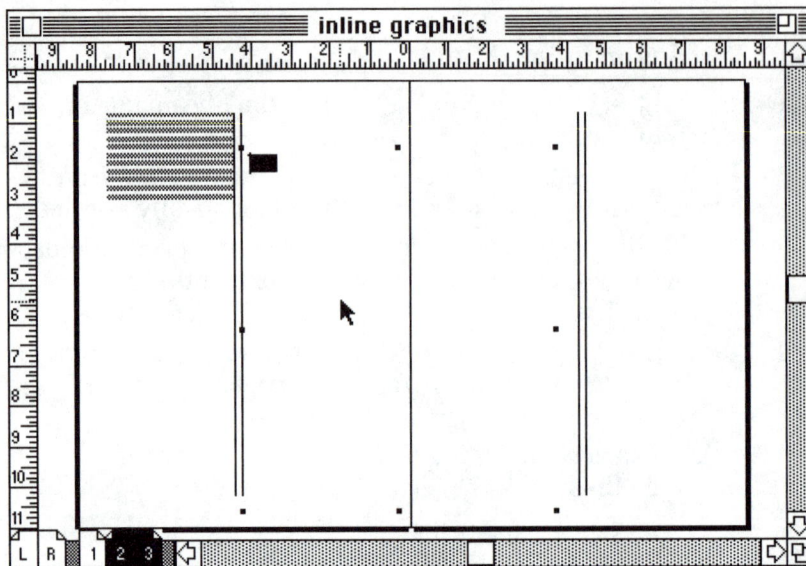

Figure 8.14 The graphic comes in with a full page of white space, moving the text off the page.

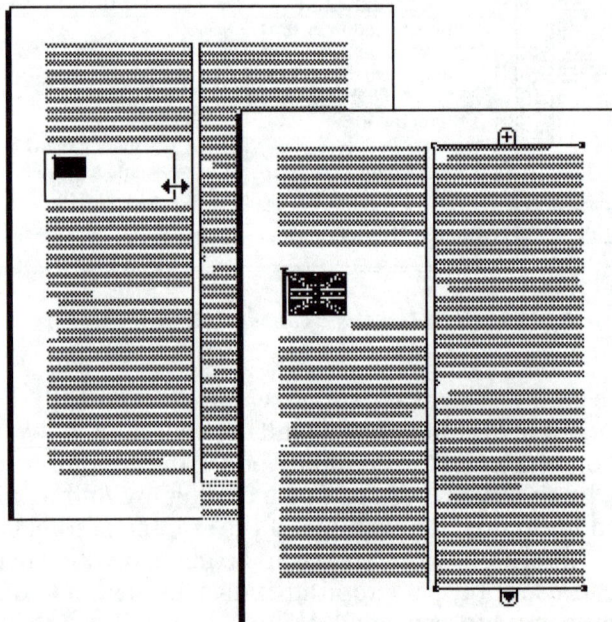

Figure 8.15 The finished inline graphic.

Yet another way to place an inline graphic involves drawing a text box with the Text tool and then pasting the graphic from the clipboard, or using the Place box. If you place an inline graphic this way, be sure to make the text box large enough to accommodate the graphic, otherwise it will not be shown completely.

If you place an inline graphic and then switch to Story view, you won't see the graphic. All you will see is a marker indicating its location. Figure 8.16 shows inline graphics markers in Story view. If you want to bring in an inline graphic while you're working in Story view, choose Import from the **Story** menu. The procedure is the same as if you were using the Place box. The difference is, you will see only a marker for the new graphic, until you return to Layout view.

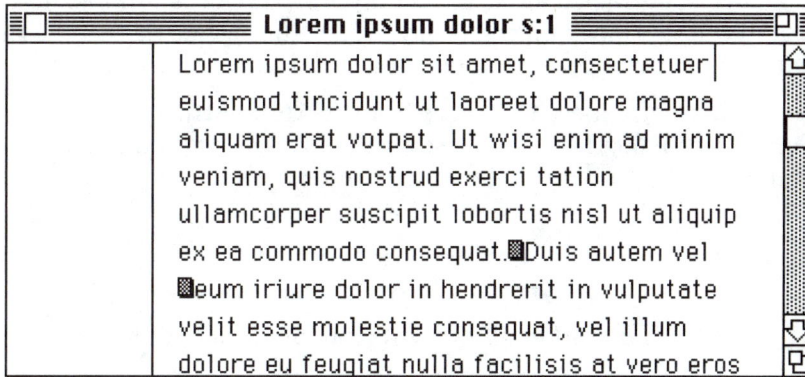

211

Figure 8.16 Inline graphics markers in Story view.

If you forgot to select an insertion point before placing the graphic, it will appear as an independent graphic. If this happens place it anywhere on the pasteboard, copy or cut it to the clipboard, use the Text tool to select your insertion point, and paste it back at the insertion point.

To remove an inline graphic, select it and delete it. To make it an independent graphic, select it with the pointer, cut it to the clipboard, and paste it where you want it.

Text Wrap

Text wrap is PageMaker's name for the function that makes text run around a graphic. Up until computer typesetting programs came along, getting this effect meant painstakingly setting each word by hand to match a tissue tracing of the graphic. It was an effect that was used rarely because it was very expensive to do. Now you can do it yourself with just a couple of mouse clicks.

Text can be wrapped around an independent graphic making it look as if it had been set inline. However, you can't wrap text around inline graphics. If it were possible to do, the picture would move whenever PageMaker tried to recompose the words around it. This would confuse the computer. Cleverly, Aldus designed the Text wrap function so that it's disabled whenever an inline graphic is selected.

When you choose **Text wrap** from the **Element** menu, you'll get the Text wrap dialog box which shows your Text wrap and Text flow options. Click on the icons that look the way you want your finished column to look.

The following are your Text wrap options:

No boundary: Text will flow over the graphic.

Rectangular boundary: The text will flow up to the rectangle around the graphic.

Custom boundary: This option lets you create a custom boundary around the graphic.

These are the text flow options:

Column break: This option lets PageMaker stop flowing text when it reaches the graphic. Text flow beg again in the next column.

Jump over: Text flow stops when it reaches the graphic and continues beyond it, leaving white space on either side.

Wrap all sides: This option flows text around all sides of the graphic.

As soon as you close the Text Wrap dialog box, a dotted line with diamond shaped handles will appear around your selected graphic. This rectangle indicates the *text wrap boundary*. It's shown in Figure 8.17.

Figure 8.17 The Text wrap boundary box is a dotted line.

213

To use text wrap with a rectangular boundary, use the following Quick Steps.

Using Text Wrap

1. Select the graphic around which the text will wrap.

2. Choose **Text wrap** from the **Element** menu.

   This opens the Text wrap dialog box.

3. Select the center Text wrap icon.

   The icon shows words around a rectangular boundary.

4. Type the desired values into the Standoff fields.

   Standoff is the distance between the text and the boundary of the graphic.

5. Click on one of the three Text
   flow icons to choose the desired
   pattern of text flow.

6. Click on OK or press Return   The text will wrap according
                                   to your specifications.   ☐

The Custom boundary icon remains disabled until you customize
the graphic's boundary. Customizing means changing the rectangular
boundary to some other shape. You can let the text follow the shape of
the graphic or leave white space in a nonrectangular shape around your
graphic. Figure 8.18 illustrates a custom boundary being placed. To
customize a boundary, use the following Quick Steps.

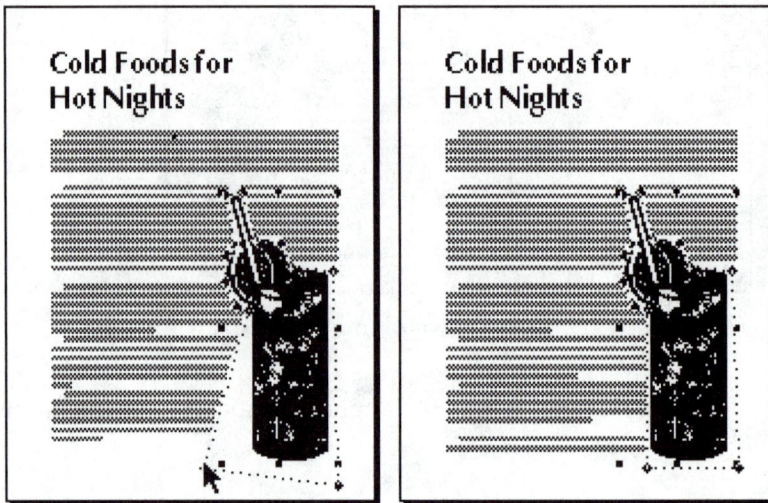

Figure 8.18 Bringing the text closer to the graphic.

Q **Customizing Text Wrap Boundaries**

1. Select the graphic to   The boundary is marked with
   customize.   a dotted line and diamond
                                     shaped handles.

2. Use the pointer to click on any The line will stretch or
   handle. Hold the mouse button   shrink to reach the handle.
   down and drag the handle to a   When you release the mouse
   new location.   button, the text will reflow to
                                    the new boundary line.

3. Create new handles by double-clicking on the dotted line.

   You can place new handles to break a line into shorter sections to fit around a curve.

4. To move a line segment, click between the diamonds and drag. The handles will move with it.

   The whole line will move when the pointer turns into a double-headed arrow. This is sometimes easier than mov ing the line by moving the handles at each end. ☐

To remove an unneeded handle, drag it over an adjacent one. As Figure 8.19 shows, you can add as many handles as you need.

Figure 8.19 A close up view of text wrapped around the graphic.

215

▶ **Tip:** Since PageMaker redraws the page each time you change the boundary on a graphic, reshaping a boundary near a lot of text can be time-consuming. To delay the redrawing, hold down the spacebar while you drag the boxes. Release it whenever you want a look at your progress.

Obviously, if you don't want type following the shape of the artwork, all you need to do is change the text flow boundary to whatever shape you want. Figure 8.20 shows a box with no outline, into which the headline for the story is set. The ball was created in SuperPaint, brought in and overlapped on the headline's box.

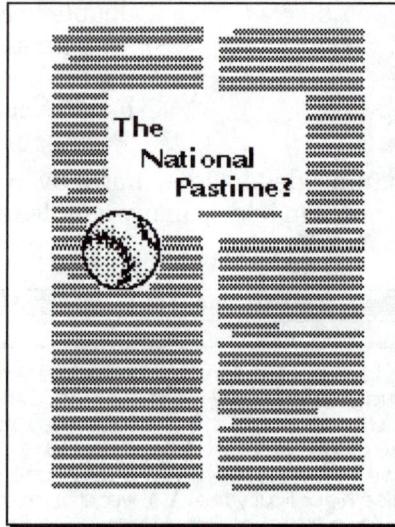

Figure 8.20 Text can be flowed around an empty space too.

Text Flow Options

The previous examples have used the Wrap all sides Text flow option. The Column break option, as shown in Figure 8.21, is very handy for laying out a yearbook, catalog, or anything where there are a lot of small pictures.

The Jump over icon, shown in Figure 8.22, indicates that the text will jump over the graphic and continue below it, leaving white space on either side.

Standoff is the distance between the boundary box and the edge of the graphic. PageMaker's default is .167 of an inch. Change the distance between the text and the graphic by entering new Standoff specifications in the Text wrap dialog box. If you want the text to overlap one side of the graphic, enter a negative number to indicate just how much.

Entering –.25 in the Left box, for instance, would give you a quarter inch of text over the left side of the art. Entering zero brings the text right to the dotted line of the boundary. If you resize the graphic, PageMaker will keep the same standoff values. To wrap text around only one side of a graphic, place the other side next to a column guide, or increase the standoff on that side so there's no room for text between the graphic and the margin.

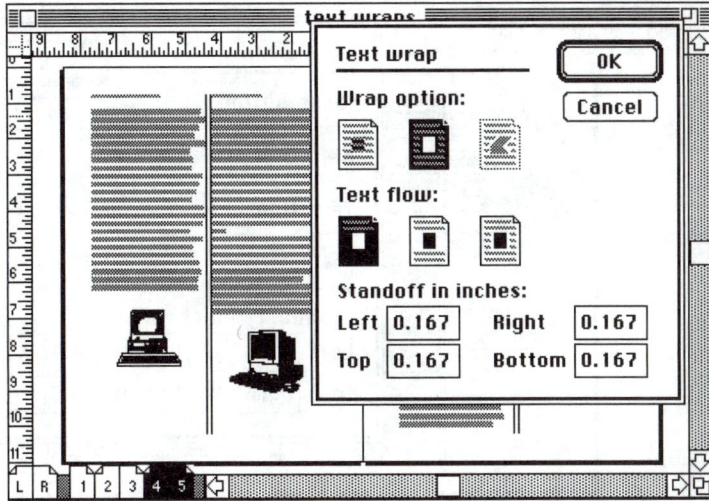

Figure 8.21 The text stops flowing when it reaches the graphic.

217

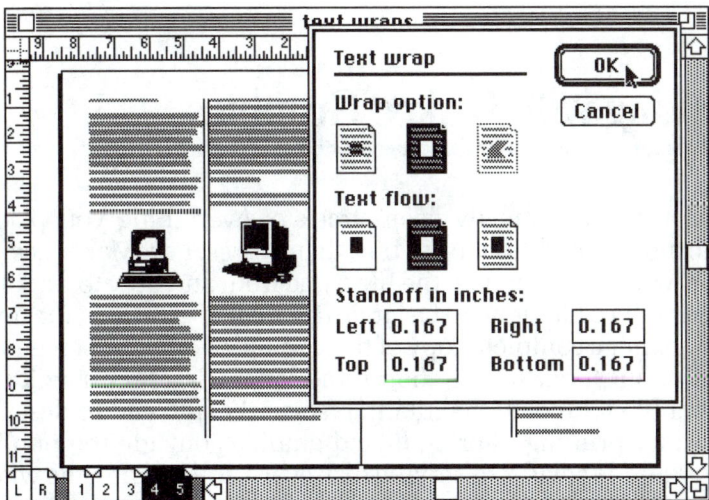

Figure 8.22 The text continues on the other side of the graphic.

When your picture has a caption, be sure to extend the graphic boundary far enough that the caption (and its handles) can be placed inside it. Otherwise, when the text wraps around, the caption will flow with the text and may get carried away. Figure 8.23 shows how captions can be treated. Notice that we've extended the bottom standoff enough to leave room for the caption, and that we've placed the caption well inside of the graphic boundary.

218

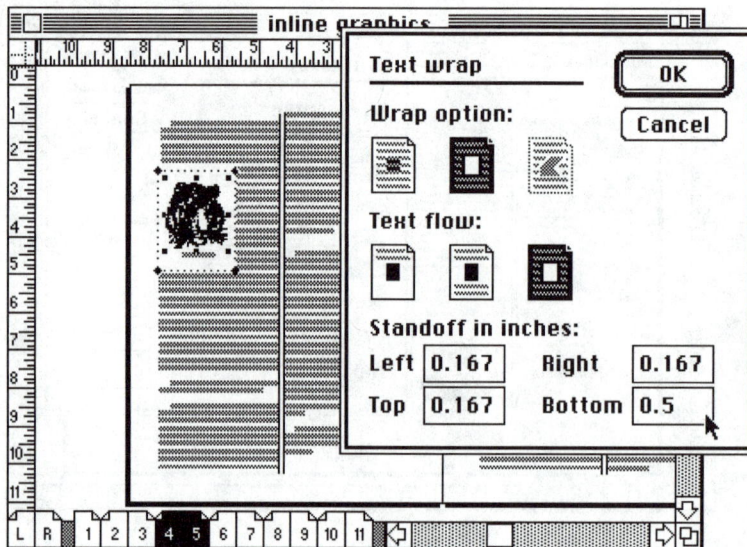

Figure 8.23 Placing the caption inside the graphic boundary.

Working with Linked Graphics

PageMaker automatically keeps track of everything you place in a publication. In addition to the files themselves, PageMaker keeps a list of *links* which tell it where the file came from and how to find it again. Since graphics files tend to be large, PageMaker gives you the option of storing either a complete copy of the graphic or only the screen version in the publication. If you choose the latter, PageMaker will use the external file to update the internal (screen) copy, and to describe the graphic for printing. Storing linked graphics outside the publication keeps your file small, conserving disk space and saving time when you open it.

EPS files are a special case. They are always automatically linked. The PostScript file includes a screen image, which is what you see in your PageMaker document, and a PostScript language description of the picture, which is what goes to the printer. PageMaker always stores a copy of EPS files with the publication. The Store copy in publication checkbox is checked and grayed-out when you look in the Link options dialog box.

By looking at the list in the Links box, shown in Figure 8.24, you can easily see all of the pieces that make up the publication. You can find out, at a glance, when each of these items was created, its most recent modification, and whether or not PageMaker's linked version is up to date. We can even use the Link info box, shown in Figure 8.25, to find out where the original document is filed.

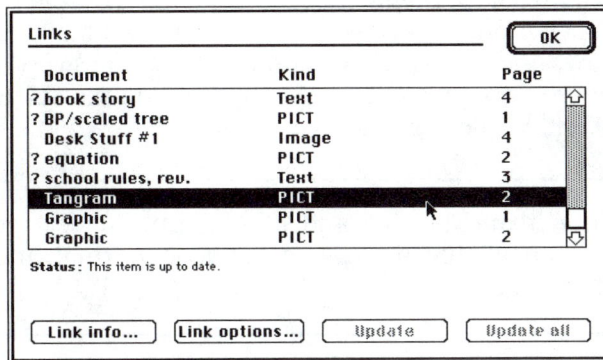

Figure 8.24 The Links dialog box.

219

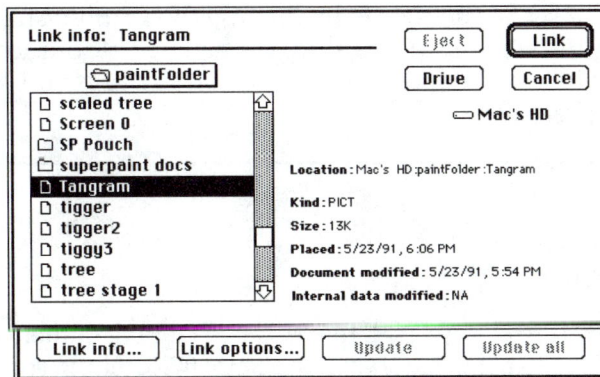

Figure 8.25 Opening the Link info box to see the location of the original document.

PageMaker will check each of these files whenever you open a publication, and will notify you if any of the linked items have been changed since you last saved the publication. You can then update them without having to replace them.

Link Defaults

In the Preferences box, you have the option of deciding how to view graphics in your publication. If you select Grayed out, you'll see a gray box called a *placeholder* in place of your graphic. This option saves a great deal of time when there are frequent page redraws. You can go back at any time and select Normal or High resolution to see the graphic.

The High resolution view supposedly gives you the best image your screen can produce, instead of the normal, bit-mapped version. Screen redraws under the High resolution setting take a very long time, however, so you won't want to use this option except to view a particularly critical piece of art.

> ▶ **Note:** With a Mac IIsi and a 13" Apple hi-res monitor, there's no visible difference between normal and high resolution viewing.

> ▶ **Tip:** You can, according to PageMaker, toggle temporarily into the High resolution view by holding down Control and forcing the screen to redraw by moving the graphic slightly or scrolling the screen up and down. The High resolution view will remain until the next redraw, when it will revert to your selected preference.

Large Graphic Files

Whenever you are using a TIFF file or a large Paint document, you may get an Alert box like the one shown in Figure 8.26, telling you that your file is larger than 256K. If so, you'll have the option of storing it externally. You can also choose to do this through the Link options box, shown in Figure 8.27.

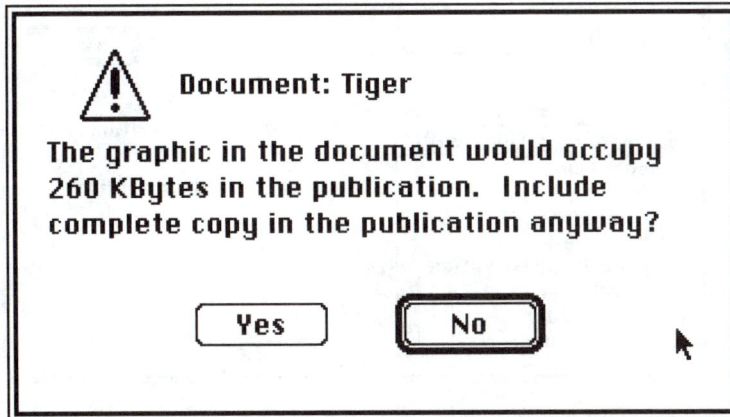

Figure 8.26 An Alert box indicating your file is too large.

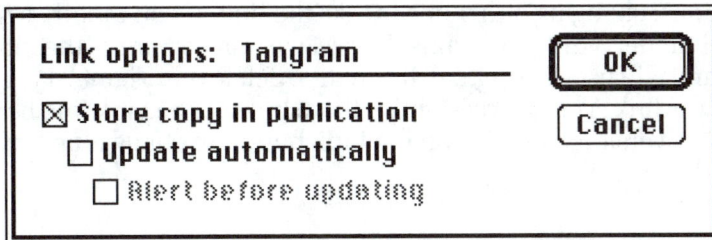

221

Figure 8.27 Clicking on this box stores graphics in the publication.

Links allow PageMaker to use the original graphics files for printing, even though they're not technically part of the document. Any changes that you've made to the screen version, within your publication, such as cropping or resizing, will be kept. If you've gone back and redrawn the original art, your cropping or other change might not look right.

Whenever you open a publication, PageMaker checks all the linked documents. If a file has been moved, PageMaker will warn you that it can't find it, and will ask for help in locating the original. Figure 8.28 shows the Cannot find box. If a link is broken, it's either because you moved the file, renamed it, or threw it away. The first two you can fix by using the menus to locate the missing file, and then clicking on Link to reestablish the connection. If you've thrown the file away, you can only ignore it. Find the new location of the file, and click on the Link button to reestablish the link. If you're not planning to print and the links aren't critical, you can just click on the Ignore button and PageMaker will open the document without updating the links.

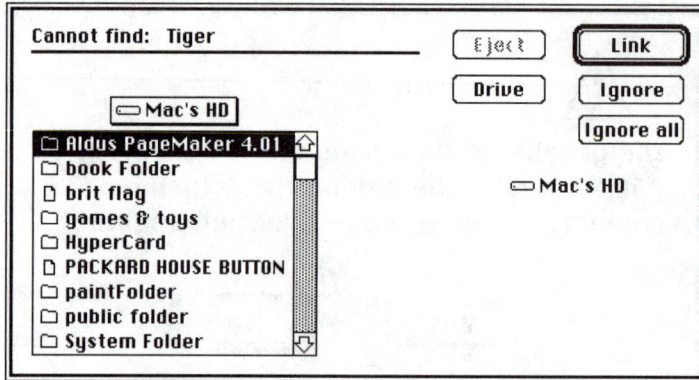

Figure 8.28 The Cannot find dialog box.

Because PageMaker keeps track of links by file names and folder locations, changing either one breaks the link. If you modify a file and save it under a different name, PageMaker isn't aware of the modification and will use the original. If you then delete the original, PageMaker loses the link. You can reestablish these links in the Link info box. Find the new version and click on the Link button to change the link to the new document.

Printing with Linked Graphics

If you're doing your own printing, either from a hard disk or from a floppy, there shouldn't be any link problems unless you've moved or thrown away your original files. The publication and all of its source files should be in the same place so PageMaker can find the information it needs to send to the laser printer. When you send a publication out on a disk for printing at a service bureau or commercial printer, be sure that you include the source files for all your linked graphics. The easy way to do this is to resave your publication using the Copy linked document option in the Save As box, shown in Figure 8.29. If Page-Maker has lost a link, it will warn you with the box shown in Figure 8.30. If you proceed, it will print from a bit-mapped version of the graphic giving you a much lower quality image.

> ▶ **Tip:** After you've copied your publication onto a blank disk, reopen the publication from the floppy to verify the links.

Save publication as

☐ **Aldus PageMaker 4.01**

[Eject] [OK]
[Drive] [Cancel]

☐ Mac's HD

☐ News #1template
☐ Aldus Installer History
☐ beethoven
☐ book story
☐ drawing for nl
☐ GT News #1

Save as:
● Publication
○ Template

GT News #1 copy

☒ **Copy linked documents**

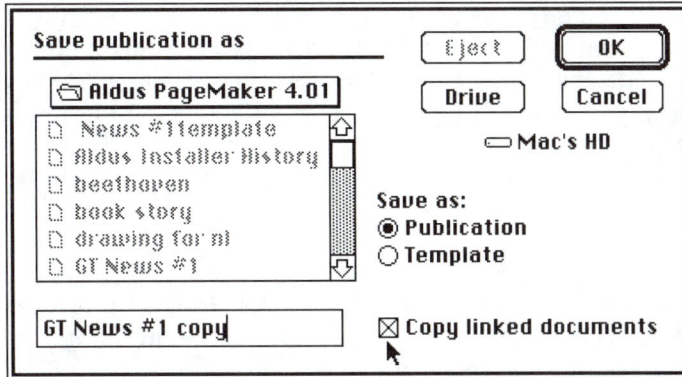

Figure 8.29 Use the Copy linked documents checkbox to make sure you've copied all of your linked files onto the disk for the service bureau.

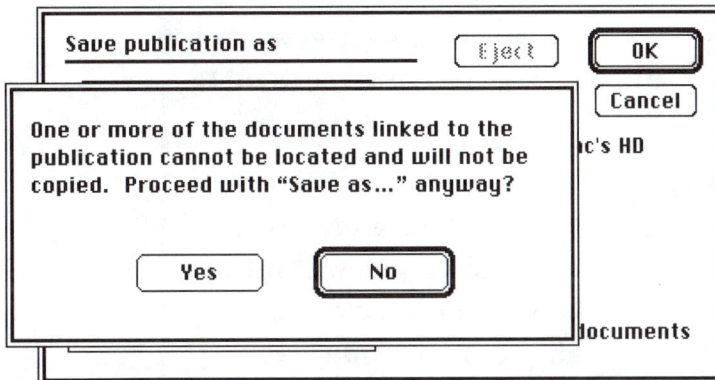

Save publication as

[Eject] [OK]
[Cancel]

c's HD

One or more of the documents linked to the publication cannot be located and will not be copied. Proceed with "Save as..." anyway?

[Yes] [No]

documents

Figure 8.30 An Alert box asking you whether or not you want to find the missing file or save anyway.

Creating Graphics in PageMaker

With PageMaker you can add quite a few graphic elements without going anywhere near your draw or Paint program. PageMaker's Toolbox includes a selection of Line and Shape tools which you can use to create some fairly complex graphics, as well as adding boxes and rules around text. The Box and Line tools work just like the ones in a graphics program. Choose line weights and styles from the **Line** menu, and any of the fill patterns (or none) from the **Fill** menu. Figure 8.31 shows how a box sets off a block of type. To place a box around a text block or graphic, use this Quick Steps.

Q Placing a Box Around Text

1. Open the **Line** menu and select a line style.

   The **Line** menu is under the **Element** menu.

2. Select **None** from the **Fill** menu.

   This makes the box transparent so the text or graphic can show through.

3. Select the Rectangle tool from the Toolbox and draw the box.

   If it's not quite the right size, use its handles to resize it. □

224

Lorem Ipsum dolor sit amet

consectetuer adipiscing elit, sed diam nonummy nibh euismod tincidunt ut laoreet dolore magna aliquam erat volutpat.

Figure 8.31 A box around the text makes it stand out.

Use the Line tools to create thin lines between columns of type and to add rules between stories. These tools are also very handy for laying out forms. Figure 8.32 shows an order form designed and created in PageMaker. Using combinations of thick and thin lines help define the different areas on the form and adds visual interest.

▶ **Tip:** If you use the Perpendicular line tool to draw lines and then move them with the pointer, PageMaker will forget to keep them perpendicular. To keep things in line, hold down Shift while you move them.

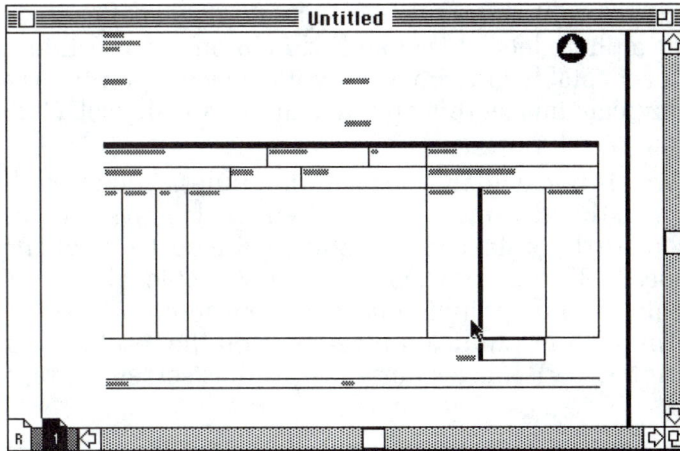

Figure 8.32 The Perpendicular line tool makes jobs like this easy.

225

Image Control: Working with Grayscale and TIFF Graphics

If you're using a scanned photograph or halftone in the TIFF format, PageMaker has a special feature which lets you alter the appearance of an image. You can increase or decrease the contrast, change a dot screen to a line screen and vice versa, and even convert a negative to a positive or posterize a photo, breaking it into black and white or one or two gray tones.

The magic happens in the Image control dialog box, shown in Figure 8.33. Select the graphic to modify and choose **Image control** from the **Element** menu. There are three modes to choose from, and all three can be applied to TIFF files.

Black and white: applies to line art and can also be used to convert grayscale photographs to high-contrast black and white images. Choosing this removes the grays from a gray scale picture. Everything lighter than middle gray is white. Everything darker than middle gray turns black.

Screened: breaks the gray image up into a pattern of black dots or lines, depending on which you've chosen. PageMaker lets you change the lines per inch and angle of halftone screens, and choose between dot and line patterns. Screening a photo lets a black and white monitor or printer produce an acceptably gray image. If your selected graphic is a grayscale image, this option is automatically selected for you.

Gray: is not available as an option unless you're working on a Mac II with a monitor which supports grayscale images. If you are, PageMaker automatically selects Gray when you select a TIFF graphic. Gray when available, gives you a realistic photographic image on your monitor. How it will print in your publication depends on the resolution of your printer. TIFF images normally print as screened graphics.

226

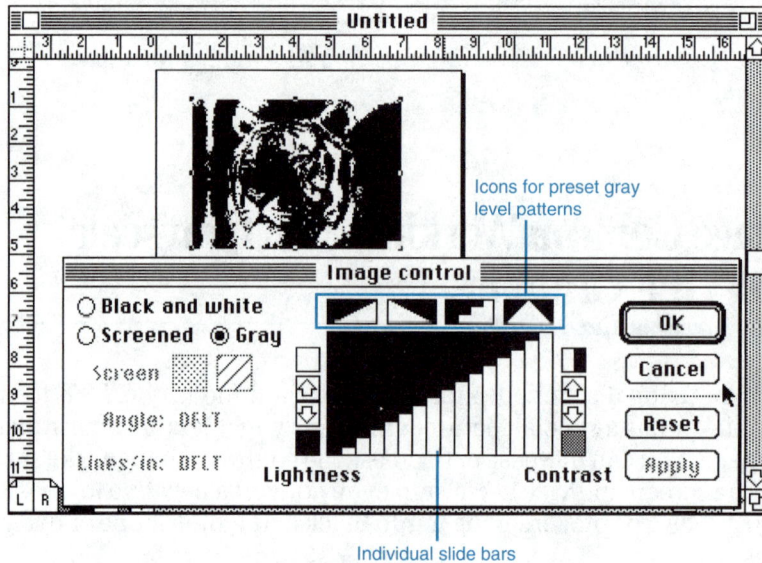

Figure 8.33 We can't change the tiger's stripes to spots, but we can make them black and white instead of black and gray.

The best way to learn how to use image control is to play with it. If you haven't saved, Reset will restore your original graphic. Within the dialog box there are four preset gray-level patterns. If you saved and then changed your mind, choosing the first preset pattern icon will restore the even gradations from light to dark. The second gives you a negative image, with even gradations from dark to light. The third reduces everything to four shades of gray (actually black, white, and two grays), and the last emphasizes the middle grays instead of the blacks and whites. Figure 8.34 shows the four possibilities.

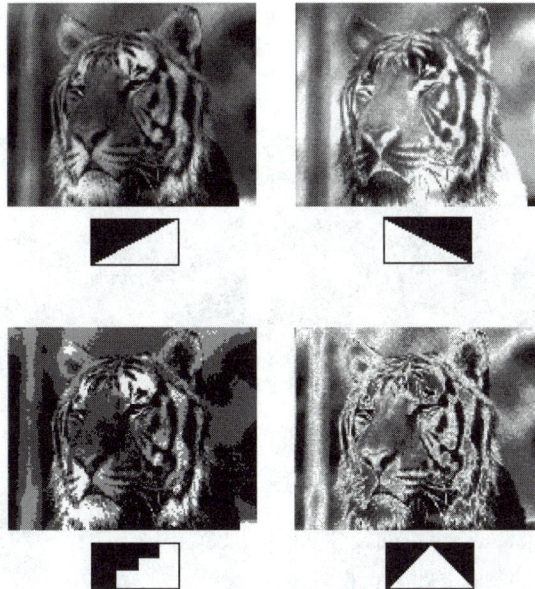

Figure 8.34 The four views correspond to the four Image control icons below them.

All the settings in the box affect the entire graphic. It's not possible to bring out just one area in PageMaker. To do so, you'd need to use a darkroom program such as PhotoShop.

The scroll bars let you adjust the values from light to dark, and the contrast from stark black and white to foggy gray. The sliding bar graph will change as you scroll up and down, or you can change individual bars to bring out particular values. Each bar represents between 4 and 16 shades of gray, depending on how the original was scanned. Again, the best way to learn what these do is to play with them. Click on Apply to see the effects of your changes, and Reset to return the TIFF to its original appearance. When you've reached a setting you like, click on OK.

Screening

Screening means transforming the gray tones of a photo into a pattern of dots or lines. You can do this within PageMaker by using Image control's screen settings. Figure 8.35 shows several different screen settings along with the original TIFF image, as a reference. Print proofs of your screened photos as you go along. PageMaker can't show you the details on your 72 dpi computer screen.

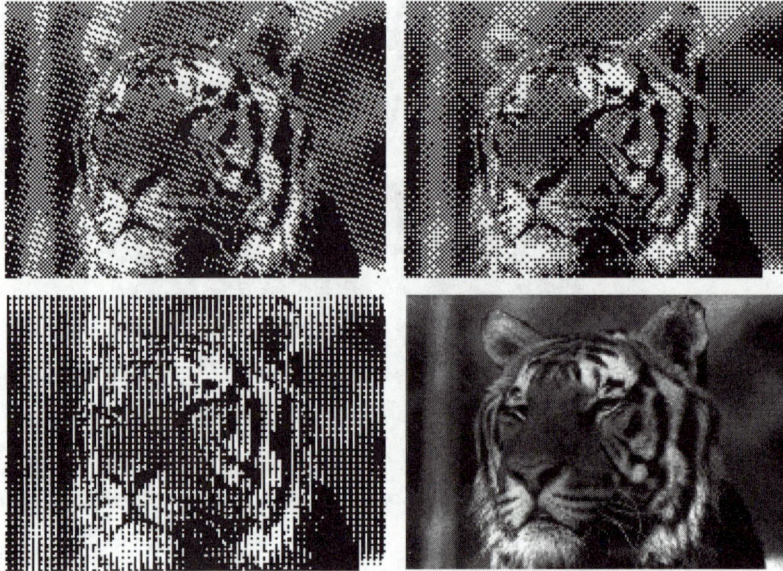

Figure 8.35 Experiment with screens until you find a combination that looks good.

One word of warning should be included here. Because of the size of the files and the complexity of translating TIFF images into PostScript, printing such a picture may tie up your Mac for several minutes. In creating the sample pages here, we needed at least two minutes to process a single tiger. (And that's with a Mac IIsi, which is a fairly fast computer.) Don't assume your system has crashed just because nothing seems to be happening. Sharpen your pencils, walk the dog (or feed the tiger), and then if nothing's happening, consider that you may have asked your Mac for more than it can handle.

What You've Learned

In this chapter, you've explored PageMaker's graphics capabilities. Specifically, you learned:

▶ About the four different formats PageMaker accepts: Paint, PICT, EPS, and TIFF. Scanners produce TIFF images. Paint and Draw programs can give you Paint and PICT graphics. Some Paint programs create EPS images.

▶ How to use the Place box to import a graphic, and how to move, resize, and crop a picture and how to use a paper colored box to cover up unwanted pieces of art.

▶ How to work with inline graphics as part of the text.

▶ How to wrap text around independent graphics, and how to use PageMaker's text wrap options, and how to flow text over or closely around irregularly shaped objects.

229

▶ How to work with linked graphics, and the advantages of storing graphics files outside the PageMaker publication.

▶ How to create some types of graphics right within the application, how to draw lines and shapes of varying thicknesses, and how to fill shapes with a choice of patterns or screen tints.

▶ How to use Image control to adjust the relationship of blacks, whites, and grays in a photo or a piece of art.

Chapter 9

Printing One Copy or Thousands

In This Chapter

▶ *Getting the Most from a Laser Printer*

▶ *Working with Downloadable Fonts*

▶ *All You Need to Know About Offset Printing*

▶ *Dealing with Service Bureaus and Printshops*

▶ *Creating Print Masters on Laser Printers and ImageSetter*

By now you've created some beautiful, persuasive pages on-screen. But publish shares the same Latin root as public, and you won't persuade anybody until you put those pages in your public's hands. That means getting them off the screen and onto paper in quantities large enough to distribute. This chapter deals with the best and most cost-effective ways to print your work.

Getting the Most from Any Laser Printer

Desktop laser printers are capable of good, relatively high-quality output. They break your page into tiny dots, (1/300th of an inch in diameter) and form letters and graphics from combinations of these dots. This is usually good enough for most business applications, but can cause noticeable patterns in photographs and gray areas. Each shade of gray requires at least four dots, so a 300 dot per inch (dpi) laser printer is really capable of only 75 dpi halftones, about the same quality as an old-fashioned newspaper photo. A few laser printers can give higher resolution, but professional typesetters and publishers rely on photographic ImageSetters with even smaller dots (as small as 1/2400th of an inch) to get fine curves in their type, and high-quality grays in their photographs. But they also rely on desktop laser printers for their proof copies.

How a Laser Prints

Yes, there really *is* a laser in the box. Laser light can be tightly focused and controlled by computer chips, so it can be shined at any one of the approximately eight million tiny locations (at 300 dpi) that make up a typical printed page. The laser scans each of these locations in turn, blinking on and off to create patterns of type and graphics. These patterns are projected onto an electrically-charged drum similar to the one in an office copier. Essentially, the drum makes a photocopy of your page, depositing black ink particles in the same pattern on the paper. Figure 9.1 illustrates, in simplified form, the laser printing process.

232

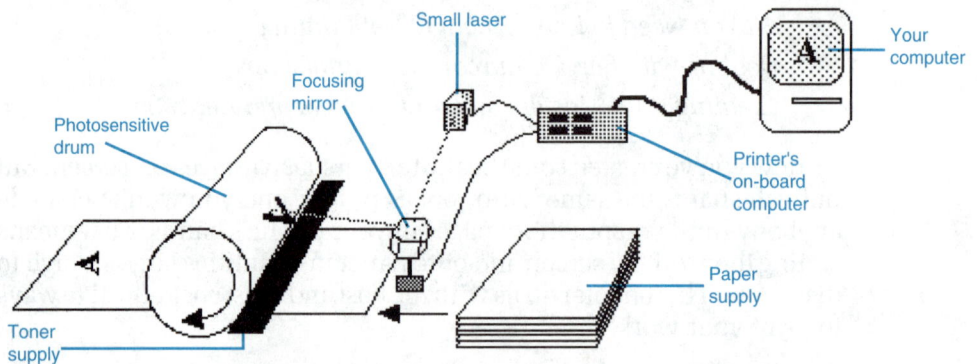

Figure 9.1 Laser printing.

Laser printers come in two different types, depending on how they get instructions from your computer. The type shown in Figure 9.1 is the most common. It has a small computer of its own, and receives relatively simple instructions sent from your Mac in the PostScript language. PostScript describes pages in terms like *put a 14-point bold Times 'A' right here*, and the printer translates that into the pattern of dots you see as **A**. This type of printing is generally called *PostScript printing*, and has several advantages:

▶ Since the page descriptions are relatively simple, they can be sent over simple networks. This makes it possible for many computers to share a single printer on a network.

▶ Most of the work is done by the printer's computer, so printing can be optimized for a specific hardware design.

▶ Almost all professional typesetting devices share this same language so you can proof a page on a 300 dpi LaserWriter, and be reasonably certain of the final output on a 2400 dpi ImageSetter.

Non-PostScript Printers

PostScript printers require an on-board computer and a license to use Adobe's copyrighted PostScript computer language. These things can add more than a thousand dollars to the printer's price tag. Apple's LaserWriter SC and GCC's Personal Laser Printer skip both language and computer, and rely on your Mac's internal brains instead. The final printed page can look just as good as a PostScript page because these companies use the same print mechanisms in their high-end printers, but the equipment is a lot cheaper.

233

Non-PostScript printers communicate through the Mac's high-speed SCSI port and are often called *SCSI Printers*. (SCSI, or Small Computer Systems Interface, is usually pronounced skuzzy.) Special software is supplied with the printer to figure out which dots go where. The software uses the Mac's built-in QuickDraw language, so these printers are also sometimes called *QuickDraw Printers*. While SCSI printers can give you excellent printouts at a reasonable cost, they do have a few disadvantages:

> ▶ **Note:** The SCSI port is a socket on the back of the computer into which the printer or other peripheral, like a hard disk, plugs. QuickDraw is the Mac's built-in graphics language.

▶ QuickDraw is anything but quick; your computer is tied up a lot longer to print the page.

▶ SCSI connections are electrically complex, so the printer can't be shared with other computers or even located more than about ten feet away.

▶ QuickDraw needs special type fonts, Adobe TypeManager (ATM) or TrueType, for high-quality text. It can't handle Encapsulated PostScript images well at all.

▶ Because of minor inconsistencies between QuickDraw and PostScript, SCSI printed proofs won't accurately preview ImageSetter pages.

Even with these disadvantages, however, the price difference can make a SCSI printer a good investment for some users. Both the Apple and GCC versions can be upgraded to full PostScript printing by installing an accessory computer card.

234   A Type of Freedom

PostScript printers usually include a few type fonts in their built-in computer, most often Times, Courier, and Helvetica. (Some higher-quality printers also include Avant Garde, Bookman, Helvetica Narrow, New Century Schoolbook, Palatino, Zapf Chancery, and Zapf Dingbats.) While it's certainly possible to create a good-looking page with just these faces, many designers prefer to work with a wider palette. Downloadable fonts can be sent, via PostScript, to the printer. Hundreds of typefaces are available, representing a good slice of the history of typography. They can be purchased on floppy disk from software dealers. Or, you can buy hard disks or CD-ROMs preloaded with hundreds of faces. Some excellent fonts are also available as shareware from user groups or computer bulletin boards. Figure 9.2 shows a few of the many available fonts.

Installing Downloadable Fonts

Downloadable fonts require two related files, a screen or bit-mapped version, and an outline version. These are always supplied together on the same disk. A pair of these files, and the Downloader utility from an Adobe font disk, are shown in Figure 9.3. (Downloader is an application that sends fonts to the printer in the same way that the Font/DA mover sends fonts to the System file.) Adobe publishes the widest selection of downloadable fonts, but you may also use disks from other publishers (and see icons like those in Figure 9.4). The *outline font file* contains a PostScript formula for each line and curve that makes up the letter. The scale isn't specified, so the same outline can serve many different point sizes. The *bit-map file* contains dot-by-dot images of each size of the letter on your screen, so you can actually see what you're typing. The outline file is useful only to a PostScript printer. These typefaces also come with AFM files (Adobe Font Metrics), which are not used by PageMaker and can be ignored.

235

Figure 9.2 A few of the many downloadable fonts.

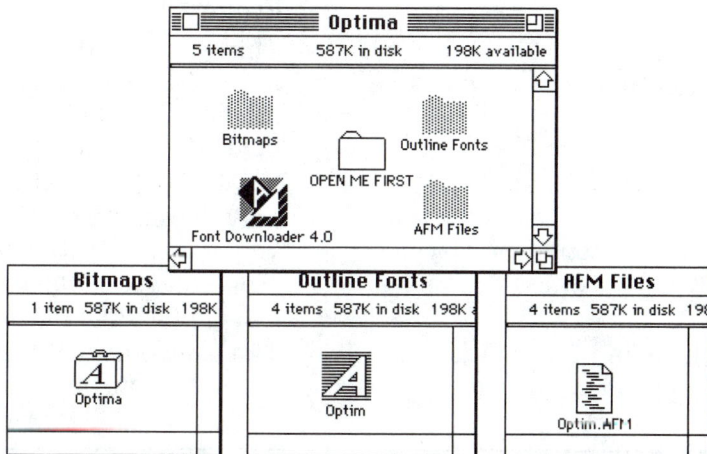

Figure 9.3 Downloadable font files and their loading software.

PreluScr   LaserWriter Font Utility

Figure 9.4 Other possible font and software icons.

Use the following Quick Steps to install downloadable fonts.

Q **Installing Downloadable Fonts**

1. Quit any applications that will use the new fonts.

   Otherwise, the applications might not recognize the new fonts.

2. Copy all of the outline font files from the font disk into your **System Folder**.

   These are the files your printer (and ATM) will actually use. You'll usually find four or more outline files with abbreviated names for each variation of the font ("Optim", "OptimBol", "OptimObli", and so on) A box containing a bar will appear to show your progress, as shown in Figure 9.5.

3. Double-click on the corresponding bit-map file.

   This will open the Font/DA mover (shown in Figure 9.6). It looks like a suitcase with the font name under it.

4. Open your System file in the Font/DA mover and use the utility to copy the fonts into your system.

   If you're using ATM, copy only the smallest sizes. If you're not, copy as many sizes and variations as you can fit onto your disk.

5. Quit Font/DA mover and reopen PageMaker.

   The new fonts will appear in the **Font** menu. □

236

> ⊘ **Warning:** Don't change the names of any of these files or move them from the **System Folder**, or your system won't be able to print the font.

> ▶ **Tip:** If you can't see your **System Folder** after you've
> selected the outline files, just drag them off of the disk's
> icon and over to the right side of your desktop. Close the font
> disk and open your hard disk's icon. You can then reselect the
> outline files and move them into the **System Folder**.

```
Files/Folders remaining to be copied:        2

Writing:        OptimBol

[████████████████████████         ]      ( Cancel )
```

Figure 9.5 Copying the outline files.

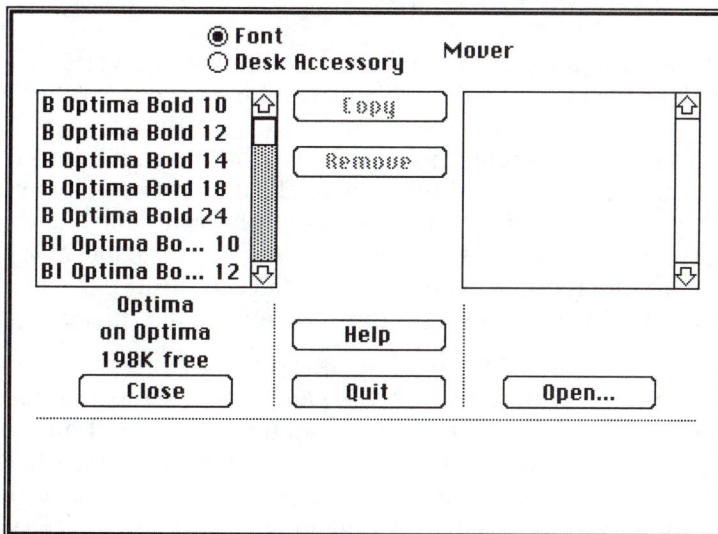

237

```
              ◉ Font
              ○ Desk Accessory      Mover

 B Optima Bold 10  ⬆      ( Copy )              ⬆
 B Optima Bold 12
 B Optima Bold 14         ( Remove )
 B Optima Bold 18
 B Optima Bold 24
 BI Optima Bo... 10
 BI Optima Bo... 12 ⬇                          ⬇

        Optima
      on Optima          ( Help )
      198K free
      ( Close )          ( Quit )        ( Open... )
```

Figure 9.6 The Font/DA mover application.

Which sizes and styles should you install? That depends on
whether you use Adobe TypeManager to help draw characters on-
screen. Here are some practical considerations:

▶ If you're not using ATM and you've got enough room on your hard disk, install all the font sizes and styles available. This will help insure that What You See is, indeed, What You Get. (If space is limited, sacrifice the bold or bold/italic versions.)

▶ If you are using ATM, then install just the smallest sizes you're likely to use for body text (usually 9, 10, and 12 point). This will let ATM create its own, more accurate versions of the font for larger sizes.

If you're running System 7 with TrueType or have a font manager program like Suitcase II, installation can be easier. For the utility, simply follow the instructions that came with the disk. For System 7, drag the Suitcase icons into the **System Folder**. If you get tired of seeing leading initials like *I Optima Oblique* or *B Optima Bold* on your **Font** menu, use a font management utility like Master Juggler or Adobe Type Reunion.

238 *Using Downloadable Fonts*

Once these fonts are properly installed, you can use them freely in your layout. PageMaker will automatically send the proper PostScript outline information to your printer's memory each time you print. This takes about twenty seconds per font. When the program thinks it won't need the font information any more, it tells the printer to forget it (but don't worry; it still lives in your Mac). Unfortunately, PageMaker doesn't look ahead to see if a typeface is used on subsequent pages and will erase a font it might need a moment later. A multi-page document can end up using quite a few of those 20-second downloads.

You can eliminate the waiting time by "permanently" downloading to the printer with a *Font Downloader*. Font Downloader is a utility that looks at the printer's memory, sees how many outline fonts the printer can hold at once, and sends you a dialog box with a list of the fonts you can move into the printer's memory for faster printing. You choose the ones you'll need to use and download them. Adobe's version is shown in Figure 9.7. Apple's Font Utility is similar. Both programs find the specific laser printer you've selected in Chooser, determine its downloading capability, and then present you with a dialog box similar to the Font/DA mover. Both can also print a catalog of available fonts. Apple's Font Utility is sometimes supplied with third-party fonts, and is available from user groups. Adobe's Font Downloader is included with Adobe font disks, but won't work with fonts from some other publishers. (When asked how to get around this, Adobe's technical representatives said, "Just buy only Adobe fonts.")

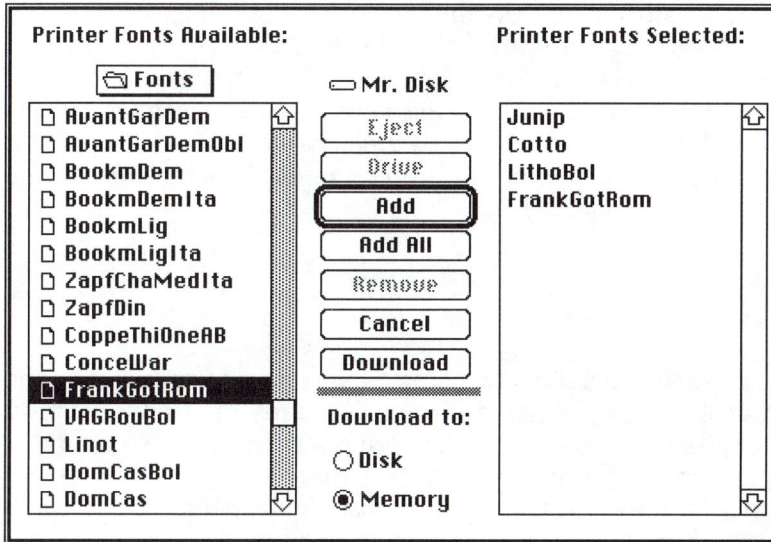

Figure 9.7 Adobe Font Downloader.

239

Not all permanent downloads are truly permanent. If you download a font to the printer's memory, it will disappear when you turn off the printer. Even so, this downloading to memory will save you time if you're going to be using the same font a lot. To permanently download a font, you'll have to use the Hard disk option available with some laser printers. It's possible to attach a hard disk to some laser printers, which the printer can use as a memory bank to keep all the outline fonts available to it, without having to download them for each page. Whether or not this can be done depends on the model of printer in use. Both Apple and Adobe's font utilities search for a printer hard disk, and let you download to it instead of the printer memory. A cheap twenty-megabyte hard disk can store hundreds of font files, saving lots of time in a busy design shop.

A Printshop on Your Desktop

Some projects require only a few copies. If you're preparing a report, a proposal, or a certificate that'll be seen by only a few people, you can get surprisingly good final copies from the same printer you've been using for proofs. With a few tricks you can produce multicolored, two-sided, professionally bound documents easily and inexpensively. Laser printed final pages usually look better than photocopies of laser printed pages, and frequently look better than offset printing, so the key question is cost. If you're using your own laser printer rather than renting time on one at a service bureau, you may find it economical to run four or five copies of a multi-page report (or a few dozen copies of a single-sided flyer) directly.

Specialty Papers

So far you've probably done most of your proof printing on standard, low-cost office copier paper. If you're using anything more expensive for PageMaker proofs, you're wasting money. Ordinary 20-pound white paper, available from most office supply stores, is fine for general purpose laser printing. It should cost about five dollars a ream (500 sheets). You don't need anything special, just look for a paper grade suitable for Xerographic office copiers.

240

For direct printing of signs, proposals, and mailers, use a slightly heavier weight paper. Most large office or printing supply houses can sell you Offset weight papers in a variety of colors for around ten dollars a ream. A 70-pound offset paper is roughly equivalent to 24-pound bond weight paper, and usually includes a polished finish on both sides that handles laser toners very well. Specify a polished, calendared or super-calendared finish, which smooths out the paper itself, rather than a coated finish, which might not react well to the heat generated by a laser printer. (Laid or textured surfaces usually don't print well. Pre-printed sheets with raised letter thermography can damage your printer.) Calendaring may also be described as *Lustre*, a reflective finish excellent for flyers and brochures, or *Vellum*, a softer finish that lends weight to proposals and correspondence. Postcards can be printed directly on 110-pound index stock with varying degrees of success, depending on the type of printer and how large the black areas are. Anything heavier will probably jam your printer.

Specialty Inks

Desktop laser printers are a little bit like Henry Ford's Model T, "You can have any color so long as it's black". But an inexpensive desktop process can convert your laser printer's print into any color of the rainbow! Letraset's ColorTag system uses sheets of specially colored dry ink that, when heated, bonds to the toner. Where there was toner, you get color. Where there was plain paper, the color peels away. The system comes with a small electrically-heated wand. To use this system, you make a sandwich of the ink sheet and a standard laser (or copier) page, and rub it with the wand to transfer the color. This can be a time-consuming process since the ink sheets have to be carefully aligned with the printout, and you have to rub with just the right pressure. On the other hand, the results look as good as professional foil-stamping and are excellent for short-run certificates and package dummies.

Of course, you can also duplicate your black and white laser pages in an office copier equipped with a colored toner cartridge. There are color PostScript printers available, but those with desktop prices use inkjets or thermal processes rather than lasers, and require special paper to produce an acceptable image.

Desktop Binderies

241

Professional reports and presentations look a lot more effective in a professional binder. Thermal binding systems use an electric heater to melt a thin strip of glue, trapping your pages in a plastic report cover. The result is far less messy than it sounds, and resembles a commercially bound magazine. Mechanical binding systems twist little plastic strips through holes punched in your pages. They can resemble the bent wire binding of your Mac's operating manual, or just appear as a plastic strip along the left edge of your publication. These manual systems can cost as little as fifty dollars.

Two-sided Printing

If you're taking the job to a print shop, they'll worry about getting the pages properly lined up so that page two appears on the back of page one and not on the back of page three. If you're publishing a short run at your desktop, you'll have to do some extra thinking. PageMaker lets you select **Print Odd (or Even) side only** from the **Options** menu in the Print dialog box, so it is possible to run one side of a stack of paper, flip it over, and then run the other side. A few warnings are in order, however:

▶ Don't try to print more than one copy of the document at a time. PageMaker's Print Odd Side Only doesn't work properly if you select multiple copies in the Print dialog box.

▶ Make sure the first print run (usually the odd-sided pages) is collated upside down.

If you're using an original LaserWriter, it spits its pages out right side up. Since page three, right side up, lands on top of page one in the output stack, it's automatically collated upside down. (This is a nuisance when printing ordinary reports but handy when printing two-sided documents.) Put the stack (of one-sided printed pages) in the paper tray, and you'll be able to print page two on the back of page one, and page four on the back of page three, just as it should be. Most modern printers flip the pages as they exit, so they're collated properly for reports. If this is the case, select Reverse Order in the Options dialog box of the **Print** menu when you print the odd-sided pages, and then deselect it before you print the even-sided pages.

242

You'll also have to figure out which side is up in the stack and which end is top. Mark a sheet of paper with an X at what you think ought to be the top, right side up, when it's printed. Then run it through and verify your guess.

How to Print All the News without Throwing a Fit

Chances are you'll need more than a few copies of your finished project. This generally means you'll have to deal with a commercial printer, whether at a copy shop or at a large, full-service printing plant. Most printers are knowledgeable, dedicated to their craft, willing to take the time to answer questions, and help you get a good job. (If you encounter one of the exceptions, look for a different print shop.) Take advantage of their experience when you're initially planning the job. A good printer will help you choose colors and formats that can avoid expensive custom work. And by all means, talk to the printer before you prepare the final output of your PageMaker design. A quick phone call or visit can make a big difference in the finished piece.

This section (about printing) was put before the section about getting final output from PageMaker for a good reason: you should be thinking about printing techniques from the first day you start a project. While you're still in the planning stages, you and your printer should pay attention to the following:

▶ *Finished size:* A stock size or easily cut variation will be much cheaper than a custom size. Depending on the printing process, bleeds (colors that extend off the edge of the page) may change the desired size.

▶ *Paper type, finish, and color:* Special effects work better on some papers than others. Screened photographs generally work best on smooth white papers. Coated or cover stocks may have different characteristics on different sides.

▶ *Printing method:* Offset printing's capabilities can vary, depending on how the printing plate is made. Sizes, bleeds, paper choices, and cost will be influenced by how the paper is fed to the press. Some of the different options are discussed later.

▶ *Binding:* Different methods require different gutters (the area that becomes difficult to read because of the stiffness of the binding). This can have a profound influence on your design, especially if you have layouts that spread across two pages.

▶ *Coverage:* Large areas of ink adjacent to fine details might print properly in some directions, and badly in others, depending on the type of press and how the paper is fed. If you're planning any large areas of black or colored ink, show a pencil sketch to your printer before you begin.

243

Offset Printing Methods

The printing plate is the most important part of the offset printing process. This is ironic since the plate never touches the paper. Offset printing is so named because the plate prints an image on a rubber blanket, which is then pressed against the paper. The image *offsets*, or transfers itself, much like a comic book page being transferred with a piece of Silly Putty. Offset just means the plate doesn't touch the paper. This process is illustrated in Figure 9.8.

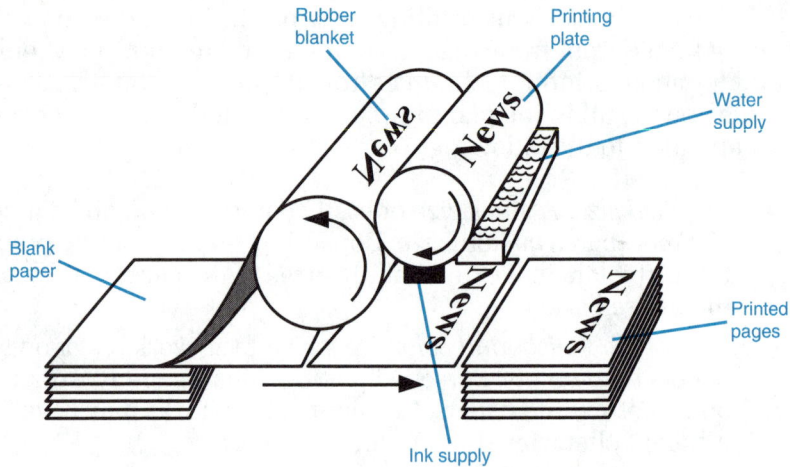

Figure 9.8 Offset printing.

244

Printing Plates

All offset plates used to be made of thin metal and were photosensitive. They were exposed through a specially prepared negative, and the resulting positive images could be inked and printed. Metal plates were durable, so the same plate could be used for hundreds of thousands of copies. The negative could be changed—or spotted—by the printer, to correct minor errors. Negatives of screened photographs could be stripped or spliced in to the main negative for extra precision and control.

Today some high-quality offset printing jobs still use negatives, but most use paper-plate printing (often called *Itek* printing). The paper plates can't print more than 10,000 copies, tend to distort or stretch, can't hold as detailed an image, and are impossible to strip or spot (what you shoot is what you print). On the other hand, Itek printing is much less expensive than metal-plate printing. There's no negative, the plate is made directly from the original. These days most small print shops can't make metal plates. They have to subcontract some of the work to a specialty shop.

The quickest and cheapest paper plates can be made on a large office photocopier or one of the high-end laser printers like a Linotronic. This is done when specially prepared plates are run through the unit, and the deposited toner does a fair job of repelling water when the page is printed. Most desktop laser printers (and small office copiers) can't handle these plates, but some service bureaus and corporate printing departments can.

Press Size

The other important consideration is the size of the printing press. Most copy shops can't print an image larger than 11x17 (and many can't print larger than 10x13). Larger presses cost more per hour to operate, but printing prices are based on the total length of time a press has to run. So even if your finished page will be only 6x9, it may be cheaper, depending on the number of pages, colors, and printed copies, to print all the pages at once on a three- or four-foot-wide piece of paper, fold them so the right pages end up in the right places, and then trim the edges to make separate sheets. Large printing presses may also be web-fed, printing giant images sequentially on a long roll of paper. There's more work involved cutting and folding but since the paper runs continuously, very large jobs use less press time than if they were sheet-fed.

245

Choosing a Printshop

Obviously there are a lot of different ways to offset print a given project. And *letterpress*, (using raised, photographically-etched plates) or *gravure*, (using plates that hold ink in tiny grooves) might be more appropriate for very large, high-quality jobs. Your local copy shop may provide the most convenient (and in some cases, the cheapest) way to print a simple newsletter. But a large commercial printer with magazine, advertising, or corporate report experience, can offer you a dazzling (and still affordable) range of printing options.

If you haven't already built a relationship with one particular printing company, it's important to shop around. Ask to see samples of similar printed pieces they've done. Decide if you're comfortable with their working style. Then prepare a careful list of specifications including paper, ink, and binding choices, the number of halftones or other special effects, trim size, and number of copies, and ask for a written estimate. Comparing estimates from two or three different printers can be very revealing.

The Ten Percent Solution

Unless you make changes in the specifications or start changing the design after the job is started, the finished printing bill should match the estimate with one exception. Printers frequently run more copies of the job than you ask for to perfect the ink distribution, and to give them spare copies in case some get damaged. If they don't need the extra copies, they'll give them to you. But even if you don't want the extras, the printer is traditionally allowed to charge you for them, up to ten percent over the agreed cost of the press run. If you're uncomfortable with or unsure of this arrangement, talk to the printer about overrun costs before you give them the job.

Printing for the Printer

246

Now that you've picked a printer and printing method, probed potential printing problems, and perfected your pages, it's time to print the master copies of the pages the printer will produce. This can be as simple as putting the proper paper in your laser printer, or it can involve service bureaus, mechanical paste ups, and photographic effects. The choice is determined by your design, printing methods, and quality standards.

Creating a Laser Master

Your 300 dpi laser printer can produce masters that are more than adequate for simple, Itek printing jobs with no photographs or fine type sizes. The process is no more complicated than pulling proof pages into PageMaker with just a few special considerations.

Using the Right Paper

Ordinary copy paper is fine for laser proofs. But for final masters, use a special laser output paper. These papers have fibers that hold a smoother line, are particularly opaque and white for maximum contrast, and are designed to stand up to the heat and pressure in laser printers without distorting or curling. Hammermill Laser Plus is preferred by many desktop publishers. It features a special coating on the back that prevents rubber cement or paste-up wax from bleeding through (the back of the paper is marked Paste-Up Side in light blue letters). Laser Plus is available at large office supply stores for about $15 a ream.

If you can't get a true laser output paper, use the smoothest, whitest paper you can find. 70-pound offset white, lustre finish will do an acceptable job. Avoid rag bond papers. Although these high-quality papers are excellent for correspondence and certificates, they have an irregular texture that can cause slight blurring of the tiny toner dots.

Treat the Paper and Your Printer Properly

Leave laser paper in its original box or ream wrapper until you're ready to use it. Open stacks of paper can accumulate moisture causing curling and distortion. Fan out the paper before loading it in the paper tray to prevent static cling. After you've printed, put the copies in a flat heavy envelope so they don't pick up any moisture.

247

You should also make sure your printer is clean. Dry toner is dusty stuff, and it can accumulate on the edges of rollers and in other unfortunate places. Run a test sheet and examine it carefully for gray smudges (especially along the edges). If you see any, try the following:

▶ Set up a page with just a single dot or small letter on it, (something that won't require much toner) and print a dozen copies of it. Chances are, the later copies won't have the smudge.

▶ Feed a Cleaning Sheet through the printer. LaserKleen has a special surface that sucks up loose toner. It costs about a dollar a sheet.

▶ Check your printer's owner's manual for cleaning instructions.

Printing Larger Pages

Some service bureaus might have laser printers capable of tabloid (11x17) output, but most laser printers can't create an image wider than eight inches. Larger pages will require tiling to break the image up into printer-sized pieces. You (or the print shop) can then assemble the pieces by hand with scissors and tape. Figure 9.9 shows a page broken up into four tiles. Notice the white margins around each printed piece. The white margin appears because a laser printer can't print up to the edge of its page. When you tape these pieces of a page together, cut the white borders off to make an unbroken image.

> ▶ **Tip:** Taping tiled pieces of a page together is a lot easier if you use a light table, available at most print shops and some service bureaus. These glass-topped tables shine a bright light up through your pages, so you can align them and then cut them with a razor blade.

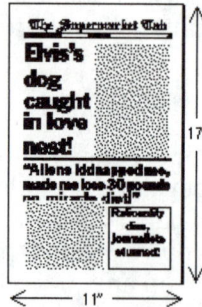

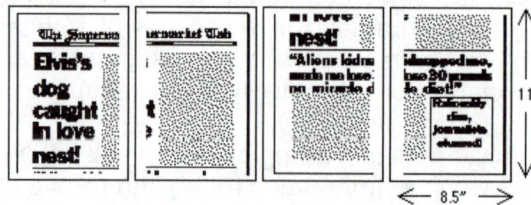

Figure 9.9 An oversized page divided into smaller chunks by tiling.

Tiling is set up through the PageMaker Print options dialog box. Use the following Quick Steps to tile pages.

Q Tiling Pages

1. If you're using a PostScript printer, select **Print** from the **File** menu to open the **Print** dialog box. Click on the **Options** button to open the **Print options** dialog box.

   The Print options dialog box is shown in Figure 9.10. (If you're using a SCSI printer, an ImageWriter, or a StyleWriter, you'll see the Tiling options as soon as you select the **Print** command.)

2. Click on the **Tile** box and select **Auto-overlap**.

Specify an auto-overlap of at least half an inch, to compensate for the unprintable borders around the edges of most laser printed pages.

3. Click on **Crop marks** and press Return, or click on OK.

PageMaker will print pages you can tile. □

▶ **Note:** Half an inch is the minimum auto-overlap, as you can see in Figure 9.9. PageMaker will try to give you as much overlap as it can for the page sizes you're working with.

▶ **Tip:** Tiled pages will be easier to align if you select Spot color overlays from the Print options box. This makes PageMaker put a registration mark on each margin of the page.

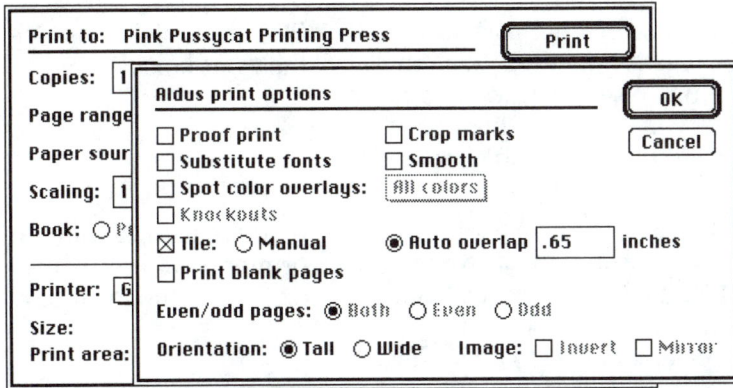

249

Print to: Pink Pussycat Printing Press   [Print]

Copies: 1

Page range   **Aldus print options**   [OK]

Paper sour   ☐ Proof print   ☐ Crop marks   [Cancel]
                ☐ Substitute fonts   ☐ Smooth

Scaling: 1   ☐ Spot color overlays: [All colors]
                ☐ Knockouts
Book: ○ P   ☒ Tile: ○ Manual   ◉ Auto overlap [.65]   inches
                ☐ Print blank pages

Printer: G   Even/odd pages: ◉ Both ○ Even ○ Odd
Size:
Print area: Orientation: ◉ Tall ○ Wide   Image: ☐ Invert ☐ Mirror

Figure 9.10 Selecting Tiling in the Aldus Print options box.

When Not To Use Auto-overlap

Most laser printers can't draw a straight line. If you hold a straight edge along the baseline of a full line of type in the middle of the page and look closely, you'll probably notice tiny hills and valleys in the line (shown in Figure 9.11). These are caused by mechanical or paper inconsistencies as the mirror scans the laser beam across the page. Usually, these variations are hardly noticeable. But if the overlap between two tiles falls in the middle of a large graphic or a column of type, and the two tiles don't line up properly, you might see a seam that looks like badly applied wallpaper.

Modern cosmetic surgery can help unsightly sags and droops, the ban swimsuits as well as in typography.

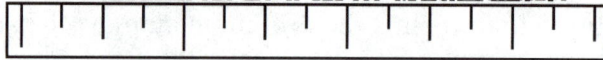

Figure 9.11 Laser printers rarely draw a straight line.

You can avoid this kind of tiling problem. If you select Manual, PageMaker will print just one tile with its upper left corner at the zero point. Then you can locate a safe place for the next tile and print it, and so on. Use the following Quick Steps for Manual tiling.

Q   Manual Tiling

1. To control what part of the image is tiled during manual tiling, reset the ruler zero point on your page to where you want the upper left corner of the tile to start.

    Place the ruler, then open the **Print** box.

2. If you're using a Post-Script printer, select **Print** from the **File** menu to open the **Print** dialog box. Click on the **Options** button to open the **Print options** box.

    If you're using a different printer, you'll see tiling options in the Print box.

3. Click on the **Tile** box and select **Manual**.

    PageMaker prints just one file at a time this way.

4. Click on OK to print the file.

    Then move the ruler and repeat the procedure for each tile.

If there are no safe places to put the boundaries, you may have to print text and graphics separately on the laser, and manually glue them together just like the pasteups we had to do before Macintoshes were invented.

Working with an ImageSetter

The best way to get large page images, finely cut type, and good-looking halftones, is to print your final copy photographically on a Linotronic ImageSetter. These devices, usually available at service bureaus or large print shops, use photographic papers and negatives instead of the office copier drum found in desktop laser printers. The resulting dot pattern is four to eight times more precise, and individual dots can be invisible to the naked eye.

ImageSetters can be connected directly to Macs via AppleTalk, and speak the same language as desktop printers. So you can make accurate proof pages on a PostScript laser printer to check your layout, and be reasonably certain the final photographic output will match. (You can't do this with SCSI or QuickDraw laser printers.) In fact, many service bureaus require you to print a proof on their laser printers before you can send a job to their ImageSetter. When you're ready to print, just select the proper printer in **Chooser** (in the **Apple** menu) and go ahead.

251

Paperless Printing

ImageSetter output is usually on light-weight, high-contrast photographic paper, similar to the paper snapshots are printed on. This copy becomes the master which is then photographed directly onto a paper printing plate, a plastic printing plate, or a negative for a high-quality metal plate. A cheaper alternative for high-quality printing is to create ImageSetter output directly onto a negative. This usually costs slightly more than paper output, but skips the photographic negative step entirely. Scanned halftones can be screened and combined with the image at the same time, eliminating the expensive stripping step at the print shop. Many publications require one of these composite negatives, including text and halftones, when you submit an ad. However, not all printing jobs (or print shops) want a negative, so check first. Before you print to a negative, select Image Invert in the Aldus Print options box. In most cases you'll be asked for a *right-reading emulsion down negative* to make the highest-quality offset plates. A right-reading emulsion down negative is a piece of photographic film with clear letters on a solid black background, designed for direct contact with the printing plate. This just means you should also select Image Mirror.

ImageSetter Concerns

ImageSetter output might not match LaserWriter output perfectly, because the image is so much more finely detailed, and the internal computer takes fewer PostScript shortcuts. Here are some things you need to watch out for when you're making the transition from Laser printer to ImageSetter:

▶ Hairline rules are considered by most drawing programs to be one dot high. On a laser printer, this is 1/300th of an inch, a nice size for ruling forms or music staves. The same rule on an ImageSetter, 1/2400th of an inch high, virtually disappears. Whenever you can, define your rules and lines in point sizes in PageMaker.

▶ Grays at both ends of the scale will fool you. A 10% gray on a laser printer, because of its nice, round dots, is a fairly usable background pattern. On an ImageSetter, it virtually disappears. Similarly, a laser's 90% gray has noticeable white dots. Anything darker than 70% on an ImageSetter appears almost black.

> ▶ **Tip:** PageMaker's Fill patterns are not true PostScript grays. If you need absolutely accurate gray-scale tones, import them from a PostScript drawing program.

▶ Very complex graphics are likely to confuse an ImageSetter because the system pays more attention to the PostScript commands that create them. Even scraps of text or graphics left outside the printing area on the pasteboard can throw off an ImageSetter. If the printer won't handle your job, make sure the pasteboard is clean. If this doesn't help, try printing one page at a time. If you still have problems, you might have to go into a drawing program and simplify your graphics.

Working with Service Bureaus

Service bureaus charge for their time, usually at a flat fee per hour for the use of their Macs, plus a small charge per laser output page (currently about eight dollars a page in the Boston area for Lino output). So if you're going to use a service bureau, you want to do it quickly and with as few mistakes as possible. A little preparation will help a lot.

Preparing Disks for a Service Bureau

Naturally, you'll want to make up a floppy disk with a copy of your PageMaker document to take to the service bureau. Even though PageMaker embeds TIFF graphics in its documents, it's also a good idea to copy any graphic files you've used in the document. Call the service bureau to make sure they have outline fonts to match all the screen fonts you've used in your layouts. If they don't have the ones you need, check your own system folder (look for icons similar to Figures 9.3 and 9.4), and put copies on your disk.

253

In fact, as a general rule of thumb when going to a service bureau, when in doubt, bring a copy. Some users bring their entire hard disk. (If you're planning to do this, check the virus warning later in this chapter.)

Some Macintosh programs used to get into trouble at service bureaus because they described fonts by number instead of by name. If the service bureau's Mac assigned the number to a different font, the results would be unpredictable. Fortunately, you probably won't encounter these font conflicts, both because Apple has changed the way it assigns font numbers and because PageMaker 4.0 refers to fonts by name instead of by number. However, you can still get some surprises. Classic type families (like Garamond) are frequently available from multiple publishers. One publisher's screen version might not line up with another publisher's outline version, wreaking havoc with column alignment and justification. There are even slight differences between the screen version of Times supplied by Apple with their systems and the one supplied by Adobe with ATM.

> ▶ **Tip:** You can avoid most spacing problems by borrowing copies of the screen versions of the fonts your service bureau uses, before you start the design. This isn't considered software piracy; it's the outline versions that count (and are usually copyrighted).

Leave Home without It

If you want to save as much time as possible at a service bureau or print shop, don't bring a PageMaker file at all. Select Print on your own computer and then click the PostScript button in the Print dialog box. The PostScript box lets you *print to disk*, which means you can save your entire publication on floppy disk as a PostScript file, which can be sent directly to the printer with no intervening software. If you check Normal in the PostScript box, you'll get a pure PostScript text file, the standard for most printing operations. (If you check EPS, you'll get an Encapsulated PostScript image of a single page attached to a low resolution screen image, which can then become part of an even larger PageMaker document.) If you have the outline fonts in your **System Folder** and want to guarantee compatibility at the service bureau, check Download PostScript fonts; this will build copies of the fonts into your PostScript file.

Again, use the telephone first. Some print shops prefer PostScript files to PageMaker files because they use less computer time to print. Some service bureaus would rather get PageMaker files to guarantee a chance to refine the proof.

Virus Warning

Computer viruses are little sections of self-copying computer code that can jump into otherwise useful software, with frequently destructive results. While they're not as much of a problem on the Macintosh as they are with other systems, service bureaus are one place they've been known to spread. Innocent (or malicious) users bring infected floppies with their applications for printing, and a copy of the virus jumps onto the service bureau's hard disk. If you're not careful, it can then jump onto your floppy and back to your hard disk when you get home.

Fortunately, viruses are fairly easy to avoid, if you follow these simple tips:

▶ Don't bring public domain (or illegally stolen) applications or HyperCard stacks home from the service bureau. Most viruses are carried by the resource forks found in applications and stacks, rather than by the data forks found in PageMaker files. (Forks are a way of organizing stuff in a Mac application. There are resource forks and data forks. The data fork is the "what", and the resource fork is the "how to.")

▶ Lock your floppy by moving the plastic tab over the little hole before you go to the service bureau. No known virus can jump to a locked disk.

▶ To be extra careful, don't put the disk back into your machine when you get home. Viruses are spread by inserting your floppy disk into your computer.

Any serious Mac owner should get a good virus protection package for his/her computer. Many users, the author included, swear by the free programs GateKeeper and Disinfectant (available from most large user groups), but you might feel more comfortable with the excellent commercial packages available at large computer stores.

255

What You've Learned

In this chapter, you learned all about the printing part of desktop publishing, and how to handle printing jobs that can't be done on your own desktop. Specifically, you learned:

▶ Desktop laser printers sell for a wide range of prices, determined (primarily) by whether or not they use the PostScript printing language. This affects printing speed and compatibility with other printers.

▶ You can expand the number of fonts in a laser printer by copying commercially available files onto your Mac, or the printer's hard disk.

▶ Paper quality affects printing quality. Papers range from very cheap (for everyday proofing) to very fancy for desktop reports, individually printed flyers, and high-quality printing masters.

▶ Cheap desktop processes can add color and professional bindings to your laser output.

▶ Offset printing methods vary greatly in price, quality, and capability. Choose carefully before you begin the design process.

▶ Your desktop laser printer can create bigger pages or effectively higher resolution output, with a few simple tricks.

▶ For the highest quality output, make a positive or negative image with an ImageSetter, available at service bureaus. If you prepare your material carefully for the service bureau, you can avoid expensive disappointments.

▶ Some reasonable, common sense precautions can protect you from most virus infections when you bring your disks to another machine.

256

Business Forms in PageMaker

In This Chapter

▶ *Using Preexisting Templates*

▶ *Designing Your Own Forms*

▶ *Invoices, Order Forms, and Ruled Forms*

▶ *Letterheads, Logos, and Business Cards*

▶ *Catalogs*

▶ *Sales Reports and Annual Reports*

Now that you've mastered the basics of PageMaker and newsletter design, it's time to take a look at some of the other tasks PageMaker can make easier. Businesses find PM a tremendous help in designing and creating all kinds of forms, stationery, and reports. If you look at the contents of an average desk drawer, virtually everything that's printed could have been done in PageMaker, and it's likely that much of it was. PageMaker has been the choice of artists and designers ever since it first appeared. Invoices, business cards, appointment slips, labels, letterheads, package designs—all these and more are at your fingertips with PageMaker and your Macintosh. So, let's get to work.

Using Premade Templates

Grampa used to say, "There's no point in reinventing the wheel." What he meant was simply that there's no good reason to redo something that's already done well. He had a point. Some things are hard to improve on, which is not to say they can't be customized. This brings us to the real point of this section: When you purchased PageMaker, the package included a set of templates. These basic layouts, for all kinds of business forms and documents, can save you hours of design time and effort. But, you still need to know how to use PageMaker to customize them. You have to insert your own company's name and address, and change the logo to yours. You should also make sure the form either fits the procedures your business already follows, or will make them more efficient.

You'll find PageMaker templates in a folder called *Templates*. There are thirty-five in all, and they range from letterheads, envelopes, and purchase orders, to multipage catalogs, brochures, and manuals. If you belong to a user group, a local group, or an on-line information service, such as America Online, CompuServe, or Delphi, you have another good source for templates. There are many generous people who are happy to share their designs, either for free or for a small shareware fee.

Working with Templates

As you know, there are two ways to open a file. You can click on its icon on the desktop, or you can open it from a menu within the application. When you're working with templates, the latter is preferable. To open a template, use these steps:

1. Open PageMaker first.
2. Choose **Open** from the **File** menu or press ⌘+O. The dialog box, shown in Figure 10.1, will appear.
3. Click on the **Copy** button at the bottom of the box to open a copy.
4. Then select the name of the template to open and double-click on it, or press Return.

```
┌─────────────────────────────────────────────────────────────┐
│  Open publication                     ┌ Eject ┐  ╔═══ OK ═══╗ │
│  ─────────────────                    └───────┘  ╚══════════╝ │
│       ┌─ 🗁 Templates ─┐               ┌ Drive ┐  ┌ Cancel ┐  │
│       └────────────────┘              └───────┘  └────────┘  │
│    ┌──────────────────────────────┬─┐                        │
│    │ 🗋 Memo                       │⬆│      ⬛ Mac's HD        │
│    │ 🗋 Newsletter 1               │ │                        │
│    │ 🗋 Newsletter 2               │ │                        │
│    │ 🗋 Newsletter 3, Tabloid      │ │                        │
│    │ 🗋 Pricelist                  │ │                        │
│    │ 🗋 Proposal                   │ │  Open:                 │
│    │ 🗋 Purchase order             │ │   ○ Original           │
│    │ 🗋 Registration form        ▸ │⬇│   ⦿ Copy               │
│    └──────────────────────────────┴─┘                        │
└─────────────────────────────────────────────────────────────┘
```

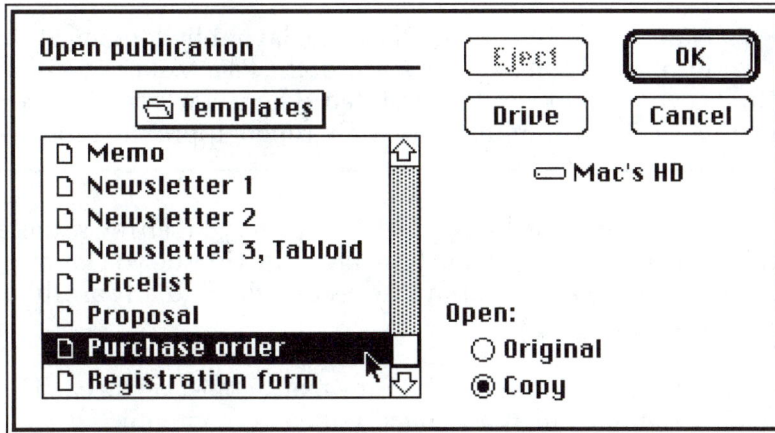

Figure 10.1 Click on the Copy button to open a copy of a template.

259

If you start PageMaker by clicking on a Template icon, you'll open the original template instead of a copy. Any changes you make will be made to the template itself. If you're not sure whether you've opened the template or a copy, look at the Title bar of the open document, or watch the screen as the publication opens. A copy will open as *Untitled*, and the legend on the opening *thermometer* will say, *Opening a copy of...*, as shown in Figure 10.2. If you accidentally open the template, close it and open a copy.

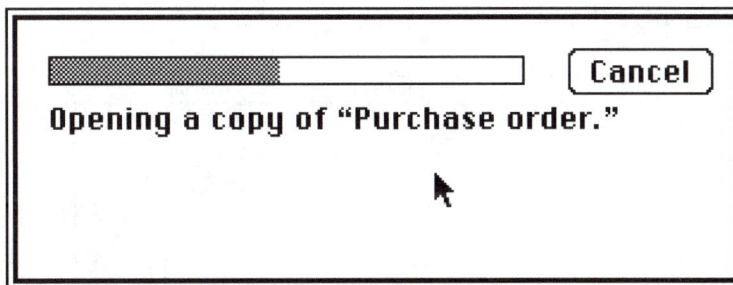

```
┌─────────────────────────────────────────────────────────────┐
│                                                              │
│   ┌──────────────────────────────────┐   ┌ Cancel ┐          │
│   │▓▓▓▓▓▓▓▓▓▓▓▓▓▓▓▓░░░░░░░░░░░░░░░░░░░│   └────────┘          │
│   └──────────────────────────────────┘                       │
│      Opening a copy of "Purchase order."                     │
│                                                              │
│                          ▶                                   │
│                                                              │
└─────────────────────────────────────────────────────────────┘
```

Figure 10.2 Opening a copy of the Purchase Order template.

> ▶ **Note:** If you select your template layout by looking at the thumbnails on pages iv and v of the PageMaker Template Guide, you might be disappointed when you open the real templates. The thumbnails are only rough approximations.

Once you've opened a copy of the template, you can revise the form to suit your needs. And, therein lies a problem. How do you know what you really need? Ask yourself and the people who regularly use the form these questions:

▶ Who uses this form? When? How many copies are needed? How is it filled in; typed, handwritten, by computer?

▶ Why are we replacing the present form? Is there a problem with the current version, or is this a cosmetic change? If this is a brand new piece of paperwork, will it solve a problem? Provide needed information? Make a process easier?

▶ Assuming this replaces a previous form, were there parts of the old one that were never filled in? Was additional information needed with no place to enter it?

Now you can take a more educated look at the form itself. Figure 10.3 shows a typical purchase order form, one of PageMaker's templates. It could be used as is, after replacing the logo, company name, and address with your own. Or, based on the information you gathered by talking to the people who would be using the form, you could make some changes that would make it even better.

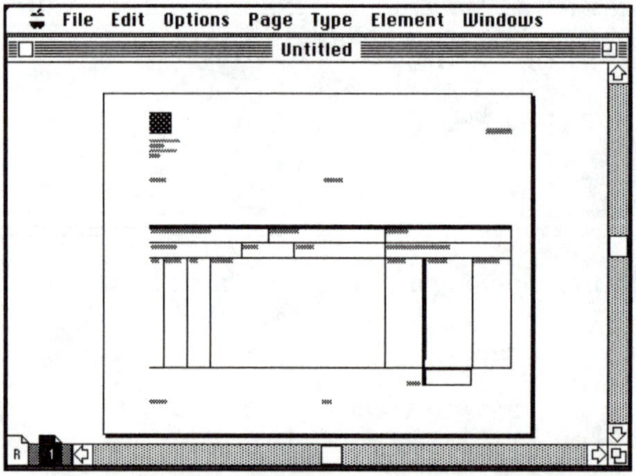

Figure 10.3 PageMaker's Purchase Order template.

For example, one problem with this particular form was that users tended to get confused and enter the vendor's name in the area which was intended for the shipping address. They would then insert the form in a window envelope meant for a different form, and end up mailing it to themselves. The close view in Figure 10.4 shows the problem and the reason. The solution: simply switch the two address boxes, an easy job in PageMaker.

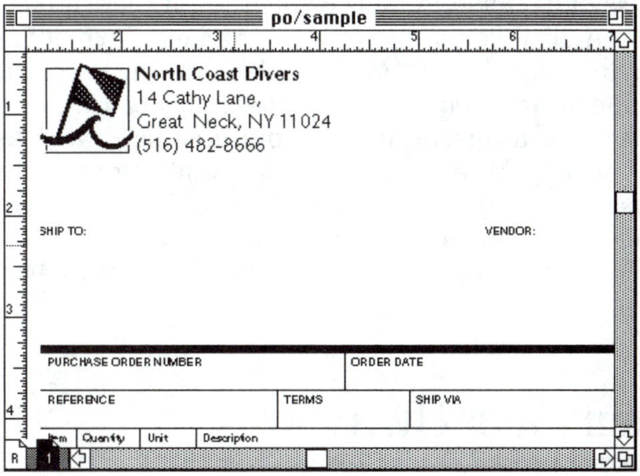

Figure 10.4 The Vendor box and the Ship to box need to be reversed.

261

To customize a template you'll need to remove the placeholders Aldus has inserted for a logo and company name. On most PageMaker templates, these are on the master page rather than on the working page, so you'll need to go to the master page in order to delete them. Use the following Quick Steps to do this.

Customizing the Logo and Address Block

1. Click on the master page icon in the lower left corner of the PageMaker window.

   This shows you only the elements on the master page.

2. Using the pointer, select the block with the address and logo and delete it.

   Now you can place your own information in the same spot, or wherever you want it. ☐

After making any other revisions to the form, print a proof copy. Don't forget to save your work. Give it a title other than the one PageMaker has assigned to the template version or else you, and your Mac, are likely to get confused.

If you like what you see in the proof version, think about the next step. If this is a brand new form, it may be a good idea to run off a dozen pages on the office copier and try them out in daily use before you go to the expense of having hundreds printed. With a small business and a low-use form, like the purchase order or an employment application, photocopying might be the most cost efficient way to continue. If your bookkeeping system requires multiple copies of invoices and other forms, have the forms printed on multiple-part NCR (No Carbon Required) paper. These are available as pinfeed forms for dot matrix printers as well as separately. NCR forms can't be run through a laser printer, however. The printer can number forms sequentially, or you can purchase a hand operated numbering stamp to do the same job.

Designing Your Own Forms

It could be there's no template readily available for the form you need, or perhaps you'd just rather have the fun of doing it yourself. Designing forms with PageMaker is simple. The biggest problem, that of drawing straight lines, is already taken care of for you. In this chapter, several different ways to lay out forms are discussed.

The considerations in designing a useful form are the same as those we discussed previously with regard to improving on an existing one. Consider the purpose and decide what information must be put into the form. Make a pencil and paper dummy, or two or three, until you find an arrangement that seems to make sense. Then open PageMaker and place guide lines, and then text and graphics, as needed, just as you would for a newsletter or any other project.

Figure 10.5 shows the grid for a form listing various items with check-off boxes. This particular page has been set up with three columns and horizontal lines placed at half inch intervals to separate the items on the list. A title, company name, and logo have also been added to the page.

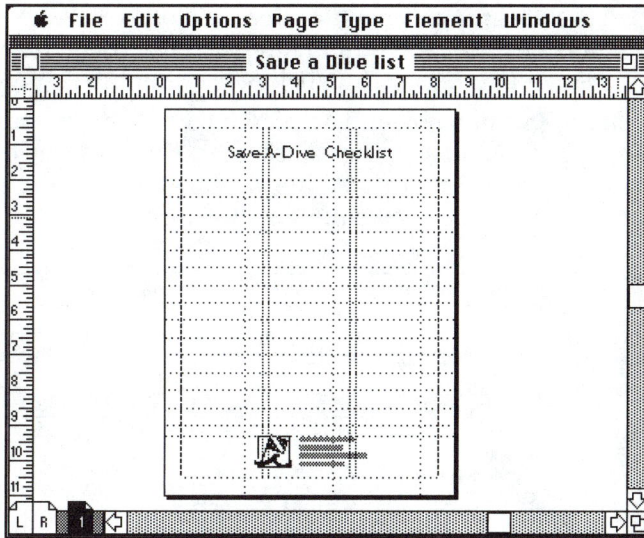

Figure 10.5 Begin by setting up a grid of column guides and ruler guides.

263

Drawing Lines Manually

To draw the lines individually, select a line weight from the **Line** menu under **Element**. Using the Perpendicular line tool, simply begin at one margin and drag a line across the page to the opposite margin. Use the ruler guides to space the lines. Be sure that Snap to Rulers is selected. It makes your ruler guides slightly magnetic-like. The lines you draw will automatically be attracted to them, making precise placement much easier.

Drawing Lines with Paragraph Rule

You can also let PageMaker draw the horizontal lines automatically. To do so, follow these steps:

1. Create your list, either in Story Editor, or in your favorite word processor. Set it up so each item is on a separate line with a single carriage return, as shown in Figure 10.6.

2. Place the list on the page and adjust the type size and leading, as needed, to correctly position the various list items within the grid.

3. Open the **Paragraph Specifications** dialog box and within it, the **Rules** box, as shown in Figure 10.7. Choose a line width and color, and click on Rule below paragraph.

4. Open the **Options** box and select **Grid**. Enter the amount of leading as the grid spacing. Close all the boxes at once by pressing Option+Return. A line appears between each pair of words. Figure 10.8 shows the finished form.

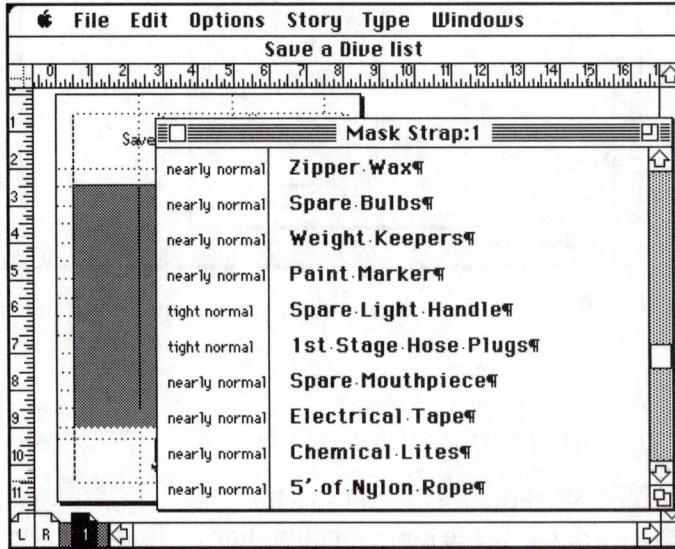

Figure 10.6 One item per line, followed by a carriage return, makes each item a separate paragraph.

Spacing Lines with Option+Paste

Here's another way to handle evenly spaced lines or other elements:

1. Create the first set. Select them and press ⌘+C to copy them.

2. Hold down Option while you press ⌘+V to paste them. They'll appear right on top of the first set. Drag them to their correct position.

3. Hold down Option while you press ⌘+V and a third set will appear. PageMaker will offset this set by the same amount as the previous one.

4. Continue this Option+Paste combination until you've placed as many offset lines or objects as you wish. Figure 10.9 illustrates the process.

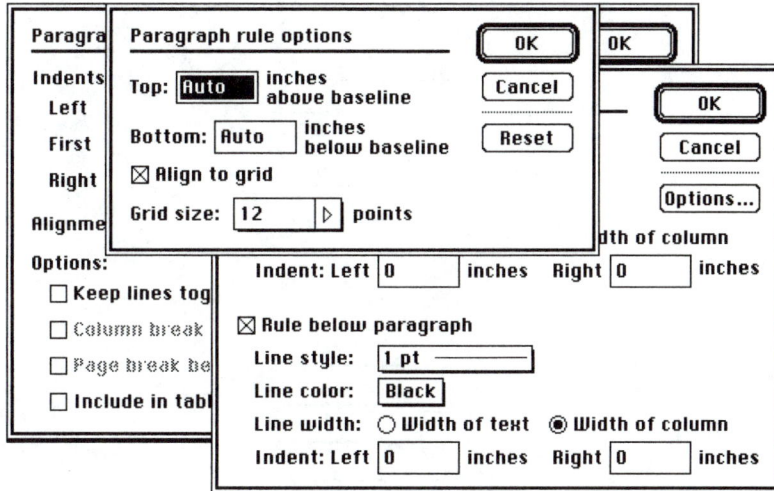

Figure 10.7 Ask PageMaker for a rule below each paragraph.

265

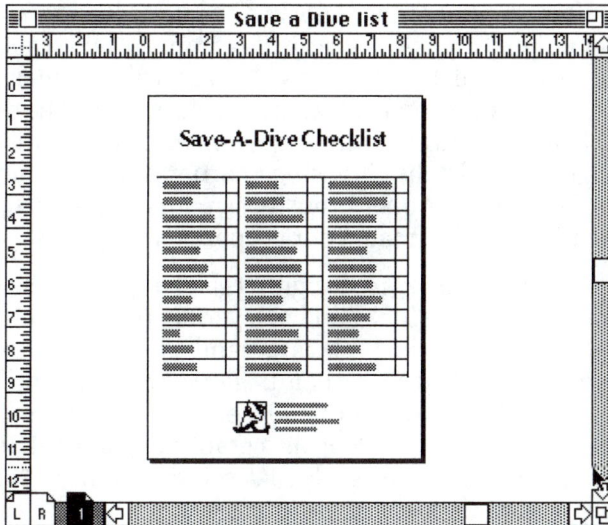

Figure 10.8 Add the vertical lines to make check boxes.

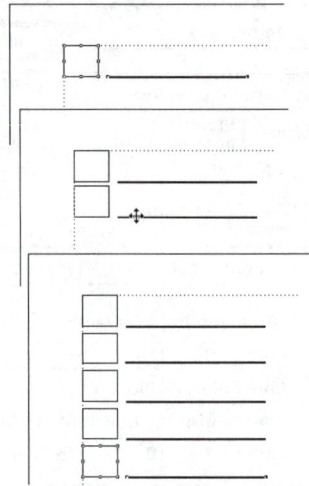

Figure 10.9 Option+Paste places elements an exact distance apart.

Quite often a business needs not just one form, but a whole package including letterheads, business cards, fax transmittal forms, invoices, purchase orders, and all the other paraphernalia of a small corporation. In order to achieve a corporate look, these pieces should be designed to relate to each other. Using the same type font and placing the corporate logo on each piece will help. Choosing a corporate color scheme for ink and paper colors on stationery, business cards, annual reports, and brochures will also help create your corporate image.

The greatest challenge in designing related pieces lies in finding combinations of type that look good in a variety of sizes, and logos that are simple, yet striking, in both large and small versions. Using a graphics program, such as SuperPaint, allows you to experiment with scaling a logo to different reductions. Of course, you can use PageMaker to experiment too. Place your logo as a graphic on a blank PageMaker page, copy it a dozen times and scale each one differently. Print the page so you can see what happens at various sizes.

> ▶ **Tip:** Create the logo as a PICT rather than a Paint file, if possible. It will reduce more smoothly.

Designing a Letterhead

Although the word letterhead somehow suggests that anything you place on the page must go at the head of it, this is an old-fashioned design rule, which you may choose to ignore. Letterheads can have type running along the side of the page and/or across the bottom as well as at the top. PageMaker is the ideal tool for this type of task as you have a great deal of flexibility with type placement. Just remember to leave at least a quarter inch of margin so your design will fall within the imaging area of your printer.

A *formal* letterhead generally has the company name and address, either centered, or set flush left at the top of the page. The logo, if any, is small, neat, and dignified. A more casual one might have the address block across the bottom or at the side of the page, and would have a larger and perhaps, less serious logo. Using PageMaker's Text rotation feature can help you produce unusual effects. Figure 10.10 shows some examples of various styles of letterhead.

267

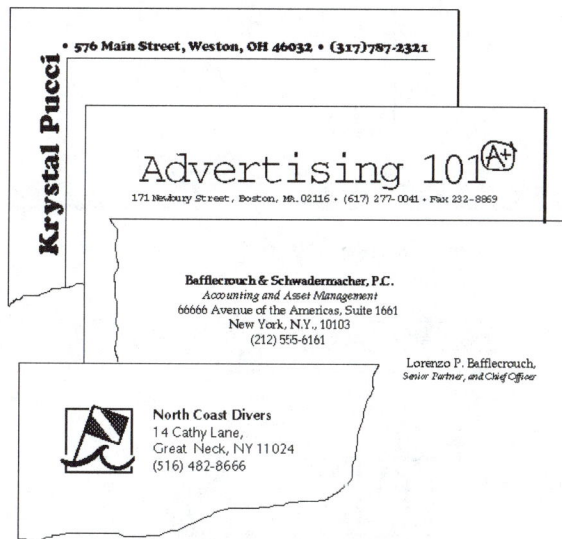

Figure 10.10 Letterheads may be formal, funky, or simply functional.

Stick with standard 8$^1/_2$-x-11-inch paper and number 10 envelopes. Other sizes will cost more and look less professional. They're also more likely to jam in your printer. Envelopes should use the same type style as the stationery, only in letters small enough to make a neat corner block. Use of a logo on the envelope is optional.

Business cards may be printed as a page of ten and cut apart. The correct measurements are 3$^1/_2$-x-2 inches, or 21-by-12 picas. Set the page up so cards are two across and five down. The grid for a page of business cards is shown in Figure 10.11. Design one card and copy it into the other nine positions. You can change the names on each card if you wish. Have business cards printed on a heavy stock. (100-pound cover is a minimum weight for cards.) Ask the printer about embossing the logo, or adding a second color to the card. Don't forget to add crop marks to show the printer where to cut the cards apart. Figure 10.12 shows the proper position for the crop marks.

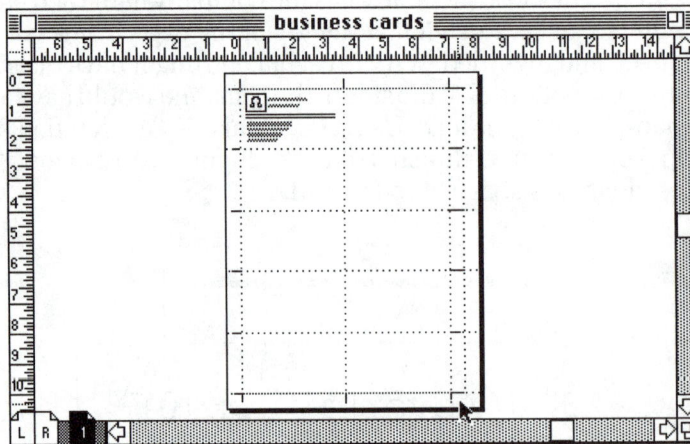

Figure 10.11 A grid for a page of business cards.

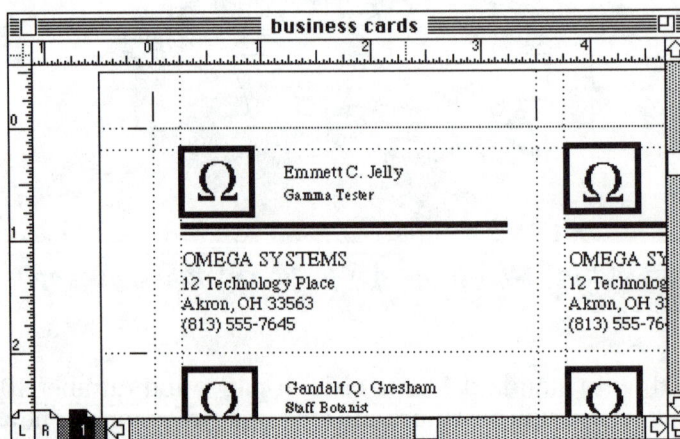

Figure 10.12 The thin black lines at the margins of the cards show the printer where to cut.

If you're having something else printed on heavy stock and trimmed to size, you can often sneak business cards in on the cropped area. Similarly, if you're having shipping labels printed and trimmed on crack & peel paper, place other odd size labels in the margins. Figure 10.13 shows a page of labels arranged to get maximum value from a single sheet of paper.

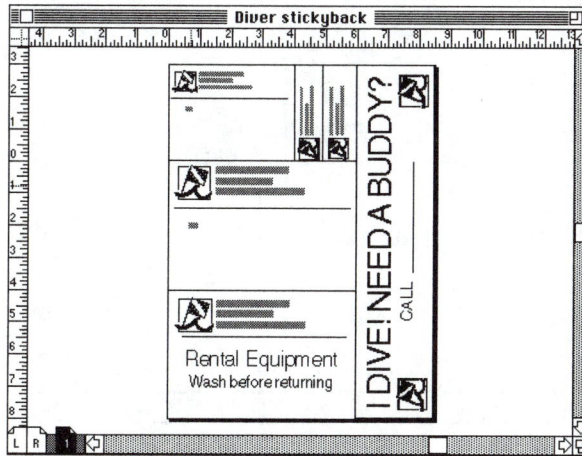

Figure 10.13 Five cuts give you six different kinds of labels.

269

Catalogs

Catalogs are one of the more complicated jobs a layout artist ever has to handle. PageMaker can make producing a catalog a good deal easier, and you can save additional time and effort by standardizing your layout. A catalog is a multipage publication, and since most of the pages can be identical in terms of layout and design, creating a master page layout is the best way to proceed. Think also about how the catalog will be printed and bound, and how many pages you'll need to produce. As always, make a dummy before you proceed.

Usually the outer covers of a catalog are printed on a heavier weight paper or even card stock. They generally contain the name of the company and a logo, or other illustration. The covers may, but not necessarily, include pictures and descriptions of merchandise. You may decide to make the catalog a self-mailer by leaving an area for an address label and mailing indicia.

Will there be an order form bound in? If so, it may be wise to let this fall on the center pages of the catalog. This way it's possible to remove it without tearing the whole catalog apart. Setup the catalog pages with a grid, perhaps mirroring left to right, as shown in Figure 10.14.

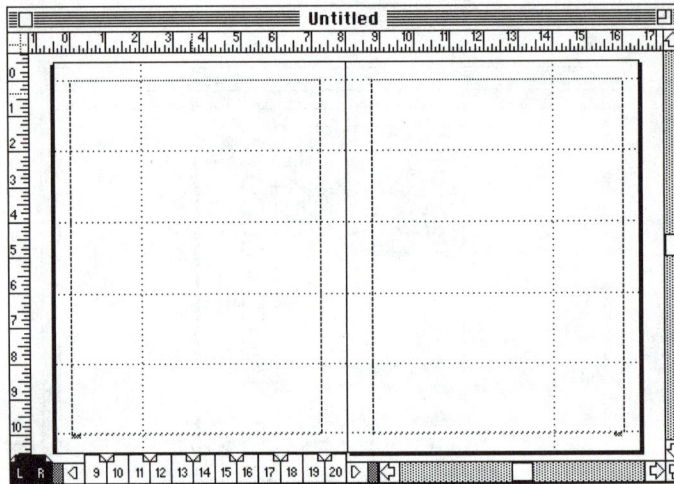

Figure 10.14 A grid for catalog pages.

For catalog work you'll need access to a scanner of some kind. To maintain a more consistent look, decide on a single type of illustration, such as line drawings, photos screened as halftones, and so on. If you're using pictures from the manufacturer's catalog sheets, trim away extraneous backgrounds and try to scale all the illustrations to the same relative size. Use the same typefaces and sizes throughout. If you keep graphics and text linked to the publication, the inevitable last minute updates will be easier to manage. Figure 10.15 shows an example of a catalog entry.

Most catalogs include an index to help users find specific items more easily. PageMaker can produce the index for you. All you need to do is highlight words to be indexed, and the list will be automatically assembled with appropriate page numbers. Chapter 12 explains, in detail, how to make index entries and assemble the index.

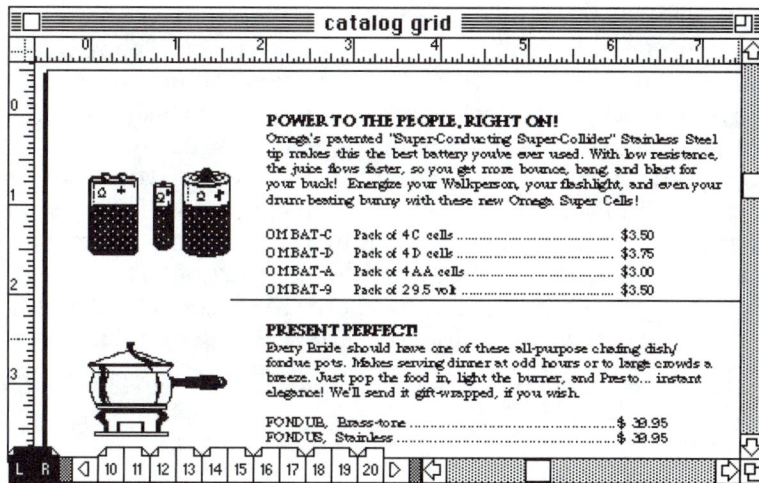

Figure 10.15 A typical catalog entry.

271

Sales Reports and Annual Reports

Large corporations often spend many thousands of dollars to produce their annual reports. These documents, sent to stockholders and potential investors, detail how well the company is doing, usually with the aid of charts, graphs, balance sheets, long blocks of copy, and lavish illustrations. Many reports include letters from the Chairman of the board or CEO. These reports generally have two things in common: they look expensive and they were (mostly) produced in PageMaker. Even if you're working on a shoestring budget, your presentation can be thoroughly professional.

Table Editor

When you must deal with numbers, tables, and graphs, PageMaker has the tools it takes. Table Editor, a separate program included with PageMaker, makes it easy to set up a good-looking chart, table, or spreadsheet. Table Editor is designed to have many of the same commands and features as PageMaker itself. You'll find it easy to learn now that you know your way around PageMaker's menus and functions.

Table Editor organizes information in rows and columns. You can easily reformat a whole table, a single cell, or a block of data, within the table. You can add shading behind the data, and define blocks with your choice of line styles and weights. Blocks are easy to resize and you can insert new blocks or delete existing ones as often as you need to. You have control over the text formatting, just as you would in a word processor or in PageMaker itself. You can export to other programs as well as to PageMaker, and you can import data from any program that saves documents as tab or comma defined text-only files. Programs with this capability include HyperCard, Microsoft Word and Excel, MacWrite II, WriteNow, Ashton-Tate's dBASE, and a great many others.

To create a table in Table Editor, use the following Quick Steps.

Q **Creating a Table**

1. Open the application Table Editor from the desktop.	If you're using Multifinder, you needn't quit PageMaker. Otherwise, you must.
2. Press ⌘+N for a new table.	The Table setup box, shown in Figure 10.16, appears.
3. Enter the desired table dimensions and number of columns and rows.	Columns are vertical and rows are horizontal.
4. Enter a distance for the gutter.	The gutter refers to the horizontal and vertical space between individual cells in the table. □

Figure 10.16 Table Editor's setup box.

If you know exactly what your settings should be, go ahead and enter them. If not, it's all right to guess. You can always come back to this box and change your settings at any time by choosing **Table setup** from the **File** menu. You can also drag the columns or rows to resize them, and add new ones if you find you need them. If you have an exact space to fill in your PageMaker document:

1. Draw a box the right size using PageMaker's Square corner rectangle tool.
2. Copy it to the clipboard.
3. Open the Table Editor. The exact dimensions will appear in the Table size fields.
4. Enter the number of columns and rows and click on OK or press Return.

Now you have a grid, as shown in Figure 10.17, with the number of columns and rows you've specified, and you can proceed to create your table. You'll notice that Table Editor has only two tools, the Text tool and the pointer. Lines and screens are added from the Menu bar. Select an individual cell by clicking within it. Select a row or column by clicking at the top or side margin. You can drag to change the size of columns or rows. To preserve the proportions, press Option as you drag a boundary.

273

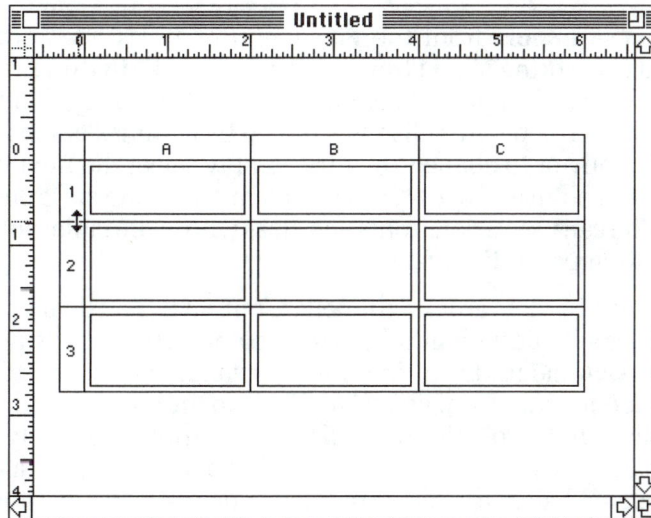

Figure 10.17 The Table Editor Grid.

> ▶ **Tip:** To select the whole table, click on the small square at the upper left corner of the grid at the intersection of the row and column labels.

Before you enter text, choose **Define flow**, from the **Edit** menu. The Define flow dialog box, shown in Figure 10.18, appears. Depending on how your text is setup, choose the appropriate flow to fill the cells by rows or columns.

274

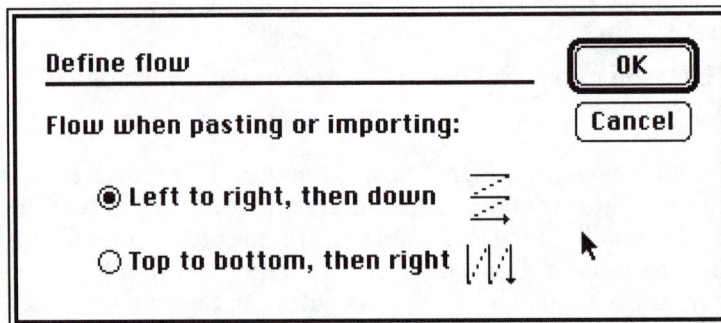

Figure 10.18. The icons in the Define flow box are self-explanatory.

Choose **Import** from the **File** menu or press ⌘+D (just as in PageMaker) to bring in text from other programs. Anything you import needs to be *tab-delimited* or *comma-delimited,* meaning that the information to go in separate cells is separated by commas or tabs. To enter data manually or to change an entry, simply select the Text tool, click an insertion point and start typing. Set font styles and sizes on the **Type** menu. You can use various fonts and sizes within the table, but only one combination per individual cell.

Placing borders around the cells is optional. You do it by selecting the table or any individual cell, row, or column, and choosing **Borders** from the **Cell** menu. Each line of the rectangle around a cell may be defined independently, if you wish. Click on the boxes to add lines, and select a line width from the menu. If you leave the boxes empty, the table won't have lines defining the cells. If you're setting up a financial statement or balance sheet, you may not want to use lines at all. Figure 10.19 shows two different types of tables that were created in Table Editor.

Hand	Number of combinations	Odds - # of hands played
Royal flush	4	1 in 649,740
Straight flush	36	1 in 72,193
Four of a kind	624	1 in 4,165
Full house	3,744	1 in 694
Flush	5,108	
Straight	10,200	
Three of kind	54,912	
Two pairs	123,552	
One pair	1,098,240	

Lucy's Lemonade   May, 1990

	Actual Income	Percent of totals
Current Assets -		
Cash on hand	$ 43.75	68
Inventory - cups, sugar	12.50	19.5
Fixed Assets - Pitchers, ladle, signs, etc. Current Assets -	8.00	12.5
Total Assets	$ 64.25	100 %

Figure 10.19 A chart and a simple balance sheet.

275

Hide the grid labels and grid lines, if you wish, to see what your table actually looks like. To hide labels and lines:

1. Press ⌘+8 to toggle grid labels on and off.
2. Press ⌘+9 to toggle grid lines.

Or,

▶ Select either or both from the **Options** menu.

You can set a title for your table when you import it into Page-Maker, or you can place one right on the table in Table Editor. To place a title across the top of your table, use the following Quick Steps.

Q Placing a Title Across the Top of a Table

1. Select a cell in the top row. Select **Insert** from the **Cell** menu or press ⌘+I.

   Add a new row of cells at the top of the table. The rows will shift down to make room.

2. Select the new row. Choose **Group** from the **Cell** menu or press ⌘+G.

   This will join the cells in this row so you can fit a long title or center a shorter one, over the table.

3. Select the Text tool and type the title into the block.

   □

Exporting Tables to PageMaker

After your table is completed, what do you do with it? You've been saving the table as you worked on it, of course, but you've been saving it to the Table Editor. In order to export it, you'll have to use the **Export** command from Table Editor's **File** menu. The dialog box, shown in Figure 10.20, appears. You can export the table as a text file, with tabs, or as a PICT image.

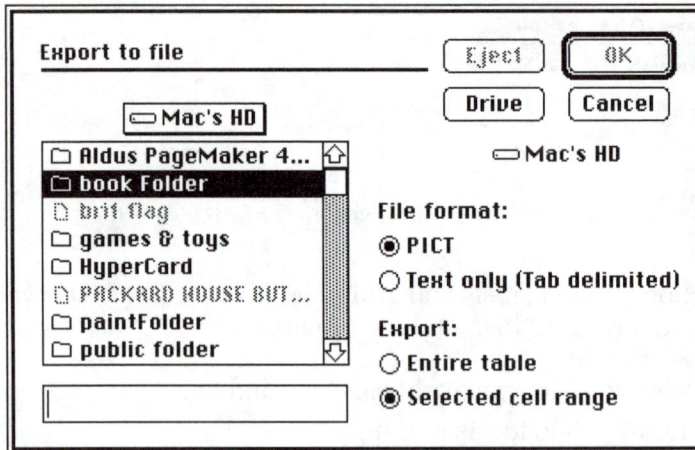

Figure 10.20 Table Editor's Export dialog box.

If you've spent time formatting the table, you'll want to bring it into PageMaker as a PICT. You can modify it within PageMaker as you would any other graphic. It can be cropped, resized, even colored. But, and this is important, you can't edit the text within the graphic. If you need to check spelling or to make changes in the PICT version of the table, you have to go back to the original table, make the changes there, and then update the export file, by exporting it again under the same name. Then when you reopen PageMaker, you'll be asked it you want to update or the graphic will be updated automatically, if you've selected Automatic update from PageMaker's Link options dialog box. PageMaker can't link to the original table, only to the export file.

> ▶ **Tip:** If links aren't important you can save time by copying the table onto the clipboard, and pasting it into PageMaker directly from the clipboard. The pasted table will look identical to the original.

If you've been using Table Editor just to organize information from a database or spreadsheet program, you might choose to bring it in as a text file. In this case, the tables, lines, shades, and text attributes are not imported. Text will be tab-delimited, meaning that columns will be separated by tabs, and rows by carriage returns. You may have to reset PageMaker's tabs to make your data line up the way it should.

You can add text files as part of an existing story, replacing an existing story, or as a new story. You can add a graphics file as an independent graphic, as an inline graphic, or replacing an existing graphic. PageMaker's Inline graphics feature lets you bring in a table and keep it with its associated text.

Directories and Address Lists

Because Table Editor can import data from databases and arrange it neatly in columns, it's a useful tool if you're creating something like a company phone directory. Figure 10.21 shows a sample page from a directory.

Omega Corp. Employees Internal Phone System, 7/91		
Anderson, Irene	Marketing	9096
Atkins, Tom	Product Dev.	6985
Atwell, Andy	Chemist	6676
Boggs, Bethany	Reception	5000
Byron, Jeffrey	Advertising	5106
Curry, Carolann	Chemist	6678
Desai, Mohandas	Research	6694
Des Ardins, Louis	Accounting	7701
Despian, Jerome	Botanist	8843
Dillys, Gwyneth	V.P.	5100
Dominici, Paola	Advertising	5107
Esterhazy, Ralph	C.E.O.	5050
Fong, How	Prod. Mgt.	8823
Ford, Fred	Transport	5902

Figure 10.21 Use Table Editor to create phone lists and other documents with columnar formats.

The data for the phone book was imported from the employee database, in HyperCard, into Table Editor. The original file included several other data fields which were inappropriate for this listing. Extraneous information was removed by deleting the columns which weren't needed, as shown in Figure 10.22.

	A	B	C	D
1	Anderson, Irene	Marketing	9096	45 Islington Rd., Aub.
2	Atkins, Tom	Product Dev.	6985	396 Glen Rd., Wes.
3	Atwell, Andy	Chemist	6676	7 Bryant Rd., Bou.
4	Boggs, Bethany	Reception	5000	253 Pheasant Ave., Aub.
5	Buskirk, Leon	Research	6693	74 Brainerd Rd., Wes
6	Byron, Jeffrey	Advertising	5106	132 Mason Terr., Bro

Figure 10.22 Delete by the row or column to remove unwanted data.

What You've Learned

In this chapter you learned how to create business forms and reports in PageMaker. You learned how to work with PageMaker's Table Editor and templates. Specifically you learned:

► How to use and customize PageMaker's predesigned templates.
► How to design a custom form, and several ways to create evenly spaced ruled lines.
► How to design letterheads, and other business and social stationery.
► How to set up pages of business cards and labels to save money on printing.
► How to design catalogs and how to set up a grid for type and graphics, to make catalog pages more uniform.
► How to work with Table Editor, how to create tables, and how to import data into them.
► How to export completed tables into PageMaker as text files or as PICT graphics, and the pros and cons of each.

Chapter 11

Other Kinds of Pages

In This Chapter

▶ *Ads "R" You*
▶ *Handbills, Flyers, and Self-mailers*
▶ *Overhead Transparencies*
▶ *Greeting Cards*
▶ *Awards and Diplomas*
▶ *Calendars*
▶ *Using Label Templates*

So far you've seen PageMaker's capabilities as a tool for newsletter production, and for designing business forms, stationery, and catalogs. However, there are lots of other kinds of pages you may have to deal with. Whatever you need to design, PageMaker can help.

Advertising for the Rest of Us

"It pays to advertise." If you've heard that once, you've probably heard it a million times, or at least a dozen or so. Sure, it pays. The advertising industry is a multibillion dollar business. Interestingly, a great many advertising agencies, as well as newspaper and magazine publishers, have turned to PageMaker. Being able to produce beautifully set type and accurate paste ups right in the computer has meant tremendous savings in both time and money. Even if you're not quite ready to be the ad agency for InterGalactic MultiFoods or Reeverse sneakers, with PageMaker and a flair for copy and design, you'll be able to put together your own ads a little more effectively and a lot easier.

The very first newspaper ad appeared in the *London Weekly Newes* in 1622, and called for the return of a stolen horse. A few years later print advertising was firmly established. In 1661, Robert Turner's *Dentifrice*, complete with trademarks, started the trend for display advertisements. A display ad, by definition, is anything that's not a classified ad. It can be as little as an inch high by a column wide, or can be a whole page, or even a double-page spread. Ads are frequently defined as a quarter page, a half page, an eighth, and so on. Obviously, you have to know the size of the page in order to set the ad up correctly. You should find the actual dimensions of the page on the publication's rate card, along with prices and other important details, such as deadlines and format specifications.

280

Typically, an ad contains the following elements:

▶ A headline—something to grab your attention.
▶ A picture—usually, but not necessarily, of the product.
▶ Some text or copy, describing the product, service, and so on.
▶ Who makes it, where to buy it, or who paid for the ad.

It doesn't matter whether you're selling shoes or insurance, soap or politicians, the basics are the same. One of the great advertising gurus has pointed out that the only effective ads are the ones that you remember when you're reaching for the product. (Well, you might not reach for the Congressman, but you'd reach for the lever under his name, or the square on the ballot next to it.) In order to have this effect, the advertisement has to: first, get noticed, and second, evoke a response. PageMaker can help you design ads that get noticed. PageMaker's flexibility lets you experiment with different placements for copy and art, and you can edit and recompose copy until each word is perfect. The response comes from the reader, who makes a mental connection with the words and/or image. Many people, when they reach for a can of soup on the grocer's shelf, subconsciously hear, "Mmm good," and pick up the one with the red and white label.

The basics of layout and design that you've already learned for newsletters and other publications apply to ads too. Remember to:

► Avoid clutter.
► Keep headlines readable.
► Follow the principles of eye-leading.
► Proof read carefully before you print!

Laying Out an Ad

One of the first things to consider in designing an ad is where it will be placed. If it's a newspaper or magazine ad, will it have a page to itself, or will it compete for the reader's eye with other ads and stories? If your ad occupies only part of the page, what else is likely to be on that page? Figure 11.1 shows a fairly typical magazine format. Each of these pages combines text and advertising, the latter in a single column. If you were to design an ad for this publication, you'd need to make it different from everything else on the page to get noticed.

281

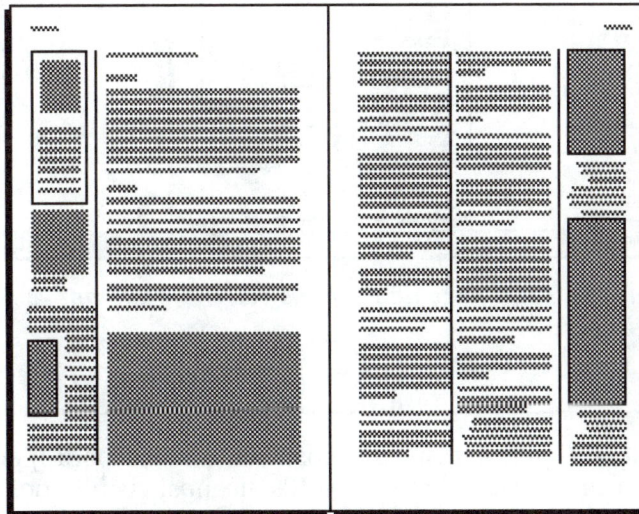

Figure 11.1 A small ad could get lost in here.

It's probably safe to say that every possible layout has already been used many times over. But, once you come up with a design that seems to work, your choice of copy and illustration can make it unique. Of course, no one formula works for every product, every time. You do need to experiment. When you design an ad in PageMaker, start with the dimensions of the page it's going on, to help you visualize your ad against the rest of the page. You may not be able to specify position, where the ad is placed on the page. However, if you know what publication the ad is going to, you can probably make an educated guess as to where it will land. For instance, if you're buying a one column ad in the *New Yorker,* it's a pretty good bet that it will be on the outside of the page, and that the rest of the page will be two columns of justified type, approximately 11 points high. Cartoons and ads never appear on the same page. Set up a page dummy with greeking so you can see the impact of the ad against the surrounding material, as shown in Figure 11.2.

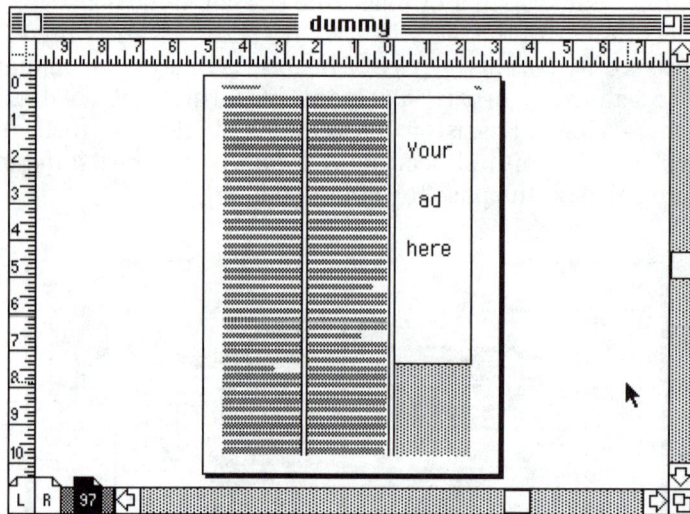

Figure 11.2 The page dummy lets you see what you've got to work with.

> ▶ **Note:** If you can specify position, ask for the upper right corner of a right-hand page. It's the most visible spot on the page, and will catch the eye of those who just flip through the magazine.

To create a page dummy, use the following Quick Steps.

Q Creating a Dummy

1. Start a new publication with the correct dimensions for the page the ad will go on.	Measure to be sure. Verify the number of columns and gutter width too.
2. Set the number of columns and pour text into them.	Use the Lorem Ipsum file from PageMaker's templates folder, or any other text files you have handy.
3. Measure and define the boundary for your ad.	If there are other ads on the same page, put them in as 20% gray boxes. □

Now you can see what space you have to fill, and how it will relate to the rest of the items on that page. When you're dealing with small space, don't try to say too much. In copywriting, the one rule is to use as few words as possible. A tiny image in a sea of white space gained attention for a certain auto maker a few years back. The accompanying headline simply urged car buyers to "Think Small." The campaign won dozens of awards and sold a lot of cars too.

283

Sometimes you can be most effective by breaking the rules. In the example in Figure 11.3, we've broken at least a half-dozen different rules: too many typefaces, too many words, no picture, it's crowded, and so on. But the ad still works because each rule was broken for a good reason. The type is the illustration, so no picture is needed. All those different faces represent different voices, and it's not afraid to laugh at itself. (This ad was designed to go into one of those yearbooks in which most of the pages just say "compliments of" or "greetings from".)

What kind of ad you design is going to depend on what you're selling. Obviously, an ad for a product like stereo speakers or mayonnaise isn't going to look like an ad for a bank or a hotel. Identify the most important point about your product or service. Make that point your headline. Follow with subheads and copy that explain and support the headline.

Find out from the publication what format they want the ad delivered in. Most will ask for it camera-ready. If you've done all the work in PageMaker, just give them a good quality print of the ad, same size. Some publications are now requesting film negatives. Your service bureau can prepare film negatives from your PageMaker files.

"You've lost weight!"*

"Nice shoes, fella."*

"I wish I'd thought of that." *

I like what you've done with this room. *

"Delicious dinner!" *

"New dress?"*

"WOW! You're totally awesome!"*

"Your hair looks great."*

You play a wicked game of tennis! *

*(Compliments of a Friend)

Jay Roz's Atic Studio
20 Mission Street
Brookline, Mass 02146
(617) 277-0041
fax (232-8861)

284

Figure 11.3 Humor helps.

Other Kinds of Ads

Of course, newspapers and magazines aren't the only way to advertise. You may need to put together a brochure or flyer. The easiest, and least costly of these is a *three-fold,* a single page flyer printed on two sides and folded in thirds. Such flyers are known variously as self-mailers, hand-outs, or stuffers, depending on how they're distributed. A stuffer goes in an envelope with other items. Banks often include stuffers with your monthly statement. Handouts are stacked on the counter or placed in displays. Self-mailers, like the newsletters and catalogs previously discussed, have a place for an address label and stamp, and can be sent without an envelope. Figure 11.4 shows a dummy for a typical three-fold.

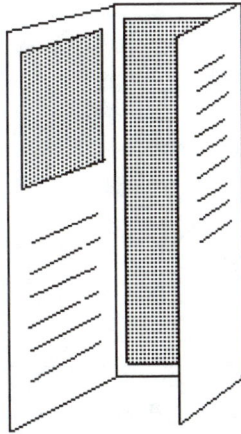

Figure 11.4 This could be a self-mailer, stuffer, or hand-out.

To set up one of these, use the following steps:

285

1. Open a new PageMaker publication.
2. In the Page setup box, choose the **Wide orientation** and click on **Double-sided**, but not Facing pages, as shown in Figure 11.5.
3. Divide the page into three columns.
4. Select **Hairline** from the **Line width** menu, and draw a vertical line from the top of the inside page extending down about an inch, at 3.66 inches and 7.33 inches across, dividing the page in thirds. Place the lines in the gutter between the columns, as in Figure 11.6. They will serve as a guide for folding, but since they'll be right on the fold no one will notice them.

Figure 11.5 Setting up a three-fold.

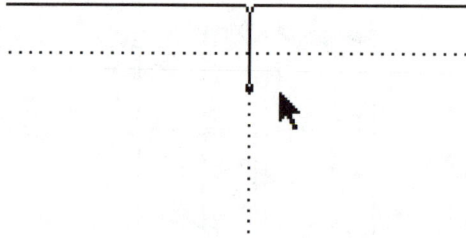

Figure 11.6 Fold on the line.

▶ **Tip:** If you're using heavy paper or light card stock to print your brochure, place your text blocks, gutters, and fold guides in a way that makes the left side just slightly wider, to compensate for the thickness of the paper when it's folded.

286

Post it?

Posters are yet another form of advertising, and one of the oldest of all. Posters for circuses and gladiator matches were found in the ruins of Pompeii, and were known to have decorated walls in Rome and Carthage well over 2000 years ago. Posters can be an inexpensive and very effective advertising medium, especially for nonbusiness ads. When you have to put together a poster, PageMaker is ready to help.

The least expensive way to make up a poster is to design it in PageMaker and have the master photocopied onto whatever stock is most appropriate. Look for bright colors, particularly if the poster is the kind that gets stapled to telephone poles or stuck on the laundromat bulletin board. Both of the posters in Figure 11.7 were low budget ads that got fast results.

▶ **Tip:** If you're a pet owner, as we are, keep scanned photos of your animals on your hard disk. Posters like the one in Figure 11.7 can be put together in a matter of minutes, alerting the neighborhood and safely returning Rover before he gets in trouble.

Figure 11.7 Low budget advertising media.

Being Your Own Advertising Agency

It's true. PageMaker makes it possible for you to produce your own newspaper and magazine ads, brochures, flyers, and other advertising pieces so you can, literally, be your own ad agency. Should you be? That's another question and one that bears some thinking.

Just as owning your own home video camera doesn't turn you into Steven Spielberg or George Lucas, having the tools to lay out an ad doesn't mean you're instantly ready to go head-to-head against the biggest names on Madison Avenue. Ad agencies know a lot more than this book, or any single book, can teach you. They have teams of experts who do everything from redesigning your corporate image to figuring out who your customers are by age, income, sex, what newspaper or magazine they read, and what radio or TV station they tune to. An advertising agency can make sure you get full value from every dollar you spend.

On the other hand, your Mac and PageMaker can turn out professional-quality work. The choice, really, is yours. If you want the know how and years of experience that an advertising agency brings to your business, hire one. The background you've gained from using

PageMaker yourself makes you a better informed client and gives you an advantage in the agency-client relationship. If you feel comfortable doing your own ads, or if there's no money in the budget to hire an expert, you have the tools to do a fine job. Apply the skills you've learned and have fun!

Overhead Transparencies

Not really in the realm of advertising, but incredibly useful in a business presentation, the classroom, or when speaking to any kind of a group about a topic, producing *overhead transparencies* gives you another opportunity to put PageMaker to work. Overhead transparencies are sheets of transparent, clear, or colored film, which can be run through a laser printer. When placed on an overhead projector, like the one shown in Figure 11.8, they give a large, very legible image. Light shines through the glass plate on which the transparency is placed. It then passes through a lens, onto an angled mirror, and bounces forward onto the screen.

288

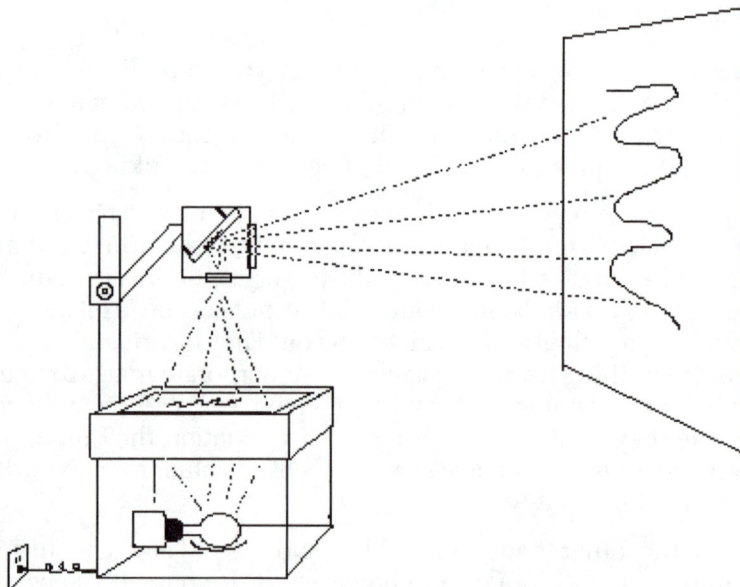

Figure 11.8 The projector is usually placed at an angle to raise the image higher on the wall over the speaker's head.

One advantage to this type of projector is that, unlike a 35mm slide show which needs darkness or a very elaborate projection system, overhead transparencies can be viewed with the room lights on. Another is that the transparency reads correctly for both the speaker and the viewer. The lecturer can draw on the transparency with grease pencil or marker as he or she speaks, and elaborate, multilayered graphs and charts can be prepared with a little bit of Scotch tape.

To create overhead transparencies you need a laser printer and one or more packages of transparency film. 3M is the popular brand. Look for 3M type PP 2950 for best results. The film comes in clear and assorted colors. If you find a different brand of transparency film, don't buy it unless it says "for use in high-temperature plain paper copiers." The operant words here are *high-temperature*. If you get the wrong kind of film, it could melt inside your laser printer, turning the printer into a very expensive paper weight. Don't even think of trying to copy on other kinds of acetate, plastic report covers, or anything other than high temperature transparency film! It will ruin your printer.

Although they're not mandatory, a package of cardboard transparency frames is helpful. Just stick the sheets of printed film into them. They'll help prevent damage to the transparencies from wrinkling and scratching. The frames also provide a convenient place to number your transparencies. Even if you're planning to use frames, you can save yourself a good deal of trouble by numbering each page. Create the whole batch of transparencies in PageMaker, and place them in the correct order as one long publication. Place a page number marker near the edge of the master page, and let PM handle the numbering for you.

289

When you're using PageMaker to lay out overhead transparencies, here are a few things to think about:

▶ Projection screens are usually horizontal. Design your pages so they'll fit the horizontal format.

▶ Overhead projectors may not have the best quality lenses. Anything near the edge of the screen could distort. Plan to put important headlines, charts, and illustrations in the middle of the screen where the image is sharpest.

▶ Creating your transparencies in PageMaker lets you use high quality TIFF and EPS images, including screened photographs and elaborate line art. Illustrations can perk up your presentation too. Use them generously.

▶ You can use PageMaker's Print Thumbnails feature to print out a numbered reference copy of the visuals. Keep one with the speaker's notes.

▶ You might even have the thumbnails photocopied as a handout for the audience. Experiment with different numbers of thumbnail pages per page, until you find a combination that's legible and efficient.

Creating a Transparency

To set up a transparency, use the following procedure:

1. Open PageMaker and start a new publication, specifying the Wide page orientation. Do not choose Double-Sided or Facing Pages from the options available since you'll be working with one page at a time.

2. The projected area of a transparency is 8 x 9³/₄ inches. Set your margins to .25 inch at the top and bottom of the page, and .625 inch at the sides. This will give you the correct frame size, centered on the page. Click on OK or press Return to see the page.

3. Open the master page. Place a page number just outside the margin, as shown in Figure 11.9. To place a page number marker, create a text block and press ⌘+Option+P. Add the company logo or anything else that will be repeated on every transparency, as an element on the master page. Save your work, and then go to the first page and start creating your presentation.

In Figure 11.9 you'll notice that we've drawn a rounded corner box as a border for our transparencies. This shape echoes the cutout area of the cardboard transparency frames and is a nice-looking way to define the screen area.

Use legible type sizes for projection. Anything between 18 and 90 points may be acceptable, depending on the font. Look for medium weight type in larger sizes and bold in smaller sizes. Big, heavy type can be hard to read when projected. Figure 11.10 shows an overhead transparency set up as a type test. As you can see, different faces have different degrees of readability at 48 points. Using bold face at smaller sizes is recommended. Be sure to kern headlines as needed and to space the lines of type so they'll look good on-screen. If your page has only one or two words on it, place them about a third of the page down, not exactly in the middle. Transparencies, by the way, are one of the places where you can use the Mac's outline and shadow type styles. They project quite nicely, although they're hard to read on the printed page.

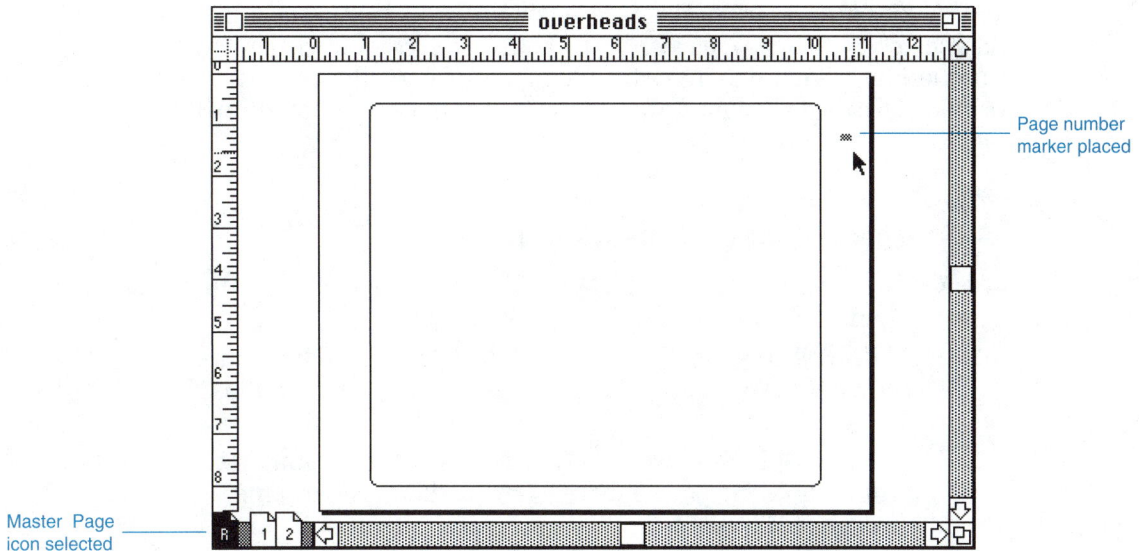

Figure 11.9 The master page for a presentation created on overhead transparencies.

291

Figure 11.10 If you're not sure how well type will project, make a type test sheet and experiment.

If you set up a series of transparencies in numbered order, and then decide to switch two pages, you needn't worry about messed up numbering or having to make the changes by hand after the sheets are printed. Use the following Quick Steps to exchange the contents of two pages.

Q Exchanging the Contents of Two Pages

1. Go to the first of the pages to be changed and press ⌘+A

   This will select everything on the page.

2. Hold down Shift while selecting **Fit in Window** from the **Page** menu.

   This lets you see the entire pasteboard. Think of it as "Fit in World".

3. Hold down Shift and drag the contents of the page onto the pasteboard to the left.

   Holding Shift as you drag keeps them in the same vertical alignment.

4. Go to the second page to be changed. Repeat the above process, dragging the page contents to the right of the pasteboard.

5. Hold Shift and drag the contents of the first page from the left pasteboard onto the new page. Figure 11.11 illustrates this process.

   Be sure to select all the elements. Using the pointer to draw a selection box around them is the easiest way. Press the mouse button and drag until the box surrounds all the items that belong on the page.

6. Align the type between the margins.

   If you kept Shift down as you dragged the page contents, vertical alignment should be no problem.

7. Repeat the procedure above to drag the contents of the second page onto the first.

□

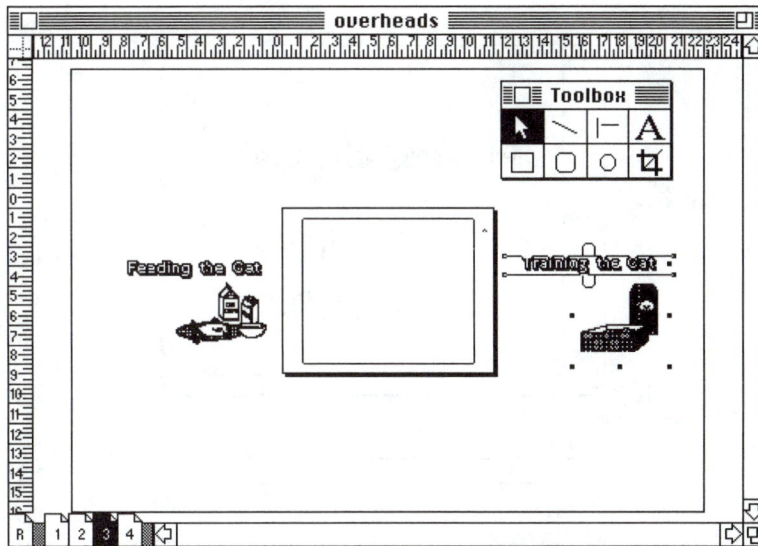

Figure 11.11 Swapping pages.

293

Multilayered Transparencies

You can achieve a sort of animated effect by starting with a headline and adding subheads below it, or bringing in the various elements of a graph or diagram one at a time. You could of course, simply recreate the headline on each page and add first one subhead on the second, and two on the third. An easier way is to place only one add-on on each page, and attach them to the main page with cellophane tape hinges, so you can flop these overlays on top of the first page as you need them. You can build up to three layers of overlay on a single page. More than four thicknesses of transparency causes problems, however. Even though the material looks clear, it absorbs some light. By the time you've added the fourth layer, the image is getting dimmer and harder to see. Figure 11.12 shows a sequence of overlays on a main page. In the first view the overlays have been flopped back. The speaker introduces the topic, then adds the left overlay and explains the subtopic. Then the right overlay is added to bring in the next subtopic, as indicated in the second view. If desired, a third overlay could be added at the bottom of the frame.

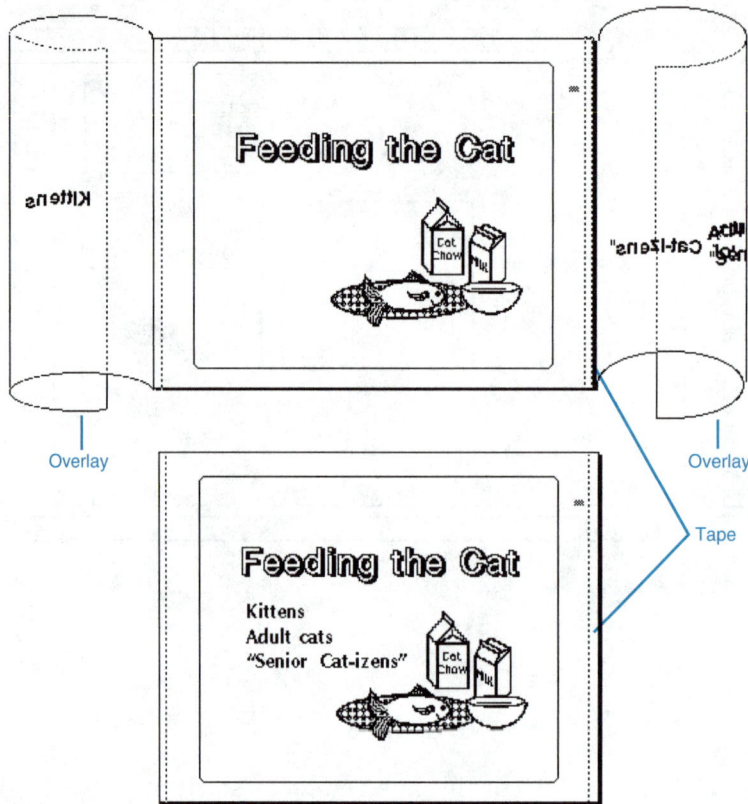

Figure 11.12 The overlays are taped to the cardboard frame.

294

> ⊘ **Warning:** Use overlay sheets full size, even if there's just a small amount of printing on them. Cut edges will show as jagged black lines on the screen.

To separate the layers of a multilayer transparency like the one in Figure 11.12, use the following Quick Steps.

Q **Multilayer Transparencies**

1. Create the page as a unit with all the layers in position.

2. Select the items to be on the overlay.

Or, on the first overlay, if there are two or three.

3. Select a color other than black from the Color palette and apply it to the overlay items, as shown in Figure 11.13

Any color will do.

4. If there's a second overlay, select the items to go on it, and apply a different color.

5. When you print, select **Spot color overlays** from the **Print options** dialog box.

PageMaker will prepare the overlays for you, exactly as if they were color separations (which is what it thinks they are).

6. Insert the main page in the frame and place the overlays on it. Tape them in place.

Tape only one side of the overlay to the frame so you can fold it back for the first step of the presentation. ☐

295

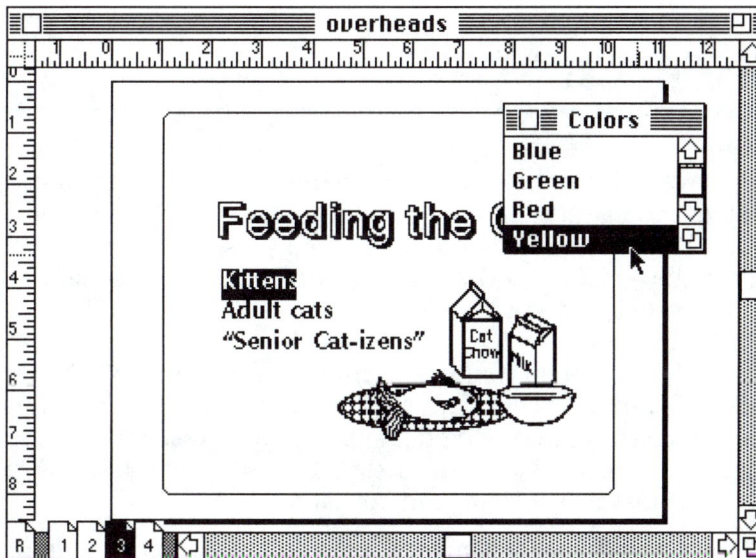

Figure 11.13 By designating the type as a spot color, you will get a separate page with just the selected words, perfect for an overlay.

> ▶ **Tip:** If the transparencies are handled a great deal or rolled up, you may have a problem with little bits of toner flaking off or smearing, especially on fine lines in a graphic. To overcome this, buy a can of artist's matte-finish spray fixative. It's the same stuff used to preserve charcoal, pastel, and pencil drawings. Spray the transparencies lightly with fixative as soon as they're printed. Too much spray will leave streaks on the toner.

You can add color to the presentation by using colored transparencies, by hand coloring them with marker (use special transparency markers for this), or by applying colored overlay sheets. These are slightly sticky sheets of evenly colored film, which are also available at your local art supply store. Letraset is one of several brands of transparent overlays. They come in a full range of Pantone PMS colors. You can colorize areas on the screen to preview the effect and then print out the transparency with black outlines on your laser printer, and add areas of the same color you applied on-screen.

296

Greeting Cards

If you have a clip art collection, or the time and patience to draw your own pictures in a graphics program, PageMaker can help you produce beautiful greeting cards. You might even personalize them with the name of the recipient as well as your own name. The simplest kind of card to create is called a *french fold*. Use a regular $8^1/_2$ x 11-inch page, but print the card on a fairly heavy weight stock. A 70-pound weight paper will run through your laser printer quite well and will fold easily, but is stiff enough to stand up so your card can be displayed. Look for paper before you plan your card design. Often the color of the paper will suggest a theme for the art. Your stationery store will have $4^3/_8$ x $5^3/_4$ inch envelopes in which to mail the cards.

Set up the page for a greeting card by following these steps:

1. Open a new publication. Set up a single letter-size page either tall or wide.

2. Position ruler guides halfway across and down the page to divide it into quarters. These guides are simply for your own

convenience in laying out the page. (You won't need to add folding guide lines since this is an easy fold.)

3. Place your text and graphics in the appropriate quarter pages according to the sample in Figure 11.14. Select **Text rotation** from the **Elements** menu to turn the type upside down.

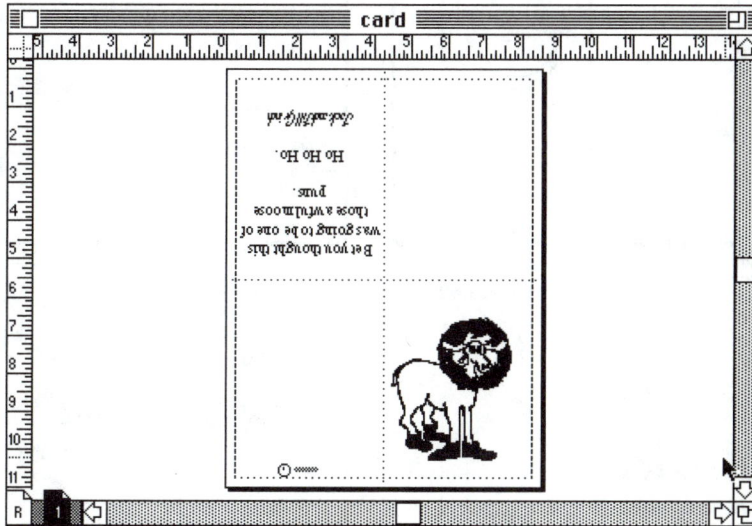

Figure 11.14 A Mac greeting card design.

You may also want to design a tall, thin, *contemporary* style card, like the ones in the rack at your local card shop. Typically these cards are about 3¹/₂ x 8 inches, and could fit in a #10 envelope. These would obviously not be folded in quarters. Instead, you'd print on both sides of a sheet of card stock and cut it down to size after printing. When you're doing this kind of a card, don't forget to add crop marks and be sure that the front and back sides of the card will line up properly. If you set the card dimensions as the margins and call for a two-sided page, Page-Maker will automatically shift the second side to align with the first. Figure 11.15 shows thumbnails of a contemporary card. Chapter 9 discusses printing for a two-sided page.

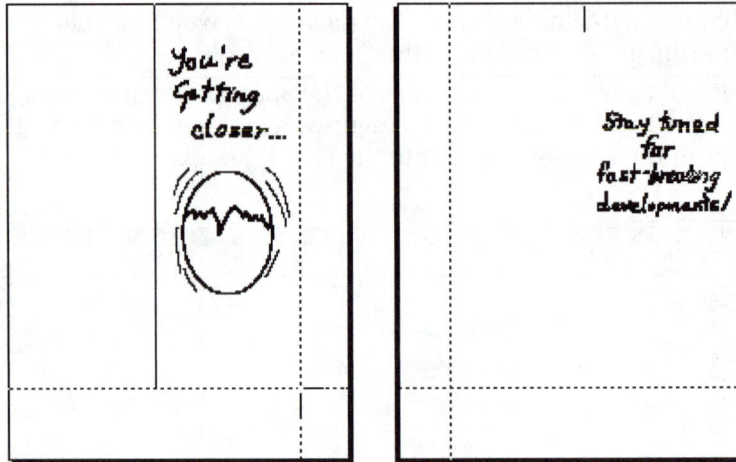

Figure 11.15 Make a card for any occasion.

298

Calendars

Customized calendars are a nice handout for businesses, a good holiday gift for the family (especially with birthdays and anniversaries noted), and a wonderful fund-raising tool for school and community groups. You can design your own calendar template and plug in the dates and data you want to include. Or, you can use PageMaker's calendar. Your PageMaker template file includes a set of calendar pages. Unfortunately, the dates currently provided run from December 1989 through January 1991, making it of somewhat limited use unless your Mac also functions as a time machine. However, there are a couple ways around this problem, if you like the general look of the calendar shown in Figure 11.16.

Of course, the first thing you have to do is to open a copy of the calendar template. Add your company logo, school name, or greeting on the master page, in place of the dummy logo Aldus pasted there. Now you need to resolve the problem of the dates. You can always put them in one number at a time. However, it takes a while.

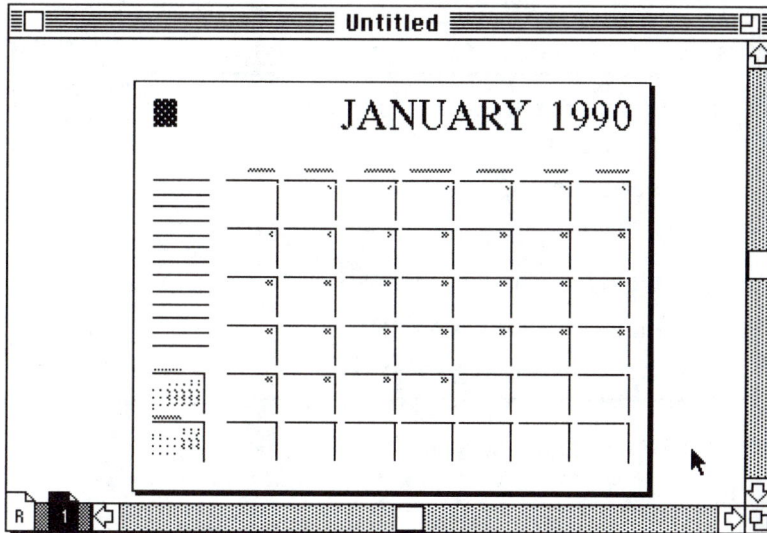

Figure 11.16 PageMaker's calendar.

299

The easiest solution to this is to pick up a copy of any good almanac, and turn to the section called perpetual calendar. Find the appropriate set of calendars for the year you're assembling and look to see what day of the week each month starts on. Now find the month in 1989 that started on the same day, and follow these steps to import the correct dates:

1. With the calendar page open, select the Text tool.

2. Click anywhere within the large dates area on the page. Press ⌘+D or select **Place** from the **File** menu.

3. Select the month you want to paste from the folder called **Calendar Dates**, and click on **Replace entire story**. Click on OK or press Return. The new dates will appear on the page, but incorrectly spaced. On top of them will be the Smart ASCII dialog box, shown in Figure 11.17. Click on OK or press Return to close it.

4. Again, use the Text tool to click anywhere within the date area and press ⌘+A to select all the dates. Apply the Dates style from the Style palette to adjust the spacing and correct the formatting.

5. Check to see what date the month ends on. Adjust the last day of the month, if necessary, so it ends on the correct day.

```
┌──────────────────────────────────────────────────────┐
│  Smart ASCII import filter, v1.2          ┌─────────┐  │
│                                           │   OK    │  │
│  Remove extra carriage returns:           └─────────┘  │
│     ☐ At end of every line                ┌─────────┐  │
│     ☐ Between paragraphs                   │ Cancel  │  │
│     ☐ But keep tables, lists and indents as is └─────┘ │
│                                                        │
│  ☐ Replace │ 3 │  or more spaces with a tab            │
│  ☐ Monospace, import as Courier                        │
│  ☒ No conversion, import as is                         │
└──────────────────────────────────────────────────────┘
```

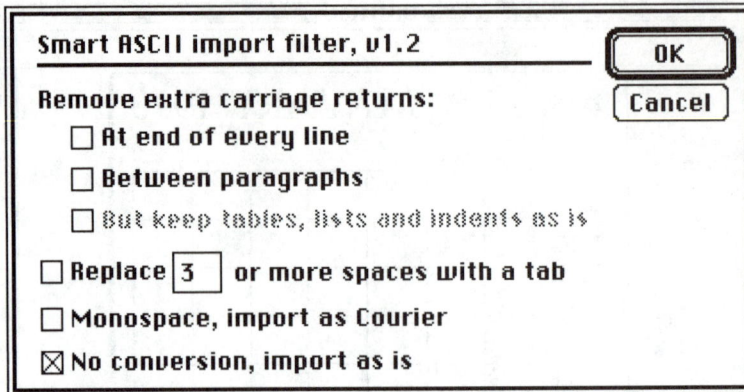

Figure 11.17 The Smart ASCII box lets you specify how Page-Maker formats the text-only files it imports from other sources.

300

Change the small date blocks in the lower left the same way. However, if you don't have a PostScript printer, you won't be able to print them properly unless your printer has a 5 point font installed. PostScript printers handle the fine print with no problems.

> ▶ **Note:** You will see the Smart ASCII dialog box above whenever you're importing a text file into PageMaker. Its options are self-explanatory. You may find, when bringing in a file originally created on a PC, that you have an extra carriage return at the end of each line. Use the options in the Smart ASCII box to strip the extra carriage returns.

If you'd rather design your own calendar, that's fine too. You might find it helpful to look at the way PageMaker's artist numbered the calendar. Open one of the calendar date pages as a text file in your word processor and use whatever command shows the tabs and spaces. In Figure 11.18, July 1990 is shown as a text file. The month began on a Sunday. The designer at Aldus started with one tab, to place the date at the right side of its block and then just placed date, tab, date, tab, and so on to the end of the first line. There they left a space after the last date on the line, then another tab, and the second row of numbers, and so on. When the dates were imported into the PageMaker calendar and the style applied, the tab spacing changed to the correct amount for the distance between two calendar numbers. There's no good reason you can't adapt these numbers to your own calendars or use the same principle to create your own text files of dates.

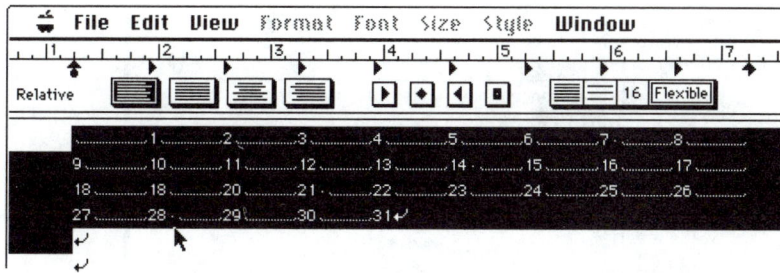

Figure 11.18 The dates are simply spaced with tabs. To align them, set appropriate tabs across the calendar page.

There are lots of calendar styles you might use. Instead of a month per page, how about a week at a glance? Figure 11.19 shows a different kind of calendar page. To create this page use several shortcuts. Rather than figuring out exactly how much space to leave between the lines, simply set the day names in a column, with two carriage returns in between each line, and adjust the position of the text block until it sits nicely on the page. Then draw the lines under each word. The date numbers are set in a different text block. Here, instead of spacing between them, I guessed at the appropriate leading and then increased it until they fell in the right spot. I borrowed a set of small calendar dates from the Calendar text files, and adjusted the type size from 5 points up to 9 points. Finally, add the gray stripes, the logo, and the month at the bottom.

301

Awards, Certificates, and Diplomas

Everybody deserves a little recognition. Maybe an "Employee of the Week" certificate isn't as rewarding as a raise, but it still goes a long way toward improving company morale. Teachers know the value of praise. Attendance awards, SuperSpeller and Math Marvel certificates are powerful motivational tools for young students. Not all awards are serious, of course. How about a "Hazardous Waste" warning on the door of a teenager's room? Or "Duffer of the Year" for the golfer who's just shanked his 1000th ball into the adjacent fairway? If you can think of a reason for an award, PageMaker can help you put together all sorts of certificates for all occasions. Figure 11.20 shows what can be done with a clip art border and a handful of type.

Monday	**10**
Advanced Open Water Class, "Y" pool, 7 pm	
Tuesday	**11**
Medic 1st Aid, 7 - 10 pm	
Wednesday	**12**
Thursday	**13**
Friday	**14**
Underwater Party, Magnolia Pt. 2-5 p.m.	**15**
Saturday	
Sunday	**16**

JUNE, 1991

Figure 11.19 A weekly calendar might have special events or class schedules included on it.

Certificates and awards are a great place to use some of the more fanciful clip art borders. Since PageMaker can't rotate graphics, you'll have better luck creating your border in a Paint program and importing it already completed. This is also the ideal spot to use the fonts you wouldn't use for more ordinary jobs. There are a number of faces that imitate hand lettering, including Zapf Chancery, included with most laser printers. The symbol set that comes with it, Zapf Dingbats, may also give you some ideas for certificate embellishments. The dingbats could even be used as a typeset border, produced quickly and easily right in PageMaker. In Figure 11.21, we've drawn some dingbat borders. The row of pencils might be used for a classroom award, the daisies and stars for more generalized applications. Use the following Quick Steps for creating dingbat borders.

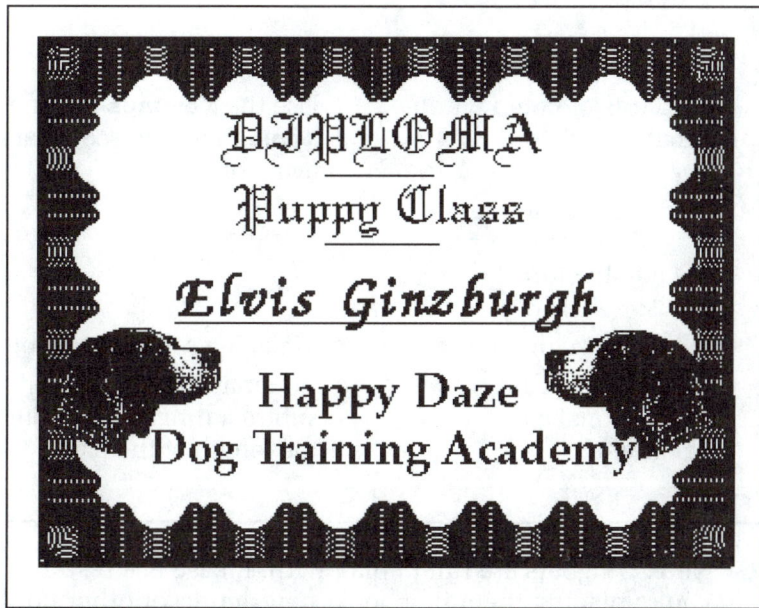

Figure 11.20 Every dog has his day, and every puppy his graduation from dog school.

Figure 11.21 Dingbats are little symbols which can be used for all sorts of purposes.

Q Creating Dingbat Borders

1. Type a row of your favorite dingbat.

    Use the **KeyCaps DA** (in the **Apple** menu) to see what's available.

2. Adjust the tracking so the row is nicely spaced and place it at the top of the page.

3. Copy it for the bottom.

    Make it a separate text block.

4. Copy it again and use text rotation to make the sides of the frame.

    You may need to add or subtract dingbats to adjust to the length of the page. ☐

304

▶ **Note:** Dingbats are fun to play with. Please use restraint if you're placing them in a book, newsletter, or other publication. Try not to use more than one or two styles per document, lest your publication look as if it's coming down with measles.

Avery Label Templates

It's not that Avery is the only label maker, or even necessarily the best label maker. But because Avery labels are available just about everywhere, Aldus has included in your template folder a set of four templates for the most commonly used sizes of Avery label. These templates will help you set up mailing lists, product labels, and all sorts of sticky little things with the greatest of ease. Your label kit includes the following:

Avery	Size
51	1 x$2^5/_8$"
5161	1 x 4"
5162	$1^1/_4$ x 4"
5163	2 x 4"

Labels come in both white paper and clear acetate. The latter is a good choice when you're doing a mailing with colored envelopes, or a self-mailer brochure or catalog. The transparent labels aren't completely invisible, but they show up a lot less than white ones against a colored background. Figure 11.22 shows a piece of the 5160 template with some of the Aldus design team's suggestions. About the only thing you may have difficulty doing within PageMaker is bringing in the mailing list to print on the stickers. I've tried everything from using the Table Editor to set names and addresses in individual cells, to copying all the data into Microsoft Word and formatting it before sending it to PageMaker. It's not worth the hassle. Use PageMaker to design custom labels which it does elegantly.

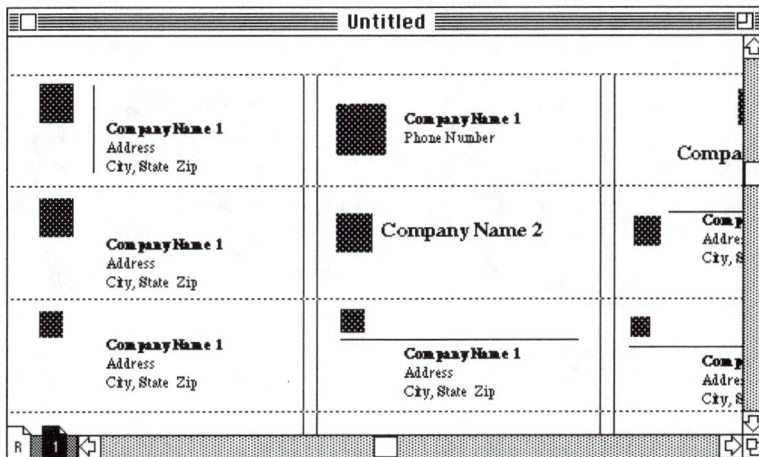

Figure 11.22 Some of the ways to use the label template.

▶ **Tip:** The best way to handle mailing lists is with Avery's MacLabelPro. For under $50, it includes templates for every kind of label Avery makes, plus a small clip art library. Most important, it has a mail merge function which lets you bring in your mailing lists and data files from Microsoft Works or Word.

Printed labels are handy for a great many tasks. For example, you can import a list of names of conference attendees or party guests, and prepare elegantly printed nametags, complete with the organization's logo or a suitably festive party design, on #5163. #5161 could also be used to label your output of homemade grape jelly, or those mysterious packages in the freezer. You could print friendly or not so friendly, reminders to stick on unpaid invoices. My son Josh, an avid cartoonist, prints sheets of transparent labels with PageMaker's various fill patterns and percent tones to use instead of the expensive, and virtually identical, shading sheets sold in the art supply store. Figure 11.23 shows a sample page and what he does with it.

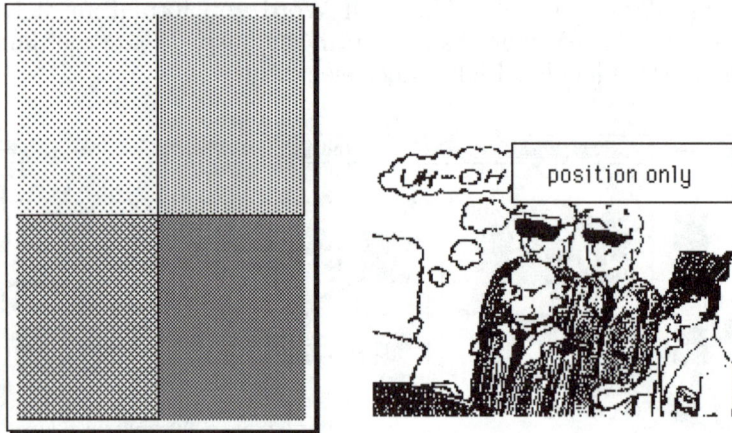

Figure 11.23 Print the tones on transparent label stock and then apply them to the drawing.

Another example of how transparent labels can be used is in the case of a dedicated electronics hacker who prints up labels with the schematics for modifications he makes to amplifiers, and other pieces of high-tech electronic gear. He then pastes one copy on the back page of the instruction book and the other inside the chassis of the equipment. Six months later, when he thinks of a new modification or when he decides to sell the stuff and upgrade his system, he's able to see what he's already done to it.

You may find templates for additional label sizes and shapes at your local computer users group, on a bulletin board, or in an online service such as CompuServe or Delphi. If you can't find a template for a particular label size, design your own. Then post it on your local user group's BBS (Bulletin Board System). If you ask for a postcard from everyone who uses it, you'll probably get mail from all over the world. There are laser-printable label pages for cassettes, videotapes, file folders, disks, and virtually anything else you can think of. Some are tricky to find. The cassette labels, for instance, are generally available only through the kind of places that sell professional audio equipment and large quantities of tapes to recording studios. Still, if you have a need for any of these less common labels, you'll probably also know where to look to find them.

Once you have the labels in hand, what should you do with them? The only limit is your own creativity. Avery even makes full-size sheets of label paper. You can use PageMaker to set up a page of bumper stickers, print them on full sheets and cut them down to size. Set the page for wide orientation and divide it into three or four stickers. A squirt of Krylon spray, available at your local art supply store, will make the bumper sticker reasonably weatherproof.

What You've Learned

307

In this chapter we looked at other uses for PageMaker. Specifically you learned about the following:

▶ How to use PageMaker to put together ads for newspapers and magazines.

▶ How to create flyers and brochures.

▶ Using PageMaker to design posters of all kinds.

▶ Advantages and disadvantages to being your own advertising agency.

▶ Creating overhead transparencies and how to make multilayer transparencies. How to use PageMaker's thumbnail printing capability to produce handouts for your presentation.

▶ Designing your own greeting cards and how to set up a french fold or a contemporary format card.

▶ How to make calendars in PageMaker using the calendar templates, or starting from scratch.

▶ Using the Avery label templates to create all kinds of labels and ideas for label uses you may not have thought of.

Longer Documents

In This Chapter

- ▶ *Book Design and Layout*
- ▶ *Managing Large Documents*
- ▶ *Creating a Table of Contents*
- ▶ *Creating an Index*

The publishing industry has become a major user of PageMaker. Books, and other long publications have similar needs. Among these are:

A consistent look—page design must remain the same page after page, chapter after chapter. Because PageMaker lets you design a master page and autoflow a whole chapter's worth of text into it in one pass, it's not only consistent, it's quick.

PageMaker can automate the previously exhausting chores of assembling an accurate table of contents and index.

PageMaker can organize the chapters and print them one at a time or as a whole book.

Planning the Book

Whether your book is a novel, instruction book, technical manual, or an annual report, you need to start thinking about designing and producing it as soon as you start to think about writing it. Creating a book length publication demands a lot of advance planning. PageMaker can assemble a book from separate chapters and this capability will save you a great deal of work. It also lets you deal with files in manageable sizes—a definite advantage, especially on a slower computer like the Mac Plus or SE.

Think of the text in sections. Call them chapters if you like or whatever division seems most appropriate. If the publication in question is a corporate report, you may be dealing with between twenty and fifty pages of material. If it's an epic novel, you may have hundreds of pages to contend with. PageMaker lets you manage up to 999 pages in one publication, and you can link publications together to maintain automatic page numbering, indexing, and printing in order for up to 9999 pages.

310

> ▶ **Note:** The longest "important" novel ever published according to the *Guinness Book of World Records*, was *Men of Good Will* by Jules Romains. Published by Peter Davies, Ltd. in 1933-46 as a 14 volume "novel cycle," the work would have been an easy job for PageMaker at 4,959 pages plus a 100-page index.

When you break down the text in chapters or sections, create a separate section for the front matter: the title page, acknowledgments, copyright statements, and table of contents. The preface or foreword, if any, should also be a separate section, as should each chapter and each appendix. Keep the index separate too. These divisions will be convenient for design and page numbering as well as for printing.

Although novels may not be profusely illustrated, reports and manuals usually are. PageMaker can handle illustrations and charts with ease. You've already learned how to import graphics into PageMaker and how to manage inline graphics, keeping charts and diagrams with the text that describes them.

> ▶ **Tip:** Be sure to keep graphics with their chapters for convenience in printing. Save each chapter and its associated graphics in a separate folder.

Designing the Book

In book design, perhaps more than in any other task in which you'll use PageMaker, you'll come to appreciate the program's capabilities for using templates, master pages, and style sheets. The way to assure consistency is to create a master page for the text and a master style sheet with the fonts and spacing attributes you'll use throughout the entire publication, and then simply not to deviate from these.

311

Begin by considering a single page of text. What size will the page be? Although normal pages are 8½ x 11" and this is the paper size that your laser printer most readily handles, few books are printed at standard size. More commonly a book will measure something like 6½ x 9", or maybe 7⅜ x 9¼ " like this one. (This is often referred to as the *trim size*.) Of course, you can set up a standard page so the margins give you an area about the right size for the book's page, but it's far better to tell PageMaker to use Custom pages and to make them the size you want them. When you print on standard 8½ x 11" paper, you can have PageMaker add the appropriate crop marks for your real page size automatically just by clicking on the Crop marks box in the Print dialog box. Crop marks will show the printer where to trim pages to get the right size.

An annual report may even use a larger size paper than normal to make it stand out from the usual stacks of stuff on a busy desk. These are frequently printed on extra heavy stock, with a textured or other special surface, and may be designed in a 9 x 12", or 11 x 14" size as well as in the more common formats.

You'll also need to think about binding the book so you'll know how much margin to assign. If you're not sure, take a look at other books or publications which use the same type of binding you're planning to use. Measure their margins. See whether they're generous enough to make reading the words at the middle of the book easy. The book should open enough that you can see the whole line of type.

In order to see what your pages are going to look like, follow these steps to create a dummy:

1. Open PageMaker and set up your page to the size and margin setting you think will work for you. Ask for several pages and be sure to select facing pages and two-sided pages. Figure 12.1 shows a typical book page setup.

2. After you've set up your pages, open the master pages, create guidelines as needed, and place page numbers. Do this by creating a text block on the left master page and pressing ⌘+Option+P. Copy this text block and drag it to the right master page. Add a chapter header if you intend to use one and any rules or other repeating graphics on the page. Remember, you can override the master pages for the first page of a chapter. Be sure to save your work.

3. Now pour some text into the page. It doesn't particularly matter what kind of text you use as long as the point size is correct. If you're going to set the book in 12 point type, use 12 point greeking. The Lorem Ipsum greeking file, from PageMaker's Templates folder, is fine if you don't already have text written and waiting to go. If the text file isn't long enough to fill two facing pages, copy and paste. Create styles on the Style palette for the text and for headlines or header/footer text blocks.

4. Add gray boxes to represent graphics if there will be a great many of them, as you'd expect to find in a technical manual or a book like this one.

5. Study what you've done and make whatever changes are needed.

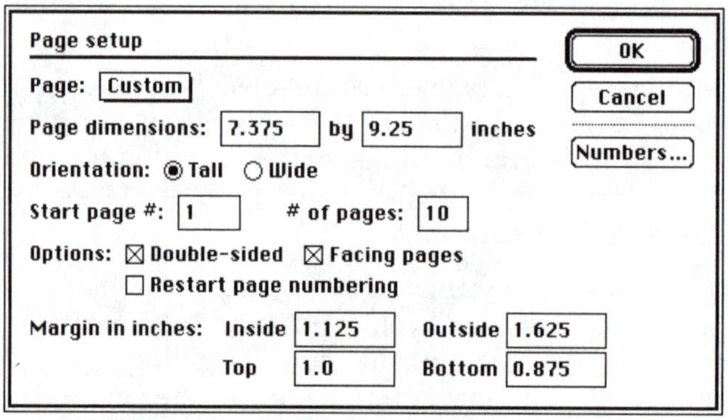

312

```
┌─────────────────────────────────────────────────────────┐
│  Page setup _____      ( OK )      │
│                                                           │
│  Page: [Custom]                              [ Cancel ]   │
│                                                           │
│  Page dimensions: [7.375] by [9.25] inches   [Numbers...] │
│  Orientation: ● Tall  ○ Wide                              │
│                                                           │
│  Start page #: [1]      # of pages: [10]                  │
│                                                           │
│  Options: ⊠ Double-sided  ⊠ Facing pages                 │
│           □ Restart page numbering                        │
│                                                           │
│  Margin in inches:  Inside [1.125]   Outside [1.625]      │
│                     Top [1.0]        Bottom [0.875]       │
└─────────────────────────────────────────────────────────┘
```

Figure 12.1 The Page setup for this page.

> **Tip:** Sometimes it's easier to evaluate your design by looking at a thumbnail instead of at the computer screen. Print thumbnails of just the pages you've poured text into, as well as full-size dummy proofs. Greeking the text lets you see the shape of it on the page so you don't get hung up on the content.

Look carefully at these dummy pages and decide whether the page design looks right or wrong. Is there enough white space to set off the text properly? Too much white space so it looks lost? Is the header in the right place? Would a footer be more effective? Figure 12.2 shows a dummy page set up in the same format as this book.

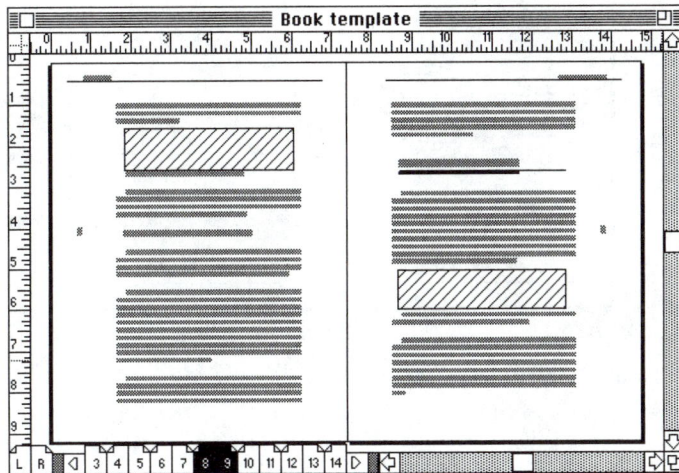

Figure 12.2 Place all elements that repeat on the master pages, then open two facing pages and import some text.

Experiment with different concepts and layouts until you find one you're satisfied with. Then remove the text from the dummy layout by selecting it all and deleting it. Remove any specific headers you've put in and leave simple place holders such as the *chapter name*, *topic*, and *text* with your style sheets applied to the appropriate place holders. Save this publication as a template. You will use the template to begin each chapter of the book or each section of the publication.

The Annual Report

In an annual report or other publication of this nature, you may wish to vary the design of the page layout. You can do this exactly as you would in a newsletter, by assigning columns differently on different pages. In such a case, you may have very little on the master pages, possibly only page numbers. Figure 12.3 shows a pair of pages from an annual report, and Figure 12.4 shows the master pages from which they were created. The items included on these master pages are the company logo at the top of both pages, the line at the bottom, and the page numbers.

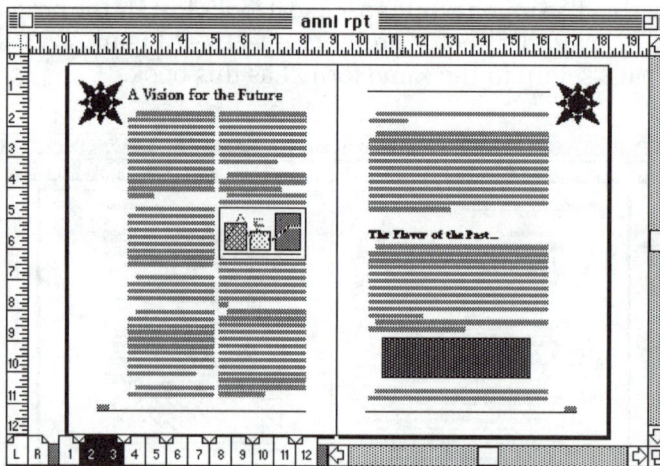

Figure 12.3 The text and figures were added on the regular pages.

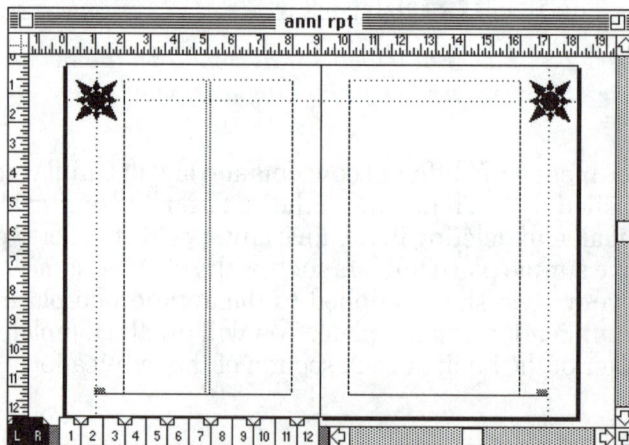

Figure 12.4 Repeating elements, column guides, and ruler guides were placed on the master pages.

Even though the number of columns changes from left pages to right pages, the overall look remains consistent. Use of the repeating logo element and rules, as well as a consistent type style, ties it all together. Remember that you can change any regular page without affecting the others. Then if you decide the changes were a mistake, you can put back the guides and redisplay the master page elements. To restore the guides on a changed page use the following Quick Steps.

Restoring the Guides on Changed Pages

1. Open the **Page** menu.

2. Click on **Copy master guides**. A checkmark will appear next to the menu entry. The screen will redraw with the master guides in place.

3. If the master guides aren't visible, press ⌘+J to see them. You may have deselected them previously. ☐

315

To redisplay master elements:

▶ Open the **Page** menu as above and click on **Display master items**.

Text and graphics for the report are best created in other programs and imported into PageMaker. You can, however, use PageMaker's Story Editor to check spelling and for final text editing. You'll find Table Editor, described in the previous chapter, very helpful for laying out spreadsheets and charts. Simple charts such as the bar graph in Figure 12.3, can be assembled right in PageMaker by using the Rectangle tool and filling with a pattern. (These obviously won't have a high degree of accuracy as they would if brought from another program.)

Programs such as Symantec's MORE 3.0, generally used for outlining and desktop presentations, can also produce charts and graphics for PageMaker. The program lets you set up pie charts, bar charts, and all sorts of other interesting graphs. Figure 12.5 shows a tree chart assembled from an outline created in MORE, and saved as an EPS file. In Figure 12.6 it's been placed in PageMaker and a headline added. The point is, practically any program you use for other purposes can also give you data you can use in PageMaker if you apply a little imagination.

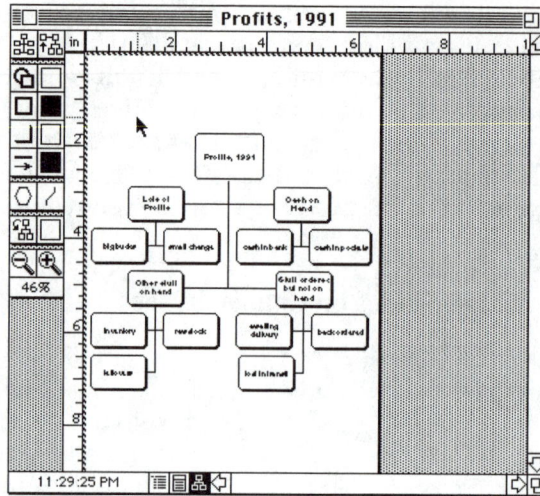

Figure 12.5 One of the many kinds of charts you can bring into PageMaker.

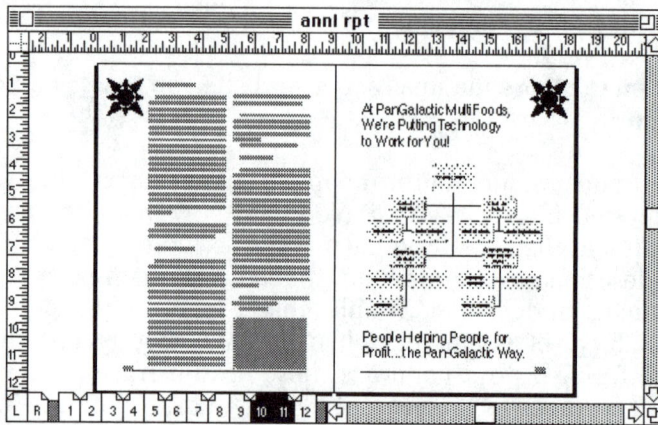

Figure 12.6 The chart has been placed in a publication. It fits with headlines and master page elements.

Preparing Text to Import

Programs such as MacWrite II, WriteNow, and Microsoft Word have much in common with PageMaker's text handling functions, so you can easily format text in any of these programs and import it into PageMaker with little or no need for additional formatting. PageMaker has a special affinity for Microsoft Word and will accept not only its style sheet definitions, but also its index entries as well.

There are several ways to save time in formatting imported text. You can do any of the following:

▶ Format text as you write it in a compatible word processing program such as WriteNow, MacWrite, or Microsoft Word.

▶ Set type specifications to apply to unformatted type before you import it.

▶ Bring in unformatted text, select it, and apply a style or create a new one for it.

▶ Enter style tags with your text, define the styles in PageMaker, and check Read tags when you place the text.

When you're preparing text to import, you can do much of your formatting in advance. Practically every word processor lets you define bold and italic type. You can also set tabs so your text and formatted tables will import into PageMaker in the correct position on the line. In Microsoft Word, you can specify a first line indent just as you can in PageMaker. If you're using some other word processor and you want first line indents, simply insert a tab. PageMaker recognizes the left margin as a starting point and will accept hanging indents (to the left of the left margin), as well as normal indents. Just be sure to click on the Retain formats checkbox in PageMaker's Place box. Otherwise your formatting will be lost.

317

> ▶ **Tip:** If you import a formatted story but forget to click on the Retain formats box, simply press ⌘+D and place the story again, this time checking both Replace existing and Retain formats.

Remember not to use carriage returns at the end of each line. Every return comes in as a line feed. This is fine at the end of a paragraph or after a fixed line of text, such as those that occur in a title or a table. But if you insert extra line feeds in your text, you'll end up with strange line spacing in your finished manuscript. Also, watch out for extra spaces after a period, the bad habit learned by anyone who was taught to type before word processors were invented.

If you're bringing in text as an ASCII (text only) file from some other word processor or from a non-Macintosh computer, you can still save time by making sure the text is clean, that it has been checked for spelling, and for stray carriage returns and spaces. Many PC-based programs have the decidedly unpleasant (for Mac users) habit of placing an extra carriage return at the end of every line. PageMaker's Smart ASCII filter will strip these off without disturbing the ones you want left behind. Just be sure the Smart ASCII filter is installed before you begin to import ASCII text. Also, since the ASCII text appears on the page pretty much unformatted, set the specifications in the Type Specifications dialog box before you place it. If you forget, then place the I-beam cursor in the text, press ⌘+A to Select All, and then enter your specifications in the Type Specifications box. The text will change when you click on OK. Both of these methods assume all the text is going to be set to the same specification. If you have heads and subheads, you'll lose them with either of these methods.

To preserve style differences, use tags. Simply decide on names for the different styles such as subhead 1, subhead 2, text, and so on. Next, type these style names in front of whatever text they're supposed to apply to, enclosed in angle brackets. For example, <text> would precede this section. Style tags apply to all the text that follows until the next style tag. Then, before you place the text, define your styles on the Style palette and check the Read tags box in the Place dialog box.

Handling Pictures

In a technical manual or how-to book, illustrations can often occupy as much space as the words that explain them. Generally, the text refers to the illustrations and it's important to keep them as close together as possible. Therefore, you may find it helpful to place them as inline graphics. Remember, there's no size limit for an inline graphic. It can, at least theoretically, be a full page. However, when you're dealing with very large graphics, you may find that they cause major disruptions in text flow. PageMaker may be forced to create new pages to accommodate your story. If the text disappears, go to Story view by pressing ⌘+E and move the cursor to the missing words. When you go back to Layout view you'll find them.

> ▶ **Tip:** If you're using a large inline graphic, you may need to adjust the page margins and/or remove master page items to make room for it.

Making a Book List

You've set up a book template to create individual chapters, and you've saved each of these chapters under its own name such as Chapter 1, Chapter 2, and so on. Now you're ready to put them together as a book. Use the **Book** command from the **File** menu to compile separate publications into a book and make up a book list of your chapters. Once your publication is in book form, PageMaker can automatically repaginate chapters, renumber pages, make up a table of contents and index, and print everything in the correct order with just one print command. To make up a book list, use this Quick Steps.

Q Making a Book List

1. Open the **Book list** dialog box shown in Figure 12.7.

   The name of the publication that's open will be automatically listed.

2. Select additional publications to insert into the book list. Click on the **Insert** button to place them.

   You can only insert one publication at a time.

3. If you wish to remove a publication from the list, select it and click on the **Remove** button.

   PageMaker will delete it from the list.

4. To change the order, select the publication to move and and click on **Move up** or **Move down**.

   Publications will be printed in the order in which they're listed so you must place them in the correct order.   □

319

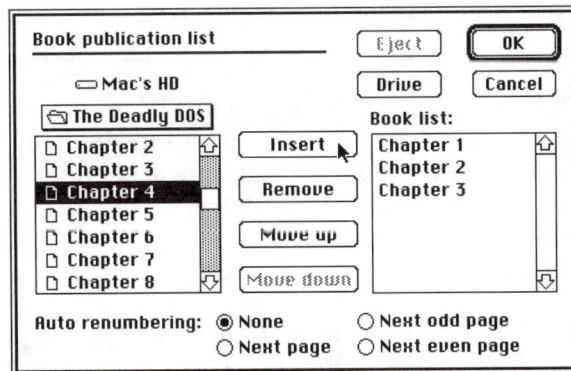

Figure 12.7 The Book List dialog box.

If you've already placed a publication and try to place it again you'll see the Alert box shown in Figure 12.8. Simply click on Continue or press Return to continue adding chapters.

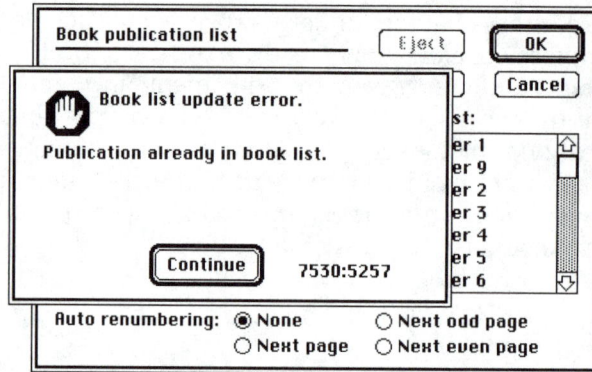

Figure 12.8 PageMaker won't let you insert the same chapter twice.

320

The logical place to compile the book list is in the table of contents publication which will by default be included in it. PageMaker always assumes that the open publication is part of the current book unless you select it from the book list and click on the Remove button. To copy a book list compiled in one publication into all others in the list, hold down ⌘ while you open **Book** from the **File** menu.

The Book dialog box also lets you tell PageMaker how to automatically renumber pages. The Auto-renumbering option you choose determines whether the first page of the next publication starts on the next page after the last page of the previous one, always on a right-hand page (next odd page), or always on a left-hand page (next even page). PageMaker will insert a blank page between chapters if one is needed.

▶ **Note:** PageMaker doesn't automatically renumber the pages until you perform a book operation such as printing, generating an index, or compiling a table of contents. When you perform any of these tasks PageMaker will follow the options you choose.

PageMaker lets you renumber pages from a given point without renumbering all the pages in the publication. For example, you may have set up a book with a separate publication for the title pages and other front material, and one for the table of contents as well as numerous chapters. The pages in the TOC have been set up with lowercase Roman numerals (i,ii,iii, and so on), and the first chapter is to start on Page 1. To renumber without losing the TOC numbers use the following Quick Steps.

Q **Renumbering without Losing TOC Numbers**

1. Make sure your publications are in the correct order in the Book list.

   If they're not, correct the order by using the Move up and Move down buttons.

2. Close that publication and open the chapter which is to start with page 1. Choose **Page Setup** from the **File** menu.

   The Page Setup box appears.

3. Click on the **Restart page numbering** option and close the box.

   When you print or perform any other "book" function, the pages will renumber. □

321

⊘ **Warning:** If you haven't placed page number markers (⌘+Option+P) on the left and right master pages of all your chapters, you won't see any page numbers.

The Table of Contents

Not all books include a table of contents. Works of fiction seldom do. Annual reports usually don't. Anthologies always do. Other types of books like technical manuals and other nonfiction works usually benefit from having one. PageMaker has eliminated much of the labor of producing a table of contents. You can generate one automatically for a single publication or for a whole book list. There are two basic steps in creating a table of contents:

▶ Specifying that a single paragraph or all paragraphs of a particular style be included in it.

▶ Using the **Create TOC** command from the **Options** menu to create the actual table and placing it as a story within the publication.

> ▶ **Note:** What PageMaker considers a paragraph for purposes of the TOC is what you might otherwise consider a chapter title or a first- or second-level subhead. (They're called paragraphs simply because they end with a carriage return.)

You need to think about how detailed you want the TOC to be. In some types of publications you might want only chapter headings, in another you might want to go all the way through a third level subhead. If you begin to plan the table of contents while you're creating the contents themselves, you can save time by marking the headings as you place them in PageMaker.

Marking Entries for the TOC

You can mark each of the paragraphs to go into the TOC in two ways: individually or as part of a paragraph style. To mark an individual entry, use the following Quick Steps.

Q Marking Paragraph Style for an Individual Entry

1. Select the paragraph to be included with the Text tool.

   It will be highlighted. Or if you wish, you can highlight a few words within a paragraph.

2. Press ⌘+M or choose the **Paragraph** command from the **Type** menu.

   The Paragraph Specifications dialog box appears, as shown in Figure 12.9.

3. Check the **Include in TOC** option and close the box.   □

The method above works fine if you're going through an existing publication. It's a lot easier, however, to decide first that you want a certain level of subhead in the TOC and to include it as it's created. This method also gives you a more consistent table of contents, as it captures all the heads at a given level, and doesn't tempt you to add extraneous items or overlook an important one. To include all the paragraphs, heads, or subheads in a particular style, use the following Quick Steps.

Q Labeling a Specific Item to be Included in the TOC

1. Choose **Define styles** from the Type menu or press ⌘+3 to open the **Define styles** dialog box.

   You'll see the list of styles on the scrolling menu.

2. Choose the name of the style whose paragraphs you want to include in the TOC and click on the **Edit** button.

   The Edit style dialog box appears.

3. In the Edit style dialog box, click on the **Para** button.

   The Paragraph Specifications box, as shown in Figure 12.9, appears.

4. Click on the **Include in TOC** box.

5. Press **Option+Return** to close all the boxes.

   All paragraphs using that type style will be included in the TOC. □

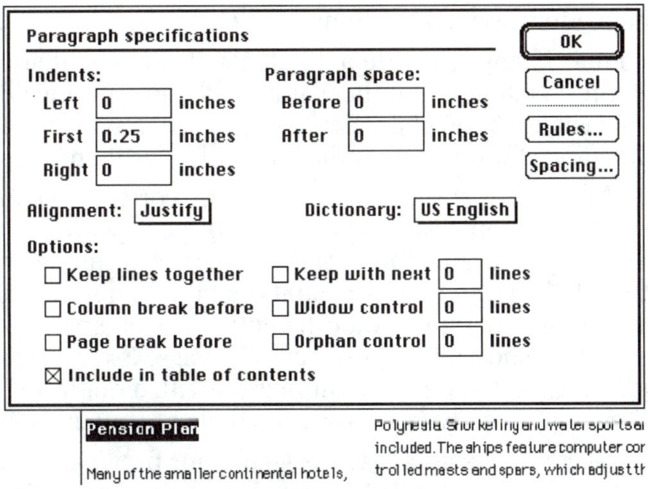

323

Figure 12.9 Choosing the TOC option.

The Table of Contents Publication

After you've identified all of the items that need to be entries in the TOC, you need to generate the publication that contains the list and place it within the book list. Although you could stick it in with the title page, dedication, and any other front material, it's better to keep the TOC as a separate publication so it can have its own set of page numbers.

> ⊘ **Warning:** Page numbers within a book may not necessarily be sequential from one publication to the next. Check your page numbers before you begin to generate a table of contents or index.

Use the following steps to create the table of contents publication:

1. Start a new PageMaker publication and title it **Table of Contents.** Give it as many pages as you think your table of contents will require.

2. From this new publication use the **Book** command to link the publications you want the TOC to include.

3. Choose **Create TOC** from the **Options** menu. The dialog box shown in Figure 12.10 will appear.

4. If the present publication is part of a book list, the Include book publications box will automatically be selected.

5. You may change the title of the table of contents if you wish, by deleting Contents from the Name field and entering whatever you wish, up to 30 characters long. If you don't want a title at all, remove *Contents* from the box and leave it empty.

6. PageMaker will automatically place the correct page numbers for your TOC entries, but you need to specify how they should be displayed. If you don't want to use page numbers in the TOC, click on the **No page numbers** box. You may place the page number before or after the entry. The character combination ^t, as shown in Figure 12.10, is PageMaker's default, a right- aligned tab on the right margin with a dot leader pattern. When you're ready to compile the table of contents click on OK.

7. PageMaker will search each page of your publication for TOC markers, compile the TOC for you, and give you a Place text icon. Place the table of contents as if it were any other story. Now you can edit it, change type styles, delete entries you've changed your mind about, and work with it in any way you like. Figure 12.11 shows a piece of an actual table of contents.

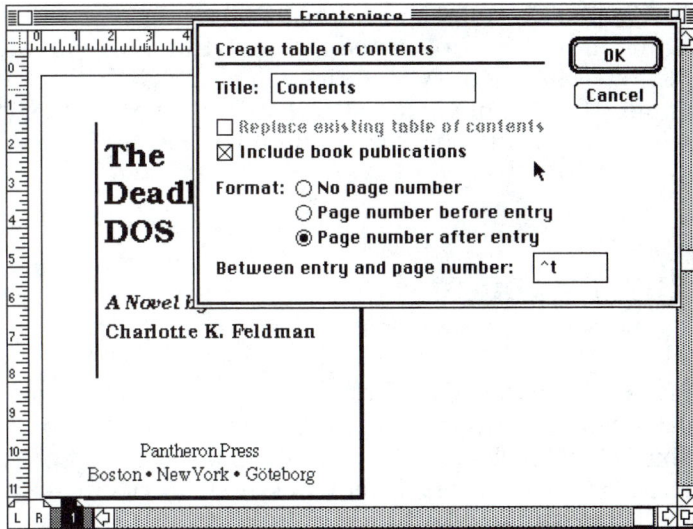

Figure 12.10 The Create table of contents dialog box.

325

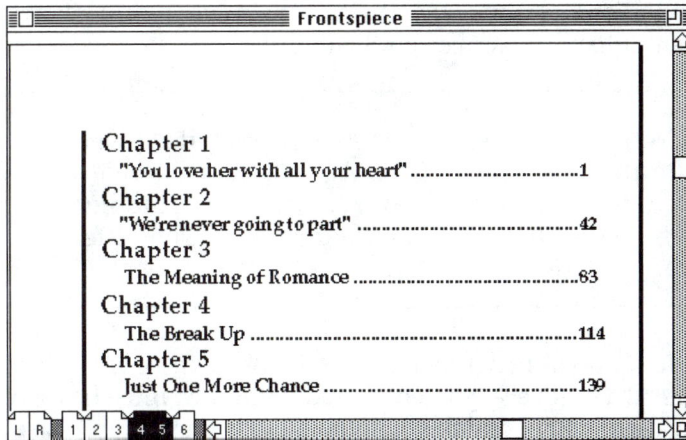

Figure 12.11 Looks like the same old story.

> ▶ **Note:** If you haven't previously created a table of contents for this book, the Replace box will be disabled. Otherwise it is selected by default so that new versions will update the previous ones.

The Create TOC command automatically assigns default styles to the TOC title and entries. You can edit these styles just as you would any others. The style names of TOC entries will have TOC in front of them, for example, TOC Headline. If you edit and rename a TOC style, you won't see the results of your changes until you recompile the TOC.

Creating an Index

The process of indexing a book is often tedious, especially when it must be done by hand. PageMaker makes indexing a great deal easier. You can define index entries as you write them, as you edit, or after the publication is finished. PageMaker will keep track of cross-references and establish up to three levels for an index entry. Once the index is complete, you place it in your document as you would any other story. You can view it and edit it in Story Editor form before placing it in the publication. PageMaker also recognizes index entries created in Microsoft Word and will incorporate them when you place a Word document into a PageMaker publication.

> **Note:** PageMaker version 4.01 has included several changes in the indexing feature. All examples shown here were created in version 4.01. If your screen looks different, you may be using version 4.0 or an earlier release. The differences are minor.

Index entries are defined in the Add index entry dialog box shown in Figure 12.12. Several choices, listed following, must be made when entering a topic to be indexed. Some of these choices will be different if you select the Cross-reference option.

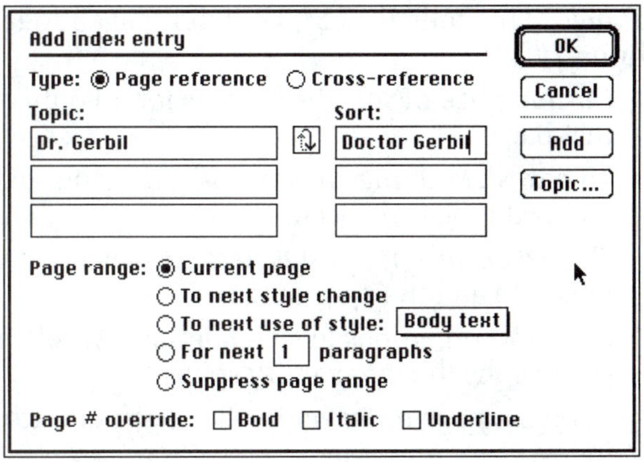

Figure 12.12 The Add index entry dialog box.

327

Page reference or Cross reference: Page reference lets you define an individual index entry. Click on the Cross-reference button if you want to cross-reference this index entry with others.

Topic: You may enter up to three index levels in the boxes. The first is the main entry and the other(s) would be entered beneath it. For example, the index entries for Lima beans might read:

Beans, 38-56

   Lima, 43-45

      cooking, 43-44

      growing, 45

Promote/Demote: The icon with the circling arrows is a button that enables you to change the hierarchy of levels of an index entry by promoting or demoting its level. Thus, the earlier entry could become:

Beans, 38-56

   cooking, 43-44, 51-52

   Lima, 43-45

      growing, 45

Sort: Entries in these boxes tell PageMaker how to sort abbreviations and nonalphabet characters. To index Dr. *Gerbil* correctly, enter *Doctor Gerbil*. It will print as Dr. but be indexed as if it were Doctor.

Page Range: This tells PageMaker what page range to assign to your entry.

> *Current page* means the entry is found only on that page.
>
> *To next style change* means the page range extends until the next type style occurs.
>
> *To next occurrence of style* lets you select a style at which to end the page range.
>
> *For next paragraphs* lets you define a whole number of paragraphs the index entry spans.
>
> *Suppress page range* omits the page range from the index.

Page # override: Lets you change the type attributes of a particular index entry to make it stand out. Otherwise it will appear in PageMaker's default index type style.

Add: Functionally the same as OK. It lets you add entries without closing the dialog box if there are several words you want to place in the index.

Topic: Takes you to the Select Topic dialog box, shown in Figure 12.13, which displays a list of current index topics. Move between sections by choosing the desired initial letter from the Topic section pop-up menu. Checking topics lets you avoid repeating index entries in slightly different ways and serves as a reminder as to whether you've previously included the topic. Choose **Repeating topics** from the **Select topic** menu to avoid misspellings in creating index entries.

When you select the Cross-reference button, some of your choices are different. Figure 12.14 shows the Add index entry box for cross-referencing. The Topic and Sort options are the same. The major difference is that you may select a way for the cross-reference to be entered. The Denoted by option gives you several choices. Select whichever seems appropriate.

```
┌─────────────────────────────────────────────┐
│  Add index entry                  ┌──────┐  │
│  Type: ◉            ┌─────────────┤  OK  ├──┐│
│  Topic:             │  Select topic          │
│  ┌──────            │  Level 1: scrapbook    │
│  │scrapb            │                        │
│  ┌──────            │  Level 2:              │
│  ┌──────            │  Level 3:              │
│  Page ra            │                        │
│                     │  Topic section: [S]    │
│                     │                        │
│                     │  Level 1    Level 2    │
│                     │  scrapbook             │
│  Page #             │  solution              │
│                     │  SuperPaint            │
└─────────────────────┴────────────────────────┘
```

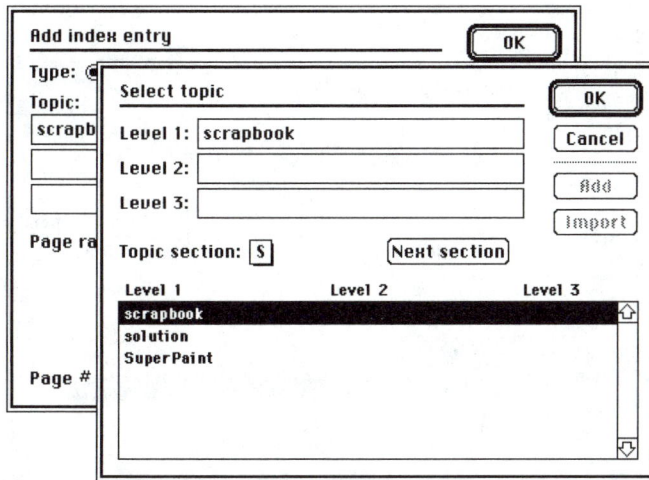

Figure 12.13 The Select topic dialog box.

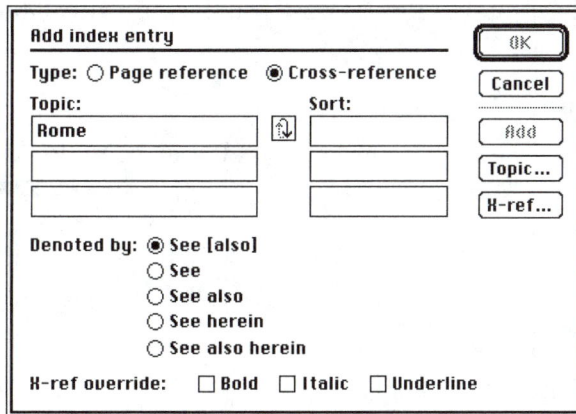

```
┌───────────────────────────────────────────────┐
│  Add index entry                  ┌────────┐  │
│  Type: ○ Page reference ◉ Cross-reference       │
│  Topic:              Sort:                      │
│  ┌──────────┐ ┌─┐   ┌──────────┐               │
│  │Rome      │ │↻│   │          │               │
│  ┌──────────┐       ┌──────────┐               │
│  ┌──────────┐       ┌──────────┐               │
│                                                 │
│  Denoted by: ◉ See [also]                       │
│              ○ See                              │
│              ○ See also                         │
│              ○ See herein                       │
│              ○ See also herein                  │
│  X-ref override:  ☐ Bold ☐ Italic ☐ Underline   │
└─────────────────────────────────────────────────┘
```

Figure 12.14 The Add index entry box for cross-referencing.

The X-ref button gives you a box much like the Topic box. It's shown in Figure 12.15. Choose and place cross-references as you did with topics, using the X-ref box to select a topic to cross-reference your entry to.

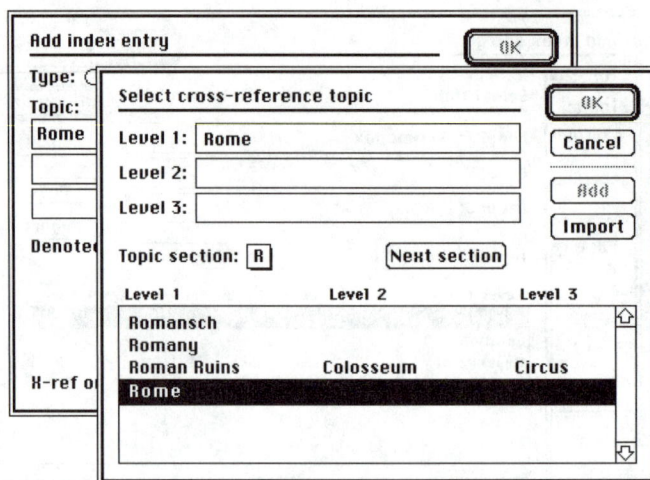

Figure 12.15 The X-ref box.

330

To make a simple index entry, use the following Quick Steps.

Q Making an Index Entry

1. Use the Text tool to select the word or phrase to enter.

   It may be up to 50 characters long including spaces.

2. Choose **Index entry** from the **Options** menu or press ⌘+;(semicolon) to open the **Index entry** dialog box shown in Figure 12.12.

   The selected word or phrase will be entered in the first Topic field.

3. If you're adding an entry to an existing topic, click on the **Promote/Demote** button to cycle the entry to the second or third field.

4. Open the **Select topic** box and locate the topic. Select it and hold down the ⌘ while you click on OK or press Return to close the box.

   The selected topic will be displayed in the first field with your entry in the field below it. If you forgot to hold down the ⌘, your entry will not appear. Retype it into the appropriate field.

5. Specify the page range for the index entry and enter any special spellings (if needed) in the Sort field.

6. When you're done defining   The entry is complete.
the index entry click on OK
or press Return.

□

▶ **Tip:** To make an even quicker entry, if all the defaults are acceptable, just highlight the word to be entered and press ⌘+Shift+;(semicolon). If you're in Story Editor you'll see the diamond symbol, which indicates an index entry.

Viewing the Index

331

Once you start defining index entries, PageMaker starts compiling the index. This means it's available so you can consult it at any time to check the list of topics and cross-references. To find out what's been indexed, select **Show index** from the **Options** menu. The Show index box is shown in Figure 12.16. As with the Topics and X-ref boxes, you move through it by using the alphabetical pop-up menu under Index section.

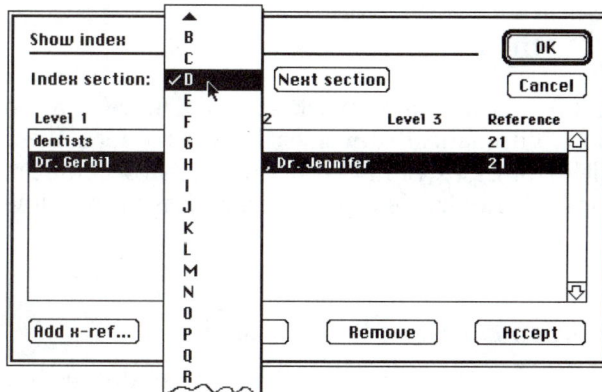

Figure 12.16 The Show index box.

You can add cross-references within this dialog box, edit and remove entries, and accept the changes without closing the dialog box after each one. The following list gives you quick keyboard/mouse combinations for many of the edit functions.

Press this	To do This
Option+Add x-ref	Deletes all cross-references since you opened the dialog box or clicked on Accept.
Option+Remove	Restores all cross-references you added since you opened the dialog box or clicked on Accept.
⌘+Option+Remove	Deletes all page references. To restore them press Option+Remove.
⌘+Shift+Remove	Deletes all cross-references. To restore them press Option+Remove.
⌘+Option+Shift+Remove	Deletes all index entries. To restore them press Option+Remove.

Indexing Names

PageMaker 4.01 allows you to mark an index entry as a proper name. After you do, it automatically reverses the word order of the name when formatting it for the index. Emily Troutwhistle will become Troutwhistle, Emily. To mark an entry as a proper name, use the following Quick Steps.

Q **Marking an Entry as a Proper Name**

1. Use the Text tool to highlight the name.	You can do this in either Story or Layout view.
2. Highlight it and press ⌘+Shift+Z.	That's all! The entry will automatically be indexed last name first. □

You can format last names with more than one word by inserting nonbreaking spaces between them. Thus, to prepare Nicolai von Stroganoff for indexing, delete the space between von and S, and press Option+Spacebar to produce a nonbreaking space. Then you can press ⌘+Shift+Z to turn it around. Use nonbreaking spaces to format names with titles and middle initials such as Sgt. Elmo Pepper and Phipps P. Phipple. In these examples, the nonbreaking spaces would need to go between Sgt. and Elmo, and Phipps and P. Names with hyphens or apostrophes don't need special treatment. PageMaker handles them automatically, as it does titles after a last name such as Jr., II, and so on. The following examples need no custom characters:

> Fenelly-Kluggman, Rebecca
> O'Reilly, Isadora
> Lavendar, Lance Jr.

If an academic degree follows a last name, it is always preceded by a comma. PageMaker, unfortunately, can't handle this, and entries such as Samuel Fullybright, Ph.D., must be typed in the Add index entry box in the form in which they should appear in the index, "Fullybright, Samuel, Ph.D."

333

Compiling the Index

The last step in producing an index is to use the Create index command to compile the actual index from all the entries, and then to adjust the formatting as needed to produce a good-looking and easily readable index. Like the table of contents, the index is created as a story and placed within the publication. Since an index generally appears at the end of the book, you can just place it and let PageMaker add as many additional pages as are needed. Figure 12.17 shows the Create index dialog box. You can give your index a name if you wish, by entering it in the box.

Replace existing index will be checked if you've previously created an index for this publication. Otherwise it will be disabled. Use the Format button to bring up the Format dialog box, shown in Figure 12.18. Index section headings are the A, B, and so on, which may be included at the head of each section of the index if you click on the box. You have the option of skipping any part of the alphabet which has no index entries.

Create index

OK

Title: | Index |

Cancel

⊠ Replace existing index
☐ Include book publications
⊠ Remove unreferenced topics

Format...

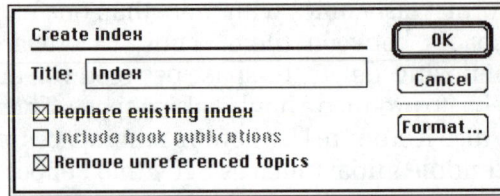

Figure 12.17 The Create index dialog box.

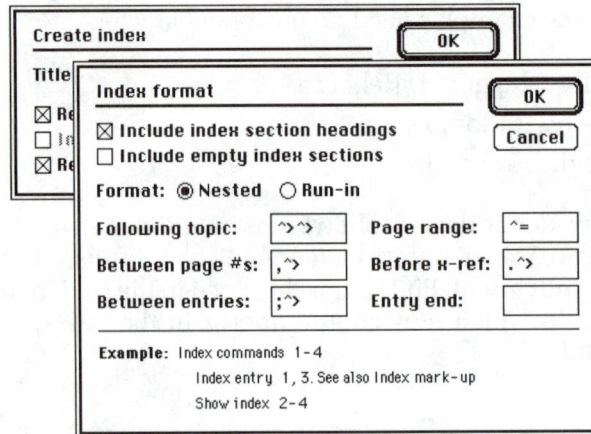

Create index

OK

Title

⊠ Re
☐ I
⊠ Re

Index format

OK

⊠ Include index section headings
☐ Include empty index sections

Cancel

Format: ⦿ Nested ○ Run-in

Following topic: | ^>^> | Page range: | ^= |

Between page #s: | ,^> | Before x-ref: | . ^> |

Between entries: | ;^> | Entry end: | |

Example: Index commands 1-4
Index entry 1, 3. See also Index mark-up
Show index 2-4

Figure 12.18 The Index format dialog box.

The strange symbols in the fields in the Index format box are called *metacharacters.* They are nonprinting characters which PageMaker inserts where you specify to leave spaces, tab across a line, and so on. When you adjust the formatting of index entries, you'll be able to preview the results immediately. The example at the bottom of the box changes whenever you change any of the metacharacter settings. The following chart of metacharacters will help you in formatting index entries.

To insert	Use metacharacter
Carriage Return	^p
Line break	^n
Tab	^t
Soft hyphen	^-
Nonbreaking hyphen	^~
Computer inserted hyphen	^c
Caret	^^
Unknown character	^?
Nonbreaking space	^s
White space or tab	^w
Thin space	^<
En space	^>
Em space	^m
En dash	^=
Em dash	^_

335

You can also use punctuation marks as shown in Figure 12.18. Commas between page numbers are helpful, as are semicolons between run-on entries. PageMaker will create and assign default styles when the index is created. You may edit these styles as you would any other. If you edit and rename an index style, PageMaker will apply the revised style the next time you create the index. However, you won't be able to see the changes unless you create the index again.

▶ **Note:** Depending on the number of entries and the length of the chapters, it may take quite a while for PageMaker to completely compile the index. An Alert box with a thermometer like the one shown in Figure 12.19, will let you know how much progress is being made.

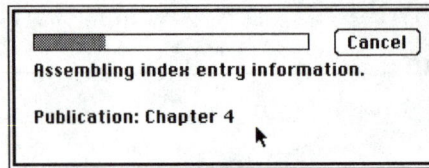

Figure 12.19 This process can take a long time.

To create the index after you've identified all the index entries, use the following Quick Steps.

Q **Compiling the Index**

1. Choose **Create index** under the **Options** menu.

   Give your index a name if you wish, or delete the default name if none is wanted.

2. Click on the box to remove unreferenced topics.

   This removes index topics whose references have been deleted, or topics imported from other publications not used as entries or cross-references.

3. Click on Format to verify formatting.

   The example in the Index format box reflects the current settings.

4. Make changes or click on OK.

   Both boxes will close. ☐

What happens next depends on whether you started to create the index from the Story Editor view or the Page layout view, and whether your index is new or replacing an existing index. PageMaker either:

▶ Opens a new Story window for the index if you're in Story view.

▶ Updates the existing Index window in Story view.

▶ Gives you a loaded Text icon so you can place the index as a new story in Layout view.

▶ Replaces the existing index and takes you to the first page of it in Layout view.

336

Figure 12.20 shows a portion of an index in Story view. The index entries have styles attached. You can edit these styles and reformat the index in any way you like. Place the index at the end of the last book chapter. PageMaker will create as many additional pages as it needs.

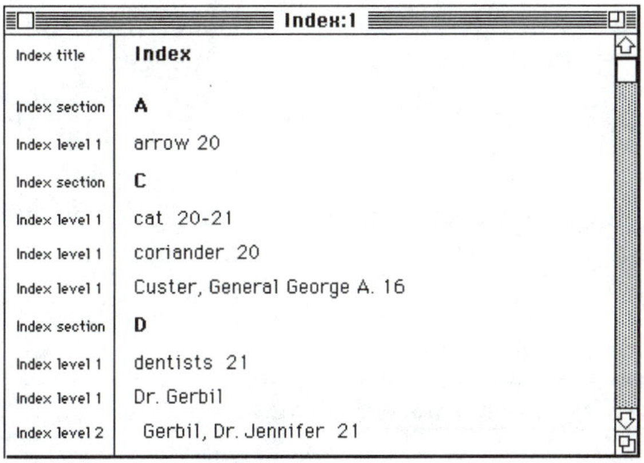

Index title	**Index**
Index section	**A**
Index level 1	arrow 20
Index section	**C**
Index level 1	cat 20-21
Index level 1	coriander 20
Index level 1	Custer, General George A. 16
Index section	**D**
Index level 1	dentists 21
Index level 1	Dr. Gerbil
Index level 2	Gerbil, Dr. Jennifer 21

Figure 12.20 The index in Story Editor.

337

Printing the Book

The job that seemed so endless and complicated has resolved itself into a series of fast and easy steps. You've created your book complete with index and table of contents. You've checked to be sure the pages are properly numbered. You've checked the spelling and made sure that your graphics are correctly placed. Your publication is ready to print!

Before you start the print run, make sure you have plenty of paper on hand and that your printer is working well. Run a single test page and check for smudges. If all is well, use the following Quick Steps to print the book.

Q **Printing a Book**

1. Open the first publication in the book.

2. Go to the Print dialog box and select **Print entire book**, as shown in Figure 12.21.

   Check the print specifications. PageMaker uses the print specifications in the current publication to print the entire book list.

3. Click on OK or press Return to print.

   Check the printer every few minutes and add paper as needed. ☐

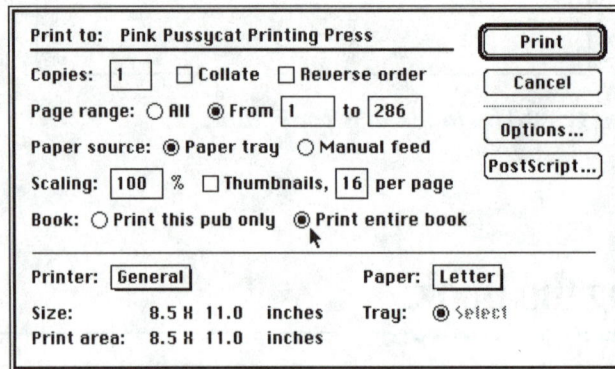

338

```
Print to:  Pink Pussycat Printing Press        ┌─────────────┐
                                               │    Print    │
Copies:  │1  │    ☐ Collate  ☐ Reverse order   └─────────────┘
                                               ┌─────────────┐
Page range: ○ All  ⦿ From │1 │  to │286│       │   Cancel    │
                                               └─────────────┘
Paper source: ⦿ Paper tray  ○ Manual feed      ┌─────────────┐
                                               │  Options... │
Scaling: │100 │ %  ☐ Thumbnails, │16│ per page  ├─────────────┤
                                               │ PostScript..│
Book: ○ Print this pub only  ⦿ Print entire book└─────────────┘

Printer: │General │            Paper: │Letter │

Size:        8.5 H 11.0  inches   Tray:  ⦿ Select
Print area:  8.5 H 11.0  inches
```

Figure 12.21 The final step is printing your book.

What You've Learned

By the end of this chapter you've learned everything you need to know to produce virtually any kind of a PageMaker publication, from a single page flyer to an entire book. In this chapter you learned all about working with longer documents. Specifically you have learned:

▶ How to plan and design a book or an annual report. You've learned about the importance of using style sheets and a book template to maintain a consistent look throughout the publication. You've seen some ways to make importing charts, text, and pictures easier.

▶ How to use the **Book** command to make a book list, and how to use the book list to link separate publications or chapters to create a continuous book.

▶ How to keep pages consecutively numbered throughout the book list. How to change page numbering to begin on designated odd or even pages, and how to keep TOC numbers separate from chapter page numbers.

▶ How to designate entries in a table of contents and why you ought to create one as a separate publication.

▶ How to define index entries and cross-references, and how to format and create an index.

▶ How to print the entire book from the book list.

339

Installing PageMaker

In This Chapter

▶ *System Requirements—Hardware and Software*

▶ *Other Programs You May Need or Want*

▶ *Making Backup Copies*

▶ *Using the Installer*

▶ *Becoming a Registered User*

PageMaker is a very versatile and complex program. As such, it requires a fairly large chunk of real estate in your computer. You must be able to give it a megabyte of memory. That's a million bytes, or 1000 K. It won't fit on a normal floppy disk, and in fact, won't fit on a high density Superdrive floppy either. You need a hard drive and a minimum of 1 MB of RAM. If you hope to run PageMaker under MultiFinder, you'll need at least twice as much RAM and you'll have to allocate 1.5 MB to PageMaker. Ideally, you'll have 4MB available (or more), so you can run PageMaker and your word processor and paint programs all at once. It can be done, but just barely and you'll have to close something before you can print or use a DA. Figure A.1 shows the Finder info box on the author's IIsi, with PageMaker, Microsoft Word, and SuperPaint, all running at once.

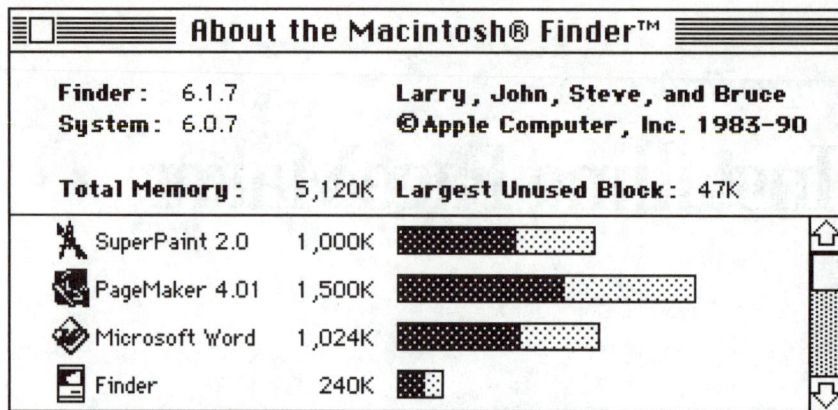

About the Macintosh® Finder™

| Finder: | 6.1.7 | | Larry, John, Steve, and Bruce |
| System: | 6.0.7 | | ©Apple Computer, Inc. 1983–90 |

Total Memory: 5,120K **Largest Unused Block:** 47K

SuperPaint 2.0	1,000K	
PageMaker 4.01	1,500K	
Microsoft Word	1,024K	
Finder	240K	

Figure A.1 This Mac is full!

It is technically possible to run PageMaker on a Mac Plus or on a Classic. Many people do and their patience is rewarded with great-looking pages. It takes a great deal of patience, however. PageMaker runs very slowly on a Plus because the computer needs to go back to the disk for information frequently. The program runs somewhat faster on an SE, and quite well on any of the Mac II's.

Of course, the top of the line (in Mac hardware) would be a IIfx with 32 megs of RAM and a huge hard drive, plus a double page, hi-res color monitor and a 1200 dpi Linotronic printer. If you don't have that kind of a computer system, rejoice in the fact that you'll have more time to study your page layouts and mentally improve them while you're waiting for PageMaker to catch up to you.

What about monitors? Of course, if you're using a Plus or an SE, you've got a built-in screen. It's hard to work with a two-page spread when you're using a small screen, however. Knowing that, several manufacturers have come out with larger screens that hook up to your Mac and give you a bigger picture. There's one that even rotates from vertical to horizontal views. Any display screen that can be used with your Mac can be used with PageMaker. If you have a Mac II, your choices are even greater—you also have the option of using a color monitor. If you're only producing black and white pages, you probably don't need a color monitor but they're nice to have.

You do need a printer and ideally it will be a PostScript laser printer, either one of the Apple models or another compatible brand. Aldus supplies Printer drivers, sort of mini-programs that let PageMaker talk directly to the printer, for most of the currently available laser printers. When you install PageMaker, you'll see a list of APD (Aldus

Printer Description) files. Choose the one(s) that you're likely to use. If you'll be sending work to a service bureau, install their APD file too. The Linotronic 100/300 APD is helpful because the Linotronic is one of the printers most commonly used by service bureaus. If your printer (or your service bureau's favorite printer) isn't on the list, check with Aldus and/or the printer manufacturer, to see if there's an APD file available for it. If not, they'll tell you which APD can be substituted.

If all you have is an ImageWriter, don't despair. With Adobe Type Manager you can still print out reasonably acceptable pages for proof-reading and then take your PageMaker publication to a service bureau for laser printing.

System Requirements

343

The good news is that PageMaker will run under System 7. The even better news for those who aren't ready to switch, is that it also runs under any system from 6.0.3 on. You'll also need Finder version 6.1 or later. You should have only one System folder installed and within it only one System file and one Finder file. To have any more than one of each is to invite disaster anyway.

What About System 7?

Aldus assures us that PageMaker will coexist quite happily with System 7, although you may have minor difficulties with installation. (If you do, see the end of this chapter for a solution.)

You'll be able to use System 7's TrueType fonts in your layout. However, there's presently no Aldus Prep print resource for TrueType, so you'll need to use the regular Apple Printer resource. (To do so, press Option while you select Print.)

You might also use a font format converter program such as FontMonger to convert TrueType fonts into PostScript versions. Aldus is developing an Aldus Prep file for TrueType fonts, and will make it available to registered users as soon as it's ready.

> ▶ **Note**: TrueType, for the benefit of those who haven't been
> following the progress of System 7, is a new feature which
> will give you nonjaggie type on your Mac screen and in print at
> all possible sizes, just as if you were using Adobe Type Man-
> ager. It requires special True Type fonts and won't work with
> PostScript fonts. There are programs that will convert your
> PostScript fonts into TrueType fonts, and vice versa.

Other Software You Need

Of course, PageMaker will run without any other programs. You
actually need very little. On the other hand, you won't be able to do
much in the way of page design without a graphics program, and you
will have a hard time doing any serious writing without a word
processor.

Choosing a Word Processor

Which programs are compatible with PageMaker? PageMaker supplies
filters which convert the output from most word processors into a
format that it can read. Microsoft Word, WriteNow, MacWrite II, and
WordPerfect are among the best-selling word processors. WriteNow
and MacWrite II have the distinct advantage of being small programs.
For example, WriteNow needs only 124K of memory, as opposed to
669K for Word. This means it will fill up less of your available RAM and
will let PageMaker work faster.

Choosing a Paint Program

As for graphics, which program to buy depends on what kind of
drawings you want to produce. Virtually every graphics program can
save files in a format PageMaker can read. (See the chapter on graphics
for a complete discussion of the differences between TIFF, PICT, Paint,
and EPSF graphic files.) Aldus Freehand is recommended by many
artists, especially those who do a great deal of color work on the Mac.
The author prefers SuperPaint for its versatility.

Extras

If you're using a scanner, a program such as Silicon Beach's Digital Darkroom or Adobe PhotoShop is a great help. These let you retouch your photos, adjust contrast, and make other helpful changes.

Adobe Type Manager is not quite a necessity, but it's a big help. What it does, basically, is to get rid of jaggies that make your type look awful on the screen. When you're trying to adjust the spacing on a headline, or to show a client, on the screen, what the page is going to look like printed, you need ATM. It also gives you better-looking type on an ImageWriter, if you happen to be using one to proof your pages before heading to the service bureau.

Clip art libraries and extra type fonts are nice to have too, and are a big help for desktop publishing. You can find all kinds of clip art, including Paint, PICT, EPS, and TIFF images. Your software dealer should have a good selection of clip art libraries and will also have additional type fonts. You can buy these either as TrueType fonts for System 7, or as PostScript files.

345

Before You Go Ahead, Back Up

The first thing you should do to your PageMaker disks is to make sure they're locked. Aldus usually ships disks locked, but you still need to check. Locking a disk protects it against being accidentally erased by the Mac or having something else written onto it that doesn't belong there, like a virus. Floppy disks have locking tabs, as shown in Figure A.2. To lock a disk, slide the plastic tab so the hole is uncovered.

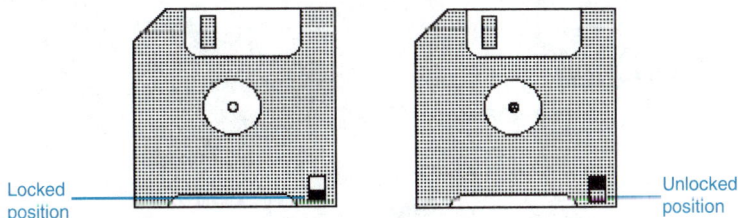

Locked position

Unlocked position

Figure A.2 Locking a disk.

Of course, disks are prone to other kinds of damage too. That's why you should make back up copies before you install the program. Aldus allows you to make one copy of your PageMaker disks for this purpose. To make backup disks, you'll need a blank, formatted disk for each disk you're copying. PageMaker comes as a set of four disks, so you'll need four new, blank disks. To format, or initialize, a disk, stick it into the disk drive. If it's blank and hasn't been used before, you'll get a series of dialog boxes like the ones in Figure A.3.

To format or initialize a disk, use the following steps:

1. Stick it into the disk drive. If it's blank and hasn't been used before, you'll get a series of dialog boxes like the ones in Figure A.3.

2. Click on Two-sided to make it an 800K disk.

3. Click on Erase, although there shouldn't be anything to erase.

4. Give the disk exactly the same name as PageMaker's original disks. Disk 1 must be Disk 1, not disk One, Copy of Disk 1, #1, or any other variation on the theme. PageMaker's Installer looks for files along very specific file paths. If you change them, it won't find the files it needs and you won't be able to install the program.

346

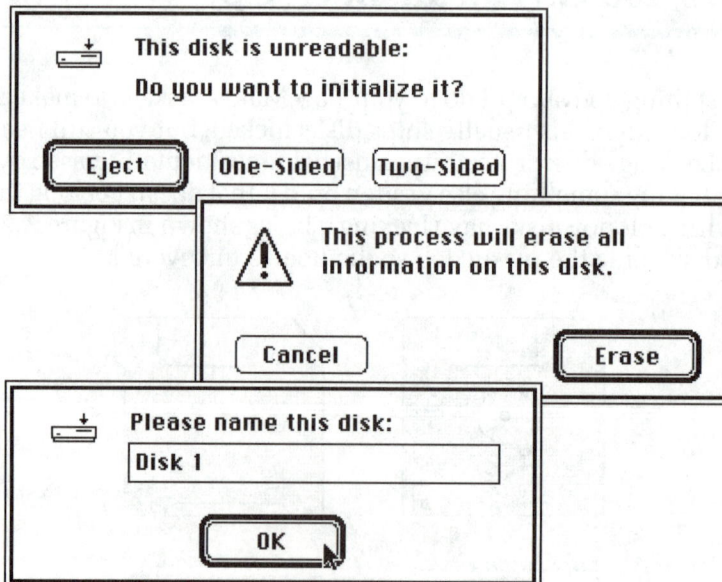

Figure A.3 Formatting a disk.

> ⊘ **Warning:** You are not allowed to make copies for your friends, co-workers, or relatives. That's software piracy and it's illegal!

How you make backup copies depends on what kind of a computer you're using. If you have an SE with two floppy drives, it's a cinch. Put the disk to be copied into one drive, and the disk you're copying to in the other drive. Drag the icon from the original disk onto the new disk and relax for a minute. That's all. Eject it and label it. Repeat until you've copied all four disks.

To make backup copies with one floppy drive, you must copy the files from the original disk in the floppy drive onto the hard drive, and then onto a new floppy in the floppy drive. Follow these steps, and repeat them for all four disks in the PageMaker package.

1. Make a new folder on your desktop by choosing New folder from the File menu or pressing ⌘+N, and call it Disk 1 or whatever you wish.

2. Drag the entire contents of the PageMaker Disk 1 into that folder. The Mac will copy the files and folders. When the copy is complete, eject the disk.

3. Put a new disk in the drive and format it, as above. Name it Disk 1.

4. Drag the contents of the Disk 1 folder into the new (floppy) disk, and wait while the Mac copies the files. Eject the copy, and label it.

5. Drag the folder into the trash. Copying the files onto the disk doesn't install PageMaker.

347

Now look for the registration cards and information that came in the PageMaker box. You should find a set of stickers with the serial number for your copy of PageMaker. It's a long number that starts with 02-. Stick one of these stickers on Disk 2, of both your back up and original sets. (Why not on Disk 1? PageMaker will ask you to enter the serial number while Disk 1 is in the drive. If you put the label on it, you won't be able to read the number.) Put the original disks in a safe place and use the copies to install PageMaker.

> ► **Note:** If you can't find the stickers, don't panic. The serial number is also on the bottom of the box. You must enter the correct number or the program won't load. It's a form of copy protection.

Installation

The Aldus Installer, provided with PageMaker will copy the various files onto your hard disk. Some of these files are always needed, others are selected for copying depending on what word processor and printer you're using. The Template and Tutorial files are optional. The Aldus Installer utility will do most of the work for you. You can relax and flip through this book while you wait, and be there to answer questions and swap disks when the Mac asks you to.

348

To install PageMaker, use the following steps:

1. Put your copy of Disk 1 in the drive. If it doesn't open automatically, double-click on the icon. If the Utilities folder doesn't open automatically, double-click it. You should see the windows shown in Figure A.4.

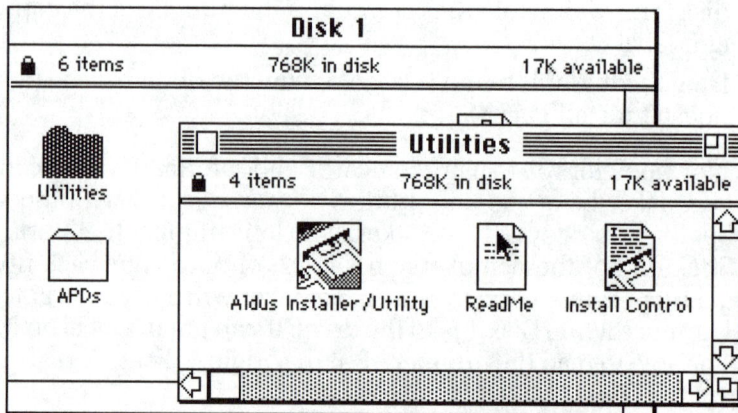

Figure A.4 When you open Disk 1, you should see these icons.

2. Double-click on the Aldus Installer/Utility icon. This will open the Main window. You'll also see three other windows. Installer History and Installer Diagnostics are empty files. The Installer will use these files to make notes for you about the system tests, and the progress of the installation. Read Me contains up to the minute information on PageMaker that's not included in your PageMaker manuals. You might find it helpful to print a copy for reference. Click on the window to select it, and choose print from the File menu to print a copy. (Be sure your printer's turned on.)

3. Select the items to be installed, PageMaker 4.0, plus the Templates and Tutorial files if you wish, and click on Install or press Return.

4. Next you'll see a dialog box asking which Aldus Printer Descriptions (APDs) you want to install. To select only one from the scrolling menu click on it. To select additional APDs, hold Shift as you click. You can select as many as you wish, as long as you hold down Shift. Selecting All installs all the APDs, which is not recommended unless you have a dozen different printers available to you. Click on OK or press Return when ready.

5. The next dialog box asks what word processor filters to install. Install an import and export filter for each word processor you're likely to use with PageMaker. In addition, install the Smart ASCII Import.flt, a general purpose filter for importing any text file as text. Again, click to select a single file or press Shift and click on as many as you want. The export filters allow you to take text files from PageMaker and return them to a word processor format. Click on OK or press Return when finished.

6. Now the Installer will run some diagnostic tests on your system and will display the results in the Diagnostics window. This file will automatically be saved on your hard disk, and you can open it and read it at any time, using the Teach Text application included with PageMaker.

7. The final dialog box in this series asks you to personalize your copy of PageMaker. Enter your name, company, and the serial number of your copy of PageMaker. The serial number is on the sticker you put on Disk 2, on the registration materials, and on a sticker on the bottom of the PageMaker box. Copy it exactly as written, with hyphens, and all the numbers. Omit any letters at the beginning of the serial number. It will repeat what you've typed and ask for verification. If you don't have the correct serial number, PageMaker will not install. Click on OK when done.

8. Now PageMaker will check the disk to make sure there's enough room for everything you've asked for, and will begin the installation. If there's not enough room on the disk, you'll get a message to that effect and you'll be asked to cancel the installation. If you need only a little more space, try again, asking for fewer filters and APDs.

9. You'll be asked where to put the PageMaker files, and given a default folder called **Aldus PageMaker 4.0**. Click on Install and the actual copying will begin.

10. You'll be asked for several disk swaps as the Installer assembles all the necessary data. When finished, you'll get a message that the installation was successful, and you'll be returned to your desktop, complete with a new PageMaker folder. There will also be a new Aldus folder inside your System folder, containing the APDs, dictionary, filters, and other files.

▶ **Note:** If you need a lot more room, you have to do some disk management before you can install PageMaker. Remove any unnecessary files and store them on floppies. Run a defragmenting program such as Norton Utilities Speed Disk for better results.

⊘ **Warning:** Do not remove or rename this folder and do not remove any of the files or folders in it. If you do, PageMaker will not work properly.

Problems?

If there's anything you're not sure about during the installation, each dialog box includes a Help button. Clicking on it will bring up a screen with the answers to most questions.

If you are installing PageMaker 4.0, 4.0.a, or 4.01, installation may be interrupted under System 7, due to a minor incompatibility. When Disk 1 has copied itself onto the hard disk, it will eject. A dialog box should appear asking you to insert Disk 2. Instead, you may get a box asking you to insert Disk 1 again. There are two ways to resolve this:

▶ Begin the installation procedure as usual. When the box asks you to insert Disk 1 again, do so. Then press ⌘+. (period). Disk 1 will eject, and you'll get the correct dialog box asking for Disk 2.

▶ Copy the Installer/Utility and Install Control files from Disk 1 onto your hard disk, and double-click on Install Control on the hard disk to start the process. This will avoid the problem.

▶ **Note**: Disk 1 sometimes fails to eject. If this happens, press ⌘+Shift+1 to eject it.

And that's all there is to it! Now you're ready to open PageMaker and explore the world of desktop publishing.

351

Index

361

Q–R

365

Reader Feedback Card

Thank you for purchasing this book from SAMS FIRST BOOK series. Our intent with this series is to bring you timely, authoritative information that you can reference quickly and easily. You can help us by taking a minute to complete and return this card. We appreciate your comments and will use the information to better serve your needs.

1. Where did you purchase this book?

☐ Chain bookstore (Walden, B. Dalton) ☐ Direct mail
☐ Independent bookstore ☐ Book club
☐ Computer/Software store ☐ School bookstore
☐ Other _____

_____

2. Why did you choose this book? (Check as many as apply.)

☐ ·Price ☐ Appearance of book
☐ Author's reputation ☐ SAMS' reputation
☐ Quick and easy treatment of subject ☐ Only book available on subject

3. How do you use this book? (Check as many as apply.)

☐ As a supplement to the product manual ☐ As a reference
☐ In place of the product manual ☐ At home
☐ For self-instruction ☐ At work

4. Please rate this book in the categories below. G = Good; N = Needs improvement; U = Category is unimportant.

☐ Price ☐ Appearance
☐ Amount of information ☐ Accuracy
☐ Examples ☐ Quick Steps
☐ Inside cover reference ☐ Second color
☐ Table of contents ☐ Index
☐ Tips and cautions ☐ Illustrations
☐ Length of book
☐ How can we improve this book?_____
☐ _____

5. How many computer books do you normally buy in a year?

☐ 1–5 ☐ 5–10 ☐ More than 10
☐ I rarely purchase more than one book on a subject.
☐ I may purchase a beginning and an advanced book on the same subject.
☐ I may purchase several books on particular subjects.
☐ (such as _____)

6. Have your purchased other SAMS or Hayden books in the past year? _____
If yes, how many _____

7. Would you purchase another book in the FIRST BOOK series? _____

8. What are your primary areas of interest in business software? _____

☐ Word processing (particularly _____)
☐ Spreadsheet (particularly _____)
☐ Database (particularly _____)
☐ Graphics (particularly _____)
☐ Personal finance/accounting (particularly _____)
☐ Other (please specify _____)

Other comments on this book or the SAMS' book line: _____
_____

Name _____
Company _____
Address _____
City _____ State _____ Zip_____
Daytime telephone number _____
Title of this book _____

Fold here

BUSINESS REPLY MAIL
FIRST CLASS   PERMIT NO. 336   CARMEL, IN

POSTAGE WILL BE PAID BY ADDRESSEE

SAMS

11711 N. College Ave.
Suite 141
Carmel, IN 46032–9839